55

WITHDRAWN

Reprinted from the edition of 1919, Boston
First AMS EDITION published 1970
Manufactured in the United States of America

International Standard Book Number: 0-404-00967-0

Library of Congress Card Catalog Number: 77-120559

AMS PRESS, INC.
NEW YORK, N.Y. 10003

A HISTORY OF AMERICAN LITERATURE

BY

PERCY H. BOYNTON

AMS PRESS
NEW YORK

PREFACE

The general purpose in the preparation of this book has been to eliminate negligible detail and to subordinate or omit authors of minor importance in order to stress the men and the movements that are most significant in American intellectual history. The book has therefore been written with a view to showing the drift of American thought as illustrated by major writers or groups and as revealed by a careful study of one or two cardinal works by each. In this sequence of thought the growth of American self-consciousness and the changing ideals of American patriotism have been kept in mind throughout. The attempt is made to induce *study* of representative classics and *extensive reading* of the American literature which illuminates the past of the country — chiefly, of course, in reminiscent fiction, drama, and poetry.

As an aid to the student, there are appended to each chapter (except the last three) topics and problems for study, and book lists which summarize the output of each man, indicate available editions, and point to the critical material which may be used as a supplement, but not as a substitute, for first-hand study. This critical material has been selected with a view, also, to suggesting books which might reasonably be included in libraries of normal schools and colleges, as well as in universities.

As further aids to the student, there have been included two maps, three chronological charts, and, in an appendix, a brief characterization of the American periodicals which have been most significant in stimulating American authorship by providing a market for fiction, poetry, and the essay.

In the writing of the book the author's chief obligation has naturally been to the many university classes who have stimulated its preparation, not only by their attention but by their free discussion.

Acknowledgment is due to the publishers of *The Nation* and *The New Republic* for portions of the chapters on Crèvecœur, the Poetry of the Revolution, Emerson, Lowell, Whitman, Sill, and Miller, which originally appeared in these weeklies.

PERCY H. BOYNTON

CONTENTS

A HISTORY OF AMERICAN LITERATURE

THE COLONIAL PERIOD

CHAPTER I

THE SEVENTEENTH CENTURY

In its beginnings American literature differs from the literatures of most other great nations; it was a transplanted thing. It sprang in a way like Minerva, full-armed from the head of Jove, — Jove in this case being England, and the armor being the heritage which the average American colonist had secured in England before he crossed the Atlantic. In contrast, Greek, Roman, French, German, English, and the other less familiar literatures can all be more or less successfully traced back to primitive conditions. Their early life was interwoven with the growth of the language and the progress of a rude civilization, and their earliest products which have come down to us were not results of authorship as we know it to-day. They were either folk poetry, composed perhaps and certainly enjoyed by the people in groups and accompanied by group singing and dancing, — like the psalms and the simpler ballads, — or they were the record of folk tradition, slowly and variously developed through generations and finally collected into continuous stories like the Iliad, the Æneid, the "Song of Roland," the "Nibelungenlied," and "Beowulf." They were composed by word of mouth and not reduced to writing for years or generations, and they were not put into print until centuries after they were current in speech or transcribed by monks and other scholars.

The one great story-poem of this sort in American literature is the "Song of Hiawatha," but this is the story of a conquered and vanishing race; it has nothing basic to do with the Americans of to-day; it is far less related to them than the earlier epics of the older European nations to whom we trace our ancestry. Except for a few place-names even the language of America owes nothing to that of the Indians, for the English tongue is a compound of Greek and Latin and French and German. Our literary beginnings, then, go back to two groups of educated English colonists, or immigrants, and our knowledge of them to conditions in the divided England from which they first came to Jamestown, Virginia, in 1607 and to Plymouth, Massachusetts, in 1620.

The English of the early seventeenth century were an eager, restless, driving people. The splendid reign of Queen Elizabeth was just past. The country was secure from foreign enemies and confident in its strength. Great naval leaders had brought new honors to her name; great explorers had planted her flag on mysterious and new-discovered coasts; a group of dramatists had made the theater as popular as the moving-picture house of to-day; a great architect was adorning London with his churches; poets and novelists, preachers and statesmen, scientists and scholars, were all working vividly and keenly. There was an active enthusiasm for the day's doings, a kind of living assent to Hamlet's commentary, on "this goodly frame, the earth, . . . this most excellent canopy, the air, . . . this brave o'erhanging firmament, this majestical roof fretted with golden fire"; and to the exclamation that follows: "What a piece of work is a man! how noble in reason! how infinite in faculty! in form and moving, how express and admirable! in action, how like an angel! in apprehension, how like a god! the beauty of the world! the paragon of animals!" And under a strong and tactful monarch the nation had been kept at peace with itself.

Yet in this fallow soil the seeds of controversy had been steadily taking root; and when Elizabeth was followed on the throne by the vain and unregal James I, the crop turned out to be a harvest of dragons' teeth. Puritan democrats and cavalier Royalists fought with each other over the body of England till it was prostrate and helpless. What followed was the rise of Puritan power, culminating with the execution of Charles I and the establishment of the Commonwealth under the Cromwells from 1649 to 1660, and the peaceful restoration of monarchy at the latter date. It was during the mid-stages of these developments that the first settlements were made in English America. Both factions included large numbers of vigorous individuals of the pioneer type. The ·Puritans were technically called "dissenters" and "nonconformists" because of their attitude toward the established Church of England; but the Royalists who came over to America were simply nonconformists of another type who preferred doing things out on the frontier to living conventional lives at home.

The Royalists, who settled in the South, came away, like other travelers and explorers of their day, to settle new English territory as a landed aristocracy. They were a mixed lot, but on the whole they were not an irreligious lot. They believed in the established church as they did in the established government, and they persecuted with a good will those who tried to follow other forms of worship than their own. They were, however, chiefly fortune hunters, just as were the men who surged out to California in 1849 or those who went to Alaska fifty years later; they hoped to make their money in the west and to spend it back in the east, and they had little thought of literature, either as a thing to enjoy or as a thing to create. When they wrote they did so to give information about the country, the Indians, and the new conditions of living, or to keep in touch with relatives, legal authorities, or sources of money supply; and always they had in mind the thought of attracting new settlers, for they needed labor more than anything else. They made no attempt at general education, adopting the now-abandoned aristocratic theory that too much knowledge would be a dangerous source of discontent among the working people. Some few individuals wrote accounts and descriptions that are interesting to the modern reader, but these were not representative of the people as a whole. They were Englishmen away from home, living temporarily in *Virgin*-ia (the province of the virgin queen, Elizabeth), in *James*-town, in the *Carolinas* (from the Latin for Charles), in *Mary*-land, and, even as late as 1722, in *George*-ia.

The nonconformists whom adverse winds drove to the North in 1620 were a very different folk. They were predominantly Puritan in prejudice and in upbringing. Many of their leaders were graduates of Cambridge University who had gone into the Church of England, only to be driven out of it because of their unorthodox preaching — born leaders who were brave enough to risk comfort and safety for conscience' sake. They came over to America in order, as Mrs. Hemans put it, to have "freedom to worship God," but not to give this freedom to others. They had endured so much for their religious faith that they wanted a place where this, and this only, should be tolerated. So they became, not illogically, the fiercest kind of persecutors, practicing with a vengeance the lessons in oppression that they had learned in England at the cost of blood and suffering. They settled in compact towns where they could believe and worship together; they put up "meeting-houses" where they could listen to the preacher on the Lord's Day and where they could transact public business, with the same man as "moderator," on week days. He was the controlling power — "pastor," or shepherd, and "dominie," or master, of the community. And when the meetinghouses were finished, the settlers erected as their next public buildings the schoolhouses, where the children might learn to read the

Scriptures so that they could "foil the ould deluder, Satan." Education became compulsory as well as public. The Puritans' place-names were Indian — Massachusetts and Agawam; derived from England of Puritan associations, like Boston, Plymouth, and Falmouth; or quaintly Scriptural, like Marthas Vineyard, Providence, and Salem. These people, unlike the settlers in the South, came over to live and die here. They wrote for the same social and business reasons that the Virginians did, but they also wrote much about their religion, compiled the "Bay Psalm Book," published sermons, and recorded their struggles, which began very early and were doomed to final failure, to keep their New England free from "divers religions." At first their writings were sent to England for publication, but before long, in 1639, they had their own printing press, and the things that were printed on it were not so much the sayings of individual men as the opinions of the community.

The history of the migrations to the North and to the South during the seventeenth century is one with the history of the civil struggle in England. Up to 1640 colonization was slow and consistent at both points. From 1640 to 1660 it increased rapidly in the South and declined in the North, for in those years the grip of the Puritans on the old country relieved them from persecution there and from the consequent need to avoid it and, at the same time, made many Royalists glad of a chance to escape to some more peaceful spot. From 1660 on, with the return of the Royalists to power in England, Puritan migration was once more started to the North, and the home country was again secure for the followers of the king. But the real characters of the two districts were unchanged. They were firmly established in the earliest years, and they have persisted during the intervening centuries clear up to the present time. The America of to-day is a compound whose basic native qualities are inherited from the oldest traditions of aristocratic Virginia and the oldest traits of democratic and Puritan Massachusetts.

In dealing with the early periods of any literature the exercise of artistic judgment is always very charitable. Rough, uncouth, fragmentary pieces are taken into account because they serve as bridges to the remoter past. Harsh critics of colonial American literature seem to forget this practice when they rule out of court everything produced in this country before the days of Irving and Cooper. A great deal of the earlier writing should, of course, be considered only as source material for the historian ; but some of it has the same claim to attention as the old chronicles, plays, and ballads in English literary history. It deserves study if it portrays or criticizes or even unconsciously reflects the life and thought of the times, and it is significant as an American product if in form or content or point of view it clearly belongs to this side of the Atlantic.

The nature of settlement and the neglect of popular education led to an early lapse in authorship in the Southern colonies, so that in a survey as brief as this chapter their writers do not come into view until they find expression in the oratory and statesmanship of the Revolutionary period. Their narratives and descriptions of colonial life, as long as they wrote them at all, were quite like most of the earliest Northern writings of the sort. The one outstanding difference is that in whatever they wrote, the religious motive for settlement and the belief in a personal Providence were less insistently recorded than by the Puritans. Thus where John Smith was content with the general phrase " it pleased God," Anthony Thacher, saved from shipwreck in Boston Harbor, wrote devoutly, " the Lord directed my toes into a crevice in the rock " ; and where Smith's companions hoped for the benevolent favor of the Most High, Thacher's fellow-worshipers were perfectly certain that every step they took was ordained by God, so that even their apparent misfortunes were His punishments for misconduct.

In all the great mass of Puritan writing in the first century of residence in America one definite current appears, and that is the quiet but irresistible current of change in human thought. The Puritans had made the profound but constantly repeated mistake of assuming that after thousands of years of groping by mankind, they had at last discovered the "ultimate truth"; that for the rest of time men need do nothing but follow the precepts which God had revealed to them about life here and life hereafter. They were, in their own serious way, happy in their confident possession of truth and sternly resolved to bestow it or, if necessary, impose it on all whom they could control. Their failure was recorded with their earliest attempts, and it came, not because of their particular weakness or the strength of their particular adversaries, but because they were trying to obstruct the progress of human thought, which is as inexorable as any other force of nature. They might as well have entered into an argument with gravitation or the tides. The most interesting and the best-written pieces of seventeenth-century New England literature all give evidence of this rear-guard action against the advancing forces of truth.

The Puritanism against which this rising tide of dissent developed was admirably embodied in William Bradford (1590–1657), the *Mayflower* Pilgrim who was more than thirty times governor of his colony and the author of "A History of Plimouth Plantation." He was a brave, sober, devout leader with an abiding sense of the holy cause in which he was enlisted. His journal of the first year in America and his history are clearly and sometimes finely written, and give ample proof of his stalwart character — "fervent in spirit, serving the Lord," and free from the personal narrowness which is often mistakenly ascribed to all Puritans. In his account, for example, of the reasons for the Pilgrims' removal from Leyden the chronicle tells of the hardships under which they had lived there, the encroachments of old age, the disturbing effects of the life on the children, and, lastly, the great hope they entertained of advancing the church of Christ in some remote part of the world. It recounts many of the objections advanced against attempting settlement in America, and concludes:

It was answered, that all great and honorable actions are accompanied with great difficulties, and must be both enterprised and overcome with answerable courages. It was granted the dangers were great, but not desperate; the difficulties were many, but not invincible. For though there were many of them likely, yet they were not certain; it might be sundry of the things feared might never befall; others, by provident care and the use of good means, might in a great measure be prevented; and all of them, through the help of God, by fortitude and patience, might either be borne or overcome. True it was, that such attempts were not to be made and undertaken without good ground and reason; not rashly or lightly, as many have done for curiosity or hope of gain, etc. But their condition was not ordinary; their ends were good and honorable; their calling lawful and urgent; and therefore they might expect the blessing of God in their proceeding. Yea, though they should lose their lives in this action, yet might they have comfort in the same, and their endeavors would be honorable.

Unhappily this heroic trait of Puritanism was coupled with a desperate religious bigotry which the world is even yet slow to forgive.

One of the earliest local dissenters was Thomas Morton (1575 ?–1646), author of the "New English Canaan," published in Amsterdam, 1637. It is a half-pathetic fact that this should stand out to-day beyond anything else written in the same decade in America, for the best of it — the third book — is a savage satire on the Puritans in Massachusetts. Morton, it is needless to say, was not a Puritan himself. He was a restless, dishonest, unscrupulous gentleman-adventurer from London who gave the best part of his life to fighting the Puritans on their own grounds. He started a fur-trading post at " Merry Mount," just southeast of Boston, sold the Indians liquor and firearms, consorted with their women, and in wanton mockery set up a Maypole there and taught the Indians the English games and dances which were particularly offensive to the grave residents of Plymouth and Boston. If he had not written his book, he would be remembered now only as one of the chief trouble-makers whom the Puritans had to fight down; but he did them more damage with his pen than with all his active misbehavior. He undermined their influence by not treating them soberly. He made fun of their costume, derided their speech, ridiculed their religious formalities, and held the valiant Miles Standish up to scorn by nicknaming him Captain Shrimp. He went further, and questioned their motives and their honesty, their integrity in business, and their sincerity in religion. A great deal of what he wrote about them was libelously unfair; he should never be taken as an authority for facts unless supported by other writers of his day. But underneath all his clever abuse of them and their ways, there is an evident basis of truth which is confirmed by the sober study of history. Although the Puritans were brave, strong, self-denying servants of the stern God whom they worshiped, they were sometimes sanctimonious, sometimes cruelly vengeful, and all too often so eager to achieve His ends on earth that they were regardless of the means they took. At the very beginning of their life in America, Thomas Morton held these characteristics up to public scorn; and in so doing he made his book an omen of the long, losing battle they were destined to fight. Morton's effectiveness as a writer lies in the fact that however ill-behaved he may have been, he was attractively — maybe dangerously — genial in character. He was in truth "a cheerful liar"; but he lied like the writer of fiction who disregards the exact facts because he is telling a good story as well as he can and because that good story is based on real life.

The next New Englander to give proof that the Puritans were not having an easy time in their "new English Canaan" was Nathaniel Ward (1578–1652?), author of "The Simple Cobler of Aggawam." In character and convictions he was as different from Morton as a man could be. When he wrote this book, which was published in London in 1647, he was an irascible old Puritan who had suffered much for his faith, and was still fighting for it, although very near to his threescore years and ten. He had been graduated at Cambridge, gone into the Church of England, been hounded there for his liberalism, come to America, and served a pastorate at Agawam (now Ipswich), Massachusetts. He had withdrawn on account of ill health, but later had served the state so well that he was granted six hundred acres as a reward, and had lived on there until his return to England at the age of seventy. He believed fiercely in the righteousness of the Puritan doctrines and in the wickedness of any departure from them; and his book was a valiant protest against any relaxation on the part of the faithful. It was written with reference to conditions in England, but it was composed after fifteen years' residence in America, and showed his unrest at conditions in the new country as well as in the old.

The book is a strange compound. In thought it is a piece of dyed-in-the-wool old fogyism, but in form and literary style it is vigorous, jaunty, and amusing. The full title is "The Simple Cobler of Aggawam in America; willing to help Mend his Native Country, lamentably tattered, both in the upper-Leather and sole, with all the honest stitches he can take. And as willing never to be paid for his work by Old English wonted pay. It is his Trade to patch all the year long, gratis. Therefore I Pray Gentlemen keep your Purses." He feared all innovations, but most of all the doctrine that men should enjoy liberty of conscience. "Let all the wits under the Heavens lay their heads together and find an Assertion worse than this [and] I will Petition to be chosen the universal Ideot of the World." "Since I knew what to fear, my timorous heart hath dreaded three things: a blazing Star appearing in the Air; a State Comet, I mean a favourite, rising in a kingdom; a new Opinion spreading in Religion." The second section of the book is devoted to fashions of dress, an evergreen subject for the satirist. Ward's attitude toward woman as an inferior creature was almost as primitive as that of the cave man, and apparently he would have liked it better if the "bullymong drossock" had dressed with the simplicity of a cave woman. As it was he felt that the lady of fashion was "the very gizzard of a trifle, the product of the quarter of a cypher, the epitome of Nothing"; and he had equal contempt for tailors who "spend their lives in making fidle-cases for futulous Women's phansies; which are the very pettitoes of Infirmity, the giblets of perquisquilian toyes." The remainder of the work is given to a discussion of affairs of English state, written with the same aggressive positiveness. The most interesting bit of it is the portion which proclaims his belief in savage oppression of the Irish, summing up the essence of the wrong-headed stupidity which has made the history of Ireland so lamentable a story even to the present time. What the old gentleman wrote is striking at points, because it seems so timely. But Ward was never up to date, in the sense of being prophetic. When he said things that apply to the twentieth century, they apply either because, like the question of extravagance in dress, the topic is a persistent trait in human nature or because, like the Irish problem, matters which should long ago have been settled have been allowed for centuries to confuse and complicate life. Yet Ward wrote with odd and striking effectiveness; and his book is far more than the "curiosity" which many critics have agreed to call it, for it is one of the best surviving records of the Puritan attempt to maintain a strangle hold on human thought.

The belief in the righteousness of persecuting dissenters was the particular ground for attack by a younger and equally vigorous man, Roger Williams (1604–1683). Williams, before he was forty years old, had been thrown out of two church establishments — first in Protestant England and then in Puritan Massachusetts. He represented what Burke termed the very "dissidence of dissent." And now, in a long and laborious argument lasting from 1644 to 1652, he fought out the issue with the Reverend John Cotton. Only by the most generous interpretation can the lengthening chain of this printed controversy be considered as literature, yet it has the same right to inclusion as the English disquisitions of Wyclif, Jeremy Taylor, and John Wesley. An English prisoner in Newgate, assailing persecution for cause of conscience, had been answered by John Cotton. Then followed Williams's "The Bloody Tenent of Persecution for cause of Conscience, discussed in a Conference between Truth and Peace" (1644); Cotton's reply "The Bloody Tenent washed and made white in the Blood of the Lamb" (1647); and Williams's rejoinder, "The Bloody Tenent yet More Bloody: by Mr. Cottons endeavor to wash it white in the Blood of the Lambe" (1652). The whole process of argument by both the reverend gentlemen was to set their literal English minds to work at analyzing and expounding Biblical passages which were full of oriental richness of imagery. It was, all things considered, rather less reasonable than it would be for the chancellors of the British and German empires to base an argument about the freedom of the seas upon definite citations from the "Rubaiyat" of Omar Khayyam.

The chief grounds of offense in the sinful unorthodoxy of Roger Williams were that he asserted two things which have become axioms to-day, and two more which will be admitted by every thoughtful and honest person. The first two were that religion should not be professed by those who did not believe it in their hearts, and that the power of the magistrates extended only to the bodies and the property of the subjects and not to their religious convictions. The second two were that America belonged to the Indians and not to the king of England, and that the established church was necessarily corrupt. By this last he meant simply that any human organization that is given complete authority, and need not fear either competition or overthrow by public opinion, is certain to decay from within. It was the idea beneath Tennyson's lines

> The old order changeth, yielding place to new,
> And God fulfils himself in many ways,
> Lest one good custom should corrupt the world.

Yet these opinions, preached and practiced by Williams, resulted in his being expelled from the community. The attempt was made to send him back to England, but he managed to get a permanent foothold in Rhode Island, where he opposed the still more liberal Quakers almost as violently as the churchmen of old and new England had opposed him. To his credit be it said, however, that he did not invoke the law against them. In action as well as in belief he marked the progress of liberal thought.

BOOK LIST

General References

EGGLESTON, EDWARD. The Transit of Civilization.

FISKE, JOHN. Beginnings of New England. Chaps. ii, iii.

HART, A. B. American History told by Contemporaries. Vol. I, pp. 200–272, 313–393.

RICHARDSON, C. F. American Literature. Chaps. i–iii.

TYLER, M. C. History of American Literature. Colonial Period. Vol. I, chaps. i–ix.

WENDELL, BARRETT. A Literary History of America. Bk. I, chaps. i–iv.

Individual Authors

CAPTAIN JOHN SMITH. A True Relation (London, 1608); A Map of Virginia, with a Description of the Country (Oxford, 1612); A Description of New England (London, 1616).

Available Editions

FORCE. Historical Tracts, Vol. II, Nos. 1 and 2. 1883.

Mass. Hist. Soc. Coll., Ser. 3, Vol. VI.

Collections

CAIRNS, W. B. Early American Writers, pp. 1–18.

DUYCKINCK, E. A. and G. L. Cyclopedia of American Literature, Vol. I, pp. 1–8, 33–43.

STEDMAN and HUTCHINSON. Library of American Literature, Vol. I, pp. 3–17.

Narratives of Early Virginia. L. G. Tyler, editor. 1907.

Sailors Narratives. G. P. Winship, editor. 1905.

WILLIAM BRADFORD. History of Plimouth Plantation. First published in *Mass. Hist. Soc. Coll., Ser. 4, Vol. III.*

Available Editions

Charles Deane, editor. 1896.

W. T. Davis, editor. 1912.

Collections

CAIRNS, W. B. Early American Writers, pp. 27–44.
STEDMAN and HUTCHINSON. Library of American Literature, Vol. I,
pp. 93–130.

THOMAS MORTON. New English Canaan, or New Canaan. Amsterdam,
1637.

Available Editions

FORCE. Historical Tracts, Vol. II, No. 5. 1883. C. F. Adams, editor.
Prince Historical Society Publications. 1888. C. F. Adams, editor.

Collections

CAIRNS, W. B. Early American Writers, pp. 60–72.
DUYCKINCK, E. A. and G. L. Cyclopedia of American Literature,
Vol. I, pp. 28–30.
STEDMAN and HUTCHINSON. Library of American Literature, Vol. I,
pp. 147–156.

NATHANIEL WARD. The Simple Cobler of Aggawam in America.
London, 1647.

Available Editions

FORCE. Historical Tracts, Vol. III, No. 8. 1906.
Ipswich Historical Society of Ipswich, Mass. *Publications.*

Biography

A Memoir of Nathaniel Ward. J. W. Dean. 1868.

Collections

CAIRNS, W. B. Early American Writers, pp. 112–124.
DUYCKINCK, E. A. and G. L. Cyclopedia of American Literature,
Vol. I, pp. 18–20.
STEDMAN and HUTCHINSON. Library of American Literature, Vol. I,
pp. 147–156.

ROGER WILLIAMS. Works. Edited by members of the Narragansett
Club, Providence, 1866–1874. 6 vols. Contains likewise J. Cotton's
contributions to the controversy with Williams, together with a
bibliography of Williams's works.

Available Edition

Letters from 1632 to 1675. *Mass. Hist. Soc. Coll., Ser. 4, Vol. VI.*

Biography and Criticism

CARPENTER, E. J. Roger Williams; a Study of the Life, etc. *Grafton
History Series.* 1909.
MASSON, DAVID. Life of John Milton, Vols. II, III.
STRAUS, OSCAR S. Roger Williams, the Pioneer of Religious Liberty.
1894.

Collections

CAIRNS, W. B. Early American Writers, pp. 94–111.

DUYCKINCK, E. A. and G. L. Cyclopedia of American Literature, Vol. I, pp. 32–38.

STEDMAN and HUTCHINSON. Library of American Literature, Vol. I, pp. 246–253.

Literary Treatment of the Period

Drama

BARKER, J. N. The Indian Princess; an Operatic Melodrama (1808), in *Representative Plays by American Dramatists* (edited by M. J. Moses), Vol. I. 1918.

CUSTIS, G. W. P. Pocahontas, or The Settlers of Virginia; a National Drama (1830), in *Representative American Plays* (edited by A. H. Quinn). 1917.

Essays

EMERSON, R. W. Discourse at Concord, 200th Anniversary. Works, Vol. XI.

LOWELL, J. R. New England Two Centuries Ago. Works, Vol. II.

WHITTIER, J. G. A Chapter of History, in *Literary Recreations and Miscellanies*.

Fiction

AUSTIN, MRS. J. G. Standish of Standish.

AUSTIN, MRS. J. G. Betty Alden (sequel).

AUSTIN, MRS. J. G. David Alden's Daughter.

HAWTHORNE, NATHANIEL. The Gray Champion and The Maypole of Merry Mount, in *Twice-Told Tales*.

HAWTHORNE, NATHANIEL. Young Goodman Brown, in *Mosses from an Old Manse*.

HAWTHORNE, NATHANIEL. The Scarlet Letter.

JOHNSTON, MARY. By Order of the Company.

JOHNSTON, MARY. The Old Dominion.

MOTLEY, J. L. Merry Mount.

Poetry

Poems of American History (edited by B. E. Stevenson), pp. 36–56.

American History by American poets (edited by N. U. Wallington). Vol. I, pp. 39–92.

TOPICS AND PROBLEMS

Read the "New English Canaan," Bk. III, with a view to deciding how far Morton's evident prejudice discredited his account of the Puritans; examine it again for its specifically literary qualities.

Read from Bradford's "History of Plimouth Plantation" for the admirable traits of Puritanism and see, also, if you find grounds for any of Morton's strictures.

Read the Hawthorne selections in the Book List — Literary Treatment of the Period — and decide how far he may have sympathized with the attitude of Morton in the " New English Canaan."

Read from " The Simple Cobler of Aggawam " for any evidence of Nathaniel Ward's residence in America ; decide on the degree to which the work is English and the degree to which it is colonial.

Compare the attitude toward Ireland of Nathaniel Ward in this work and of Jonathan Swift in his " Modest Proposal."

Make comparisons in diction from a corresponding number of pages in " The Simple Cobler " and in Carlyle's " Sartor Resartus."

CHAPTER II

Although it is generally said of the Puritans that they were actually hostile to all the arts, there is abundant proof that they had a liking for verse and a widespread inclination to try their hands at it. They wrote memorial verses of the most intricate and ingenious sorts, sometimes carving them in stone as epitaphs. There is less verse sprinkled through the unregenerate Morton's "Canaan" than there is in the intolerant Ward's "Cobler." The old conservative never wrote more wisely than in this so-called "song":

> They seldom lose the field, but often win,
> Who end their Warres, before their Warres begin.
>
> Their Cause is oft the worse, that first begin,
> And they may lose the field, the field that win.
>
> In Civil Warres 'twixt Subjects and their King,
> There is no conquest got, by conquering.
>
> Warre ill begun, the onely way to mend,
> Is t' end the Warre before the Warre do end.
>
> They that will end ill Warres, must have the skill,
> To make an end by Rule, and not by Will.
>
> In ending Warres 'tween Subjects and their Kings,
> Great things are sav'd by losing little things.

The first whole volume in English printed in the Western Hemisphere (printing of Spanish books in Mexico had long preceded) was "The Bay Psalm Book," Cambridge, 1640. This represented a conscientious attempt to put into the service of worship a literal translation of the Psalms. The worst passages are all too frequently cited as evidence of the inability of the Puritans to compose or appreciate good verse. And this in spite of the often-quoted and charmingly written prose comment in the editors' preface :

If therefore the verses are not alwayes so smooth and elegant as some may desire or expect; let them consider that God's Altar needs not our pollishings: Ex. 20. for wee have respected rather a plaine translation, then to smooth our verses with the sweetness of any paraphrase, and soe have attended Conscience rather than Elegance, fidelity rather then poetry, in translating the hebrew words into english language, and David's poetry into english meetre; that soe wee may sing in Sion the Lords songs of prayse according to his owne will; untill hee take us from hence and wipe away all our teares, & bid us enter into our masters joye to sing eternall Halleluliahs.

Some historians, moreover, seem to derive satisfaction from quoting passages from Michael Wigglesworth's (1631–1705) "Day of Doom" as added proof that the Puritans were never able to write verse that was beautiful or even graceful. It must be admitted that this grave and pretentious piece of work was hardly more lovely than the name of the author. Wigglesworth was a devoted Puritan who came to America at the age of seven; graduated from Harvard College ; qualified to practice medicine; and then became a preacher, serving, with intermissions of ill health, as pastor in Malden, Massachusetts, from 1657 until his death in 1705. He was a gentle, kindly minister, unfailing in his care for both the bodies and the souls of his parishioners.

He had the "lurking propensity" for verse-writing which was common among the men of his time, but instead of venting it merely in the composing of acrostics, anagrams, and epitaphs, he dedicated it to the Lord in the writing of a sort of rimed sermon on the subject of the Day of Judgment. The full title reads, "The Day of Doom or, a Description Of the Great and Last Judgment with a short discourse about Eternity. Eccles. 12. 14. For God shall bring every work into judgment with every secret thing, whether it be good, or whether it be evil." It was printed, probably in Cambridge, Massachusetts, in 1662.

The poem is composed of two hundred and twenty-four eight-line stanzas. After an invocation and the announcement of the day of doom, the dead come from their graves before the throne of Christ. There the "sheep" who have been chosen for salvation are placed on the right, and the wicked "goats" come in groups to hear the judge's verdict. These include hypocrites, civil, honest men, those who died in youth before they were converted, those who were misled by the example of the good, those who did not understand the Bible, those who feared martyrdom more than hell-torment, those who thought salvation was hopeless, and, finally, those who died as babes. All are sternly answered from the throne, and all are swept off to a common eternal doom except the infants, for whom is reserved "the easiest room in hell."

Two facts should be remembered in criticizing "The Day of Doom" as poetry. The first is that Wigglesworth wrote it consciously as a teacher and preacher and not as a poet. In his introduction he said :

> Reader, I am a fool
> And have adventurèd
> To play the fool this once for Christ,
> The more his fame to spread.
> If this my foolishness
> Help thee to be more wise,
> I have attainèd what I seek,
> And what I only prize.

The second point is that in writing a rimed sermon for Christian worshipers he had a model supplied him in the popular "Bay Psalm Book," which had appeared some twenty years before and which was familiar to all the people who were likely to be his readers. The translators of the 121st Psalm wrote, for example :

> 1 I to the hills lift up mine eyes,
>   from whence shall come mine aid
> 2 Mine help doth from Jehovah come,
>   which heav'n and earth hath made.

And Wigglesworth took up the strain with

> No heart so bold, but now grows cold,
>   and almost dead with fear;
> No eye so dry but now can cry,
>   and pour out many a tear.

To any modern reader the use of this light-footed meter for so grave a subject seems utterly ill-considered, and the whole idea of the day of doom as he presented it seems so unnatural as to be amusing. But Wigglesworth was trying to write a rimed summary of what everybody thought, in a meter with which everybody was familiar, and he was unqualifiedly successful. A final verdict on Michael Wigglesworth is often superciliously pronounced on the basis of this one poem, or, if any further attention is conceded him, the worst of his remaining output is produced for evidence that he and all Puritan preachers were clumsy and prosaic verse-writers.

Yet in the never-quoted lines immediately following " The Day of Doom " — a poem without a title, on the vanity of human wishes — Michael Wigglesworth gave proofs of human kindliness and of poetic power. In these earnest lines Wigglesworth showed a mastery of fluent verse, a control of poetic imagery, and a gentle yearning for the souls' welfare of his parishioners which is the utterance of the pastor rather than of the theologian. For a moment God ceases to be angry, Christ stands pleading without the gate, and the good pastor utters a poem upon the neglected theme " The Kingdom of Heaven is within you " :

> Fear your great Maker with a child-like awe,
> Believe his Grace, love and obey his Law.
> This is the total work of man, and this
> Will crown you here with Peace and there with Bliss.

" The Day of Doom," however, was far more popular than the better poetry that Wigglesworth wrote at other times. It was the most popular book of the century in America. People memorized its easy, jingling meter just as they might have memorized ballads or, at a later day, Mother Goose rimes; and the grim description became "the solace," as Lowell says, "of every fireside, the flicker of the pine-knots by which it was conned perhaps adding a livelier relish to its premonitions of eternal combustion." The popularity of "The Day of Doom" shows that in the very years when the Royalists were returning to power in England the Puritans were greatly in the majority in New England. The reaction marked by Morton, Ward, and Roger Williams was only beginning. Moreover, if it had been the only "poetry" of the period, we should have to admit that the Puritans were almost hopelessly unpoetical.

Anne Bradstreet (1612–1672) proves the contrary, and in doing so she proves how the love of beauty can manage to bloom under the bleakest skies. Her talent was assuredly a "flower in a crannied wall." She was born in England in 1612 and was married at the age of sixteen, as girls often were in those days, to a man several years older, Simon Bradstreet. In 1630 she came to Massachusetts with her husband and her father. Both became eminent in the affairs of the colony. In the family they were doubtless sober and probably dull. Mrs. Bradstreet kept house under pioneer conditions in one place after another, and when still less than forty years old had become the mother of eight children. Yet somewhere in the rare moments of her crowded days — and one can imagine how far apart those moments must have been — she put into verse "a compleat Discourse and Description of The Four Elements, Constitutions, Ages of Man, Seasons of the Year; Together with an exact Epitome of the four Monarchies, viz., the Assyrian, Persian, Grecian, Roman" [this means *five* long poems, and not two]; "also a dialogue between Old England and New concerning the late troubles; with divers other pleasant and serious poems." All these she wrote without apparent thought of publication, for the purely artistic reason that she enjoyed doing so; and in 1650 — halfway between "The Bay Psalm

Book " and " The Day of Doom " — they were taken over to London by a friend, and there put into print as the work of " The Tenth Muse Lately Sprung up in America."

Poetry was more than a diversion for Anne Bradstreet; it must have been a passion. As a girl she had been allowed to read in the library of the Puritan Earl of Lincoln, over whose estate her father was steward. And here she had fallen under the spell of the lesser poets of her age, naturally not the dramatists, whom the Puritans opposed. So, after their fashion, and particularly in the fashion of a Frenchman, Du Bartas, whose works were popular in an English translation, she wrote her quaint "quarternions," or poems on the four elements, the four seasons, the four ages, and the four "humours," and capped them all with the four monarchies. These are interesting to the modern reader only as examples of how the human mind used to work. Chaucer had juggled with the same materials; Ben Jonson had been fascinated with them. It was a literary tradition to develop them one by one, to set them in debate against each other, and to interweave them into corresponding groups : childhood, water, winter, phlegm ; youth, air, spring, blood ; manhood, fire, summer, choler; and old age, earth, autumn, melancholy.

Yet her chief claim on our interest is founded on the shorter poems, in which she took least pride. In these she showed her real command of word and measure to express poetic thought. Her " Contemplations," for example, is as poetic in thought as Bryant's " Thanatopsis," or as Lanier's " The Marshes of Glynn," to which it stands in suggestive contrast (see pp. 161 and 357). The former two are on the idea that nature endures but man passes away. This was never long absent from the Puritan mind, but when it came to the ordinary Puritan it was likely to be cast into homely and prosaic verse, as in the epitaph :

> The path of death it must be trod
> By them that wish to walk with God.

Anne Bradstreet, taking the same observation, wrote with noble dignity :

> O Time the fatal wrack of mortal things,
> That draws oblivions curtain over kings,
> Their sumptuous monuments, men know them not,
> Their names without a Record are forgot,
> Their parts, their ports, their pomp's all laid in th' dust
> Nor wit, nor gold, nor buildings, scape time's rust;
> But he whose name is grav'd in the white stone [1]
> Shall last and shine when all of these are gone.

Yet as a strictly Puritan poetess she did only one part of her work. She was even more interesting as an early champion of her sex. She did not go so far as to assert equality of the sexes; that was too far in advance of the age for her imagination. But she did contend that women should be given credit for whatever was worth "small praise." This appears again and again in her shorter poems.

> Let Greeks be Greeks, and women what they are
> Men have precedency and still excell,
> It is but vain unjustly to wage warre;
> Men can do best, and women know it well;
> Preheminence in all and each is yours;
> Yet grant some small acknowledgment of ours.

Naturally she was full of pride in the achievements of Queen Elizabeth, a pride which she expressed in a fine song "In Honour of that High and Mighty Princess":

> From all the Kings-on earth she won the prize.
> Nor say I more then duly is her due,
> Millions will testifie that this is true.
> She hath wip'd off th' aspersion of her Sex,
> That women wisdom lack to play the Rex:
> Spains Monarch, sayes not so, nor yet his host:
> She taught them better manners, to their cost.

[1] Rev. ii, 17.

> The Salique law, in force now had not been,
> If France had ever hop'd for such a Queen.
> But can you Doctors now this point dispute,
> She's Argument enough to make you mute.
> Since first the sun did run his nere run race,
> And earth had once a year, a new old face,
> Since time was time, and man unmanly man,
> Come shew me such a *Phœnix* if you can?

Then follows a recital of Elizabeth's proudest triumphs, and assertions of how far she surpassed Tomris, Dido, Cleopatra, Zenobya, and the conclusion:

> Now say, have women worth? or have they none?
> Or had they some, but with our Queen is't gone?
> Nay Masculines, you have thus taxt us long,
> But she, though dead, will vindicate our wrong.
> Let such as say our Sex is void of Reason,
> Know tis a Slander now, but once was Treason.

Anne Bradstreet foreshadowed the "woman's movement" of to-day by two full centuries, and thus showed how even the daughter of one Puritan governor of Massachusetts and the wife of another could be thinking and aspiring far in advance of her times.

BOOK LIST

General References

OTIS, W. B. American Verse, 1625–1807. 1909. (A full and valuable bibliography appended.)

TUCKER, S. M. In chap. ix of Cambridge History of American Literature, Vol. I, Bk. I.

TYLER, M. C. A History of American Literature. Colonial Period (1607–1765), Vol. I, chaps. x, xi. 1878.

Individual Authors

The Bay Psalm Book. The Whole Booke of Psalmes Faithfully Translated into English Metre, etc. 1640.

Available Editions

A Reprint, 1862.

Facsimile Reprint for the New England Society in the City of New York, 1903.

Collections

CAIRNS, W. B. Early American Writers, pp. 73–81.
DUYCKINCK, E. A. and G. L. Cyclopedia of American Literature, Vol. I, pp. 16–18.
STEDMAN and HUTCHINSON. Library of American Literature, Vol. I, pp. 211–216.

MICHAEL WIGGLESWORTH. The Day of Doom; or, a Description of the Great and Last Judgment, etc. (1662). Meat out of the Eater: or, Meditations concerning the necessity, end and usefulness of Afflictions unto God's Children, etc. (1670). God's Controversy with New England (1662). Vanity of Vanities (appended to 3d edition of The Day of Doom).

Available Editions

The Day of Doom, 1867.
God's Controversy with New England. *Proceedings of the Mass. Hist. Soc.*, 1871.

Biography

Memoir of Michael Wigglesworth. J. W. Dean. 1871. See also M. W.,* earliest poet among Harvard graduates. *Proceedings of the Mass. Hist. Soc.*, 1895.

Collections

BOYNTON, PERCY H. American Poetry, pp. 18–23, 598–600.
CAIRNS, W. B. Early American Writers, pp. 163–177.
DUYCKINCK, E. A. and G. L. Cyclopedia of American Literature, Vol. I, pp. 57–59.
STEDMAN and HUTCHINSON. Library of American Literature, Vol. II, pp. 3–19.

ANNE BRADSTREET. The Tenth Muse lately sprung up in America, or Several Poems, compiled with great Variety of Wit and Learning, full of Delight — by a Gentlewoman in those parts. 1650.

Available Editions

The Club of Odd Volumes, 1897.
The Works of Anne Bradstreet, in Prose and Verse. J. H. Ellis, editor. 1867. This contains a valuable memoir.
The Works of Mrs. Anne Bradstreet, together with her prose remains, and with an introduction by Charles Eliot Norton.

Biography and Criticism

CAMPBELL, HELEN. Anne Bradstreet and her Time. 1891.
TYLER, M. C. American Literature. Colonial Period, Vol. I, chap. x.

Collections

BOYNTON, PERCY H. American Poetry, pp. 1–8, 594–598.
CAIRNS, W. B. Early American Writers, pp. 146–164.

DUYCKINCK, E. A. and G. L. Cyclopedia of American Literature,
Vol. I, pp. 47–52.
STEDMAN and HUTCHINSON. Library of American Literature, Vol. I,
pp. 311–315.

TOPICS AND PROBLEMS

Confirm the comparison of meters in the " Bay Psalm Book "
and " The Day of Doom."

Read the opening and closing passages in " The Day of Doom "
(Boynton, "American Poetry," pp. 18–21) for the genuinely poetic
material. Compare with Milton's use of the same material in
" Paradise Lost," Bk. I.

Read Anne Bradstreet's verses to Queen Elizabeth, the Prologue
to the long poems, the rimed epistles to her husband, and the tribu-
tary poems of Nathaniel Ward and others (Boynton, "American
Poetry," pp. 1–13 passim) for the difference — even with her libera!-
ism — between her point of view and that of the modern woman.

Read " Contemplations " and a passage of equal length from
"The Faerie Queene " for likenesses and differences in versification.

Compare the ideas of God and of nature in " Contemplations " (of
the later seventeenth century), "Thanatopsis " (of the early nineteenth),
and " The Marshes of Glynn " (of the later nineteenth) and note how
far they are personal to Anne Bradstreet, Bryant, and Lanier and
how far they represent the spirit of their respective periods.

CHAPTER III

THE TRANSITION TO THE EIGHTEENTH CENTURY

As the end of the seventeenth century approached, the Puritans were still in an overwhelming majority in New England, but the hold of the churchmen on the government of the colonies was, nevertheless, being slowly and reluctantly relaxed. Government in America has always, in its broad aspects, reflected the will of the people. If legislators and legislation have been vicious, it has been because the majority of the people have not cared enough about it to see that good men were chosen. If stupid and blundering laws have been passed, it has been because the people were not wide awake enough to analyze them. On the other hand old laws, unadjusted to modern conditions, have often become "dead letters" because the majority did not wish to have them enforced, even though they were on the statute books ; and new and progressive legislation has been imposed on reluctant lawmakers by the pressure of public opinion. Now the Puritan uprising in England had been a democratic movement by a people who wanted to have a hand in their own government. It was a religious movement, because in England Church and State are one and because the oppression in religious matters had been particularly offensive. And in England it had been on the whole successful in spite of the restoration of kingship in 1660, for from that time on the arbitrary power of king and council were steadily and increasingly curbed. As a consequence there was a parallel movement in the democracy across the sea. American colonists with a highly developed sense of justice resented a bad royal governor like Andros, and were able to force his withdrawal; and they resented unreasonable domination by the

27

clergy, and were independent enough to shake it off. Between 1690 and 1700 Harvard College became for the first time something more than a training school for preachers; the right to vote in Boston was made to depend on moral character and property ownership instead of on membership in the church; and in the midst of the Salem witchcraft hysteria judges and grand-jurymen caught their balance and refused any longer to act as cat's-paws of the clergy. The passage to the eighteenth century was therefore a time of transition in common thinking; and the record of the change is clearly discernible in the literary writings of the old-line conservatives Cotton and Increase Mather, in the Diary of Samuel Sèwall, who was able to see the light and to change slowly with his generation, and in the Journal of Sarah Kemble Knight, who represented the silent unorthodoxy of hundreds of other well-behaved and respectable people.

The Mathers, Increase (1639–1723) and Cotton (1663–1728), were the second and third of a succession of four members of one family who were so popular and influential as to deserve the nickname which is sometimes given them of the "Mather Dynasty." These two were both born in America, educated in Boston and at Harvard, and made church leaders while still young men. In age they were only twenty-four years apart, and from 1682 to 1723 they worked together to uphold and increase the power of the church in New England. Because of their prominence as preachers they inherited the "good will" which had belonged to their greatest predecessors, and by their own industry, learning, eloquence, and general vigor they added to their ecclesiastical fortunes like skillful business men. Their congregations were large and respectfully attentive; scores of .their sermons were reprinted by request; on all public occasions and in all public discussions they were at the forefront. They were great popular favorites, and in the end they suffered the fate of many another popular favorite. For the deference which was given to them year after year made them vain and domineering; they talked too much and too long and too confidently, and they made the mistakes of judgment which men who talk all the time are bound to make. When Increase Mather lost the presidency of Harvard in 1701 they both acted like spoiled children ; their prestige was already on the wane, for when the reaction had followed the witchcraft delusion, to which they had fanned the flames, the caution which they had advised was forgotten, and the encouragement which they had given was held up against them. To the ends of their lives, in 1723 and 1728, they were proudly unrelenting, but their last years were embittered by the knowledge that their power was departed from them.

The bulk of their authorship was prodigious, even though most of it was in the form of pamphlets or booklets, for it amounted in the case of Increase to about one hundred and fifty titles, and in the case of Cotton to nearly four hundred. But they are chiefly remembered for three books : " An Essay for the recording of Illustrious Providences," by the elder ; and " The Wonders of the Invisible World " and the " Magnalia Christi Americana : Or the Ecclesiastical History of New-England," by the younger. The first two of these are unintended explanations to the twentieth-century reader as to how a whole community could ever have been swept into the Salem witchcraft excesses of 1692. Any educated man who should advance the theories to-day which were soberly expounded by these two really learned men would be held up to scorn and very possibly be made subject of a sanity investigation. Yet two hundred years ago the world was ignorant of the commonplaces of science. Popular superstition therefore ran riot ; and the belief that God would interpose in the affairs of daily individual life, and that a personal devil was walking up and down the earth seeking whom he might devour, added to the confusion. Medicine in those days was hardly a science even in the broadest sense of the word. Physicians depended for honest effects on a few simple herb remedies and on powerful emetics and the letting of blood. The populace believed

in curatives which still are resorted to only by children and
the most ignorant of grown-ups — like anointing implements
with which they had been injured, in order to heal cuts and
bruises, or like being touched by the monarch as a remedy
for scrofula, the " king's evil." Sir Kenelm Digby, a well-
known subject of Charles II, reported that he overcame a
persistent illness by having the fumes of camomile poured into
his ear. The same sort of speculation prevailed in all the other
sciences; and side by side with it superstition flourished. Between 1560 and 1600 in the little kingdom of Scotland, which
had a population no larger than that of Massachusetts to-day,
there were eight thousand executions for witchcraft, — an average of nearly four a week; and James I, who was Scotland's
gift to England, was the author of a work on demonology.

What the New Englanders, and among them the Mathers,
believed was, therefore, not unusual at the time. In fact the
Mathers were both somewhat less credulous than their fellows,
but they only substituted one superstition for another. Their
way of casting off the old and vulgar beliefs which were pagan
in origin was to contend that these vain and foolish ideas
were put into Christian minds by Satan and his emissaries.
Said Increase Mather in his " Illustrious Providences " :

> Some also have believed that if they should cast Lead into the
> Water, then *Saturn* would discover to them the thing they inquired
> after. It is not *Saturn* but *Satan* that maketh the discovery, when
> anything is in such a way revealed. And of this sort is the foolish
> Sorcery of those Women that put the white of an Egg into a Glass
> of Water, so that they may be able to divine of what Occupation their
> future husbands shall be. It were much better to remain ignorant
> than thus to consult with the Devil. These kind of practices appear
> at first blush to be Diabolical; so that I shall not multiply Words in
> evincing the evil of them. It is noted that *the Children of Israel did
> secretly those things that are not right against the Lord their God* 2 King.
> 17. 9. I am told there are some who do secretly practice such Abomi-
> nations as these last mentioned, unto whom the Lord in mercy give
> deep and unfeigned Repentance and pardon for their grievous Sin.

These preachers thus turned superstition into an enemy of the true religion, as it assuredly is; but they regarded it not as the fruit of ignorance, to be remedied by education and intelligence, but as a device of Satan which could be offset by preaching and prayer. The two books are cut from the same cloth, so that an indication of the contents of the one just mentioned will give an idea of them both. The chapter headings run as follows: Of Remarkable Sea Deliverances; Preservations; Lightening; Philosophical Meditations; Things Preternatural [voices of invisible speakers and doings of mysterious mischief-makers]; That there are Daemons and Possessed Persons [three main arguments: (1) Scripture forbade witchcraft, therefore there must be such a thing; (2) experience has made it manifest; (3) convicted maldoers have confessed it]; Apparitions; Conscience; Deaf and Dumb Persons; Tempests; Earthquakes; and Judgments. As a whole the book is a collection of curious anecdotes taken on almost any hearsay, but almost all at second or third hand. They resemble some of the most popular of the atrocity stories which have been told during every war that history chronicles, but which no investigator has been able to run down in any single instance. In point of superstition the Mathers, to repeat, should be considered in two lights: compared with educated men of the twentieth century they were almost incredibly primitive in what they were willing to believe, but considered with reference to their own generation they fought the wiles of the devil as soldiers of the Lord.

The most ambitious work that either produced was Cotton Mather's "Magnalia," a history of the Church in New England. This was a bulky two-volume effort, divided into seven parts, or books. As a matter of fact it was really a general history of the region by a man who regarded the existence of New England as identical with the existence of the Church. In this basic assumption as well as in many of his details Cotton Mather revealed himself as a hopeless conservative of his day — hopeless because it was already evident to all but him and his kind that the State was shaking off the control of the Church leaders. One can get a fair idea of the bias of the book from the opening paragraph :

It is the Opinion of some, though 't is *but* an *Opinion*, and *but* of *some* Learned Men, That when the Sacred Oracles of Heaven assure us, *The Things under the Earth* are some of those, *whose Knees are to bow in the Name of Jesus*, by those *Things* are meant the Inhabitants of *America*, who are Antipodes to those of the other *Hemispheres*. I would not quote any words of *Lactantius*, though there are *some* to countenance this Interpretation, because of their being so *Ungeographical*: nor would I go to strengthen the Interpretation by reciting the Words of the *Indians* to the first *White Invaders* of their Territories, *We hear you are come from under the World, to take our World from us*. But granting the *uncertainty* of such an Exposition, I shall yet give the Church of God a certain account of these *Things*, which in *America* have been Believing and Adoring the glorious *Name* of Jesus ; and of that Country in America, where those *Things* have been attended with Circumstances most remarkable.

The "Magnalia" is really an attempt at a general history of New England from 1620 to 1698, containing classified material on the governors, magistrates, and preachers, a history of Harvard, a collection of reports of church transactions, an account of the Indian Wars, and "A Faithful Record of many Illustrious Wonderful Providences." Yet for historical data it is almost as unreliable as the libelous "New English Canaan" of Thomas Morton. For Morton was no more eager to turn the facts to the discredit of the Puritans than Mather was to interpret them to the glory of the Church; and the consequence was that neither could be absolutely trusted. The historians have abandoned Mather as a safe authority. His sin has found him out, even though he committed it in the name of the Lord.

The man in this period in whom complete faith can be put is Samuel Sewall, who did not profess to be an author except in an incidental way. He lived from 1652 to 1730 and kept a very full diary from 1673 to 1729. This was written with no thought of publication, and actually was not printed until a hundred and fifty years later, when it was given to the world by the Massachusetts Historical Society. In American literature Sewall's Diary occupies a place almost exactly parallel to that of John Evelyn's in English letters. Their lives and their long diaries covered about the same years, and they held corresponding positions in the communities. Both were educated men — Sewall was a graduate of Harvard — and both were highly respected and trusted. Sewall held a minor position at Harvard connected with the library, was prominent in church affairs, and was a judge, officiating at the time of the Salem witchcraft trials. An informal journal written without prejudice, by such a man as he, gives material of the greatest value for a picture of the times. It is material of course and not the picture itself, for it lacks anything in the way of composition, just as do the facts of ordinary daily life in the order of their occurrence. But out of it two main threads of interest may be unwoven. One is the sober but not unrelieved background of the times, itself a composite of various strands. Religion was its strongest fiber. Few weeks pass in which there is no record of sermon, fast, christening, wedding, funeral, or special celebration. These were among the chief social happenings of the calendar. Funerals as well as more festive occasions were accompanied with gifts of gloves and rings; refreshments were ample if not lavish; and the bill for strong drinks was always a heavy item, for it must be remembered that prohibition is of recent origin, and that among the Puritans self-control made drunkenness as infrequent as drinking was common. Against frivolity too they set their minds; and Sewall's Diary gives a protest at " tricks " and dancing and May festivals, and even Christmas and Easter, which were triply hated because they had their origins in pagan tradition and had come to the present through the Church of Rome and the Church of England. Yet the objections to these practices and festivals show that they were real disturbances in Sewall's Boston, as were the roistering of sailors and other strangers in town.

The other and more important thread is the revelation of the inner mind of a flesh-and-blood colonial American. It takes patient reading to recreate the real man; but he is here in these pages, with all the inconsistencies that make up life out of story-books. He was all in all a fine, devout, broad-gauge man — and this is what any biographer would tell of him — with a moderate supply of littleness and petty vanity, which the biographer would be almost certain to suppress. And he was in himself a record of the public opinion of his generation. He wrote two other things besides his Diary. One is a theological treatise which was as uninspired as the quoted paragraph from Mather's "Magnalia," and on much the same theme. It shows him to be an apparently hopeless old fogy. The other is a pamphlet called "The Selling of Joseph," which was probably the first antislavery utterance printed in America, and implies that Samuel Sewall was centuries ahead of the times. There is at second glance nothing perplexing in this contradiction. Sewall was a normal man who stood between the oldest-fashioned and the newest-fashioned thinkers. Sometimes he leaned backward, and sometimes forward ; but on the whole he was inclined to advance. Of this he gave one famous proof. Five years after the Salem trials he had the honesty to admit to himself that he had been all wrong in his judgment, and the courage to make a public confession of his repentance. He chose one of the hardest ways of doing it. Among the "curious punishments of bygone days," one was the humiliation of disreputable persons by forcing them to sit at the foot of the church pulpit while the minister read a public reproof. On Fast Day, 1697, Samuel Sewall of his own choice posted a bill which could be read by any who would, and, giving a copy of it to the Reverend Mr. Willard, stood up at the reading before the congregation. The method of atoning for his mistake proves that he was still a devout and faithful Puritan worshiper, but the fact that he did so at all shows that he could confess errors, even when they had been committed in behalf of the Church. The Mathers could neither have seen nor acknowledged such mistakes. They were too cocksure of being always right. So life passed on, leaving them by the wayside ; and Samuel Sewall was with the quiet majority who sadly left them behind.

A third representative of the attitudes of mind at the changing of the centuries was a genial woman, Mrs. Sarah Kemble Knight (1666–1727). She was not in any sense a public figure, like the preachers and the judge just mentioned, nor did she pursue the habit of writing a continued diary like Sewall's. Most emphatically she was not given to the unwholesome recording, like many other women in her day, of "itineraries of daily religious progress, aggravated by overwork, indigestion, and a gospel of gloom." But there was one itinerary which she did record for her own satisfaction and which was published more than a century later, in 1825, — her " Journal of a Journey from Boston to New York in 1704." At this time a vigorous woman of thirty-eight, a wife and a mother, she set out alone on the ten-day journey, taking such guides as she could engage from one stage to the next. The hardships were considerable and the discomforts and inconveniences very great ; and the striking fact about them is that she bore up under them in a good-humored, matter-of-fact, sort of twentieth-century way. An accident was an accident and not a visitation from on high ; a disagreeable or churlish or even a dishonest person was somebody to be put up with and not to be moralized on as unscriptural. The worst innkeeper she encountered was a man to avoid in the future rather than a man to convert ; she did not seem shocked by a drunken quarrel late one night, but she was annoyed, because she wanted to go to sleep.

She was at times positively frivolous and irreverent in her allusions. Crossing a river one day she was very near to being tipped over.

The canoe was very small and shallow, so that when we were in [it] seemed ready to take in water, which greatly terrified me, and caused me to be very circumspect, sitting with my hands fast on each side, my eyes steady, not daring so much as to lodge my tongue a hair's breadth more on one side of my mouth than t' other, nor so much as to think on Lot's wife; for a wry thought would have overset our wherry.

Her jests about the name of the innkeeper, Mr. Devil, would have landed her in the stocks had she made them publicly in Boston.

The post encouraged me by saying we should be well accommodated at Mr. Devil's, a few, miles further; but I questioned whether we ought to go to the Devil to be helped out of affliction. However, like the rest of the deluded souls that post to the infernal den, we made all possible speed to this Devil's habitation; where, alighting in good assurance of good accommodations, we were going in.

The accommodations turned out to be anything but good; and she left her host with a sigh of relief, and the thought " He differed only in this from the old fellow in t' other country — he let us depart," following the observation with a rimed warning for subsequent travelers to avoid this earthly hell. These are quoted not because they are admirable or worthy of imitation but because they give an indication of what was going on under one very respectable bonnet when Mrs. Knight was sitting decorously in her Boston pew. She was a highly respected woman in the Puritan community. She was accustomed to its ways. There is no word of motherly regret that she was away from her little daughter on Christmas Day, for Christmas was not a festal day in her calendar. Of the people who were coming into manhood and womanhood when Sarah Kemble Knight was born, Hawthorne wrote in " The Scarlet Letter ": " The generation next to the early immigrants wore the blackest shade of Puritanism, and so darkened the national visage with it, that all the subsequent years have not sufficed to clear it up. We have yet to learn again the forgotten art of gayety."

It was men like the author of the "Magnalia" who had darkened the national visage, but women here and there, like the writer of this Journal, who had already returning gleams of gayety. Of the three people whom we have taken as types of New-England thought at this period, Cotton Mather may fairly be regarded as representing the faith of a declining theology, Samuel Sewall the hope of a broader and more generous civic attitude, and Mrs. Knight as the flicker of charity or warm-hearted and genial fellow-feeling which had been almost extinguished in the seventeenth century.

BOOK LIST

General References

CHAMBERLAIN, N. H. Samuel Sewall and the World he Lived in. 1897.

COBB, S. H. Rise of Religious Liberty in America. 1902.

DEXTER, HENRY M. The Congregationalism of the Last Three Hundred Years as Seen in its Literature. With a bibliographical appendix. 1880. (An excellent history, and indispensable for its bibliographical information.)

EARLE, ALICE MORSE. Child Life in Colonial Days. 1904.

EARLE, ALICE MORSE. Curious Punishments of Bygone Days. 1896 and 1907.

EARLE, ALICE MORSE. Customs and Fashions in Old New England. 1893.

EARLE, ALICE MORSE. Home Life in Colonial Days. 1898.

EARLE, ALICE MORSE. Stage-Coach and Tavern Days. 1900.

FISKE, JOHN. New France and New England, chap. v.

MASSON, DAVID. Life of John Milton. 1859–1880. 6 vols. (Valuable for the English backgrounds of Puritanism.)

RICHARDSON, C. F. American Literature, chap. iv.

TYLER, M. C. A History of American Literature. Colonial Period. Vol. I, chaps. xii, xiii.

WALKER, W. Ten New England Leaders. 1901.

WENDELL, BARRETT. Literary History of America, Bk. I, chap. v. 1901.

Individual Authors

INCREASE MATHER. An Essay for the Recording of Illustrious Providences. 1684.

Available Edition

With introductory preface by George Offor. London, 1890.

Collections

CAIRNS, W. B. Early American Writers, pp. 199–216.

DUYCKINCK, E. A. and G. L. Cyclopedia of American Literature, Vol. I, p. 59.

STEDMAN and HUTCHINSON. A Library of American Literature, Vol. II, pp. 75–106.

COTTON MATHER. The Wonders of the Invisible World. 1693. Magnalia Christi Americana: or, The Ecclesiastical History of New England, 1620–1698. 1702.

Available Editions

Magnalia. With notes, translations, and life. 1853.

The Wonders, etc. Reprints, Cambridge, 1861, 1862.

Biography and Criticism

MARVIN, Rev. A. P. The Life and Times of Cotton Mather. 1892.

PARRINGTON, V. L. Cambridge History of American Literature. Vol. I, Bk. I, in chap iii.

SPRAGUE, W. B. Annals of the American Pulpit, Vol. I, pp. 189–195. 1857.

TYLER, M. C. History of American Literature. Colonial Period. Vol. I, chaps. xii, xiii.

Collections

CAIRNS, W. B. Early American Writers, pp. 217–237.

DUYCKINCK, E. A. and G. L. Cyclopedia of American Literature, Vol. I, pp. 59–66.

STEDMAN and HUTCHINSON. Library of American Literature, Vol. II, pp. 114–166.

SAMUEL SEWALL. Diary from 1673 to 1729. The only edition is *Mass. Hist. Soc. Coll., Ser. 5, Vols. VI–VIII.*

Collections

CAIRNS, W. B. Early American Writers, pp. 238–251.

STEDMAN and HUTCHINSON. Library of American Literature, Vol. II, pp. 188–200.

History and Criticism

CHAMBERLAIN, N. H. (See General References.)

TYLER, M. C. (See General References.)

SARAH KEMBLE KNIGHT. Journals of Madame Knight. From the original manuscripts written in 1704. T. Dwight, editor. 1825.

Available Editions

A Reprint, Albany, 1865.

A Reprint, Norwich, Conn., 1901.

Collection

STEDMAN and HUTCHINSON. Library of American Literature, Vol. II, pp. 248–264.

History and Criticism

TYLER, M. C. (See General References.)

Literary Treatment of the Period

Drama

BARKER, J. N. Superstition, a Tragedy (1824), in *Representative American Plays* (edited by A. H. Quinn). 1917.

LONGFELLOW, H. W. The New England Tragedies.

WILKINS, MARY E. Giles Corey, Yeoman.

Essays

LOWELL, J. R. Witchcraft. Works, Vol. V.

WHITTIER, J. G. Charms and Fairy Faith, and Magicians and Witch Folk in *Literary Recreations and Miscellanies*.

Fiction

AUSTIN, MRS. J. G. A Nameless Nobleman.

AUSTIN, MRS. J. G. Dr. Le Baron and his Daughter (sequel).

COOPER, J. F. The Wept of Wish-ton-Wish.

SIMMS, W. GILMORE. The Yemassee.

WILKINS, MARY E. The Heart's Highway.

Poetry

Poems of American History (edited by B. E. Stevenson), pp. 71–97.

TOPICS AND PROBLEMS

Read the introduction to the "Magnalia" or a chapter from "Illustrious Providences," or "The Wonders of the Invisible World," for evidence of superstition based on Scriptural authority and of vulgar, or folk, superstition.

In the *Nation* of August 17, 1918, pp. 173–175, there is an article in review of five new books under the title "Spirit Communication." Establish the differences and the likenesses between the modern attitude and the attitude of the seventeenth century toward "the invisible world."

Read Fitz-Greene Halleck's "Connecticut," stanzas xiii–xxvi, and Whittier's "The Double-Headed Snake of Newbury," ll. 71–85, as well as Irving's "The Legend of Sleepy Hollow" (see p. 129 in this volume), for typical literary expressions of aversion to Cotton Mather.

The best method of approaching Samuel Sewall's Diary is to read some fifty pages — preferably between 1680 and 1710 — for the references to a definite topic. This may best be selected from promising suggestions in the first few pages of reading. If none appears, look for any of the following or others like them: Sunday observance; funerals, weddings, and christenings; the pastor and his people; holidays; parents and children; self-analysis; religious discipline; law and order. Comparisons on a given topic with the entries for the same period in Evelyn or for an equal number of pages in Pepys are fruitful.

A similar approach may be made to Mrs. Knight's compact and consecutive Journal. Her humor, irreverence, tolerance, independence, timidity, or her use of exaggeration, mock-heroics, Scriptural allusion, personal description, social analysis, are rich in their possibilities.

Read in Andrew Macphail's " Essays in Puritanism " the essay on John Winthrop, and then the exchange of opinions between Messrs. White and Hackett in the *New Republic*, May 17, 1919. Do either or both throw light on the chief characters discussed in this chapter?

CHAPTER IV

JONATHAN EDWARDS AND BENJAMIN FRANKLIN

The danger in drawing conclusions about a whole century, as we have been doing, is that the facts may be forced to seem far simpler than they were. It should be kept in mind that these are only certain broad currents of thought, tendencies which were obscured by all sorts of cross waves and chop seas. And it should be mentioned that the Puritan with the greatest mind of them all, Jonathan Edwards, was only a year old when Mrs. Knight made her journey to New York, and that to the end of his life, in 1758, he struggled in vain to keep alive the logic of the old religious doctrines.

He was born in 1703 with a rich heritage from the learned aristocracy. As a youth he showed extraordinary precocity, which appeared in his early excursions into philosophy and natural science and developed further in the unfulfilled promise of religious radicalism.

From my childhood up, my mind had been full of objections against the doctrine of God's sovereignty, in choosing whom he would to eternal life, and rejecting whom he pleased; leaving them eternally to perish, and be everlastingly tormented in hell. It used to appear like a horrible doctrine to me. But I remember the time very well, when I seemed to be convinced, and fully satisfied, as to this sovereignty of God. . . . I have often, since that first conviction, had quite another kind of sense of God's sovereignty than I had then. I have often since had not only a conviction, but a delightful conviction. The doctrine has very often appeared exceedingly pleasant, bright, and sweet. Absolute sovereignty is what I love to ascribe to God. But my first conviction was not so.

The first instance that I remember of that sort of inward, sweet delight in God and divine things that I have lived much in since, was on

POINTS OF LITERARY INTEREST IN NEW ENGLAND

reading those words, 1 Tim. i. 17, *Now unto the King eternal, immortal, invisible, the only wise God, be honor and glory for ever and ever, Amen.* As I read the words, there came into my soul, and was as it were diffused through it, a sense of the glory of the Divine Being. . . .

Not long after I first began to experience these things, I gave an account to my father of some things that had passed in my mind. I was pretty much affected by the discourse we had together ; and when the discourse was ended, I walked abroad alone, in a solitary place in my father's pasture, for contemplation. And as I was walking there, and looking up on the sky and clouds, there came into my mind so sweet a sense of the glorious *majesty* and *grace* of God, that I know not how to express. I seemed to see them both in a sweet conjunction ; majesty and meekness joined together ; it was a sweet and gentle, and holy majesty ; and also a majestic meekness ; an awful sweetness ; a high, and great, and holy gentleness.

The striking fact about Edwards's later development, however, is that he passed entirely from poetic mysticism to a championship of the theology of Calvin. His great period of influence was during his pastorate in Northampton, Massachusetts, from 1727 to 1750, and during his following six years at Stockbridge, Massachusetts. He was a preacher of extraordinary power — the more extraordinary because his command of audiences was obtained by the sheer quality of his discourse and not, as in the case of John Cotton and the Mathers, by pulpit presence or flights of eloquence. His sermons were at once irresistible in their logic (provided his auditors were willing to start with his assumptions) and, at the same time, irresistibly cogent in their simple, concrete methods of illustration. His most famous discourse, "Sinners in the Hands of an Angry God," is a complete illustration of his method. Notwithstanding his sincerity and his talents as a preacher his ministerial experience was ended with a tragic downfall. His parishioners could not endure the rigor of his teachings, agreeing perversely with Dr. Johnson's later dictum on his "Freedom of the Will" — that all theory might be for it but all experience was against it. During his residence in Stockbridge he continued with the writing of discourses which philosophers have agreed at once to applaud and reject. He died in 1758 shortly after his inauguration as president of the College of New Jersey.

His failure lay in the fact that his religion was a religion of logic rather than of faith. It was based on what learned men had theorized out from the Bible, and in a great many cases from the least important passages of the Bible, and it sternly rejected what many other equally learned men had found in the same book. Moreover, it was concerned with life on earth chiefly as a prelude to a future life of reward or punishment. In all the tide of human event which was making the eighteenth century each year more interesting as a matter of present living, men could not go on indefinitely looking everywhere but at life itself. Oliver Wendell Holmes summed up the situation in his "Wonderful ' One-Hoss Shay' " (see p. 305). This is a pleasant story for children, but a comment on life for grown-ups ; and to the grown-ups Holmes addressed his concluding couplet:

> End of the wonderful one-hoss shay :
> *Logic* is *logic*. That's all I say.

Benjamin Franklin (1706–1790) is the man who reflected better and earlier than other Americans the complete change from the Puritan point of view — reflecting it so unqualifiedly that he must be understood as an extreme case and not a typical one. In education and character he offered a succession of contrasts to the leaders of seventeenth-century New England. He did not come of a cultured family ; he was not a college man ; he did not enter any of the learned professions — ministry, law, or teaching ; he was not an active supporter of the church ; he did not live in the New England where he was born. In fact he was one of the first to act on the much-quoted principle, " Boston is a very good place — to come from."

Franklin was born in Boston in 1706, the youngest son of a tallow-chandler and the fifteenth of seventeen children. He was industrious and bookish as a boy, and before he was seventeen years old he had trained himself to write in the fashion of the English essayist Joseph Addison, had been apprenticed in his brother's printing shop, and had written many articles published in his brother's paper, *The New England Courant*. In 1723, as the result of troubles with his brother, he ran away to Philadelphia. From there he went to London for two years, on the promise of the irresponsible Governor Keith to set him up in the printing business on his return. The failure of the governor to keep his word did him no harm in the end, for he established his own printing house in 1728, and in 1748, at the age of forty-two, he was able to retire with a moderate fortune. During this time he had not only succeeded in Philadelphia but had combined with partners in New York, Newport, Lancaster (Pennsylvania), Charleston (South Carolina), Kingston, Jamaica, and Antigua.

The activities of his life were so crowded and interwoven that they may best be summarized under a few simple heads. As a public-spirited citizen of Philadelphia he organized a debating society, the Junto, in 1727; published *The Pennsylvania Gazette* in 1729; founded the first circulating library in America in 1731; conducted *Poor Richard's Almanac* from 1732 to 1748; organized the American Philosophical Society in 1744; and in 1749 founded the academy which developed into the University of Pennsylvania. As an inventor he perfected the Franklin stove in 1742 and contrived methods of street paving and lighting which were widely adopted. As a scientist he proved the identity of lightning and electricity in 1752, and went on from that to further investigations which sooner or later brought him election to the Royal Academy of London and their Copley gold medal, an appointment as one of the eight foreign associates of the French Academy of Sciences, and medals and diplomas from other societies in St. Petersburg, Madrid, Edinburgh, Padua, and Turin. As a holder of public trusts and offices he became clerk of the Assembly of Pennsylvania in 1736; postmaster of Philadelphia in 1737; deputy postmaster-general of the colonies in 1753 ; commissioner from Pennsylvania to the Albany Congress in 1754 ; colonial agent to London from Pennsylvania in 1757 and 1764 and for Massachusetts in 1770 ; one of the framers of the Declaration of Independence ; minister to the French court from the United States in 1778; a signer of the Peace Articles in 1783; president of the Commonwealth of Pennsylvania in 1785–1787; and a framer of the Constitution of the United States. Such a catalogue is not a thing to be exactly memorized. Its value is like that of an entry in " Who's Who in America " — it should be referred to when needed. Yet it is worth reading and rereading as an evidence of the almost unparalleled variety and usefulness of occupations which filled this man's life.

Usefulness is, without question, the idea which Franklin most emphasized in his writings and exemplified in his conduct. In comparison with the Puritan fathers he was more interested in the eighteenth century than in eternity, more actively concerned with Philadelphia and Pennsylvania and the United States of America than with the mansions prepared above. This attitude of mind was not a freakish or accidental one ; it can be accounted for in the influences which affected him when he was a boy and in the kind of English and American thinking which characterized his whole century.

He came of what he himself called an " obscure family," his ancestors in the near generations having been hard-working, intelligent English clerks and artisans. They were nonconformists, and independent enough to take their chances in the new world for the sake of liberty of conscience. But the lesson that he learned from his parents was rather more practical than theological and was, perhaps unconsciously, attested to in the epitaph which he wrote for them. At two points in it he recorded his belief that God helps them who help themselves, laying special stress on the degree to which they help themselves :

> By constant labor and industry,
> With God's blessing,

he says, and again :

> Be encouraged to diligence in thy calling
> And distrust not Providence.

Cotton Mather, whom Franklin quoted with respect, would have reversed the ideas in order and importance ; but it was Cotton Mather's " Essays to Do Good " that Franklin quoted, and his ability to draw a practical inference from some slight event ("Be not too proud," he said, when he bumped his head against a beam), and not any of his sermons. Franklin's early reading was almost wholly in the field of what might be called common-sense literature — discussions of different aspects of daily life and how to get on in it. He read " Pilgrim's Progress," which of all religious books is one of the most definite on questions of earthly conduct. He read a great deal of history and biography : Defoe " Upon Projects," Locke " Concerning Human Understanding" and " The Art of Thinking," and Addison on all the common-sense subjects that make up the contents of the *Spectator*. He read the rimed " Essays " of Alexander Pope, too, using a quotation from one of them to confirm his belief in a system of arguing by means of asking questions, which is known as the " Socratic method."

In a word, he filled his boyish mind with the special kind of writing which belonged to the first half of the eighteenth century in England, and this was exactly the kind to be valuable to a youth who was destined to work his way unaided to prosperity. For this period was a particularly prosaic and practical one. In the two generations just gone England had passed through the Puritan uprising against Charles I, the return of the Stuarts to the throne, and the further rebellion against James II. Religious enthusiasm had risen to its height in the middle of the century, but had already waned by the years when John Milton received only ten pounds for the manuscript of " Paradise Lost." By the end of the century politics had definitely overthrown religion as a subject of popular

discussion. Little newspapers had sprung up in surprising numbers, the coffeehouses had provided centers for conversation,
and a common-sense age was settling down to a rather sordid
and common-sense existence. Sometimes under the impulse
of a world movement a few leaders of thought have a great
deal to do with actually molding the character of the period in
which they live, but in less inspiring times the popular writers
produce just about "what the public wants." The period of
Franklin's youth was one of the latter kind, and Addison, Pope,
and their followers were writing for a public who wanted to
keep on the surface of life. It was as if the people had said:
"All this religious zeal of the last century only made England
uncomfortable. Just see what confusion it threw us into! Now
we are back about where we were when the trouble started.
Let's be sensible and stick to facts, and stop quarreling with
each other." So the populace, who began reading in greater
numbers than ever before, read the little newspapers; and the
various groups of congenial people talked things over in the
coffeehouses; and Addison made it his ambition to bring
"philosophy" (by which he meant a simple theory of everyday
living) down from the clouds and into the field of ordinary
thinking. The plays of Shakespeare would have helped Franklin very little in the early stages of the printing business; so
would the poems of Milton; but the essays of Addison, Pope,
and Defoe made for him what would be called to-day "excellent vocational reading." And he profited by it to the limit.

Moreover, if literature helped to make him a good printer,
printing was no less helpful toward making him a good writer.
There are few trades or crafts which demand so high a degree
of accuracy. A boy or girl who achieves a grade of 95 per cent
in any study, even in mathematics, is well above the average;
but a typesetter or proofreader who avoids error in only nineteen out of every twenty operations will have a short career in
any printing house. Most people do not know of the extreme
care which is given to assure correctness in the simplest

product which is put into type. A textbook, for example, after being written, revised, recopied, and revised is criticized by a special expert and once more revised before the publisher's editor goes over it word by word. Then when it goes to the printer it is set up in long strips, or galleys, from these into pages (still in type), and from these is cast into plates, and after each of these three operations is read over with microscopic care by both an editorial proofreader and the author. During the printing experience a liberal allowance is made to the author for actual changes from his original copy, but the printer is held responsible for any slightest departure from the manuscript that is supplied him. The boy who, like Franklin, has spent some years in the printing room and the editorial office has received a discipline which is miles beyond that which can ever be given in any school or college composition course.[1]

To this important training Franklin added a conscious attempt to develop his own powers. Printing and the love of books led the horse to water, but his desire for self-expression made him drink. Of this he tells in an early passage of the "Autobiography." His daily work had taught him to spell and punctuate correctly, but he was faulty in choice of words and in "perspicuity," or clearness of construction. So he took Addison's *Spectator* as his model, put paragraphs into his own words, then tried to set them back into the original form, compared the two products, and made up his mind wherein Addison's versions were better than his and wherein, as he sometimes thought, his were better than his teacher's. He also followed up the art of discussion both in speech and in writing, making it always a point to convince his opponents without antagonizing them. These things he did, not in order to become a professional writer but solely

---

[1] This same discipline was enjoyed — among later American authors — by Mark Twain, Bret Harte, William Dean Howells, and Walt Whitman, all of whom were scrupulously careful writers.

in order to utter or write his ideas to the best effect. " It has ever since," he says, "been a pleasure to me to see good workmen handle their tools; and it has been useful to me, having learned so much by it as to be able to do little jobs myself." Prose writing was simply a tool for him — the most useful one that he ever mastered and, as he says elsewhere, the principal means of his advancement.

As long as he was a printer (until he was forty-two years old) he employed his prose composition in writing copy which was clear and interesting and therefore salable — chiefly in the *Pennsylvania Gazette* and in *Poor Richard's Almanac*; but during and after that time he put his powers to even greater use as a speaker and as a writer of articles and pamphlets on affairs of public interest. He was almost always simple, definite, and practical, for he wrote to the mass ot people with little education. He realized that if he was to bring his points home to them he must not write "over their heads," and that he must appeal to their common sense and their self-interest; and he was invariably good-humored, for he knew that good humor makes more friends than enemies.

Out of the great mass of Franklin's published writings — and they run to a dozen large volumes — two deserve special attention as pieces of American literature: *Poor Richard's Almanac* and the " Autobiography." The former of these was a commercial undertaking; it was written to sell. The almanac, an annual publication of which the calendar was a very small part, had been popular in England and America for many generations before Franklin started his own. It preceded the newspaper and until 1800, or even later, reached a wider public. The second piece of printing in this country was *Pierce's Almanack*, printed in Cambridge, Massachusetts, in 1639. Others followed: in Boston, 1676; in Philadelphia, 1676; in New York, 1697; in Rhode Island, 1728; and in Virginia, 1731. There had been, however, only one great almanac editor to precede Franklin in America — Nathaniel Ames, who began publishing his series in Dedham, Massachusetts, in 1726. Besides the calendar, the astronomical data for the year, and the half-jocular weather predictions, the chief feature of Ames's was the poetry, very considerable in bulk, and the "interlined wit and humor," which was brief and usually rather pointless. Franklin, realizing the fondness of his generation for the wise sayings of which Alexander Pope was then the master-hand in the English-speaking world, dropped the poetry and studied to expand the interlined material of Ames into the chief contribution of his "Richard Saunders." "I endeavored to make it both entertaining and useful," he said in the "Autobiography," "and it accordingly came to be in such demand, that I reaped considerable profit from it; vending annually near ten thousand. And observing that it was generally read, scarce any neighborhood in the province being without it, I considered it as a proper vehicle for conveying instruction among the common people, who bought scarcely any other books. I therefore filled all the little spaces, that occurred between the remarkable days in the Calendar with proverbial sentences, chiefly such as inculcated industry and frugality, as the means of procuring wealth, and thereby securing virtue; it being more difficult for a man in want, to act always honestly, as, to use here one of those proverbs, *it is hard for an empty sack to stand upright.*"

In the Almanac of 1757 he collected the sayings of the last twenty-five years into a timely essay on "The Way to Wealth," making an old man deliver a speech filled with quotations from "Poor Richard." This contained not only sound practical advice for any time but was also pertinent to a political issue of the moment, and so applied to the state as well as to all the people in it. It was reprinted by itself and had an immense circulation in America and abroad, in the original and in several translations. Very likely since "The Day of Doom," in 1662, nothing had been so influential in the colonies as "The Way to Wealth," in 1757; and no contrast could better indicate the change that had taken place between those two dates. Said Father Abraham, the old speaker :

It would be thought a hard Government that should tax its People one-tenth Part of their Time, to be employed in its Service. But *Idleness* taxes many of us much more, if we reckon all that is spent in absolute *Sloth*, or doing of nothing, with that which is spent in idle Employments or Amusements, that amount to nothing. Sloth, by bringing on Diseases, absolutely shortens Life. *Sloth, like rust, consumes faster than Labour wears; while the used Key, is always bright*, as *Poor Richard* says. *But dost thou love life, then do not squander Time, for that 's the stuff Life is made of*, as *Poor Richard* says. How much more than is necessary do we spend in sleep, forgetting that *The sleeping Fox catches no Poultry*, and that *There will be sleeping enough in the Grave*, as *Poor Richard* says.

This was the sort of workaday advice that was shouldering the old-time theology into modest Sabbath-day retirement.

Franklin's "Autobiography" is the greatest of his writings if not the greatest of all his achievements. "Poor Richard" and "The Way to Wealth" are full of good common sense, but they belong only to the "efficiency" school of ideas and morality; they are neither distinguished in form nor inspiring in content, and they are chiefly interesting because they so well mirror what was in the eighteenth-century mind. The "Autobiography" has a larger claim to attention than these, for by general consent it has come to be regarded as one of the great classics of literature. Several features have combined to make it deserve this high place. Simply stated they are all nothing more than ways of explaining that this book is the simple, definite, honest life-story of an eminent man, as he recalled it in his old age.

In the first place, it is simple and uncalculated. It was not composed, like "Poor Richard," to sell, nor, like many of Franklin's speeches and pamphlets, to convince by skillful argument. As a matter of fact, Franklin did not want to write it at all, and consented only when the insistence of his friends and relatives made it easier to do it than to leave it undone.

Moreover, he dropped it for the thirteen years from 1771 to 1784, took it up again when wearied, old, and ill, and left it at his death hardly more than well started, with all the most celebrated part of his life still to be recounted. It is simple therefore because it was done with no desire to create an impression or to be "literary," and is the unadorned narrative of an old man familiarly told to those who knew him best.

For the same reason it is definite and homely in what he chose to record. It is the "little, nameless, unremembered" episodes not set down in more pretentious histories for which the "Autobiography" is itself best remembered. Some of the details make real the conditions of living in those simple times — the invention of the stove named after him, the improvements in street lighting and paving, the organization of a fire company. Others are typical of human nature in any age, as his portrait of the croaker, Samuel Mickle, who sadly predicted Franklin's failure as a printer, or as his jocular account of the entrance of luxury into his own household.

We have an English proverb that says, *He that would thrive, must ask his wife.* It was lucky for me that I had one as much disposed to industry and frugality as myself. She assisted me cheerfully in my business, folding and stitching pamphlets, tending shop, purchasing old linen rags for the paper-makers, etc., etc. We kept no idle servants, our table was plain and simple, our furniture of the cheapest. For instance, my breakfast was a long time bread and milk (no tea), and I ate it out of a twopenny earthen porringer, with a pewter spoon. But mark how luxury will enter families, and make a progress, in spite of principle: being called one morning to breakfast, I found it in a China bowl, with a spoon of silver! They had been bought for me without my knowledge by my wife, and had cost her the enormous sum of three and twenty shillings, for which she had no other excuse or apology to make, but that she thought *her* husband deserved a silver spoon and China bowl as well as any of his neighbors. This was the first appearance of plate and China in our house, which afterward in a course of years, as our wealth increased, augmented gradually to several hundred pounds in value.

Many and many of the simplest episodes reveal how shrewd, penetrating, and, above all, how clear-headed he invariably was. Such, for example, was the hour when he was listening to the great evangelist, Whitefield, and while all his other auditors were being thrilled by the speaker's eloquence, Franklin was backing away from him step by step, in order to estimate how far his voice would carry, and thus to verify the newspaper accounts of his having preached to twenty-five thousand people in the fields. Franklin went away full of admiration for the preacher's voice, but with no word of comment on his sermon. He went often to hear Whitefield, but always as a very human public speaker and never as a "divine." A biographer, even one of his associates, could not have known many of the intimate facts that Franklin included, and he would almost surely have left out other details as irrelevant or impertinent. Franklin himself, in contrast, wrote the things which still clung in his old man's memory and which must have been important in his development, or he would have forgotten them.

Another striking feature of the "Autobiography" is its honesty, for he did not hesitate to record happenings which revealed defects in his character—defects which nine out of ten admiring biographers would have been inclined to omit or even actually to cover up. Franklin knew that his life had not been all admirable, that many times it had not been above reproach; but, all things considered, he was willing to let it stand for what it was. In consequence, if one reads his story as honestly as Franklin wrote it,—and few people do,—it will appear that not only was he disorderly and unmethodical but that he was not always truthful, that he was sometimes unscrupulous in business, and that he was at times self-indulgent and immoral. In fact too often the editing of Franklin's life-story seems to have been done on the principle laid down by Dr. Samuel Johnson about Chesterfield's "Letters to his Son"—that they should be put into the hands of every young man after the immorality had been taken out of them. This is not honest teaching and does not lead to honest habits of study.

The truth is that Franklin was like other people in being a combination of virtues and defects. He was unlike other people in having extraordinary talents and virtues and in owning up to his defects. For the two great "errata" of his life — the use of money intrusted to him for Mr. Vernon and his unfaithfulness while in London to Miss Read, his betrothed — he afterward made the fullest possible atonement. In his glorification of usefulness at every turn he was at once the greatest expounder and the greatest example of his century. He made a religion of usefulness, putting it into a simple creed which gives less heed to the spirit of worship than many of us need, but far more to the spirit of service than most of us follow :

It is expressed in these words, viz. :
That there is one God, who made all things.
That he governs the world by his providence.
That he ought to be worshipped by adoration, prayer and thanksgiving.
But that the most acceptable service of God is doing good to man.
That the soul is immortal.
And that God will certainly reward virtue and punish vice, either here or hereafter.

In the third of these articles Franklin recommended a worship which he did not practice, but in the fourth he presented a doctrine of service of which his life was a remarkable fulfillment. In his theory of life Franklin seemed to make no claims for the finer emotions, but in his actual citizenship in all its public aspects he was so far above the average man as to serve as a pretty safe "working model" for this and coming generations.

If he had not written this uncompleted life-story we should not know the man as intimately as we do, for to read the "Autobiography" is to read Franklin himself.

Since the "Autobiography" brings the story of Franklin only up to 1757, it gives no hint of the Revolutionary struggle in which as negotiator and diplomat he was hardly less important than was Washington as military leader. The America presented in these pages is loyal and contented. The rising voices of discomfort from 1765 to 1775, of doubt during the next year, and of decision for revolt in 1776 were all echoed and often led by Franklin in his political writings. Moreover, it is of especial significance in these days to recall another fact unrecorded in his own story — that he was the first American to represent his nation among other nations, and that in his feeling for America as a member of the great world-family he was a hundred years and more ahead of his countrymen. The new marshaling of forces in 1917 which brought about the celebration of the Fourth of July in London and the arrival of allied American troops in Paris recalled from hour to hour the name of Franklin as our first great international figure.

BOOK LIST

General References

BROOKS, VAN WYCK. America's Coming of Age, chap. i. 1915.
DUNNING, A. E. Congregationalists in America. 1894.
FISKE, JOHN. New France and New England, chap. vi. 1902.
WALKER, W. History of the Congregational Churches in the United States. 1894.

Individual Authors

JONATHAN EDWARDS. There have been at least twenty-two editions and printings of Edwards's collected work. The most accessible is that in four volumes which appeared originally in 1843 and has been reprinted nine times, the last in 1881. In these volumes the most important pages are in Vol. I, pp. 1–27 (biographical), and in Vol. IV (sermons).

Biography and Criticism

DWIGHT, TIMOTHY. Travels in New England and New York (1822), Vol. IV, pp. 323 ff.
HOLMES, O. W. Pages from an Old Volume of Life. 1891.
JAMES, WILLIAM. The Varieties of Religious Experience. 1902.
MACPHAIL, ANDREW. Essays in Puritanism. 1905.
SANBORN, F. B. *Journal of Speculative Philosophy*, Vol. XVII, No. 4. October, 1883.
STEPHEN, LESLIE. *Littell's Living Age*, Vol. V (*ser. 5*), No. 1546. Jan. 24, 1874.
WALKER, WILLISTON. Ten New England Leaders. 1901.
WARD, W. H. *The Independent*, Vol. LV, No. 2861. Oct. 1, 1903.

WOODBRIDGE, F. J. E. *Philosoph. Rev.*, Vol. XIII, No. 4. July, 1904. *The Congregationalist and Christian World*, Edwards number, Vol. LXXXVIII, No. 40. Oct. 3, 1903.

BENJAMIN FRANKLIN. There are eleven editions of Franklin's collected works in English, French, and German, dating from 1773 to 1905. The best of these is the one compiled and edited by John Bigelow. 1889. 10 vols. Poor Richard Improved, 1757. This was latei issued as Father Abraham's Speech, over 150 editions and reprints of which are recorded. Autobiography. First issued in Paris, 1791. Best recent editions: John Bigelow, editor, 1874; H. E. Scudder, editor, *Riverside Literature Series*, 1886; William MacDonald, editor, *Temple Autobiography Series*, 1905; William MacDonald, editor, *Everyman's Library*, 1908.

History and Biography

BRUCE, W. C. Benjamin Franklin Self-Revealed: A Biographical and Critical Study based mainly on his own Writings. 1918. 2 vols.

FORD, P. L. The Many-Sided Franklin. 1899.

HALE, E. E. and E. E., Jr. Franklin in France; from original documents most of which are now published for the first time. 1887–1888. 2 vols.

McMASTER, J. B. Benjamin Franklin (*A. M. L. Series*). 1887.

McMASTER, J. B. Franklin in France. *Atlantic Monthly*, Vol. LX. September, 1887.

SHERMAN, STUART P. Cambridge History of American Literature, Vol. I, chap. vi.

SWIFT, LINDSAY. Catalogue of works relating to Benjamin Franklin in the Boston Public Library. 1883.

COLONIAL ALMANACS

KITTREDGE, G. L. The Old Farmer and his Almanack. 1904.

COLONIAL JOURNALISM

COOK, E. C. Cambridge History of American Literature, Vol. I, chap. vii.

HUDSON, F. Journalism in the United States, 1690–1872. 1873.

THOMAS, I. History of Printing in America. 1871.

Literary Treatment of the Period

Fiction

COOPER, J. F. Satanstoe.

COOPER, J. F. The Chainbearer.

COOPER, J. F. The Deerslayer.

COOPER, J. F. The Redskins.

THACKERAY, W. M. The Virginians.

Poetry

Poems of American History (edited by B. E. Stevenson), pp. 99–125

TOPICS AND PROBLEMS

Few modern readers can regard the sermons of Jonathan Edwards as anything but documents of historical interest. It is quite worth study to read at first-hand one or two sermons about which so many careless generalizations have been made. The chief points of interest are the theology as it stands in his own living words, and his rhetorical method, which is an admirable exercise of forensic discourse.

Read Harriet Beecher Stowe's "The Minister's Wooing" and "Oldtown Folks" (especially chap.   ) for a faithful portrait of one of Edwards's chief successors (see pp. 305–308).

Read Franklin's "Autobiography" for its revelation of personal characteristics: his continued emphasis on usefulness; his refusal to allow his emotions to carry him away (whether anger, love, religious fervor, or desire for revenge); his willingness to act unscrupulously for what he felt was a good end; his self-analysis (in other places than the passage on the virtues); his public spirit.

Read Franklin's "Autobiography" for its literary characteristics: his emulation of Addison's style (compare passages of this and the *Spectator*); his respect for Pope and his likeness in use of apothegms; his similarity to Chesterfield in point of view and use of homely detail. Contrast Franklin's style with Irving's or Cooper's.

CHAPTER V

CRÈVECŒUR, THE "AMERICAN FARMER"

By 1750 the thirteen colonies had all been long established, and the straggling community on the Atlantic seaboard from Maine to Georgia had an individuality of its own. The America-to-be was at once young and old. There were old towns, old churches, old homes, old families. There was an aristocracy with memories that went back to England, but with roots firmly planted in American soil. Yet, withal, the country was so vast and the people on it so few that there was unlimited chance for the energetic man of real ability. It was a new land of untold opportunities; all its apparent maturity was the maturity of a well-born young gentleman who has just become of age and whose real career is all before him. The old age of the Old World was something very different, for it was based chiefly on the control of the land — of the actual soil and stream and forest. Edmund Burke in 1775 said in his "Speech on Conciliation of the American Colonies" that if the attempt were made to restrict the population of the colonies the people could swarm over the mountain ranges and resettle there in a vast plain *five hundred miles square*. However fair the estimate was to the land in actual English possession, that statement was about as far as the imagination of an Englishman accustomed to smaller dimensions could then go, or as big a figure as he could dare to hope his fellow-members of Parliament would believe ; for in those days, as to-day, there were not in England or France five square miles of land out of owner-ship, and very little that was not in the possession of a few great proprietors. As the control of government was largely in the same hands, the great mass of the people could neither freely enjoy the fruits of their own labor, which were pitilessly reduced by rents and taxes, nor make any effective peaceful protest in behalf of political change. The American Revolution was the voice of the colonies protesting against the possible repetition of such conditions on this side the water, and the French Revolution was the harsh voice of a downtrodden people calling for redress.

No man could better appreciate the promise of life in America than one who had felt the oppression of the old conditions and had then enjoyed the freedom of the new ones. In the same years when the wiser leaders in the colonies were viewing with alarm the aggressive and mistaken policies of George III and his ministers, a young Frenchman, educated in England, came over to this country, settled and prospered on his own land, and was so delighted with his life as a farmer and a citizen that he could not refrain from making a record of his happy circumstances. This was Michel Guillaume St. John de Crèvecœur, and his book was the " Letters from an American Farmer," published in London in 1782, though written almost entirely before the outbreak of the Revolution. It is made up of twelve so-called letters addressed to an imaginary English friend. Two of these are about his direct experience on his own acres in the middle colonies ; five are on the people and the country in northern colonies, as he found them in Marthas Vineyard, Nantucket, and Cape Cod ; one is drawn from observations in South Carolina ; and the other four are less related to definite places, three being on nature themes, and one — the most important of all — on the ever-new question, " What is an American ? "

With industry and frugality hardly less than Franklin's, Crèvecœur had also a certain power of poetic imagination and fresh enthusiasm. He was writing from a kind of earthly paradise. Seen against the background of unhappy France, the rights to own, to earn, and to have a voice in governing himself seemed almost too good to be true. He had no misconceptions about the hard labor which was necessary to make a farm productive; but he enjoyed work because he knew that he could enjoy the fruits of it, and he enjoyed it all the more because he knew that in making an ear of corn grow where none had grown before he was the best kind of pioneer. To his sorrow he knew much about the ugliness of an old civilization; it was with the zest of a youthful lover that he wrote about the beauty of this new country's inexperience.

He felt a perfect satisfaction in his own state of mind and body. Although he was a newcomer, he had a sense of belonging to the district as complete as Emerson, with two centuries of ancestry, was later to have; and, with a pride equal to Emerson's in " Hamatreya," could "affirm, my actions smack of the soil." With his baby boy ingeniously rigged before him on the plow, he reckoned the increase of his fields, herds, flocks, — even his hives, — and acknowledged his inferiority "only to the Emperor of China, ploughing as an example to his kingdom." Then, looking beyond his own little acreage, he hinted at future industries. He was tilling the surface; there must be further treasures below. He and his neighbors were weaving the natural wool; some chemist must make and prepare colors. Commerce must follow on the heels of abundant production; "the avenues of trade are infinite." And in time the deep vast of the West, about which men had yet such feeble and timid fancies, must be explored and subjugated in its turn.

Here we have, in some measure, regained the ancient dignity of our species: our laws are simple and just; we are a race of cultivators; our cultivation is unrestrained, and therefore everything is prosperous and flourishing. For my part I had rather admire the ample barn of one of our opulent farmers, who himself felled the first tree in his plantation, and was first founder of his settlement, than study the dimension of the temple of Ceres. I had rather record the progressive steps of this industrious farmer, throughout all the stages of his labor and other operations, than examine how modern Italian convents can be supported without doing anything but singing and praying.

Moreover, above all the material resources of field, forest, and mountain, he was glad for the human stream which was flowing into America to fertilize them. The thrifty people who were shrewd and bold enough to come over from Great Britain and northern Europe were to profit by nature's gifts, and in the experience were to be welded "into one of the finest systems of population which has ever appeared." If it is fair to say that the history of immigration to America falls into three general periods, Crèvecœur was writing about the very midst of the middle period, from 1675 to 1875. First had been a half century when only the strongest spirit of adventure or the strongest desire for freedom could impel men to attempt the conquest of an untried world. Every Englishman who came over and every American born here was conscious of the need of more hands to work, and all were eager for more Englishmen, and yet more, to help in the gigantic undertaking. In the last forty years, with the taking up of all the available land and the manning of the industries, the millions who have flooded in, not alone from England or Great Britain but mainly from southern Europe and the near East, have arrived as new mouths to feed. The problem has been not so much how they could help America as how America could take care of them; and with their arrival a feeling of perplexity and alarm has arisen such as was expressed in 1892 by Thomas Bailey Aldrich in his "Unguarded Gates":

> . . . Wide open and unguarded stand our gates,
> And through them presses a wild motley throng —
> Men from the Volga and the Tartar steppes,
> Featureless figures of the Hoang-Ho,
> Malayan, Scythian, Teuton, Kelt, and Slav,
> Flying the Old World's poverty and scorn;
> These bringing with them unknown gods and rites,
> Those, tiger passions here to stretch their claws.
> In street and alley what strange tongues are loud,
> Accents of menace alien to our air,
> Voices that once the Tower of Babel knew!

O Liberty, white Goddess! is it well
To leave the gates unguarded? . . .
                    Have a care
Lest from thy brow the clustered stars be torn
And trampled in the dust. . . .

But Crèvecœur was living between these two periods. The first conquest of the Eastern woods and fields had been made. America was known to be a land of plenty, and as yet there was more than plenty for all the newcomers from England and the neighboring countries of northern Europe. There seemed to be no limit to its resources. And so he wrote:

What, then, is the American, this new man? He is neither a European, nor the descendant of a European: hence that strange mixture of blood, which you will find in no other country. I could point out to you a family, whose grandfather was an Englishman, whose wife was Dutch, whose son married a Frenchwoman, and whose present four sons have now four wives of different nations. He is an American, who, leaving behind him all his ancient prejudices and manners, receives new ones from the new mode of life he has embraced, the new government he obeys, and the new rank he holds. He becomes an American by being received in the broad lap of our great "alma mater." Here individuals are melted into a new race of men, whose labors and posterity will one day cause great changes in the world. Americans are the western pilgrims, who are carrying along with them that great mass of arts, sciences, vigor and industry, which began long since in the East. They will finish the great circle.

There was an artistic strain in this man who could so easily kindle with enthusiasm and who could express his enthusiasms with such rhythmic eloquence. The special subjects on which he could best vent his poetic powers were found in his passages and his occasional whole chapters on nature themes — in particular the letters on "John Bartram, Botanist," and "The Snakes and the Humming Bird." In these it is impossible not to feel the resemblances between this early naturalist and his successor, Thoreau (see.pp. 222–229). While neither was a scientist in the strict sense of the word, neither was content to dismiss nature subjects with mere words of general appreciation. Both were interested enough to observe in detail and to record with some exactness the ways of plants, flowers, birds, and insects ; but both were at their best when they were giving way to the real zest they had in the enjoyment of the out of doors.

Who can listen unmoved to the sweet love-tales of our robins, told from tree to tree, or to the shrill cat-birds ? The sublime accents of the thrush, from on high, always retard my steps, that I may listen to the delicious music. . . . The astonishing art which all birds display in the construction of their nests, ill-provided as we may suppose them with proper tools, their neatness, their convenience, always make me ashamed of the slovenliness of our houses. Their love to their dame, their incessant, careful attention, and the peculiar songs they address to her while she tediously incubates their eggs, remind me of my duty, could I ever forget it. Their affection to their helpless little ones is a lovely precept ; and, in short, the whole economy of what we call the brute creation, is admirable in every circumstance ; and vain man, though adorned with the additional gift of reason, might learn from the perfection of instinct, how to regulate the follies, and how to temper the errors, which this second gift often makes him commit. . . . I have often blushed within myself, and been greatly astonished, when I have compared the unerring path they all follow, — all just, all proper, all wise, up to the necessary degree of perfection — with the coarse, the imperfect, systems of men.

For generations the beauties of nature had held small place in English literature, because the English men of letters were a completely citified set of writers ; and they had received little attention in America, partly because England gave American writers no reminder and partly because nature in America had been chiefly something to struggle with.

So enthusiastic was Crèvecœur over conditions in America, and so certain was he that they never would be disturbed in any unfortunate way, that the twentieth-century reader looks over his pre-Revolution pages with a kind of wistful impatience. About many aspects of the material development of the country

Crèvecœur was keenly prophetic. Throughout eleven of the letters, evidently written before 1775, he continued in an exalted and confident mood. Whether he was presenting the "provincial situations, manners and customs" of Nantucket and Marthas Vineyard, or of the central Atlantic, or of the Southern colonies, his senses and his judgment were equally satisfied. Industry prevailed. The wilderness was being converted into towns, farms, and highways. "A pleasing uniformity of decent competence" was a rule of the democracy. The indulgent laws were fair to the laborer and the voter. He seemed to feel that the era of prosperity would last till the end of the world. His vision of the future was the vision of a man perched in the small end of an infinite horn of plenty, with a vista unclouded by the hint of any limit to the supply or of any possible conflict between gluttony and hunger.

In fact, along the whole coast there was only one practice which deserved the name of a problem, and that was the institution of slavery. Against this, which existed both North and South, Crèvecœur protested just as Samuel Sewall and John Woolman had done before him, and as Timothy Dwight and Joel Barlow in Connecticut and William Pinkney and other lawmakers and abolitionists in Maryland and Virginia were to do soon after him. Yet, however sincere he was, he regarded slavery only as an external blemish rather than as a national danger. It was a mistake, but not a menace. It was typical of the America of the future that Crèvecœur should have had so unquestioning a confidence in the prospect. The belief in a "manifest destiny" for America, which is finely inspiring for all who will work to bring about a glorious future, has been demoralizing to millions who have used a lazy belief in it to excuse them from feeling or exercising any responsibility.

With the twelfth letter came a total change of key. It was evidently written long after all the others, after the outburst of war, perhaps after his New Jersey property had been burned, possibly even during his return voyage to France in the autumn of 1780. As a naturalized subject of King George, when well on in middle life he had been forced to choose between his sworn allegiance and the interests of his fellow-colonists. He sympathized with the American cause, though he did not enlist. And then in the years that followed he learned (the perennial lesson of war time) of the " vanity of human wishes." Unhappily for the moral of the tale, the latter part of his life was far from heroic. In the concluding letter, written quite after the fashion of the most sentimental and unreal eighteenth-century nature lovers, Crèvecœur decided to abandon the struggle in the war zone and to take up life anew with his family among the Indians in the West. He would forswear all talk of politics, " contemplate nature in her most wild and ample extent," and formulate among his adopted neighbors a new system of happiness. As a matter of fact, however, his retreat was even more complete than this ; for he returned permanently to the Continent, lived contentedly in Paris, London, and Munich, married his daughter to a French count, wrote volumes on Pennsylvania and New York, and memorialized his career as a farmer by inditing a paper on potato culture.

Although such a turn of events resulted in very much of an anticlimax, this fact should not make one forget the prophetic quality in his " Letters," nor should his failure to predict every aspect of modern life throw any shadow on the clearness with which he foretold some of the most important of them. It is true, of course, that he did not appreciate how tragic were to be the fruits of slavery ; that he saw immigration only as a desirable supply of labor to a continent which could never be overpopulated ; that, writing before the earliest chapter of the factory era, he did not dream of the industrial complexities of the present. But when he said that the American, sprung from Europe but here adopted into a new nation, " ought therefore to love this country much better than that wherein either he or his forefathers were born," he was saying something that has been repeated with new conviction ten thousand times since the outbreak of the Great War. And when he declared that "the American is a new man, who acts upon new principles" he was foreshadowing national policies which the world has been slow to understand. The possibility of a nation's being too proud to fight at the first provocation, and the subordination of national interest to the interest of mankind — this is the language of the new principles that Crèvecœur was invoking. It is nearly a century and a half since he tried to answer the question "What is an American?" Much has happened since then. Internally the country has developed to the extent of his farthest dreams, and in the world-family, after five great wars, it has become one of the greatest of the powers, fulfilling so much of his predictions that one speculates in all humility on what may be the next steps "for that new race of men whose labours and posterity will one day cause great changes in the world."

BOOK LIST

Individual Author

MICHEL GUILLAUME ST. JEAN DE CRÈVECŒUR. Letters from an American Farmer. Written for the information of a friend in England. Edited by J. Hector St. John. 1782.

Available Editions

Letters from an American Farmer. Ludwig Lewisohn, editor. With prefatory note by W. P. Trent. 1904.

W. B. Blake, editor. In *Everyman's Library*.

Biography and Criticism

BOYNTON, PERCY H. A Colonial Farmer's Letters. *New Republic*, June 19, 1915.

MITCHELL, JULIA POST. St. Jean de Crèvecœur. 1916.

TYLER, M. C. Literary History of the American Revolution (1765–1783), Vol. II, chap. xxvii. 1897.

TOPICS AND PROBLEMS

Read the characterization of the American colonies in Burke's "Speech on Conciliation."

Read the letter entitled "What is an American?" and see how far its generalizations apply to the America of to-day.

Read Zangwill's play " The Melting Pot " in the light of this letter on " What is an American ? "

Read passages which deal with nature for Crèvecœur's observation on plant and animal life.

Read the closing essay in comparison with Rousseau's " Émile " for its romantic idealization of primitive life. Compare this essay with the picture of frontier life as presented in " The Deerslayer " or " The Last of the Mohicans." Note the resemblances to Châteaubriand's " René."

Read the opening chapters or divisions of Thoreau's " Walden " and compare with the Crèvecœur "Letters" in point of the contrasting views on property, labor, and citizenship.

Read Mary Antin's " The Promised Land " for the differences in the America to which Crèvecœur came and the America which she found.

CHAPTER VI

THE POETRY OF THE REVOLUTION AND PHILIP FRENEAU

With the Revolutionary War there was naturally a great output of printed matter. Controversial pamphlets, state papers, diaries, letters, and journals, plays (with prologues and epilogues), songs, ballads and satires, all swelled the total. No one can fully understand the Revolution or the period after it who does not read extensively in this material; yet, taken in its length and breadth, the prose and most of the verse are important as history rather than as literature. Out of the numerous company of writers who were producing while Franklin was an aging man and while Crèvecœur was an American farmer, one, Philip Freneau, may be considered as chief representative, and two others, Francis Hopkinson and John Trumbull, deserve a briefer comment.

Francis Hopkinson (1737–1791), the Philadelphian, was well characterized in a much-quoted letter from John Adams to his wife in August, 1776:

At this shop I met Mr. Francis Hopkinson, late a mandamus councillor of New Jersey, now a member of the Continental Congress, who . . . was liberally educated, and is a painter and a poet. . . . He is one of your pretty little, curious, ingenious men. . . . He is genteel and well-bred and is very social. I wish I had leisure and tranquillity of mind to amuse myself with those elegant and ingenious arts of painting, sculpture, statuary, architecture and music. But I have not.

Undoubtedly Hopkinson's work savors of the dilettante throughout; yet part of its historical significance is inherent in this fact, for Hopkinson is one of the earliest examples of talented versatility in American life. He had virtues to complement the accomplishments half enviously cited by John

Adams. He was a learned judge, a stalwart revolutionist, a practical man of affairs, and a humorist.

His collected writings in three volumes were done in the best manner of eighteenth-century England. Five sixths of them are essays, written not in series, but quite of the *Spectator* type. Three prose satires — "A Pretty Story" (1774), "A Prophecy" (1776), and "The New Roof" (1778) — are as important a trio as any written by one man in the Revolutionary days. The other sixth — his verse — belonged no less to the polite literature of the period. There are Miltonic imitations, songs, sentiments, hymns, a fable, and a piece of advice to a young lady. There are occasional poems, including birthday and wedding greetings, dramatic prologues and epilogues, elegies, and rimed epitaphs. Verses of these kinds, if they were all Hopkinson had written, would indicate a hopeless subservience to prevailing English fashions. But Hopkinson was nobody's vassal. When he wrote

> My generous heart disdains
> The slave of love to be,
> I scorn his servile chains,
> And boast my liberty,

he might as truly have asserted his refusal to submit to any sort of trammels except at his own option. Into a few imitation ballads he poured the new wine of Revolutionary sentiment, one of which, "The Battle of the Kegs," with its mocking jollity, put good cheer in all colonial hearts in the times that tried men's souls. It was his jaunty self-control, the quality of heroism without its pompous mannerisms, that set Hopkinson off in contrast with his fellows. He was almost the least pretentious of them all, yet few were more effective.

John Trumbull (1750–1831), most talented of the "Hartford Wits," tried his hand, like Hopkinson, at the conventional poetical subjects, but, unlike him, the bulk of his verse was contained in two long satirical essays: "The Progress of Dulness " (1772 and 1773) and "M'Fingal" (1776 and 1782). Apparently he had no further ambition for himself or other American poets than to

> bid their lays with lofty Milton vie;
> Or wake from nature's themes the moral song,
> And shine with Pope, with Thompson and with Young.
> This land her Swift and Addison shall view,
> The former honors equalled by the new;
> Here shall some Shakspeare charm the rising age,
> And hold in magic chains the listening stage;
> A second Watts shall strike the heavenly lyre,
> And other muses other bards inspire.

Nevertheless, in these two satires he wrote first from a provincial and then from an early national point of view. "The Progress of Dulness" is a disquisition on how not to bring up children. He chose for his examples Tom Brainless, Dick Hairbrain, and Harriet Simper. He put the boys through college (Trumbull was a graduate of Yale), making one a dull preacher and the other a rake. Harriet, the American counterpart of Biddy Tipkin in Steele's "Tender Husband" or Arabella in Mrs. Lennox's "The Female Quixote," is fed on flattery, social ambition, and the romantic fiction of the hour (see p. 103), becomes a coquette and a jilt, and, thrown over by Dick, sinks into obscurity as the faded wife of Parson Tom. This was homemade satire, democratic in its choice and treatment of character, and clearly located in and about New Haven, Connecticut.

So also, and much more aggressively, was the rimed political document "M'Fingal," an immensely popular diatribe at the Tory of the Revolution — his attitude, his general demeanor, and his methods of argument. It recounts the events of a day in a New England town which was torn by the dissensions between the rival factions in the opening days of the conflict, and describes in detail the ways in which this particularly offensive Tory was driven to cover. The modern reader must bring to it a good deal of student interest if he expects to complete the reading and understand it, even with the aid of Trumbull's copious footnotes. For the moment it was a skillful piece of journalistic writing. Trumbull knew how to appeal to the prejudices of his sympathizers (for controversial war writing confirms rather than convinces); he knew how to draw on their limited store of general knowledge ; and he knew how to lead them on with a due employment of literary ingenuities like puns, multiple rimes, and word elisions, and a judicious resort to rough jocosity and vituperation. "M'Fingal" was war literature with all its defects of passion, uncandor, and speciousness, but the score or more of editions through which it ran before 1800 are evidence that it reached the low mark at which it was aimed. If it had the faults of its kind, so in later years did "Uncle Tom's Cabin" and "Mr. Britling sees it Through."

The most representative poet of the Revolutionary period was Philip Freneau, who lived from 1752 to 1832 and who was active in authorship for forty-five years, from 1770 on. He was a graduate of Princeton College in 1771, gained a sudden reputation as a political satirist in 1775, and lived a strangely varied life from then till well into the nineteenth century. For three years he lived in Santa Cruz and Bermuda. In 1779 he sailed to the Azores, and for a six-year period at a later time he was engaged in Atlantic coast trade. From 1784 to 1807 he went the circle in five stages as editor, seaman, editor, farmer, and seaman again. Everything he did he seems to have done hard, and nothing held him long. It is a kind of life which does not seem surprising in a man who has often been called "Poet of the Revolution," for he wrote as vigorously as he sailed or farmed or edited, and he plowed his political satires quite as deep and straight as he plowed the seas and the furrows of his fields. After his bitter experience of three months on a British prison ship, he blazed out with a savage flame of verse which has carried the horrors of this particular form of war brutality down the centuries to greet the "atrocities" of the present. When the editors of rival papers and rival parties annoyed him he scourged them with a savageness of attack which was notable even in a day when journalism knew no restraint and recognized no proprieties. Freneau had at least one title to the friendship of Dr. Samuel Johnson, who loved "a good hater."

This vehement side of his life resulted in a generous amount of war poetry which would be remembered — or forgotten — with the best of the rest of its kind if it were all that he had written. In a brief survey like the present chapter it can therefore serve the double purpose of illustrating the verse of the Revolution and of representing a less important aspect of his whole work. In this respect it is comparable to the Civil-War and anti-slavery poetry of Whittier. Sometimes this verse is full of scorn, as in "The Midnight Consultations," in which Lord Howe is ridiculed as presiding over a council which arrives at the following heroic conclusion :

> Three weeks — ye gods ! — nay, three long years it seems
> Since *roast beef* I have touched, except in dreams,
> In sleep, choice dishes to my view repair,
> Waking, I gape and champ the empty air, —
>
> . . . .
>
> On neighbouring isles uncounted cattle stray,
> Fat beeves, and swine, an ill-defended prey —
> These are fit victims for my noonday dish,
> These, if my soldiers act as I would wish,
> In one short week should glad your maws and mine ;
> On mutton we will sup — on roast beef dine.

Sometimes it is full of the hate which war always engenders. Freneau wrote no more bitterly about the king, Lord North, and the leading generals in active service against the colonists than did Jonathan Odell — the foremost Tory satirist — about Washington and his associates. As the war went on, and the likelihood of American success became stronger, Freneau's tone softened, as he could well afford to have it, and in such a product as "The Political Balance" he wrote with nothing more offensive than the mockery of a rather ungenerous victor. This poem, characterized by well-maintained humor, is one of the best of its kind. It represents Jove as one day looking over the book of Fate and of coming to an incomplete account of Britain, for the Fates had neglected to reveal the outcome of the war. In order to find out for himself, he directs Vulcan to make an exact model of the globe, borrows the scales from Virgo, and plans to foretell the future by setting the mother country on one side and the States on the other. When, after many difficulties, the experiment is tried, of course the States overbalance the little island. Then, to make sure, he adds the foreign dominions on Britain's side,

> But the gods were confounded and struck with surprise,
> And Vulcan could hardly believe his own eyes!

> For (such was the purpose and guidance of fate)
> Her foreign dominions diminish'd her weight —
> By which it appeared, to Britain's disaster,
> Her foreign possessions were changing their master.

> Then as he replac'd them, said Jove with a smile —
> " Columbia shall never be rul'd by an isle —
> But vapours and darkness around her shall rise,
> And tempests conceal her a while from our eyes ;

> " So locusts in Egypt their squadrons display,
> And rising, disfigure the face of the day ;
> So the moon, at her full, has a frequent eclipse,
> And the sun in the ocean diurnally dips.

> " Then cease your endeavors, ye vermin of Britain —
> (And here, in derision, their island he spit on)
> 'T is madness to seek what you never can find,
> Or think of uniting what nature disjoin'd ;

> " But still you may flutter awhile with your wings,
> And spit out your venom, and brandish your stings,
> Your hearts are as black, and as bitter as gall,
> A curse to yourselves, and a blot on the Ball."

After the successful completion of the war it was only natural that Americans in their rejoicing should imagine the glorious future that awaited their new independence. The more vivid their imaginations were, the more splendid were the prophecies they indulged in. As we read over the records of their lofty hopes we are reminded of commencement oratory; and the likeness is not unreal, for these post-Revolution poets were in fact very like eager college graduates, diploma in hand, looking forward to vague but splendid careers. It was in these poems too that the germs of Fourth of July oratory first took root — the oratory described by James Fenimore Cooper in his " Home as Found " (chap. xxi) :

There were the usual allusions to Greece and Rome, between the republics of which and that of this country there exists some such affinity as is to be found between a horse-chestnut and a chestnut horse, or that of mere words; and a long catalogue of national glories that might very well have sufficed for all republics, both of antiquity and of our own time. But when the orator came to speak of the American character, and particularly of the intelligence of the nation, he was most felicitous, and made the largest investments in popularity. According to his account of the matter, no other people possessed a tithe of the knowledge, or a hundredth part of the honesty and virtue of the very community he was addressing; and after laboring for ten minutes to convince his hearers that they already knew everything, he wasted several more in trying to persuade them to undertake further acquisitions of the same nature.

These elephantine poems were written each in several " books," to each one of which was prefixed an outline which, in the language of the day, was called " the argument." Here is a part of the outline for Book VII of Timothy Dwight's " Greenfield Hill " (1794) :

Happiness of U. S. contrasted to Eastern Despotism. Universal Prevalence of Freedom. Unfortified, and therefore safe, state of U. S. Influence of our state of Society on the Mind. Public Property employed for the Public Benefit. Penal Administrations improved by Benevolence. Policy enlarges its scope. Knowledge promoted. Improvements in Astronomical and other Instruments of Science. Improvements of the Americans, in Natural Philosophy — Poetry — Music — and Moral Science. State of the American Clergy. Manners refined. Artificial Manners condemned. American Women. Cultivation advanced. Other Nations visit this country, and learn the nature, and causes, of our happiness. Conclusion.

And here is a part of the argument to Book IX of Joel Barlow's " Columbiad," in which he demonstrates that the present government of America is a culmination of all human progress :

. . . the ancient and modern states of the arts and of society, Crusades, Commerce, Hanseatic League, Copernicus, Kepler, Newton, Galileo, Herschel, Descartes, Bacon, Printing Press, Magnetic Needle, Geographic Discoveries, Federal System in America.

Freneau had shared all this prophetic enthusiasm, and had expressed it even before the war, partly in an actual commencement poem on " The Rising Glory of America " and partly in a series of eighteen " Pictures of Columbus." Just after graduation he had written :

> I see, I see
> A thousand Kingdoms rais'd, cities and men
> Num'rous as sand upon the ocean shore ;
> Th' Ohio then shall glide by many a town
> Of note ; and where the Mississippi stream
> By forests shaded now runs weeping on,
> Nations shall grow, and States not less in fame
> Than Greece and Rome of old ; we too shall boast
> Our Alexanders, Pompeys, heroes, kings,
> That in the womb of time yet dormant lye
> Waiting the joyful hour of life and light.

After the war, however, he did not rejoin the increasing choir who were singing this kind of choral. His most interesting bit of prophecy, which must have seemed to his contemporaries to be a piece of the airiest fancy, has been amazingly verified more than a century after he wrote it. This is

"The Progress of Balloons," written in the jaunty tone of
"The Political Balance":

> The stagemen, whose gallopers scarce have the power
> Through the dirt to convey you ten miles in an hour,
> When advanc'd to balloons shall so furiously drive
> You 'll hardly know whether you 're dead or alive.
> The man who at Boston sets out with the sun,
> If the wind should be fair, may be with us at one,
> At Gunpowder Ferry drink whiskey at three
> And at six be at Edentown, ready for tea.
> (The machine shall be order'd, we hardly need say,
> To travel in darkness as well as by day)
> At Charleston by ten he for sleep shall prepare,
> And by twelve the next day be the devil knows where.
> .   .   .   .
> If Britain should ever disturb us again,
> (As they threaten to do in the next George's reign)
> No doubt they will play us a set of new tunes,
> And pepper us well from their fighting balloons.
> .   .   .   .
>   Such wonders as these from balloons shall arise —
> And the giants of old that assaulted the skies
> With their Ossa on Pelion, shall freely confess
> That all they attempted was nothing to this.

This, of course, was newspaper poetry, and Freneau, for long
years of his life, was a newspaper man. Even his lines "To
Sir Toby," a slaveholding sugar-planter in Jamaica, spirited as
they are, are in effect an open letter in protest against human
slavery, and they were printed in the *National Gazette* in 1792.
The really poetical work of Freneau, however, which entitles
him to an attention greater than that for his fellows, had nothing
to do with political or military events of the day. They were
his shorter poems on American nature and American tradition ;
and a distinguishing feature of them was that they were different from the English poetry of the time, in form as well as in
content. As a young man Freneau had set out on his career

by writing after the style of Milton and Dryden and Pope and their lesser imitators. This was absolutely natural. Until after the Revolution, America was England; and it was more nearly like England in speech and in thought than much of Scotland and Ireland are to-day. All the refinements of America were derived from English sources; practically all the colonists' reading was from English authors. But after the Revolution there came a strong reaction of feeling. We can look to Freneau's own rimes (journalistic ones again) for an explanation of the new and native quality of his later verse; they are called " Literary Importation," and they conclude as follows :

> It seems we had spirit to humble a throne,
> Have genius for science inferior to none,
> But hardly encourage a plant of our own:
>   If a college be planned
>   'T is all at a stand
> 'Till to Europe we send at a shameful expense,
> To send us a bookworm to teach us some sense.

> Can we never be thought to have learning or grace
> Unless it be brought from that horrible place
> Where tyranny reigns with her impudent face ;
>   And popes and pretenders
>   And sly faith-defenders
> Have ever been hostile to reason and wit,
> Enslaving a world that shall conquer them yet.

> 'T is a folly to fret at the picture I draw :
> And I say what was said by a Doctor Magraw ;
> " If they give us their Bishops, they 'll give us their law."
>   How that will agree
>   With such people as we,
> Let us leave to the learned to reflect on awhile,
> And say what they think in a handsomer stile.

As a consequence of this feeling that America should be different, the tendency grew to seek out native subject matter and to cease conscious imitation of English literary models.

For the next half century American authors were contending, every now and then, that native themes should occupy their attention, and a good deal of verse and prose was written with this idea in mind. Most of it was more conscientious than interesting, for literature, to be genuinely effective, must be produced not to demonstrate a theory but to express what is honestly in the author's mind. The first step toward achieving nationality in American writing was, therefore, to achieve new and independent habits of national thinking. The Irish mind, for example, is basically different from the English mind, and Irish literature has therefore a long and beautiful history of its own, in spite of the fact that Ireland is near to England and subject to it. But the Australian is simply a transplanted English-speaking, English-thinking mind, and Australia has consequently produced no literature of which the world is yet aware.

Now Freneau was a naturally independent thinker. He was educated and well read in the best of English and classical literature. But unlike most of his fellow authors, he was not a city man, nor a teacher, preacher, or lawyer. His hands were hardened by the steersman's wheel and the plow, and doubtless much of his verse — or at least the inspiration for it — came to him on shipboard or in the field rather than in the library. In the midst of the crowd he was an easy man to stir up to fighting pitch. All his war verse shows this. Yet when he was alone and undisturbed he inclined to placid meditation, and he expressed himself in the simplest ways. As a young man he wrote a little poem called " On Retirement." It is the kind of thing that many other eighteenth-century poets — confirmed city dwellers — wrote in moments of temporary world-weariness; but Freneau's life-story shows that he really meant it :

> A cottage I could call my own
>   Remote from domes of care ;
> A little garden, wall'd with stone,
> The wall with ivy overgrown,
>   A limpid fountain near,

> Would more substantial joys afford,
>   More real bliss impart
> Than all the wealth that misers hoard,
> Than vanquish'd worlds, or worlds restor'd —
>   Mere cankers of the heart!

And there was another poem of his youth which told a secret of his real character. This was "The Power of Fancy," an imitation of Milton in its form, but genuinely Freneau's in its sentiment. The best of his later work is really a compound of these suggestions — poems of fancy composed in retirement. Thus he wrote on "The Indian Burying Ground," interpreting the fact that

> The Indian, when from life releas'd,
>   Again is seated with his friends
> And shares again the joyous feast,

instead of being buried recumbent as white men are. And thus he wrote in "To a Caty-did," "The Wild Honeysuckle," and "On a Honey Bee," little lyrics of nature and natural life, which were almost the first verse written in America based on native subject matter and expressed in simple, direct, and unpretentious form.

Nathaniel Ames, in one of his early almanacs, recorded soberly:

MAY

> Now Winters rage abates, now chearful Hours
> Awake the Spring, and Spring awakes the Flowers.
> The opening Buds salute the welcome Day,
> And Earth relenting, feels the genial Ray.
> The Blossoms blow, the Birds on Bushes sing;
> And Nature has accomplish'd all the Spring.

This was perfectly conventional and perfectly indefinite; not a single flower, bud, blossom, bird, or bush is specified. The six lines amount to a general formula for spring and would apply equally well to Patagonia, Italy, New England, or northern

Siberia. Mr. R. Lewis, who wrote on "A Journey from Patapsco to Annapolis" in 1730, improves on this:

> First born of *Spring*, here the *Pacone* appears.
> Whose golden Root a silver Blossom rears.
> In spreading Tufts see there the *Crowfoot*, blue,
> On whose green Leaves still shines a globous Dew;
> Behold the *Cinque-foil*, with its dazling Dye
> Of flaming Yellow, wounds the tender Eye.
> But there enclos'd the grassy Wheat is seen
> To heal the aching Sight with cheerful Green.

Lewis mentions definite flowers, colors, and characteristics, but he never misses a chance to tuck in a conventional adjective or participle, and he is led by them into weaving the extravagant fancy of an eye made to ache by flaming and dazzling colors, and healed by the cheerful green of the wheat field. In contrast to these, Freneau's little nature poems are as exact as the second and as simple as the subject on which he writes:

> In a branch of willow hid
> Sings the evening Caty-did:
> From the lofty locust bough
> Feeding on a drop of dew.
> In her suit of green array'd
> Hear her singing in the shade,
> Caty-did, Caty-did, Caty-did.

Such simplicity as this does not seem at all remarkable to-day, but if it be compared with the fixed formalities that belonged to almost all the verse of Freneau's time it will stand out as a remarkable exception.

On account of the two kinds of poetry which Freneau published he has often been given misleading titles by his admirers. Those who have been interested in him mainly or exclusively from the historical point of view have christened him the " Poet of the American Revolution." This is unfair because of the implication that he gave his best energy to this and had no other right to distinction. Even as a journalist he was more than poet of the Revolution, since he wrote on local and timely themes for many years after its close. This designation does not claim enough for him. The other title is defective for the opposite reason, that it claims too much. This is the " Father of American Poetry." Such a sweeping phrase ought to be avoided resolutely. It is doubly false, in suggesting that there was no American poetry before he wrote and that everything since has been derived from him. The facts are that he had a native poetic gift which would have led to his writing poetry had there never been a war between the colonies and England, but that when the war came on he was one of the most effective penmen on his side ; that entrance into the field of public affairs diverted him from the paths of quiet life ; that after the war he continued both kinds of writing. He never ceased wholly to think and write about "affairs," but more and more he speculated on the future, dreamed of the picturesque past, and played with themes of graceful and tender sentiment. He is very much worth reading as a commentator on his own times, and he is no less worth reading for the beauty of many poems quite without reference to the time or place in which they were written.

The long and fruitful colonial period must not be overlooked by any honest student of American literature, yet it may fairly be regarded as no more than a preparatory stage. It has the same relationship to the whole story as do the ancestry, boyhood, and education to the development of an individual. In the broad and brief survey attempted in these chapters a few leading facts have been reviewed about the youth of America : (1) Everything characteristic of the early settlers was derived directly from England, those in the South representing the aristocratic traditions of king and court, and those in the North reflecting the democratic revolt of the Puritans. As a natural consequence of these differences the writing of books soon waned in Virginia and the neighboring colonies, but developed consistently in Massachusetts and New England. (2) The attempt of the Puritans to force all New Englanders to think the same thoughts and worship in the same way was unsuccessful from the start, and the most interesting writers of the seventeenth century reveal the spread of disturbing influences. The first three chosen as examples are Thomas Morton, the frank and unscrupulous enemy of the Puritans; Nathaniel Ward, a sturdy Puritan who was alarmed at the growth of anti-Puritan influences; and Roger Williams, a deeply religious preacher, who rebelled against the control of the Church in New England just as he and others had formerly rebelled in the mother country. (3) Even in the first half century a good deal of verse was written: sometimes, as in the case of "The Day of Doom," as a mere rimed statement of Puritan theology; but sometimes, as in the case of Anne Bradstreet and her followers, as an expression of real poetic feeling. (4) With the passage to the eighteenth century the community was clearly slipping from the grasp of the Puritans. Evidence is ample from three types of colonists: the Mathers, who were fighting a desperate but losing battle to retain control; Samuel Sewall, who, although a Puritan, was willing to accept reasonable changes; and Mrs. Sarah Kemble Knight, who said little at the time, but in her private journals showed the existence of growing disrespect for the old habits of thought. (5) Benjamin Franklin, whose work is more valuable than that of any of his predecessors, is also completely representative of the complete swing away from religious enthusiasm to a hard-headed worldliness which was prevailing in England in the eighteenth century. (6) On the other hand, Crèvecœur, writing just before the Revolution, sounded the note of thanksgiving to the Lord that America was different from the Old World, and emphasized what were the conditions of life that were worth fighting to save. (7) Finally, out of all the roster of talented writers during the Revolutionary War, Freneau was selected as the most gifted poet of the period, both as an indirect recorder of the conflict and as an author of poetry on native themes in no way related to the war.

BOOK LIST

General References

ADAMS, H. B. Thomas Jefferson and the University of Virginia. 1888.

FISKE, JOHN. The Critical Period of American History. Chap. ii. 1888.

OTIS, WILLIAM BRADLEY. American Verse, 1625–1807. 1909.

PATTERSON, SAMUEL WHITE. The Spirit of the American Revolution as Revealed in the Poetry of the Period (contains good bibliography). 1915.

RICHARDSON, C. F. American Literature. Chaps. i, vi, viii. 1887.

TUCKER, S. M. In chap. ix of Cambridge History of American Literature, Vol. I, Bk. I.

TYLER, M. C. The Literary History of the American Revolution, chaps. ix, xix, xx, xxi, xxvi, xxviii, xxix, xxxi, xxxii. 1897.

VAN TYNE, C. H. The Loyalists in the American Revolution. 1902.

WENDELL, BARRETT. Literary History of America, chaps. vii, viii, ix. 1900.

For spirit of the times read Familiar Letters of John and Abigail Adams. 1876.

General Bibliography

Cambridge History of American Literature, Vol. I, pp. 457–467.

Individual Authors

FRANCIS HOPKINSON. Miscellaneous Essays and Occasional Writings. 1792. 3 vols. The latter half of the third volume contains in separate paging (1–204) his Poems on Several Subjects. (There has been no reprinting.)

Available Edition

The Old Farm and the New Farm: a Political Allegory (edited by B. J. Lossing). 1864.

Biography and Criticism

HILDEBURN, C. R. A Biographical Sketch of Francis Hopkinson. 1878.

MARBLE, MRS. A. R. Francis Hopkinson, Man of Affairs and Letters. *New England Magazine*, Vol. XXVII, p. 289.

TYLER, M. C. The Literary History of the American Revolution, Vol. I, chap. viii, pp. 163–171; chap. xii, pp. 279–292; chap. xxii, pp. 487–490; and Vol. II, chap. xxx, pp. 130–157.

Collections

BOYNTON, PERCY H. American Poetry, pp. 35–42, 604–606.

CAIRNS, W. B. Early American Writers, pp. 372–383.

DUYCKINCK, E. A. and G. L. Cyclopedia of American Literature, Vol. I, pp. 209–219.

STEDMAN and HUTCHINSON. Library of American Literature, Vol. III, pp. 236–251.

JOHN TRUMBULL. Poetical Works. 2 vols. Hartford, 1820. Progress of Dulness. Part I, The Rare Adventures of Tom Brainless, 1772; Part II, The Life and Character of Dick Hairbrain of Finical Memory, 1773; Part III, The Adventures of Miss Harriet Simper, 1773. M'Fingal: a Modern Epic Poem. Canto I; or, The Town Meeting (includes what is now Cantos I and II). 1776. Completed with Cantos III and IV. 1782.

Available Edition
M'Fingal; an Epic Poem (edited by B. J. Lossing). 1860, 1864, 1881.

Collections
BOYNTON, PERCY H. American Poetry, pp. 43–57, 58–88, 606–610, 611–614.

CAIRNS, W. B. Early American Writers, pp. 395–408.

DUYCKINCK, E. A. and G. L. Cyclopedia of American Literature, Vol. I, pp. 308–319.

STEDMAN and HUTCHINSON. Library of American Literature, Vol. III, pp. 422–429; Vol. IV, pp. 89–92.

PHILIP FRENEAU. Poems. Printed for the Princeton Historical Association. F. L. Pattee, editor. 1902–1907. 3 vols.

Available Edition
Poems of Philip Freneau relating to the American Revolution. E. A. Duyckinck, editor. 1865.

Bibliography
A volume compiled by Victor H. Paltsits. 1903.

Biography and Criticism
AUSTIN, MARY S. Philip Freneau, the Poet of the Revolution. 1901.

DELANCEY, E. F. Philip Freneau, the Huguenot Patriot-Poet, etc. *Proceedings of the Huguenot Soc. of Amer., Vol. II, No. 2.* 1891.

FORMAN, SAMUEL E. The Political Activities of Philip Freneau. *Johns Hopkins University Studies, Ser. 20, Nos. 9, 10.* 1902.

Collections
BOYNTON, PERCY H. American Poetry, pp. 89–117, 614–618.

CAIRNS, W. B. Early American Writers, pp. 431–448.

DUYCKINCK, E. A. and G. L. Cyclopedia of American Literature, Vol. I, pp. 327–348.

STEDMAN and HUTCHINSON. Library of American Literature, Vol. III, pp. 445–457.

TIMOTHY DWIGHT. There are no recent editions of Dwight. These appeared originally as follows: The Conquest of Canaan, 1785; The Triumph of Infidelity, 1788; Greenfield Hill, 1794; Travels in New England and New York, 1823.

Biography and Criticism

DWIGHT, W. T. and S. E. Memoir prefixed to Dwight's Theology. 4 vols.

SPRAGUE, W. B. The Life of Timothy Dwight, in Vol. XIV of Sparks's *Library of American Biography*.

SPRAGUE, W. B. Annals of the American Pulpit, Vol. II.

TYLER, M. C. Three Men of Letters, pp. 72–127. 1895.

Introduction to the Poems of Philip Freneau (edited by F. L. Pattee), Vol. I, pp. c, ci. 1902.

Collections

BOYNTON, PERCY H. American Poetry, pp. 118–124, 618–621.

CAIRNS, W. B. Early American Writers, pp. 409–420.

DUYCKINCK, E. A. and G. L. Cyclopedia of American Literature, Vol. I, pp. 357–365.

STEDMAN and HUTCHINSON. Library of American Literature, Vol. III, pp. 426–429 and 463–483.

JOEL BARLOW. His epic is accessible only in early editions. His poetical work appeared originally as follows: The Vision of Columbus, 1787; The Columbiad, 1807; Hasty Pudding, 1847.

Biography and Criticism

TODD, C. B. Life and Letters of Joel Barlow. 1886.

TYLER, M. C. Three Men of Letters, pp. 131–180. 1895.

Collections

BOYNTON, PERCY H. American Poetry, pp. 125–135, 621–624.

CAIRNS, W. B. Early American Writers, pp. 421–430.

DUYCKINCK, E. A. and G. L. Cyclopedia of American Literature, Vol. I, pp. 391–404.

STEDMAN and HUTCHINSON. Library of American Literature, Vol. III, pp. 422–429, and Vol. IV, pp. 46–57.

Literary Treatment of the Period

Drama

In *Representative Plays by American Dramatists* (edited by M. J. Moses), Vol. I. 1918.

The Group; a Farce, by Mrs. Mercy Warren.

The Battle of Bunker's Hill, by H. H. Brackenridge.

The Fall of British Tyranny; or, American Liberty, by John Leacock.

The Politician Outwitted, by Samuel Low.

The Contrast, by Royall Tyler.[1]

André, by William Dunlap.[1]

[1] Also in *Representative American Plays* (edited by A. H. Quinn). 1917.

Fiction

CHURCHILL, WINSTON. Richard Carvel.
COOPER, J. F. Lionel Lincoln; or, The Leaguer of Boston.
COOPER, J. F. The Pilot.
COOPER, J. F. The Spy.
FORD, P. L. Janice Meredith.
HARTE, BRET. Thankful Blossom.
JEWETT, SARAH ORNE. The Tory Lover.
KENNEDY, J. P. Horse Shoe Robinson.
MITCHELL, S. WEIR. Hugh Wynne.
SIMMS, W. GILMORE. The Partisan.
SIMMS, W. GILMORE. The Scout.

Poetry

Poems of American History (edited by B. E. Stevenson), pp. 125–265.
American History by American Poets (edited by M. V. Wallington), Vol. I, pp. 125–293.

TOPICS AND PROBLEMS

In a survey course enough material is presented for Hopkinson, Trumbull, Dwight, and Barlow in the collections mentioned in the Book List for this chapter. The only reprint available of Lewis's interesting "Journey from Patapsco to Annapolis" is in "American Poetry" (P. H. Boynton, editor), pp. 24–29. These poems are chiefly significant for the combination of English form and American subject matter.

Compare Trumbull's comments on the education of girls with the corresponding passage by Mrs. Malaprop, in Sheridan's "The Rivals," and with Fitz-Greene Halleck's comments on the education of Fanny, in the poem of that name (see "American Poetry," pp. 127, 128, and 155, 156).

Compare Dwight's "Farmer's Advice to the Villagers," "Greenfield Hill," Pt. VI, with Benjamin Franklin's "The Way to Wealth."

Compare the nationalistic note in the seventh and ninth books of Barlow's "Vision of Columbus" with that in Timrod's "Ethnogenesis" and that in Moody's "Ode in Time of Hesitation." Do the dates of the three poems suggest a progressive change? (See "American Poetry," pp. 123, 349, and 577.)

Read Freneau's more bitter war satires in comparison with Jonathan Odell's "Congratulation" and "The American Times," for which see "American Poetry," pp. 78–83.

Read Freneau's more jovial war satires in comparison with Whittier's " Letter from a Missionary of the Methodist Episcopal Church " (" American Poetry," p. 255); John R. Thompson's " On to Richmond " ("American Poetry," p. 325); Edmund C. Stedman's " How Old Brown took Harper's Ferry " ("American Poetry," p. 317); and Lowell's " Biglow Papers."

Read Freneau's " Pictures of Columbus " in comparison with Lowell's "Columbus" ("American Poetry," p. 382); Lanier's "Sonnets on Columbus " ("American Poetry," p. 458); and Joaquin Miller's " Columbus " ("American Poetry," p. 564).

" The Progress of Balloons " derives its title from a whole series of preceding " progress " poems. Cite others and compare them as you can.

With reference to Freneau's diction in nature passages as compared with that of Ames and Lewis in the text, read Wordsworth's essay on " Poetic Diction " prefatory to the lyrical ballads of 1798, with which Freneau agreed and which he anticipated in certain of his poems.

CHAPTER VII

THE EARLY DRAMA

In the growth of most national literatures the theater has developed side by side with the drama, the stage doing for the play what the printing press did for the essay, poem, and novel. But in America, the land of a transplanted civilization, the order was changed and the first plays were supplied from abroad just as the other forms of literature were. In the history of the American stage, therefore, the successive steps were the presentation of English plays by American amateurs in regular audience rooms with improvised stages; then the development of semiprofessional and wholly professional companies who played short seasons at irregular intervals; then the erection of special playhouses; and finally the formation of more permanent professional companies, both English and American,—all of which took place in the course of nearly two generations before the emergence of any native American drama. Recent investigations have so frequently pushed back the years of first performances, playhouses, and plays that now one can offer such dates only as subject to further revision.

According to the "Cambridge History of American Literature," "there seem to have been theatrical performances in this country since 1703." Paul Leicester Ford in his "Washington and the Theater" says, "that there was play-acting in New York, and in Charleston, South Carolina, before 1702, are unquestioned facts." In 1718 Governor Spottswood of Virginia gave an entertainment on the king's birthday, the feature of which was a play, probably acted by the students of William and Mary College, as there are references to later events of this sort. The Virginia governor's patronage bore different

CHRONOLOGICAL CHART I. AMERICAN LITERATURE, 1600–1800

	JAMES I	CHARLES I	PRO-TECTOR-ATE	CHARLES II	JAS. II	WM.-MARY	ANNE	GEORGE I	GEORGE II	GEORGE III
	1603→	→1625	1649↔1660	→1685	1689	→1702	→1714	→1727	→1760	→1820

1600 1610 1620 1630 1640 1650 1660 1670 1680 1690 1700 1710 1720 1730 1740 1750 1760 1770 1780 1790 1800

Thomas Morton (1575?–1646?)
Nathaniel Ward (1578–1652?)
Roger Williams (1604–1683)
Michael Wigglesworth (1631–1705)
Anne Bradstreet (1612–1672)
Increase Mather (1639–1723)
Cotton Mather (1663–1728)
Samuel Sewall (1652–1730)
Sarah Kemble Knight (1666–1727)
Jonathan Edwards (1703–1758)
Benjamin Franklin (1706–1790)
Michel de Crèvecœur (1731–1813)
Francis Hopkinson (1737–1791)
John Trumbull (1750–1831)
Philip Freneau (1752–1832)
Timothy Dwight (1752–1817)
Joel Barlow (1754–1812)
Brockden Brown (1771–1810)
Washington Irving (1783–1859)
Fitz-Greene Halleck (1790–1867)
Joseph Rodman Drake (1795–1820)
J. Fenimore Cooper (1789–1851)
Wm. Cullen Bryant (1794–1878)

AMERICAN REVOLUTION

fruit from the early indorsement of playing in staid Massachusetts, for Samuel Sewall recorded in his diary of March 2, 1714, a protest at the acting of a play in the council chamber. " Let not Christian Boston," he admonished, " goe beyond Heathen Rome in the practice of Shamefull Vanities." On the other hand, Williamsburg, Virginia, had its own theater before 1720, New York enjoyed professional acting and a playhouse by 1732, and in Charleston, South Carolina, the use of the courtroom was frequent in the two seasons before the opening of a theater in the winter of 1736. These slight beginnings, with further undertakings in Philadelphia, doubtless gave Lewis Hallam, the London actor, courage to venture over with his company in 1752. With his twelve players he brought a repertory of twenty plays and eight farces, the majority of which had never been presented in America ; and since the year of their arrival the American theater has had a consecutive and broadening place in the life of the people.

The beginnings of drama in America, to distinguish them from the early life of the theater, are not quite clearly known. The first romantic drama, and the first play written by an American and produced by a professional company, was Thomas Godfrey's " The Prince of Parthia," completed by 1759 and acted in 1767 at the Southwark Theater, Philadelphia. The first drama on native American material — an unproduced problem play — was Robert Rogers's " Ponteach," published in London in 1766. The first American comedy to be produced by a professional company was Royall Tyler's " The Contrast," acted in 1787 at the John Street Theater, New York. The first professional American playwright was William Dunlap (1766–1839), author and producer, who wrote, adapted, and translated over sixty plays, operas, sketches, farces, and interludes, of which at least fifty were produced and nearly thirty have been published. The first actor and playwright of more than local prominence was John Howard Payne (1791–1852), more original than Dunlap and equally prolific, with one or two great successes and eighteen published plays to his credit. The history of the American drama, as yet unwritten, will be a big work when it is fully done, for the output has been very large. Three hundred and seventy-eight plays are known to have been published by 1830 and nearly twice that number to have been played by 1860. In the remainder of this chapter, the aim of which is to induce study of plays within the reach of the average college class, four dramas will be discussed because they are interesting in themselves and because they are early representatives of types which still prevail.

The first is "The Prince of Parthia," a romantic tragedy by Thomas Godfrey (1736–1763). He was the son of a scientist, a youth of cultured companions, West the painter and Hopkinson the poet-composer, and his almost certain attendance at performances of the American company of actors led him, in addition to his juvenile poems, to make his ambitious attempt at drama. "The Prince of Parthia" is evidently imitative, and yet no more so than most American poems, essays, novels, and plays written in the generation to which Godfrey belonged until his early death at the age of twenty-seven. The Hallam and American companies had played more of Shakespeare than any other one thing, somewhat of Beaumont and Fletcher, and more or less of Restoration drama; and these combined influences appear in Godfrey's work. There are traces from "Hamlet," signs of "Macbeth," evidences of "The Maid's Tragedy," and responses to the Restoration interest in pseudo-oriental subjects. Yet the play should not be dismissed with these comments as though they were a condemnation. What is more to the point is the fact that "The Prince" is very admirable as a piece of imitative writing. The verse is fluent and at times stately. The construction as a whole is well considered. The characters are consistent, and their actions are based on sufficient motives. Many a later American dramatist fell far short of Godfrey both in excellence of style and in firmness of structure and characterization. Had Godfrey lived and had he passed out of his natural deference for models, he might have done dramatic writing quite equal to that of many a well-known successor. The twentieth-century mind is unaccustomed to the "tragedy of blood." A play with a king and two princely sons at once in love with the same captive maiden, a jealous queen, a vengeful stepson, and a court full of intriguing nobles, a story which ends with the accumulating deaths of the six leading characters, hardly appeals to theatergoers accustomed to dramas which are more economical in their material. But Godfrey should be compared with his own contemporaries, and, all things considered, he stands the comparison well. The type of poetic drama he attempted reoccurs later in the work of Robert Montgomery Bird, Nathaniel Parker Willis, George Henry Boker, and Julia Ward Howe, and reappears in the present generation in plays by such men as Richard Hovey and Percy Mackaye.

The second notable play was Robert Rogers's (1730?–1795) "Ponteach: or the Savages of America," published in London in 1766. The fact that it was not produced at the time must be laid to managerial timidity rather than to defects in the play, for it has some of the merits of Godfrey's work in the details and construction. Two reasons sufficient to put a cautious manager on guard were its criticism of the English and its treatment of the churchman. For the play as a whole is a sharp indictment of the white man's avarice in his transactions with the Indians, in the course of which a Roman Catholic priest is by no means the least guilty. Traders, hunters, and governors combine in malice and deceit, undermining the character of the Indians and at the same time embittering them against their English conquerors. A play with this burden, written so soon after the Seven Years' War, had no more chance of being produced than a pacifist production did from 1914 to 1918. Godfrey's treatment of the Indians seems at first glance unconvincing, but this is chiefly because of the way he made them talk. All the savages and all the different types of white rascal hold forth in the same elevated rhetorical discourse. This fact, which constitutes a valid criticism, should be tempered by the recollection that generations were yet to pass before anything lifelike was to be achieved in dialect writing. Cooper's Indians are quite as stately in speech as Rogers's. Yet, like Cooper, Rogers endowed them with native dignity, self-control, tribal loyalty, and reverence for age as well as with treachery and the lust for blood. If " Ponteach " had been an indictment of the French instead of the English, it is a fair guess that American audiences would have seen it and greeted it " with universal applause." As an Indian play it was followed by many successors — Pocahontas alone was the theme of four plays between 1808 and 1848. As a race play it broke the trail not only for these but for others which branched off to the negro theme — from " Uncle Tom's Cabin" and " The Octoroon," before the Civil War, to Sheldon's " The Nigger," of 1911. As a problem-purpose play it was the first American contribution to a long series which never flags entirely and which always multiplies in years when class or political feeling runs high.

The third notable American play — a success of 1787 and the first of many successes in its field — was " The Contrast," a comedy by Royall Tyler (1757–1826). Its purport is indicated in the opening lines of the prologue :

> EXULT each patriot heart ! — this night is shewn
> A piece, which we may fairly call our own ;
> Where the proud titles of " My Lord ! Your Grace ! "
> To humble Mr. and plain Sir give place.
> Our Author pictures not from foreign climes
> The fashions, or the follies of the times ;
> But has confin'd the subject of his work
> To the gay scenes — the circles of New York.

There is a complacency of pioneership in this and a hint at servility among other playwrights which are not strictly justified by the facts, but the prologue is none the less interesting for this. It is quite as true to its period as the content of the play is, for it displays the independence of conscious revolt, exactly the note of Freneau's " Literary Importation " written only two years earlier (see p. 78) and a constantly recurrent one in American literature for the next fifty years.

Tyler's play is a comedy of manners setting forth " the contrast between a gentleman who has read Chesterfield and received the polish of Europe and an unpolished, untraveled American." This is reënforced by the antithesis between an unscrupulous coquette and a feminine model of all the virtues, and between a popinjay servant and a crude countryman, the original stage Yankee. As far as the moral is concerned the play makes its point not because the good characters are admirable but because the bad ones are so vapid. Manly, the hero, is well disposed of by his frivolous sister's statement : " His conversation is like a rich, old-fashioned brocade, it will stand alone ; every sentence is a sentiment " ; and Maria, the heroine, is revealed by her own observation that " the only safe asylum a woman of delicacy can find is in the arms of a man of honor." Yet the contrasts lead to good dramatic situations and to some amusing comedy, and the play is further interesting because of the fund of allusion to what Tyler considered both worthless and worthy English literary influences. The extended reference to " The School for Scandal " as seen at the theater by Jonathan is acknowledgment enough of Tyler's debt to an English master. " The Contrast " is the voice of young America protesting its superiority to old England and old Europe. It had been audible before the date of Tyler's play, and it was to be heard again and again for the better part of a century and in all forms of literature. In drama the most famous play of the type in the next two generations was Anna C. O. Mowatt's " Fashion " of 1845. " Contrast " was furthermore a forerunner of many later plays which were descriptive without being satirical, a large number of which carried New York in their titles as well as in their contents. These doubtless looked back quite directly to the repeated successes of Pierce Egan's " Life in London," but they had all to acknowledge that Tyler was the early and conspicuous playwright who had

> confin'd the subject of his work
> To the gay scenes — the circles of New York.

The fourth and last play for any detailed comment here is "André" (1798) by William Dunlap (1766–1839). Dunlap asked for recognition, as Tyler had done, on nationalistic grounds,

> A Native Bard, a native scene displays,
> And claims your candour for his daring lays;

and he took heed, as Rogers seems not to have done, of the risk he was running in entering the perilous straits of political controversy in which "Ponteach" was stranded before it had reached the theater:

> O, may no party spirit blast his views,
> Or turn to ill the meanings of the Muse;
> She sings of wrongs long past, Men as they were,
> To instruct, without reproach, the Men that are;
> Then judge the Story by the genius shown,
> And praise, or damn it, for its worth alone.

Party feeling was high at the time over the opposing claims of France and England — "The Rival Suitors for America," as Freneau called them in his verses of 1795. "Hail Columbia," by Joseph Hopkinson, made an immediate hit when sung at an actors' benefit less than four weeks after the production of "André," and made it by an appeal to broad national feeling. And Dunlap, after a slip of sentiment in the first performance, kept clear of politics, and showed tact as well as daring by making the Briton heroic, though a spy, and by his fine treatment of the unnamed "General," who was evidently Washington. Dunlap's play showed a ready appreciation of theatrical effectiveness. It was the work of a playmaker rather than a poet, and the verse had none of the elevation of Godfrey's or Rogers's.

It was far better than the declamatory stage efforts of the Revolutionary years by Brackenridge, Leacock, Low, and Mercy Warren, and it was the best early specimen of the historical romance for which there is always a ready patronage.

Dunlap is more significant as an all-round man in the early history of the American theater than as a pure dramatist. He was a good judge of what the public wanted, and fairly able to achieve it. What he could not write he could translate or adapt. He turned Schiller's " Don Carlos " into English, and it failed ; but he made a great success of Zschokke's " Abaellino " and translated no less than thirteen plays of Kotzebue. A comic opera, a dramatic satire, a farce, or an interlude seemed all one to him in point of ease or difficulty. From 1796 to 1803 he produced more than four plays a year under his own manage- ment at the Park Theater in New York. He continued as a manager till 1805 and was connected with the theater again in 1810–1811. Finally, to cap all, in 1832 he published in two volumes his " History of the American Theater," which, though inaccurate in many details, is full of the personal recollections of men and events that no amount of exact scholarship could now unearth.

The really auspicious beginnings in American play-writing up to 1800 were hardly followed up in the period before the interruption of the drama by the Civil War. One man stands out, John Howard Payne (1791–1852). Starting as a precocious boy actor and a dramatist whose first play was staged at the age of fifteen, he developed into a reputation greater than that of Dunlap, but in the perspective of time little more enduring. His " Brutus " was played for years by well-known tragedians, and his " Charles II," in which Washington Irving had a hand, was long successful as a comedy. But he was too prolific for high excellence, and he did nothing new. Now and then men who wrote abundantly produced single plays of rather high merit though of imitative quality, such as Robert Montgomery Bird's " Broker of Bogota." There was a generous output, but a low level of production ; tragedies, historical plays, comedies of manners, local dramas, social satires, melodramas, and farces followed in steady flow. Successful novels of Cooper, Simms, Mrs. Stowe, and writers of lesser note were quickly staged, but no one of undoubted distinction came to the fore. Writers in other fields, like Nathaniel Parker Willis, the essayist, George Henry Boker, the poet, and Julia Ward Howe, turned their hands at times to play-writing with moderate success. But it is significant that the conspicuous names of the period were names of actors and producers rather than of playwrights. The history of the American stage has been unbroken up to the present time, but it was not until near the end of the century that the literary material presented on the stage became more than a vehicle for the enterprise of managers and the talents of actors. This later stage will be briefly discussed in one of the closing chapters of this book.

BOOK LIST

General References

CRAWFORD, M. C. The Romance of the American Theater. 1913.

DUNLAP, WILLIAM. History of the American Theater. 1832.

HUTTON, LAURENCE. Curiosities of the American Stage. 1891.

MOSES, MONTROSE J. Famous Actor-Families in America. 1906.

MOSES, MONTROSE J. The American Dramatist. 1911.

SEILHAMER, G. O. History of the American Theater, 1749–1797. 3 vols. 1888–1891.

TYLER, MOSES COIT. Literary History of the American Revolution, 2 vols. Vol. II, chap. xxxii.

WINTER, WILLIAM. The Wallet of Time. 2 vols. 1913.

Collections

MOSES, MONTROSE J. Representative Plays by American Dramatists, Vol. I. 1918. Vols. II and III in press.

QUINN, ARTHUR H. Representative American Plays. 1917.

Special Articles

GAY, F. L. An Early Virginia Play. *Nation*, Vol. LXXXVIII, p. 136. 1909.

LAW, ROBERT A. Early American Prologues and Epilogues. *Nation*, Vol. XCVIII, p. 463. 1914.

LAW, ROBERT A. Charleston Theaters, 1735–1766. *Nation*, Vol. XCIX, p. 278. 1914.

MATTHEWS, ALBERT. Early Plays at Harvard. *Nation*, Vol. XCVIII, p. 295. 1914.

NEIDIG, W. J. The First Play in America. *Nation*, Vol. LXXXVIII, p. 86. 1909.

QUINN, ARTHUR H. The Early Drama, 1756–1860. Cambridge History of American Literature, Vol. I, Bk. II, chap. ii.

TOPICS AND PROBLEMS

The best available sources of material are the collection of A. H. Quinn, which contains three of the plays mentioned in detail, and the first volume of the collection of M. J. Moses, which contains all four, and a half dozen more from the early period.

There is no need of suggesting specific topics in connection with the different plays. Each one may be read with reference to its story content — the kind of plot, of characters, of scenes, of episodes — or with reference to the skill with which it was written — the construction, the characterization, the supply of motives for action, the dialogue, the prose or verse style — or with reference to the personality of the author and the " signs of the times " — the purpose of the play, the moral, intellectual, and æsthetic character and prejudices of the author.

If the student is working toward a report — written or oral — he will arrive at a satisfactory result only as he limits himself to one very definite subdivision and presents his findings in detail.

CHAPTER VIII

CHARLES BROCKDEN BROWN

The first professional man of letters in America, and the last of note who was born before the Revolution, was Charles Brockden Brown. His short life, from 1771 to 1810, was almost exactly contemporary with the productive middle half of Freneau's long career. That he earned his living by his pen is a matter of incidental interest in American literary history ; the more important facts are that he looms large in the chronicles of the American novel and that he was a factor in the development of the American periodical.

He was born in Philadelphia. "His parents," says Dunlap, whose whole biography is written with the same labored elevation, "were virtuous, religious people, and as such held a respectable rank in society ; and he could trace back a long line of ancestry holding the same honorable station." He was a delicate, precocious child, and under the prevalent forcing process of the day was cultivated into an infant prodigy. By the time that he was sixteen he was well schooled in the classics ; he had versified parts of Job, the Psalms, and Ossian ; he had sketched plans for three epic poems ; and he had permanently undermined his health. At eighteen he was studying law, indulging in debate and in philosophical speculation, and was the author of his first published magazine article. In the next few years — the dates are not exactly recorded — he abandoned the law ; at one time gave thanks that because of his feeble health he was free from the ordinary temptations of youth, and at another, for the same reason, contemplated suicide ; and finally, to escape the urgent counsels of his advisers, he left his home city for New York. Here he fell in with congenial literary companions, joined the Friendly Club, in which among other benefits he was the recipient of friendly criticism for his "disputatiousness and dogmatism," and in the stirring period of the '90's began to dream Utopian dreams of a new heaven on the old earth.

His active authorship, which began with 1797, was varied and incessant. It included between then and 1810 a large number of magazine contributions (many of them serials), six novels (all published between 1798 and 1801), several other volumes more or less in the nature of hack work, and nine years of periodical editorship. He wrote with the confidence of youth for a youthful and uncritical reading public, with the natural result that his output was more bulky than distinguished. He was immensely communicative: filled with "the rapture with which he held communion with his own thoughts"—committing them to paper in a copious journal, in circumstantial letters, and in the rivulet which flowed from his pen into the forgotten gulf of magazinedom. In 1799 he was working on five different novels, although from April until the end of the next year he was editing *The Monthly Magazine and American Review*. Before he was thirty his reputation was established and his important work was done. In 1801 he returned to Philadelphia with achieved success as a reply to the friends who had tried to dissuade him from professional writing. There he undertook in 1803 another editorial venture in *The Literary Magazine and American Register*. From the excited young radical of a half-dozen years earlier, disciple of William Godwin, he had become by some reaction a fulfiller of his pious ancestry. In his statement of principles he made it clear that he would rather be respectable than disturbing in his sentiments. He referred to the recent bold attacks on "the foundations of religion and morality," declared that he would conserve these and proscribe everything that offended against them, and concluded (using the editorial third person): "His poetical pieces may be dull, but they at least shall be free from voluptuousness or sensuality; and his prose, whether seconded or not by genius and knowledge, shall scrupulously aim at the promotion of public and private virtue." Even under the weight of this unmitigated morality the magazine was continued for four years. Brown had, however, stepped down from the level of an author who was in any degree creative to a platform for dispensing commonplace conservatism and useful knowledge. The decline is further proven by the nature of his last industrious ventures: "The American Register, or General Repository of History, Politics and Science" (Philadelphia, 1807–1811, seven vols.) and a prospectus in 1809 of an unfinished "System of General Geography; containing a Topographical, Statistical and Descriptive Survey of the Earth." With the handicap of his early impaired health and under the burden of his self-imposed schedule his strength failed him, and he died in 1810, an overworked consumptive. It is quite evident, however, that his distinctive work was done. If old age had been granted him, unless some amazing reversal of form had taken place, it would have been a long, industrious, and ultraconventional anticlimax to the rather brilliant promise of his young manhood.

In entering the field of fiction-writing Brown took his place in the newest literary movement in America. For nearly two centuries, as the preceding chapters have shown, poetry and expository prose had been the only accepted forms. Some years after the beginnings of a native theater in the middle of the eighteenth century the first attempts were made in a native drama, but they were faint and scant and were looked on with indifference, if not with disapproval, by most of the country. The chief tide of composition after the war for independence was controlled by the twin moons of Pope and Addison. The triumph of the English novel had occurred in the twenty-five years after the death of Pope, however, and its influence could not be long unfelt. In fact the six years of controversy which led to the dismissal of Jonathan Edwards

from his Northampton church in 1750 (see p. 43) suggest that
Richardson achieved a furtive reading almost at once; for
it was Edwards's protest against certain books which led to
"lascivious and obscene discourse" among the young people
that started the whole trouble — and "Pamela" was the
sensation of the day. A later disapproval of Richardson was
based merely on his encouragement of frivolity. Says Trumbull
of Harriet Simper, in "The Progress of Dulness" of 1773 :

> Thus Harriet reads, and reading really
> Believes herself a young Pamela,
> The high-wrought whim, the tender strain
> Elate her mind and turn her brain :
> Before her glass, with smiling grace,
> She views the wonders of her face ;
> There stands in admiration moveless,
> And hopes a Grandison, or Lovelace.

And by 1804 so strait a conservative as President Dwight of
Yale could refer with complacency to novelists in general, and
to Sterne in particular : "Our progress resembled not a little
that of my Uncle Toby; for we could hardly be said to
advance at all."

The earliest American novels were tentative beginnings of
several sorts. The first was "The Power of Sympathy," by a
Lady of Boston (Mrs. Sarah Wentworth Morton), in 1789.
It was soon overshadowed by Susanna Rowson's extremely
popular "Charlotte" in 1790. Both were highly-seasoned
love stories. Of a different kind was H. H. Brackenridge's
"Modern Chivalry" (1792–1793–1797), a rollicking satire
on democracy carried on a narrative thread, with about the
same right to be termed a novel as Pierce Egan's "Life in
London" of a generation later. Different again was G. Imlay's
"The Emigrants" (1793), a tale of the West with a conventional London plot and set of characters. And different again
was Royall Tyler's "The Algerine Captive" (1797), a contemporary story combining social satire, travel, and international

politics, with significant witness in the preface to the growing American vogue of the novel.

When Brown came to the point of telling his own stories, however, he did not follow in the footsteps of any American predecessors, but turned to a type for which he was especially fitted — the Gothic romance. This was the first extravagant contribution of fiction to the Romantic movement, — the tale of wonder and horror, of alternating moonlit serenities and midnight storms, of haunted castles and secret chambers, of woods and vales and caves and precipices, of apparent supernaturalism which was explained away in a conscientious anticlimax, and of the same seraphic heroine and diabolical villain who had played the leading rôles for Richardson. It had been developed by Horace Walpole and Mrs. Anne Radcliffe and "Monk" Lewis and finally by William Godwin, who combined all this machinery into a kind of literary "tank" for the conveyance of a didactic gun crew, for his "Caleb Williams" was in fact little more than "Political Justice" in narrative camouflage. This was a formula exactly to Brown's taste, since he had both a strong ethical bias and a liking for the mysterious. His particular undertaking was to translate it into American terms, a task that he carried through in his extraordinary output of 1798 to 1801.

The first to be published was "Wieland," a gradually increasing succession of horrors which are brought about through the influence of a mysterious voice. By the oracular commands of the unseen speaker Wieland's double tendency to superstition and melancholy is deepened into a calm and steady fanaticism. At the end, in obedience to what he thinks is the voice of God, he murders his wife and children and, confessing, is acquitted on grounds of insanity. The horrid chapter of mishaps is explained by the repentant villain, Carwin, a ventriloquist, who accounts for the stupendous wickedness of his achievement by nothing more convincing than an irresistible inclination to practice his talent. "Ormond," of the next year, is a story of feminine virtue triumphant over obstacles, which is complicated by the employment of two heroines, two victimized fathers, and two villains. The element of horror is supplied in the background of the yellow-fever plague; and the mystery, by the apparent omniscience of the worse of the malefactors, who is simply an ingenious resorter to false doors and secret partitions.

Brown's most ambitious novel was "Arthur Mervyn," which appeared in two volumes in 1799 and 1800. It carries as a subtitle "The Memoirs of 1793." These days, according to the preface, were suggestive to "the moral observer, to whom they have furnished new displays of the influence of human passions and motives." He has used "such incidents as appeared to him most instructive and remarkable," believing that "it is every one's duty to profit by all opportunities of inculcating upon mankind the lessons of justice and humanity." He believes in tragic realism on account of the "pity" which it may inspire. As a matter of fact the plague seems rather incidental than integral to the story. It gives rise to the introduction of Arthur Mervyn on the scene and to the long piece of retrospective narrative which occupies all of the first volume. This tells of the experiences of Arthur, three days long, with a consummate villain, Welbeck, just as the sins of the latter return to him in a dozen ways. The second volume pursues certain unfinished stories begun in the first, the general motives being to show how completely the innocent Arthur Mervyn is misunderstood and to present his efforts to atone in some degree for the offenses of the real sinner. The structure is by no means as firm even as this analysis would seem to indicate. It is an endless ramification of stories within stories, and stops at last without any sufficient conclusion.

"Arthur Mervyn" is evidently indebted to William Godwin, of whose "transcendent powers" in "Caleb Williams" Brown was an ardent admirer. But it is hard for the modern reader to see why either book is strikingly individual. Godwin's feelings about the travesties on justice indulged in by the English courts had been anticipated by Smollett in " Roderick Random " (chap. lxi ff.) ; and Caleb's hard times as a fugitive from a false charge are very similar to Roderick's. In the light of history it seems apparent that Brown was impressed by the book because it was widely popular when he was writing, and that its popularity was due not so much to its merits as to its political timeliness at a moment of revolutionary excitement. Of Brown's three remaining novels only one, " Edgar Huntly," is of any importance. This is a good detective story, fresher than any of his others. A somnambulist who murders while walking in his sleep supplies the horror and creates the mystery; and certain pictures of frontier life and Allegheny Mountain scenery, with an Indian massacre and a panther fight, are effectively homemade.

Brown's novels should naturally be estimated in comparison with the works of his contemporaries rather than with the crisp and clean-cut narrative of the present, but even so they are burdened with very evident defects. The most flagrant of these are the natural fruits of hasty writing. He is quoted as saying to one of his friends, " Sir, good pens, thick paper, and ink well diluted, would facilitate my composition more than the prospect of the broadest expanse of clouds, water or mountains rising above the clouds." This suggests the steady craftsmanship of Anthony Trollope with his thousand words an hour. Yet he was in no respect of style or construction the equal of Trollope. His novels are full of loose ends and inconsequences. He is unblushing in his reliance on "the long arm of coincidence." Even when one untangles the plots from the maze of circumstance in which he involves them, they are unconvincing because they are so deficient in human motive. Moreover, in style they are expressed in language which is dizzily exalted even for the formal period in which they were written. "I proceeded to the bath, and filling the reservoir with water, speedily dissipated the heat that incommoded me." "I had been a stranger to what is called love. From subsequent reflection I have contracted a suspicion that the sentiment with which I regarded the lady was not untinctured from this source and that hence arose the turbulence of my feelings."

As he never wrote — never had time to write — with painstaking care, his best passages are those which he set down with passionate rapidity. When the subject in hand rapt him clean out of himself so that he became part of the story, he could transmit his thrill to the reader. The horrors of a plague-stricken city such as he had survived in New York made him forget to be " literary." And the tense excitement of an actor in moments of suspense he could recreate in himself and on paper. His gifts, therefore, were such as to strengthen the climaxes of his stories and to emphasize the flatness of the long levels between. He had the weakness of a dramatist who could write nothing but "big scenes," but his big scenes were thrillers of the first magnitude. He was a journalist with a ready pen ; his best work was done in the mood and manner of a gifted reporter. He had neither the constructive imagination nor the scrupulous regard for details of the creative artist.

Although in his Gothic tales Brown was a pioneer among American novelists, he was like many another American of early days in trailing along after a declining English fashion. By 1800 the great day of the Gothic romance was over. Within a few years it was to become a literary oddity. Scott was to continue in what he called the "big bow-wow" strain but was to make his romances rational and human, and Jane Austen was to describe the feelings and characters of ordinary life with the hearty contempt for the extravagances of the Radcliffe school which she expressed throughout " Northanger Abbey " (chaps. I, xx ff.). Yet in his own period Brown was recognized in England as well as in America. The best reviews took him seriously, Godwin owed a return influence from him,

Shelley read him with absorbed attention, Scott borrowed the names of two of his characters. In these facts there is evidence that he was American not only in his acceptance of foreign influence but in his conversion of what he received into a product that was truly his own and truly American. There are more or less distinct hints of Cooper and Poe and Hawthorne in the material and the temper of his writings, and there is more than a hint of Mrs. Stowe and Lew Wallace and the modern purpose-novelists in the grave intention to inculcate "upon mankind the lessons of justice and morality" with which he undertook his labors.

BOOK LIST

General References

CROSS, W. L. The Development of the English Novel, pp. 98–109. 1899.
LOSHE, L. D. The Early American Novel. 1907.

Individual Author

CHARLES BROCKDEN BROWN. The Novels of, with a Memoir of the Author. Boston, 1827; Philadelphia, 1857, 1887. These appeared originally as follows: Alcuin, 1798; Wieland, 1798; Ormond, 1799; Arthur Mervyn, 1799–1800; Edgar Huntly, 1799; Clara Howard, 1801; Jane Talbot, 1801.

Bibliography

WEGELIN, O. Early American Fiction, 1774–1830. 1913. See also Cambridge History of American Literature, Vol. I, pp. 527–529.

History and Criticism

DUNLAP, WILLIAM. Life of Charles Brockden Brown: with selections. 1815. 2 vols.
ERSKINE, JOHN. Leading American Novelists. 1910.
HIGGINSON, T. W. Charles Brockden Brown, in Carlyle's *Laugh and Other Surprises*. 1909.
MARBLE, ANNIE R. Charles Brockden Brown and Pioneers in Fiction, in *Heralds of American Literature*. 1907.
PRESCOTT, W. H. Life of Charles Brockden Brown, in Sparks's *Library of American Biography*, Vol. I. 1834. Also in Prescott, *Biographical and Critical Miscellanies*. 1845.
VAN DOREN, C. Early American Realism. *Nation*, Nov. 12, 1914. (The Source of Wieland.)

VAN DOREN, C. Minor Tales of Brockden Brown, 1798–1800. *Nation*, Jan. 14, 1915. (A detailed study, adding several titles not before ascribed to Brown.)

VAN DOREN, C. In chap. vi of Cambridge History of American Literature, Vol. I, Bk. II.

TOPICS AND PROBLEMS

Read W. L. Cross's "Development of the English Novel" for general characterization of the Gothic romance, and for contemporary reaction against this type of fiction read Jane Austen's "Northanger Abbey," chaps. i, xx ff.

Brown and his work are so remote from the present that they challenge inevitable comparisons with other authors who preceded, accompanied, or followed him in literary history. For example:

Read "Arthur Mervyn," Bk. I, for a comparison in handling similar material with Defoe's "Journal of the Plague Year" and the entries in Pepys's Diary on the plague of 1666.

Read "Arthur Mervyn" for a comparison of subject matter, plot, and purpose with Godwin's "Caleb Williams."

Read "Edgar Huntly" for a comparison as a detective story with any modern story, as, for example, one of Conan Doyle's.

Read the great suspense passages in "Wieland" for a comparison with similar passages in the tales of Edgar Allan Poe.

CHAPTER IX

IRVING AND THE KNICKERBOCKER SCHOOL

The turn to Washington Irving and his chief associates in New York — James Fenimore Cooper and William Cullen Bryant — is a turn from colonial to national America and from the eighteenth to the nineteenth century. This is not to say that what they wrote was utterly and dramatically different from what had been written in the colonial period; yet there are many points of clear distinction to be marked. With them, for one thing, New York City first assumed the literary leadership of the country. It was not a permanent conquest, but it was notable as marking the fact that the new country had a dominating city. As a rule the intellectual and artistic life of a country centers about its capital. Athens, Rome, Paris, London, are places through which the voices of Greece, Italy, France, and England have uttered their messages. These cities have held their preëminence, moreover, because, in addition to being the seats of government, they have been the great commercial centers and usually the great ports of their countries. In the United States, then, the final adoption of Washington in the District of Columbia as the national capital was a compromise step; this could not result in bringing to it the additional distinction which natural conditions gave to New York. Washington has never been more than the city where the national business of government is carried on; locating the center for art and literature has been beyond the control of legislative action. For the first third of the nineteenth century New York was the favored city. Here Irving was born, and here Cooper and Bryant came as young men, rather than to the Philadelphia of Franklin and his contemporaries.

For these men of New York, America was an accomplished fact — a nation slowly and awkwardly taking its place among the nations of the world. To be sure, the place that Americans wanted to take, following the advice of George Washington, was one of withdrawal from the turmoil of the Old World and of safety from " entangling alliances " which could ever again bring it into the warfare from which it was so glad to be escaping. The Atlantic was immensely broader in those days than now, for its real breadth is to be measured not in miles but in the number of days that it takes to cross it. When Irving went abroad for the first time in 1804 he was fifty-nine days in passage. To-day one can go round the world in considerably less time, and the average fast Atlantic steamship passage is one tenth of that, while the aëroplane flight has divided the time by ten again. So the early Americans rejoiced in their " magnificent isolation " and wanted to grow up as dignified, respected, but very distant neighbors of the Old World.

It was an unhappy fact, however, that America — or the United States — was not notable for its dignity in the early years of the nineteenth century ; for the finest dignity, like charity, " is not puffed up, doth not behave itself unseemly," whereas the new nation was very self-conscious, quickly irritated at foreign criticism, and uncomfortably aware of its own crudities in manner and defects in character. As far as foreign criticism was concerned, there were ample reasons for annoyance in America. Even as early as 1775 John Trumbull[1] had felt that it was hopeless to expect fair treatment at the hands of English reviewers, warning his friends Dwight and Barlow,

> Such men to charm could Homer's muse avail,
> Who read to cavil, and who write to rail ;
> When ardent genius pours the bold sublime,
> Carp at the style, or nibble at the rhyme ;

[1] Lines addressed to Messrs. Dwight and Barlow.

and the mother country, after the Revolution and the War of 1812, was less inclined than before to deal in compliment. Man after man came over,

> Like Fearon, Ashe, and others we could mention;
> Who paid us friendly visits to abuse
> Our country, and find food for the reviews.[1]

Moreover, all the time that England was criticizing her runaway child, she was maddeningly complacent as to her own virtues. Americans could not strike back with any effect, because they could not make the English feel their blows. So they fretted and fumed for half a century, their discomfort finding its clearest expression in Lowell's lines[2]:

> She *is* some punkins, thet I wun't deny
> (For ain't she some related to you 'n' I ?)
> But there's a few small intrists here below
> Outside the counter o' John Bull an' Co,
> An' though they can't conceit how 't should be so,
> I guess the Lord druv down Creation's spiles
> 'thout no *gret* helpin' from the British Isles,
> An' could contrive to keep things pooty stiff
> Ef they withdrawed from business in a miff;
> I ha'n't no patience with sech swellin' fellers ez
> Think God can't forge 'thout them to blow the bellerses.

A further reason for uneasiness in the face of foreign comment was that honest Americans were aware that their country suffered from the crudities of·youth. It is unpleasant enough for "Seventeen" to be nagged by an unsympathetic maiden aunt, but it is intolerable if she has some ground for her naggings. In small matters as well as great "conscience doth make cowards of us all." In a period of such rapid expansion as prevailed in the young manhood of Irving, Cooper, and Bryant it was unavoidable that most of the population were

---

[1] Fitzgreene Halleck, "Fanny," stanza lviii.
[2] Mason and Slidell, ll. 155–165.

drawn into business undertakings that were usually eager and hurried and that were often slipshod or even shady. The American colleges and their graduates were not as distinguished as they had been in the earlier colonial days, and the new influence of European culture from the Old World universities was yet to come. In the cities, and notably in New York, the vulgar possessors of mushroom fortunes multiplied rapidly, bringing up vapid daughters like Halleck's " Fanny," [1] who in all the modern languages was

> Exceedingly well-versed; and had devoted
> To their attainment, far more time than has,
>   By the best teachers, lately been allotted;
> For she had taken lessons, twice a week,
> For a full month in each; and she could speak
>
> French and Italian, equally as well
>   As Chinese, Portuguese, or German; and,
> What is still more surprising, she could spell
>   Most of our longest English words off-hand;
> Was quite familiar in Low Dutch and Spanish,
> And thought of studying modern Greek and Danish;

and whose father, a man of newly affected silence that spoke " unutterable things," was established in a mortgaged house filled with servants and " whatever is necessary for a 'genteel liver' " and buttressed with a coach and half a dozen unpaid-for horses. At the same time the countryside was developing a native but not altogether admirable Yankee type. At their best, Halleck [2] wrote,

> The people of today
> Appear good, honest, quiet men enough
>   And hospitable too — for ready pay;
> With manners like their roads, a little rough,
> And hands whose grasp is warm and welcoming, though tough.

---

[1] " Fanny," stanzas cxxi, cxxii.   [2] " Wyoming," stanza iv.

And at their worst Whittier[1] looked back a half century, to 1818, and recalled them as

> Shrill, querulous women, sour and sullen men,
> Untidy, loveless, old before their time,
> With scarce a human interest save their own
> Monotonous round of small economies,
> Or the poor scandal of the neighborhood;
> .   .   .   .
> Church-goers, fearful of the unseen Powers,
> But grumbling over pulpit tax and pew-rent,
> Saving, as shrewd economists, their souls
> And winter pork, with the least possible outlay
> Of salt and sanctity; in daily life
> Showing as little actual comprehension
> Of Christian charity and love and duty
> As if the Sermon on the Mount had been
> Outdated like a last year's almanac.

A natural consequence of such criticism from without, and such raw and defective culture within the country, was that American writers of any moment bided their time as patiently as they could, recognizing that for the moment America must be a nation of workers who were

> rearing the pedestal, broad-based and grand,
> Whereon the fair shapes of the Artist shall stand,
> And creating, through labors undaunted and long,
> The theme for all Sculpture and Painting and Song.[2]

Finally, it is worth noting that the first three eminent writers in nineteenth-century America were themselves not university products. Bryant withdrew from Williams College at the end of the first year, and Cooper from Yale toward the end of the second. The real education of these two and of Irving, who did not even enter college, was in the world of action rather than in the world of books, and their associates were for the most part men of affairs.

---

[1] " Among the Hills " (Prelude, 71 ff.).   [2] Lowell, " Fable for Critics."

WASHINGTON IRVING

Many of the facts about the boyhood and youth of Washington Irving (1783–1859) are typical of his place and his period as well as true of himself. The first is that he was born (in New York City) of British-American parents, his father a Scotch Presbyterian from the Orkney Islands and his mother an Englishwoman. His father's rigid religious views dominated in the upbringing of himself and his six brothers and sisters. Two nearly inevitable results followed : one, that as a boy he grew to believe that almost everything that was enjoyable was wicked, and the other, that as he came toward manhood he was particularly fond of the pleasures of life. A boy of his capacities in Boston at this time would have been more than likely to go to Harvard College, which was a dominating influence in eastern Massachusetts, but King's College (Columbia) occupied no such position in New York. Irving's higher education began in a law office, and then, when his health seemed to be failing, was continued by travel abroad. The long journey, or series of journeys, that he took from 1804 to 1806 were of the greatest importance. They were important to Irving because he was peculiarly fitted to get the greatest good from such informal education. He was an attractive young fellow, so that it was easy for him to make and to hold friends ; and he was blessed with his father's moral balance, so that he did not fall into bad habits. He was so far inclined to laziness that it is doubtful if he would have achieved much if he had gone to college, but he was wide-awake and receptive, so that he absorbed information wherever he went. Furthermore, he had a mind as well as a memory, and he came back to America stocked not merely with a great lot of miscellaneous facts but with a real knowledge of human nature and of human life.

From the day of his return to New York in 1806 to the day of his death, in 1859, Washington Irving had an international point of view and developed steadily into an international character. His first piece of writing was that of a very young man, but a young man of promise. Like the other Americans of his day he had read a good deal of English literature written in the eighteenth century; and among the essayists of that century who had attracted his attention one was Oliver Goldsmith. New York supplied him with his subjects and Goldsmith with his method of attack, for he wrote, in company with one of his brothers and a mutual friend, a series of amusing criticisms on the ways of his townsmen, modeling his *Salmagundi Papers* after Goldsmith's *Citizen of the World*. This was at once independent and imitative. The youthful authors blithely announced in their introductory number that they proposed to "instruct the young, reform the old, correct the town, and castigate the age." In the twenty-two papers that came out at irregular intervals between January, 1807, and January, 1808, they criticized everything that struck their attention, and they had their eyes wide open. The American love of display, the inclination to indulge in fruitless discussion which made the country a "logocracy" rather than a democracy, the lack of both judgment and order which marked their political elections, and their social and literary fashions make just a beginning of the list of subjects held up to genial ridicule. Yet, though the criticism was fair and to the point, it was an old-fashioned kind of comment, the kind that England had been feeding on for the better part of a century, ever since Addison and Steele had made it popular in the *Tatler* and the *Spectator*. Moreover, it was done in an old-fashioned way, for in making Mustapha Rub-a-Dub Keli Khan, the Tripolitan, the foreign commentator on American life as he saw it with a stranger's eyes, they were using a device that was old even before it was employed by the Englishman from whom they borrowed it. The *Salmagundis* are interesting, however, as early representatives of a longish succession of satires on the life of New York, all pleasant and rather pleasantly superficial. Three years later Irving, this time alone, followed up this initial success with his "Knickerbocker's

History of New York," not as serious a piece of work as its title at first suggests, for it was a burlesque of a heavy and pretentious history on the same subject which had appeared just before. Like the *Salmagundis* it was vivacious and impertinent, the very clever work of a very young man.

Now for ten years Washington Irving produced nothing as a writer. He was engaged in business with his brothers, and proved himself the most level-headed member of a pretty unbusinesslike combination. In 1815, in connection with one of their many ambitious and unsuccessful schemes, he went abroad, probably without the least suspicion that he would be absent from his own country for seventeen years and that he would return to it as a celebrated writer widely read in two continents. The first step toward his wider reputation came in 1819 with the publication in London of "The Sketch Book," the best known of all his works. This was followed in 1822 by "Bracebridge Hall" and in 1824 by "Tales of a Traveller," both similar in tone and contents to "The Sketch Book." With a reputation as a graceful writer of sketches and stories now thoroughly established, he turned to a more substantial and ambitious form of work in the composition of "The History of the Life and Voyages of Christopher Columbus," living and writing in Madrid for the two years before its publication in 1828 ; and this book he followed quickly, as in the case of "The Sketch Book," with two other productions of the same kind — "The Conquest of Granada" in 1829 and "The Voyages and Discoveries of the Companions of Columbus" in 1831. For three years before his return to America, Irving served as Secretary of Legation to the court of St. James, London, and then came back to enjoy at home a popularity which had been almost wholly earned abroad. Out of his career thus far four main facts deserve attention. First, that his literary work began with two pieces of social satire, written in a boyish, jovial manner which he largely abandoned in later years ; second, that his fame was established on works of "The Sketch Book" type, made up of short units, gracefully written, and full of quiet humor and tender sentiment (now and again he continued in this sort of composition up to the end of his life); third, that in his maturer years he resorted to the writing of formal history, and that he followed the first three studies, done in Spain, with "Oliver Goldsmith" in 1849, "Mahomet and his Successors" in 1850, and "The Life of Washington," completed in 1859, the year of his death. To these literary facts should be added a fourth which is both literary and political and of no small significance in history — the fact of Irving's appointment to a post in the foreign diplomatic service. This was to be followed in his own life by his four years as Minister to Spain in 1842–1846, under President Harrison, and in the next fifty years by a distinguished list of other appointments to the consular and diplomatic staffs. No single group has done more to bring honor to the United States in the courts of Europe during the nineteenth century than writers like Irving, Hawthorne, Motley, Howells, Bayard Taylor, Lowell, Hay, and their successors down to Thomas Nelson Page and Brand Whitlock.

To return to "The Sketch Book." By 1818, three years after Irving had gone abroad for the second time, the business in which he had been engaged with his brothers had utterly failed, and he was forced to regard writing not merely as an attractive way of diverting himself but as a possible source of income. The new articles which he then wrote, together with many which had been accumulating in the leisure of his years in England, were soon ready for publication, but they found no English publisher ready to risk putting them out. Even the powerful influence of Sir Walter Scott, Irving's cordial friend, could not prevail at first with John Murray, "the prince of publishers." In 1819 Sidney Smith's contemptuous and famous query, "Who reads an American book?" was fairly representative of the English-reading public. Murray was interested in Irving's manuscript, but did not see any prospect of selling enough books to justify the risk of publication. Irving had wanted the indorsement of Murray's imprint to offset the severity of the kind of English criticism deplored years earlier by John Trumbull (see p. 111). As soon, however, as the sketches were printed in New York in a set of seven modest installments, the attention of English readers was attracted to them, and Irving heard rumors that a "pirated" English edition was to appear. There was no international copyright in those days, and no adequate one until as late as 1899; so that a book printed on one side of the Atlantic was fair game for anyone who chose to steal it on the other. If an author wanted his works to appear correctly and to get his full money return for them, it was necessary for him to go through all the details of publishing independently in both countries. After a great deal of difficulty, therefore, Irving contrived to get out an English edition through an inefficient publisher, but the success of it was so marked that Murray soon saw the light and from then on was eager to get the English rights for everything that Irving wrote and to pay him in advance five, ten, and, in one case, as much as fifteen thousand dollars.

With the appearance of "The Sketch Book" England arrived at a new answer for Sidney Smith's question. Irving was sought as a celebrity by the many, in addition to being loved as a charming gentleman by his older friends. Few tributes are more telling than that contained in a letter written many years later by Charles Dickens in which he refers to the delight he took in Irving's pages when he was "a small and not over particularly well taken care of boy." Even the austere *Edinburgh Review* indorsed the American as a writer of "great purity and beauty of diction." From the most feared critic in the English-speaking world to the neglected boy whose father was in debtors' prison Irving received enough applause quite to turn the head of a less modest man.

"The Sketch Book" includes over thirty papers of four or five different kinds. About fifteen are definite observations on English life and habits as seen in country towns and on country

estates. Of the remainder six are literary essays of various
kinds; four are in the nature of personal traveling reminiscences; three are the famous short stories — "Rip Van Winkle,"
"Sleepy Hollow," and the "The Spectre Bridegroom"; and
five so far defy classification as to fall under the convenient
category of "miscellaneous."

As a document in literary history the sixth paper deserves
far more notice than is usually conceded to it, for as a rule
it is totally neglected. This is entitled "English Writers on
America." The tone of English literary criticism has already
been referred to. Irving called attention to the fact that all
English writings on America and the Americans were equally
ill-natured. He pointed out that ordinarily English readers demanded strictest accuracy from author-travelers; that if a man
who wrote a book on the regions of the Upper Nile or the
unknown islands of the Yellow Sea was caught in error at a
few minor points, he was held up to scorn as careless and unreliable, and another English traveler who could convict him
of mistakes or misstatements could completely discredit him.
But in marked contrast to this, no such scrupulousness was
demanded of visitors to the United States. Books on the new
nation in the Western World were written and read to satisfy
unfriendly prejudice rather than to supply exact information
and honest opinion. Against a continuation of such a practice
Irving gave warning, not merely because it was uncharitable
but because in time it would estrange the two peoples and
lose for England a friend with whom she could not afford to
be at loggerheads.

Is all this to be at end? Is this golden band of kindred sympathies,
so rare between nations, to be broken forever? Perhaps it may be
for the best. It may dispel an illusion which might have kept us in
mental vassalage; which might have interfered occasionally with our
true interests, and prevented the growth of proper national pride.
But it is hard to give up the kindred tie! and there are feelings dearer
than interest — closer to the heart than pride — that will make us cast

back a look of regret as we wander farther and farther from the paternal roof, and lament the waywardness of the parent that would repel the affections of the child.

There were probably many other Americans capable of making the warning prophecy so notably fulfilled nearly a hundred years later, though few, perhaps, who would have put it in such temperate language; but Irving went further in following with a warning to his fellow-countrymen:

Shortsighted and injudicious, however, as the conduct of England may be in this system of aspersion, recrimination on our part would be equally ill-judged. . . . Let us guard particularly against such a temper, for it would double the evil instead of redressing the wrong. Nothing is so easy and inviting as the retort of abuse and sarcasm, but it is a paltry and unprofitable contest. . . . The members of a republic, above all other men, should be candid and dispassionate. They are, individually, portions of the sovereign mind and sovereign will, and should be enabled to come to all questions of national concern with calm and unbiased judgments. . . . Let it be the pride of our writers, therefore, discarding all feelings of irritation, and disdaining to retaliate the illiberality of British authors, to speak of the English nation without prejudice and with determined candor.

If there is any justification for calling an American essay "The American Declaration of Literary Independence" the title should be conferred on this neglected number in "The Sketch Book." It was long before either English or American writers were wise enough to follow Irving's counsels, but he himself was always as tactful as he was honest.

"The Sketch Book" as a whole, then, can best be understood as an American's comments on English life and custom, made at a time when "the retort of abuse and sarcasm" would have been quite natural. In the opening paper, as well as in the sixth, there is a gentle reminder that the literary east wind had felt rather sharp and nipping in New York. Irving is describing himself after the fashion of the eighteenth-century essayists at the introduction of a series, and at the end indulges in this little nudge of irony :

A great man of Europe, thought I, must . . . be as superior to a great man of America, as a peak of the Alps to a highland of the Hudson ; and in this idea I was confirmed by observing the comparative importance and swelling magnitude of many English travelers among us, who, I was assured, were very little people in their own country. I will visit this land of wonders, thought I, and see the gigantic race from which I am degenerated.

His summarized impressions of the typical Englishman are contained in the thirtieth paper, on " John Bull." This keen analysis will bear the closest reading and study, and the more one knows of English history the more interesting it becomes. In this respect it is like " Gulliver's Travels," for it is full of double meanings. To the inattentive or the immature it is simply a picture of a bluff, hearty, quick-tempered, over-conservative average English country gentleman, but to the intelligent and attentive reader this gentleman turns out to be the embodiment of the English government and the British Empire. The character of Parliament, the relation between Church and State, the condition of the national treasury, the attitude of the rulers toward reform legislation and toward the colonies, dependencies, and dominions are all treated with kindly humor by the visiting critic. The picture is by no means a flattering one, but it was Irving's happy gift to be able to indulge in really biting satire and yet to do so in such a courteous and friendly way that his words carried little sting. Part of the concluding paragraph to this essay will illustrate his method of combining justice with mercy :

Though there may be something rather whimsical in all this, yet I confess I cannot look upon John's situation without strong feelings of interest. With all his odd humors and obstinate prejudices, he is a sterling-hearted old blade. He may not be so wonderfully fine a fellow as he thinks himself, but he is at least twice as good as his neighbors represent him. His virtues are all his own ; all plain, home-bred, and unaffected. His very faults smack of the raciness of his good qualities. His extravagance savors of his generosity; his quarrelsomeness of his courage; his credulity of his open faith; his vanity of his pride; and his bluntness of his sincerity. They are all the redundancies of a rich and liberal character.

In this spirit Irving wrote the other sketches of John Bull as he appears in "Rural Life," "The Country Church," "The Inn Kitchen," and the group of five Christmas pictures.

To judge from these eight scenes of English country life, Irving, a visitor from a new and unsettled land, was chiefly fascinated by the evidences of old age and tradition on every side. For this reason, if for no other, he delighted in the customs of the country squires who had not been swept out of their ancient order by the tide of modern trade. Even the English scenery was in his mind "associated with ideas of order, of quiet, of sober, well-established principles, of hoary usage and reverend custom. Everything seems to be the growth of ages of regular and peaceful existence." As Irving observed it, it was still the "Merrie England" of song and story, an England, therefore, beautifully typified in the celebration of the Christmas festivities. There is a touch of autobiography in his comment on the good cheer that prevailed at Bracebridge Hall, — a home that Squire Bracebridge tried to make his children feel was the happiest place in the world, — it was so utterly different from the suppressed family circle over which his Presbyterian father had ruled. As a guest he enjoyed all the picturesque and quaint merrymaking at the Hall, and re-conjured up pictures like those which Addison had previously drawn at Sir Roger de Coverley's. Yet all the while he was aware that the old English gentleman was a costly luxury for England to maintain, that Squire Bracebridge was after all nothing but John Bull, and that John Bull was inclining to lag behind his age. As a student of Goldsmith, Irving had read "The Deserted Village"; the thought of it seems to have come back to him while writing "Rural Life";

for a moment the usurpation of the land by the wealthy disquieted him, but then he consoled himself with the comforting thought that abuses of this sort were "but casual outbreaks in the general system." Irving was writing as an observer who found much to admire in the external beauty of the old order of things, but at the bottom of his American mind it is quite apparent that there was a silent approval of gradual reform in "the good old ways." Squire Bracebridge was delightful to Irving, but on the whole he was a delightful old fogy.

Irving's papers on London — "The Boar's Head Tavern," "Westminster Abbey," and "Little Britain" — are full of a similar reverence for old age in the life of the community. In the same mood in which he laughed at the pranks of the Christmas Lord of Misrule, he made his way to Eastcheap, "that ancient region of wit and wassail, where the very names of the streets relished of good cheer, as Pudding Lane bears testimony even at the present day"; and he took much more evident satisfaction in his recollection of Shakespearean revelries than in his hours in Westminster, the "mingled picture of glory and decay." Once again in "Little Britain" Irving was in more congenial surroundings, for he preferred to smile at the echoes of dead laughter than to shudder at the reminders of vanished greatness.

Little Britain may truly be called the heart's core of the city; the strong-hold of true John Bullism. It is a fragment of London as it was in its better days, with its antiquated folks and fashions. Here flourish in great preservation many of the holiday games and customs of yore. The inhabitants most religiously eat pancakes on Shrove Tuesday, hot-cross-buns on Good Friday, and roast goose at Michaelmas; they send love-letters on Valentine's Day, burn the Pope on the fifth of November, and kiss all the girls under the mistletoe at Christmas. Roast beef and plum-pudding are also held in superstitious veneration, and port and sherry maintain their grounds as the only true English wines.

In more than casual respect for such traditions Irving goes on to introduce the rival oracles of Little Britain, to escort us to Wagstaff's and the Roaring Lads, to act as personal conductor to Bartholomew Fairs and a Lord Mayor's Day, and finally to lament the baleful influence of the socially ambitious Misses Lamb and the decline of the choice old games All-Fours, Pope Joan, and Tom-come-tickle-me. It is no wonder that the youthful Dickens loved these papers, for the same England appealed to both Irving and Dickens throughout their lives. It was a rough, boisterous, jolly England, with a good deal of vulgarity which they were ready to forgive and a good many vices which they chose to overlook in favor of its chief virtues — a blunt honesty, a hearty laugh, and a full stomach.

There is another side of old England that was dear to those two — that John Bull could "easily be moved to a sudden tear" (see p. 109, first topic). In the old days of even a hundred years ago men of Saxon stock were much more ready to express themselves than they are to-day, for the accepted manners of the present are comparatively reserved and impassive. If a man was amused he laughed loud and long; if he was angered he came up with "a word and a blow"; and if his deeper feelings were touched he was not ashamed of a tear. In fact he seemed almost to feel a certain pride in his "sensibility," as if his power to weep proved that his nature was not destitute of finer feeling and made up for his quickness to wrath and his fondness for a broad joke. In perhaps unconscious recognition of this habit of mind the literature of a century ago contained a great many frank appeals to the reader's feeling for pathos, appeals which the modern reader would be likely to condemn as unworthily sentimental.

In the history of literature a distinction is made between "sentiment" — the ability to respond to the finer emotions, such as love, sorrow, reverence, patriotism, worship — and "sentimentalism" — the unrestricted expression of these emotions by eloquence, tears, and feminine sighs, blushes, and swoonings. For this sentimentalism, which was a literary fashion of his period, Irving found an outlet in sketches like "The Wife," "The Broken Heart," "The Widow and her Son," and "The Pride of the Village." The first is on "the fortitude with which women sustain the most overwhelming reverses of fortune," a sketch in which the husband is the sentimentalist. He has lost his money and is afraid to shock his wife with the revelation, but his "altered looks and stifled sighs" half betray him. In "an agony of tears" he tells a friend, and by him is persuaded to be honest with her. Her latent heroism comes out in the face of his announcement; and on her welcome to him at his first homecoming to the modest cottage he is rendered speechless, and tears once more gush into his eyes. The second is a direct attempt to shame "those who have outlived the susceptibility of early feeling, or have been brought up . . . to laugh at all love stories." The third, on "The Widow and her Son," is more convincing to the reader of to-day, for it is on the tragic picture of a fond parent's bereavement. The fourth is the best example of all. The pride of the village is introduced as "blushing and smiling in all the beautiful confusion of girlish diffidence and delight." She falls in love with a gallant young soldier, who begs her to accompany him when he is ordered to the front. Shocked at his perfidy she clasps her hands in agony, then succumbs to "faintings and hysterics," and then goes into a decline. After some time her lover returns to her and rushes into the house. "She was too faint to rise — she attempted to extend her trembling hand — her lips moved as if she spoke, but no word was articulated — she looked down upon him with a smile of unutterable tenderness — and closed her eyes forever!" If these sketches seem unreal and even amusing to the student, it is partly because they are actually overdrawn and partly because the present generation has repressed, if it has not "outlived, the susceptibility of early feeling."

Two other types of work remain to be mentioned. The first is the literary essay, in which the chief interest arises from Irving's sympathetic appreciation of his English masters. From these essays — there are five of distinct importance — it appears that he was especially well-read in the writings of a much earlier period and that he took pleasure in dwelling on passages which were characterized, as his own work came to be, by "great purity and beauty of diction." The other group is the most famous in "The Sketch Book," the three stories of which "Rip Van Winkle" is the best known. This is extremely interesting for several reasons. The first is that it is a good story, which will long be read for its own sake, and as such it needs no comment, for it is familiar to everyone. But it is also a milestone in literary history. One reason for this is that it carries into practice a principle that American authors had long been talking and writing about — the principle of using native material. It is located in the Catskill Mountains and in the years before and after the Revolutionary War. It introduces real colonial and early American people. Although it is a far-fetched romance in its theme, it makes use of homely, realistic details. Jonathan Doolittle's hotel was just the sort of shabby boarding house that marred the countryside during the slipshod years after the Revolution and that survived into Irving's youth. "A large rickety wooden building . . . with great gaping windows, some of them broken and mended with old hats and petticoats." The sign was strangely changed from pre-Revolution days. "The red coat was changed for one of blue and buff, a sword was held in the hand instead of a sceptre, the head was decorated with a cocked hat, and underneath was painted in large characters, GENERAL WASHINGTON." The fact that the folk story about Hendrick Hudson and his crew had some basis in a German superstition does not affect the fact that Irving completely localized it and gave it its enduring fame as an American tale.

Another reason why this story stands out in literary history is that it is one of the first really successful examples of the modern short story, and that in this sense it represents America's chief contribution to the types of literature. We are likely to take for granted that all the popular forms of literature have existed since the beginning of time. Yet prose stories of any kind were comparatively modern a hundred years ago, and most of them were long narratives in two or three and sometimes as many as six or seven volumes. What short stories existed were merely condensed novels, not limited to any brief period and not developed with any definite detail. " Rip Van Winkle " was strikingly different from its vague and shapeless forerunners. After the introduction it was limited to two short passages of time — the few hours just before and the few hours just after Rip went to sleep on the mountain. And the whole story was composed to lead up to the main point, — the chief point of this history and of all history, — the relentless way in which life moves on, regardless of the individual who falls asleep and is left behind. All the details in the story help to develop this idea. Rip, the ne'er-do-well, was the sort of man to serve as the central character, for he was more anxious to escape life than to take his part in it. His eager, querulous, sharp-tongued wife reminded him of the burden of living only to make him avoid it the more ; her loss was the only one which he did not regret on his return. His dog and gun, which he missed first and missed most keenly, were the pride of the old-fashioned trapper out of place in the up-to-date American village. The years bridging the Revolution were the most natural and effective ones to mark the kind of change that is always taking place ; and Rip's experience in finding that loyalty to a discarded monarchy was treason to a new republic was simply an emphatic illustration of what will usually happen to a man who lives in the past instead of in the present. It is not at all necessary to assume that Irving chose the old folk-legend in order to expound this theme, or even that he was conscious of the completeness with which he was doing it. The fact remains that it was remarkable in its day for its clear compactness, and that it meets one of the tests of enduring fiction in telling a good story well and of building that story out of elements that convey some truth about life.

" The Legend of Sleepy Hollow " is comparable to " Rip Van Winkle " only in its use of native American character, scenes, and tradition. It is hardly a short story at all, but rather a prolonged sketch full of " local atmosphere " and partly strung on a narrative thread. Ichabod Crane and his townsmen, except for Brom Bones and his gang, are like Rip in one respect, for they are representative citizens in a town where " population, manners and customs remain fixed ; while the great torrent of migration and improvement, which is making such incessant changes in other parts of this restless country, sweeps by them unobserved." Ichabod was an interesting survival, too, because his combination of learning and superstition had come to him from a distinguished source, for he " was a perfect master of Cotton Mather's history of New England witchcraft, in which, by the way, he most firmly and potently believed. He was, in fact, an odd mixture of small shrewdness and simple credulity. His appetite for the marvellous, and his powers of digesting it, were equally extraordinary, and both had been increased by his residence in this spellbound region. No tale was too gross or monstrous for his capacious swallow. It was often his delight, after his school was dismissed in the afternoon, to stretch himself on the rich bed of clover, bordering the little brook that whimpered by his schoolhouse, and there con over old Mather's direful tales, until the gathering dusk of the evening made the printed page a mere mist before his eyes." Ichabod, moreover, is a comic type in American life in the early nineteenth century, who seems to have been equally disliked by all the New Yorkers — the Puritan descendant strayed from home. Cooper's David Gamut is one of the same crop. The story of the Headless Horseman, like that of the Spectre Bridegroom, is, of course, only a make-believe ghost story, neither important nor well told. The real interest in the sketch lies in its picture of simple country life. The whole scene at Baltus Van Tassel's house is as clear and vivid as the contrasting scenes at Bracebridge Hall or as Whittier's picture of another family scene in " Snow-Bound." The third well-known story in " The Sketch Book," " The Spectre Bridegroom," is, like " The Legend of Sleepy Hollow," more of a sketch than a story, and does not pretend to be laid on American soil.

It is a common experience of schoolboys and schoolgirls to feel on reading Irving for the first time that his way of writing is stiff and unnatural. Compared with the fashion of to-day the wording and sentence structure of " The Sketch Book " deserve such a verdict. But to render it against the writing of a hundred years ago, without comparing the book in question with others of its own generation, is to ignore the very point of " Rip Van Winkle " — that fashions change. Assuming, then, that styles do change, and that Irving was no more formal than other authors of his day, it is still worth while to see what some of the main points of contrast are between 1819 and 1919. Here are two passages that will serve as a basis for comparison. The first is from " Philip of Pokanoket," one of the two " Sketch Book " essays written in America.

It is to be regretted that those early writers, who treated of the discovery and settlement of America have not given us more particular and candid accounts of the remarkable characters that flourished in savage life. The scanty anecdotes which have reached us are full of peculiarity and interest ; they furnish us with nearer glimpses of human nature, and show what man is in a comparatively primitive state, and what he owes to civilization. There is something of the charm of discovery in lighting upon these wild and unexplored tracts of human nature ; in witnessing, as it were, the native growth of moral sentiment, and perceiving those generous and romantic qualities which have been artificially cultivated by society, vegetating in spontaneous hardihood and rude magnificence.

The second is from G. S. Lee's "Crowds," Bk. I, chap. viii :

The future in America cannot be pictured. The only place it can be seen is in people's faces. Go out into the street, in New York, in Chicago, in San Francisco, in Seattle ; look eagerly as you go into the faces of the men who pass, and you feel hundreds of years — the next hundred years — like a breath swept past. America, with all its forty-story buildings, its little play Niagaras, its great dumb Rockies, is the unseen country. It can only as yet be seen in people's eyes. Some days, flowing sublime and silent through our noisy streets, and through the vast panorama of our towers, I have heard the footfalls of the unborn, like sunshine around me.

These passages have almost exactly the same number of words, — the former one hundred and fifteen and the latter one hundred and seventeen, — but a glance at the printed page shows that Irving's words take up one fifth more space than Lee's do. The reason is that Irving uses twenty-six words of more than two syllables, and Lee, aside from place-names, only two. Although both passages are written in analysis of American conditions, Irving, who is discussing the past, employs abstract or general words — to use the nouns alone, words like *discovery*, *anecdotes*, *peculiarity*, *civilization*, *sentiment*, *qualities*, *magnificence* ; Lee, who is looking to the future, uses definite and picturesque terms like *faces*, *street*, *buildings*, *eyes*, *panorama*, *towers*, *footfalls*, — uses these words even though he admits the idea he is dealing with cannot be pictured. Again, Irving cast his one hundred and fifteen words into three sentences averaging nearly forty words in length, and Lee put his into six, averaging a fraction less than twenty. Finally, all Irving's sentences are "loose," or so built that the reader may rest or even stop with a completed sense before he comes to the end ; but four out of six in Lee's passage are "periodic," or so constructed that you must read to the end or be left hanging in mid-air.

It would, of course, be forcing the issue absurdly far to insist or even suggest that so broad a comparison would apply
without exception to the writers of a hundred years ago and
of to-day, but in general there is a fair deduction to be drawn.
Irving belonged to a group who were still addressing an
eighteenth-century audience, an audience made up of "gentle
readers " — men who enjoyed the rhythmical flow of a courtly
and elegant style, who felt that there was a virtue in purity and
beauty of diction apart from any idea the diction was supposed
to express ; but the modern reader esteems literature as a means
rather than an end. It must catch and hold his attention ; it
must be clear and forcible first, and elegant as a secondary
matter ; and its words and sentences must be chosen and put
together as a challenge to a reader in the midst of a restless,
driving, twentieth-century world. With these facts in mind
one may say, if he will, that Washington Irving was stiff and
formal, but he should say this as marking a difference and not
a necessary inferiority in Irving.

Irving lived until 1859, but the richly fruitful part of his
life was from 1819, the year in which the serial publication of
"The Sketch Book" began, to 1832, the year of his return
from abroad. In this period he published ten books and all
the best known of his works but the lives of Goldsmith and
Washington. When he came back after seventeen years' absence
he was known and admired in England, France, and Germany,
and the most popular of American authors. Irving was one of
the first to profit, American fashion, by a European reputation
reflected and redoubled at home. At the dinner of welcome
tendered him soon after his arrival he showed how absence
had made the heart grow fonder :

I come from gloomier climes to one of brilliant sunshine and
inspiring purity. I come from countries lowering with doubt and
danger, where the rich man trembles and the poor man frowns —
where all repine at the present and dread the future. I come from

these to a country where all is life and animation ; where I hear on every side the sound of exultation ; where everyone speaks of the past with triumph, the present with delight, the future with growing and confident anticipation.

And here, he went on to say, he proposed to remain as long as he lived. These last twenty-seven years were filled with honors. He had already received the gold medal from the Royal Society of Literature and the degree of Doctor of Laws from Oxford University. Now he was to have the refusal of a whole succession of public offices and the leadership of a whole " school " of writers. Diedrich Knickerbocker had become a household word, which was applied to the Knickerbocker school of Irving's followers and used in the christening of the *Knickerbocker Magazine* (1833–1865). Irving was in truth a connecting link between the century of his birth and the century of his achievements. He carried over the spirit and the manners of Addison and Goldsmith into the New World and into the age of steam. With him it was a natural mode of thought and way of expression, but with his imitators it was affected and superficial — so much so that the Knickerbocker school declined and the *Knickerbocker Magazine* went out of existence shortly after Irving's death.

The leading figure in the Knickerbocker school was Fitz-Greene Halleck, who was born in Connecticut in 1790 but spent his active life in New York. When he came up to the city, at the age of twenty-one, he fell in with the literary people of the town and shared their eager interest in the current English output. According to his biographer they were absorbed in " The Lady of the Lake " and " Marmion," in Campbell's " Pleasures of Hope," Rogers's " Pleasures of Memory," Moore's " Melodies," Miss Porter's " Scottish Chiefs " and " Thaddeus of Warsaw," and, a little later, in " Waverley," " Guy Mannering," and " The Antiquary " — works that in Halleck's opinion produced "a wide-spread enthusiasm throughout Great Britain and this country which has probably never been equalled in the history of literature."

Halleck (as already cited on page 113) was uncomfortably conscious of the prosaic commercial drive of American life and disposed to lament the wane of romance. His regret for the passage of "the good old days" he frequently expressed in the poems he wrote between the ages of twenty-five and thirty — "Alnwick Castle," "Red-Jacket," "A Sketch," "A Poet's Daughter"; and in "Wyoming" he sometimes grieved for the old and sometimes protested at the new. When in 1823 he wrote "Marco Bozzaris," he lived up to his own thesis, taking an heroic episode of immediate interest — August 20, 1823 — and putting it into a ballad for freedom that has probably been declaimed as often as "The Charge of the Light Brigade" or "How They Brought the Good News from Ghent to Aix."

In the meanwhile he had become the intimate of the talented young Joseph Rodman Drake. Their friendship had sprung from a common love of romantic poetry, but the joint work which they undertook was a series of contemporary satires. These were printed in *The National Advocate* and the New York *Evening Post* between March and July, 1819. Thirty-five of them appeared over the signature of "Croaker," from which they became known as the "Croaker Papers." They were both pertinent and impertinent, aided by the mystery of their authorship and accumulating in interest through the uncertainty as to when the next would appear and whom it would assail. The more general in theme had the same underlying good sense which belonged to the earlier *Salmagundis* (see p. 116), and in their simple and often brutal directness they must have offered then, as they do now, a relief from the fashionable echoes of secondary English poets. Later in 1819 Halleck resumed the same strain in "Fanny" — the account in about a thousand lines of the rise and fall of Fanny and her father in New York finance and society.[1] Among many efforts of the sort Stedman's " Diamond Wedding " and Butler's " Nothing to Wear " have been the only later approach, and all have been true not merely of New York but of the same stage in most quick-growing American cities.

In 1820 Drake died at the age of twenty-five, leaving as his literary bequest the inspiration for Halleck's memorial verses,

> Green be the turf above thee
> Friend of my better days !

as well as his share in the " Croaker Papers," and " The Culprit Fay," and certain shorter poems which give promise of things much greater than this overrated attempt. The " Fay," according to a letter by Halleck, was a three-day production of 1816, written to demonstrate that the Hudson River scenery could be turned to literary account. Whether or no the anecdote is true, Drake wrote to this point in his " To a Friend," and in " Niagara " and " Bronx." Yet the fact is worth remark that nothing in " The Culprit Fay " is any more explicitly true of the Hudson region than of the Rhine country or the Norwegian fiords. The poem reads like a pure fantasy, hurriedly and carelessly written by an inexperienced hand. Nevertheless, when published it was extravagantly praised. Halleck said, " It is certainly the best thing of the kind in the English language, and is more strikingly original than I had supposed it was possible for a modern poem to be." [2]

---

[1] An interesting tribute is paid this poem by Ezra Pound in a footnote to " L'Homme Moyen Sensuel," in " Pavannes and Divisions," p. 33. " I would give these rhymes now with dedication ' To the Anonymous Compatriot Who Produced the Poem " Fanny " Somewhere About 1820,' if this form of centennial homage be permitted me. It was no small thing to have written, in America, at that distant date, a poem of over forty pages which one can still read without labor."

[2] It was reserved for Poe to write a genuinely critical estimate of it. See *The Southern Literary Messenger*, Vol. II, pp. 326 ff. Reprinted in " The Literati," p. 374.

In Halleck's exclamatory surprise at originality in any modern poem is to be found the vital difference between the two friends. Halleck seemed to believe that the final canons for art had been fixed, and could hardly conceive of originality in a nineteenth-century poet; but Drake tried new things and rebelled at the old. His best efforts, however qualified their success, were strainings at the leash of eighteenth-century convention.

> Go! kneel a worshipper at nature's shrine!
> For you her fields are green, and fair her skies!
> For you her rivers flow, her hills arise!
> And will you scorn them all, to pour forth tame
> And heartless lays of feigned or fancied sighs?
> And will you cloud the muse? nor blush for shame
> To cast away renown, and hide your head from fame?

As "The Culprit Fay" shows, Drake's idea was to escape from the drawing-room into the open, but when in the open to weave, as it were, Gobelin tapestries for drawing-room use. He saw no gleam of essential poetry in democracy or the crowded town, yet in his vague craving for something better than Georgian iterations he showed that the revival of individualism was at work in him. The story is told that his intimacy with Halleck began in his accord with the latter's wish that he could " lounge upon the rainbow, and read ' Tom Campbell.' " In his aspirations he seems to have been nearer to the spirit of Keats and Shelley.

As fate would have it, the more independent of the two was taken off before his prime, and Halleck, the survivor, settled down into complacent Knickerbockerism. With his nicety of taste, his keen eye, his fund of humor, and his frankness, he was an established literary and social favorite. He was the kind of handsome and courtly gentleman of the old school, as Irving was also, who became a friend and associate of the leading financier of the day. There was nothing restless or disconcerting about him. He was a critic of manners, but not of the social order. He probably knew little of Emerson, and he certainly disapproved of Whitman. In 1848, when less than sixty years of age, he went back to his native town in Connecticut and lived there till after the Civil War, totally unaffected as a man of letters, except as the conflict seems to have silenced him. But he was not alone, for when he sank into eclipse all the Knickerbockers disappeared with him. Their vogue was over.

BOOK LIST

Individual Authors

WASHINGTON IRVING. First posthumous complete edition. New York, 1860–1861. 21 vols. These appeared originally as follows: Salma-gundi, 1807–1808; History of New York, 1809; The Sketch Book, 1819; Bracebridge Hall, 1822; Jonathan Oldstyle, 1824; Tales of a Traveller, 1824; Columbus, 1828; Conquest of Granada, 1829; Companions of Columbus, 1831; The Alhambra, 1832; The Crayon Miscellany, 1835; Astoria, 1836; Captain Bonneville, 1837; Gold-smith, 1849; Mahomet, 1839–1850; Wolfert's Roost, 1855; Washington, 1855–1859; Uncollected Miscellanies, 1866.

Bibliography

Compiled by Shirley V. Long for Cambridge History of American Literature, Vol. I, pp. 510–517.

Biography and Criticism

The standard life of Washington Irving is by P. M. Irving, The Life and Letters of Washington Irving. 1862–1864. 1864, 1879, 1883. 4 vols.

BOYNTON, H. W. Washington Irving. Boston, 1901.

BRYANT, W. C. A Discourse on the Life, Character, and Genius of Washington Irving. 1860.

CURTIS, G. W. Irving's Knickerbocker. *Critic*, Vol. III. 1883.

CURTIS, G. W. Washington Irving, in *Literary and Social Essays*. 1894.

HAZLITT, WILLIAM. Elia, and Geoffrey Crayon, in *The Spirit of the Age*. 1825.

HOLMES, OLIVER WENDELL. Irving's Power of Idealization. *Critic*, Vol. III. 1883.

HOLMES, OLIVER WENDELL. Tribute to Irving. *Mass. Hist. Soc. Proceedings.* 1858–1860.

HOWELLS, WILLIAM DEAN. My Literary Passions. 1895.

LONGFELLOW, H. W. Tribute to Irving. *Mass. Hist. Soc. Proceedings.* 1858–1860.

LOWELL, J. R. A Fable for Critics. 1848.

PAYNE, W. M. Leading American Essayists. 1910.

POE, E. A. Irving's Astoria. *Southern Literary Messenger*, Vol. III. 1837.

PUTNAM, G. H. Cambridge History of American Literature, Vol. I Bk. II, chap. iv.

THACKERAY, W. M. Nil Nisi Bonum. *Cornhill Magazine*, Vol. I. 1860. *Harper's*, Vol. XX. 1860.

WARNER, C. D. *American Men of Letters Series.* 1881.

WARNER, C. D. Irving's Humor. *Critic*, Vol. III. 1883.

WARNER, C. D. Washington Irving. *Atlantic*, Vol. XLV. 1880.

WARNER, C. D. The Work of Washington Irving. 1893.

FITZ-GREENE HALLECK, The Poetical Works of. New York, 1847, 1850, 1852, 1853, 1854, 1855, 1858, 1859. Poetical writings with extracts from those of Joseph Rodman Drake. J. G. Wilson, editor. 1869, 1885. (These editions include the Croaker Papers.) These appeared originally as follows: Fanny, 1819; Alnwick Castle with Other Poems, 1827; Fanny and Other Poems, 1839; Young America, a Poem, 1865; Lines to the Recorder, 1866.

Biography and Criticism

The standard life is The Life and Letters of Fitz-Greene Halleck. J. G. Wilson. 1869.

BRYANT, W. C. Some Notices on the Life and Writings of Fitz-Greene Halleck. 1869.

DENNETT, J. R. The Knickerbocker School. *Nation*, Dec. 6, 1867.

DUYCKINCK, E. A. Fitz-Greene Halleck, in *Putnam's Magazine.* 1868.

LEONARD, W. E. Cambridge History of American Literature, Vol. I, Bk. II, in chap. v.

POE, E. A. Fitz-Greene Halleck, in *Complete Works*, Vol. VIII. 1902.

TUCKERMAN, H. T. Reminiscences of Fitz-Greene Halleck, in *Lippincott's Magazine.* 1868.

WILSON, J. G. Bryant and his Friends. 1886.

Collections

BOYNTON, PERCY H. American Poetry, pp. 147–168, 626–629.

DUYCKINCK, E. A. and G. L. Cyclopedia of American Literature, Vol. II, pp. 207–212.

GRISWOLD, R. W. Poets and Poetry of America. 1842.

STEDMAN and HUTCHINSON. Library of American Literature, Vol. V, pp. 216–225.

JOSEPH RODMAN DRAKE. Poems by Croaker, Croaker and Co., and Croaker, Jr. First printed in the New York *Evening Post.* 1819. Reprinted as a pamphlet, 1819. The Culprit Fay and Other Poems. 1835. The American Flag. 1861.

Biography and Criticism

CORNING, A. L. Joseph Rodman Drake. *Bookman.* 1915.

HOWE, M. A. DEW. American Bookmen. 1898.

POE, E. A. Fancy and Imagination. *Complete Works*, Vol. VII. 1902.
WELLS, J. L. Joseph Rodman Drake Park. 1904.
WILSON, J. G. Bryant and his Friends. 1886.
WILSON, J. G. Joseph Rodman Drake, in *Harper's Magazine*. June, 1874.

Collections

BOYNTON, PERCY H. American Poetry, pp. 136–153, 624–626.
DUYCKINCK, E. A. and G. L. Cyclopedia of American Literature, Vol. I, pp. 201–207.
GRISWOLD, R. W. Poets and Poetry of America. 1842.
STEDMAN and HUTCHINSON. Library of American Literature, Vol. V, pp. 363–379.

TOPICS AND PROBLEMS

Read the " Salmagundi Papers " and " The Citizen of the World " for evident influences. Close attention will reveal obligations not merely in the use of a foreign observer, a slight narrative thread, and the kind of topics treated, but also in actual detail passages.

Read passages covering the education of Goldsmith in Irving's Life, in Macaulay's essay, and in Thackeray's " English Humourists," and compare the degrees of sympathy with which Goldsmith is presented.

In connection with the problems of international copyright, see passages indicated in the table of contents or index of the following volumes : " Matthew Carey, Publisher," by E. L. Bradsher ; " Letters of Richard Watson Gilder " (edited by Rosamond Gilder, 1916); " These Many Years," by Brander Matthews, 1917; " Memories of a Publisher " and " The Question of Copyright," by George Haven Putnam, 1915 ; "Mark Twain, a Biography," by A. B. Paine, 1912.

Read " John Bull " in " The Sketch Book " for the passages in specific reference to the English government.

Read " Rural Life " in "The Sketch Book" for a further obligation to Goldsmith — the influence of " The Deserted Village."

Read " Bracebridge Hall" for a further development of English life and character begun in the " Sketch Book " essays discussed in the text.

Read "The Alhambra" for a comparison in subject matter, method, and tone with the three stories in " The Sketch Book."

Pick out the five essays in literary criticism in "The Sketch Book" for the light they throw on Irving's literary likings and critical acumen.

Read in "The Legend of Sleepy Hollow" the description of the domestic group at the Van Tassels for comparison with similar pictures in the English sketches.

Compare the "Croaker Papers" with the "Salmagundi Papers."

Read Halleck's "Fanny" (see Boynton, "American Poetry," pp. 154–158) for comparison in method with the "Croaker Papers."

Read Joseph Rodman Drake's "To a Friend" for an appeal for originality characteristic of the period and then read "The Culprit Fay" ("American Poetry," pp. 136–146) for a nonfulfillment of the authors' own appeal.

CHAPTER X

JAMES FENIMORE COOPER

Cooper's life (1789–1851) was inclosed by Irving's, for he was born six years later and died eight years earlier. When he was a little more than a year old his father took his large family — Cooper was the eleventh of twelve children — to the shore of Otsego Lake, New York, where he had bought a tract, after the Revolution. It was uncleared country, but here Judge Cooper laid out what developed into Cooperstown, established a big estate, and built a pretentious house. His scheme of life was aristocratic, more like that of the first Virginia settlers than like that of the Massachusetts Puritans. Here the boy grew up in an ambitious home, but among primitive frontier surroundings, until he needed better schooling than Cooperstown could offer. To prepare for Yale College he was sent to Albany and put in charge of the rector of St. Peter's Church. Under this gentleman he gained not only the "book learning" for which he went but also a further sense of the gentry's point of view — a point of view which throughout his life made him frankly critical of the defects in America even while he was passionately loyal to it. At thirteen he was admitted to Yale. This sounds as if he were a precocious child, but there was nothing unusual in the performance, for the colleges were hardly more than advanced academies where most of the students received their degrees well before they were twenty. This was the institution which John Trumbull — who had passed his examinations at seven! — had held up to scorn in his "Progress of Dulness," and where his hero, Tom Brainless,

> Four years at college dozed away
> In sleep, and slothfulness and play,

141

but even from here Cooper's unstudious and disorderly ways caused his dismissal in his second year. His formal education was now ended, and in his development as a writer it was doubtless much less important than his earlier years in the wilderness west of the Hudson River or those that were to follow on the ocean. In 1806 he was sent to sea for a year on a merchant vessel, and on his return was commissioned a midshipman in the United States Navy. His service lasted for three years, from January 1, 1808, to May, 1811, and was ended by his marriage to the daughter of a Tory who had fought on the British side in the Revolutionary War. Then for nine years he settled down to what seemed like respectable obscurity, living part of the time at his father-in-law's home, part of the time at Cooperstown, and the last three years at Scarsdale, New York.

From these first thirty years of his life there seemed to be little prospect that he was to become a novelist of world-wide and permanent reputation. There is no record that anyone, even himself, expected him to be a writer. Yet it is quite evident, as one looks back over it, that his preparation had been rich and varied. He had lived on land and on sea, in city and country, in New York, New Jersey, and Connecticut. He had breathed in the stories of the Revolutionary days, grown up on the frontier, and been a part of America in the making. And from his father, his tutor, and his wife and her family, as well as from his travel, he had learned to see America through critical eyes. He had the material to write with and the experience to make him use it wisely. The one apparently missing factor was the most important of all — there was not the slightest indication that he had either the will or the power to use his pen.

The story of how he began to write is a familiar one. Out of patience with the crudity of an English society novel that he had been reading, he said boastfully that he could write a better one himself. Many another novel-reader and playgoer has talked with equal recklessness after a literary disappointment in the library or the theater, but the remarkable part of the story is that in 1820 Cooper made his boast good. The resultant novel, "Precaution," was successful in only one respect — that it started Cooper on his career. It was a colorless tale with an English plot, located in English scenes of which he had no first-hand knowledge. It made so little impression on public or publishers that when his next novel was ready, in 1821, he had to issue it at his own expense; and he made this next venture, "The Spy," in part at least because of his friends' comment — characteristic of that self-conscious period — that he would have been more patriotic to write on an American theme. To let Cooper tell his own story:

The writer, while he knew how much of what he had done was purely accidental, felt the reproach to be one that, in a measure, was just. As the only atonement in his power, he determined to inflict a second book, whose subject should admit no cavil, not only on the world, but on himself. He chose patriotism for his theme; and to those who read this introduction and the book itself, it is scarcely necessary to add that he [selected his hero] as the best illustration of his subject.

By means of this story of war times, involving the amazing adventures of Harvey Birch, the spy, Cooper won his public; a fact which is amply proven by the sale of 3500 copies of his third novel, "The Pioneers," on the morning of publication. This story came nearer home to him, for the scenery and the people were those among whom he had lived as a boy at Cooperstown. Working with this familiar material, based on the country and the developing life which was a part of his very self, Cooper wrote the first of his famous "Leatherstocking" series. The five stories, taken together, complete the long epic of the American Indian to which Longfellow was later to supply the earlier cantos in "Hiawatha." For Cooper took up the chronicle where Longfellow was to drop it (see p. 276):

> Then a darker, drearier vision
> Passed before me, vague and cloud-like;
> I beheld our nation scattered,
> All forgetful of my counsels,
> Weakened, warring with each other:
> Saw the remnants of our people
> Sweeping westward, wild and woful,
> Like the cloud-rack of a tempest,
> Like the withered leaves of Autumn.

It was not a deliberate undertaking, planned from start to finish; it was not written in the order in which the stories occurred — like the long series by Winston Churchill; it did not even conceive of the scout as the central character of the first book, much less of the four which were to follow it. Cooper did not even seem to appreciate after he had written "The Pioneers" how rich a vein he had struck, for within the next two years he wrote "The Pilot" a sea story, and "Lionel Lincoln, or the Leaguers of Boston," supposed to be the first of a series of thirteen colonial stories which were never carried beyond this point. However, in 1826 he came back to Leatherstocking in "The Last of the Mohicans," second both in authorship and in order of reading, and in 1827 he wrote "The Prairie," the last days of the scout. It was not till 1840 and 1841 that he completed the series with the first and third numbers, "The Pathfinder" and "The Deerslayer." To summarize: the stories deal in succession with Deerslayer, a young woodsman in the middle of the eighteenth century; then Hawkeye, the hero of "The Last of the Mohicans," a story of the French and Indian War; next, Pathfinder; fourth, Leatherstocking, the hero of "The Pioneers," in the decade just before 1800; and finally, with the trapper, who in 1803 left the farming lands of New York to go westward with the emigrants who were attracted by the new government lands of "The Prairie."

With the writing of the second of the series, Cooper concluded the opening period in his authorship. In a little over six years he had published six novels and had shown promise of all that he was to accomplish in later life. He had attempted four kinds : stories of frontier life, in which he was always successful ; sea tales, for which he was peculiarly fitted ; historical novels, which he did indifferently well ; and studies in social life, in which he had started his career with a failure but to which he returned again and again like a moth to the flame.

To " The Last of the Mohicans " the verdict of time has awarded first place in the long roster of his works. It is the one book written by Cooper that is devoted most completely to the vanishing race. Three passages set and hold the key to the story. The first is from the author's introduction : " Of all the tribes named in these pages, there exist only a few half-civilized beings of the Oneidas on the reservation of their people in New York. The rest have disappeared, either from the regions in which their fathers dwelt, or altogether from the earth." The second is a speech from Chingachgook to Hawkeye in the third chapter, where they are first introduced : " Where are the blossoms of these summers ? — fallen, one by one : so all of my family departed, each in his turn, to the land of the spirits. I am on the hilltop, and must go down into the valley ; and when Uncas follows in my footsteps, there will no longer be any of the blood of the Sagamores, for my boy is the last of the Mohicans." The third is the last speech of the book, by the sage Tamenund : " It is enough," he said. " Go, children of the Lenape, the anger of the Manitou is not done. Why should Tamenund stay ? The pale-faces are masters of the earth, and the time of the red-men has not yet come again. My day has been too long. In the morning I saw the sons of Unamis happy and strong ; and yet, before the night has come, have I lived to see the last warrior of the wise race of the Mohicans."

For many years it was a habit of critics to scoff at Cooper's Indian characters as romantic and idealized portraits of the red man. This judgment may have arisen during the period of Cooper's great unpopularity, when nothing was too unfair to please the American public; but, once said, it persisted and was quoted from decade to decade by people who cannot have read his books with any attention. It was insisted that the woodcraft with which Cooper endowed the Indians was beyond possibility, yet later naturalists have recorded time and again marvels quite as incredible as any in Cooper's pages. It was reiterated that their dignity, self-control, tribal loyalty, and reverence for age were overdrawn, yet many another authority has testified to the existence of these virtues. And, finally, it was charged that they were never such a heroic and superior people as Cooper made them, though study of his portraits will show that Cooper did not make them half as admirable as he is said to have done. Tamenund is simply a mouthpiece; Uncas and Chingachgook are the only living Indian characters whom he makes at all admirable, but he acknowledges the differences between their standards and the white man's in the murder and scalping of the French sentinel after he had been passed in safety: " 'T would have been a cruel and inhuman act for a white-skin; but 't is the gift and natur' of an Indian, and I suppose it should not be denied." All the other Indians, beneath their formal ways in family, camp, and council, Cooper presents as treacherous and bloodthirsty at bottom, a savage people who show their real natures in the Massacre of Fort William Henry, the chief historical event in the book. On this ground he partly explains and partly justifies the conquest of the red men by the white.

The other people of the story are types who appear in all Cooper's novels. Most important is the unschooled American:

> He has drawn you *one* character, though, that is new,
> One wildflower he 's plucked that is wet with the dew
> Of this fresh Western world.

He is an out-of-door creature, intolerant of town life, skeptical of any book but the book of nature, a lover of the woods and mountains, and a worshiper of the God who made them. He has no "theory of life" or of government or of America, but he is just as truly a product of American conditions as the mountain laurel or the goldenrod. Natty Bumppo, central figure of the "Leatherstocking" series, is blood brother to Harvey Birch in "The Spy," to Long Tom Coffin in "The Pilot," to Captain Truck in "Homeward Bound" and "Home as Found," and to a similar man in almost every one of the other stories. Quite in contrast to this "wildflower" is a potted plant, of whom Cooper is almost equally fond. This is the polished gentleman of the world, such as Montcalm, who embodies the culture and manners that the New World needed. Cooper admired such a man almost to the point of infatuation, but presented him very badly; he made an idea of him rather than a living character, a veneer of manners without any solid backing, superficial, complacent, and hollow. One feels no affection for him and very little respect. He annoys one by so evidently thanking God that he is not as other men. Another type is the pedant David Gamut, a man who is made grotesque by his fondness for his own narrow specialty. David, a teacher of psalm-singing, bores the other characters by continually "talking shop," and breaks into melody in and out of season, capping the climax by chanting so vociferously during the massacre that the Indians regard him as a harmless lunatic and spare him then and thereafter. Dr. Sitgreaves of "The Spy," and Owen Bat, the doctor of "The Prairie," are struck from the same die. Finally, among the leading types, must be mentioned the "females."

The use of this word, which sounds odd and uncouth to-day, was general a hundred years ago, when "lady" was reserved to indicate a class distinction, and "woman" had not become the common noun; but the change is not merely one of name, for the women of books and the women of life were far less self-reliant than the women of the twentieth century. Then they were frankly regarded not only as dependents but as inferiors. A striking evidence of this can be found in the appropriate pages in Bartlett's "Familiar Quotations." The majority of the quoted passages are culled from poets who wrote before the rise of the woman's movement, and the tone of the passages taken as a whole is distinctly supercilious and condescending. "Women are lovely at their best," the poets seemed to agree, "but after all, they are merely — women. And at less than their best, the least said about them the better." Cooper was by no means behind his time in his attitude; indeed, he was, if anything, rather ahead of it. His feeling for them seems to have been that expressed in the famous passage from "Marmion" of which the first half is usually all that is quoted :

> O woman! in our hours of ease
> Uncertain, coy, and hard to please,
>
> .   .   .   .
>
> When pain and anguish wring the brow,
> A ministering angel thou!

In the ordinary situations in Cooper's novels his "females" were things to patronize and flatter, — for flattery never goes unattended by her sardonic companion, — but in times of stress they showed heroic powers of endurance. The three introduced in the first chapter of "The Spy" were endowed, according to the text, with "softness and affability," "internal innocence and peace," and expressed themselves by blushes and timid glances. The two "lovely beings" of "The Last of the Mohicans" are even more fulsomely described. "The flush which still lingered above the pines in the western sky was not more bright nor delicate than the bloom" on Alice's cheeks; and Cora was the fortunate possessor of "a countenance that was exquisitely regular and dignified, and surpassingly beautiful." In the passage that follows they are not referred to simply, but always with a bow and a smile — "the reluctant fair one," "the dark-eyed Cora," and as they finally disappear on horseback through the woods, the reader is expected not to laugh at the final ridiculous tableau of "the light and graceful forms of the females waving among the trees." Of course the readers to whom Cooper addressed this did not laugh. They realized that in speaking of women he was simply using the conventional language of the day, which was not intended to mean what it said ; that he was introducing a pair of normal, lovely girls, and that the best to be required of a normal girl was that she should be lovely — "only this and nothing more." There was no evidence that Cora and Alice had minds ; they were not expected to ; instead they had warm hearts and "female beauty." Lowell was probably not unfair in his comment :

> And the women he draws from one model don't vary,
> All sappy as maples and flat as a prairie.

But it must be admitted that in Cooper's time the model was a prevailing one, and that it was only in his old age that women began in any large numbers to depart from it.

Cooper was all his life a more and more conscious observer and critic of American character and American conditions. As a result his stories take hold of the reader for the very simple reason that they are based on actual life and real people. They had, moreover, and still have, the added advantage that they are based on a life that was fascinatingly unfamiliar to the great majority of his readers, and so, though realistic in their details, they exert the appeal of distant romance. All through the eighteenth century, and particularly through the last third of it, literature had been inclining to dwell on the joys of life in field and forest. Addison and his followers had handed on the spell of the old ballads of primitive adventure. Pope had dabbled with the "poor Indian" and Goldsmith had written his celebrated line about "Niagára's . . . thundering sound." Collins and Gray had harked back o the romantic past, and Burns and Wordsworth had confined their poems to the peasantry among whom they lived. Irving's reply to " English Writers on America " (see p. 120) alluded to the frequency of books on distant lands and peoples. So when Cooper began publishing his stories of adventure in untrodden lands, he found an attentive public not only in America but in England, and not only in England but all over Europe, where, as soon as his novels appeared, they were reprinted in thirty-four different places.

With the literary asset of this invaluable material Cooper combined his ability to tell an exciting story. There is nothing intricate or skillful about his plots as pieces of composition. In fact they seldom if ever come up to any striking finish. They do not so much conclude as die, and as a rule they "die hard." They are made up of strings of exciting adventures, in which characters whom the reader likes are put into danger and then rescued from it. "The Last of the Mohicans" has its best material for a conclusion in the middle of the book, with the thrilling restoration of Alice and Cora to their father's arms at Fort William Henry ; but the story is only half long enough at that point, so the author separated them again by means of the massacre and carried it on more and more slowly to the required length and the deaths of Cora and the last of the Mohicans. For "The Spy," the last chapter was actually written, printed, and put into page form some weeks before the latter part had even been planned. Cooper's devices for starting and ending the exciting scenes seem often commonplace, partly because so many later writers have imitated him in using them. Mark Twain, in " Fenimore Cooper's Literary Offenses," said derisively that the " Leatherstocking Tales " might well have been named "The Broken Twig " series, because villain and hero so often discover each other as the result of a misstep on a snapping branch. He might have substituted " A Shot Rang Out " as his title, on account of the frequency with which episodes are thus started or finished. Bret Harte's burlesque in his "Condensed Novels" shows how broadly Cooper laid his methods open to attack from the scoffers. Yet the fact remains that few who have come to scoff could have remained to rival Cooper. He has enlisted millions of readers in dozens of languages; he has fascinated them by the doings of woodsmen who were as mysteriously skillful as the town-bred Sherlock Holmes; he has thrilled by the genuine excitement of deadly struggles and hairbreadth 'scapes; and the sale of his books, a hundred years after he first addressed the public, would gladden the heart of many a modern novelist.

As a chapter in the literary history of America there is another side of Cooper's career which is intensely interesting. It has already been mentioned that he did not abandon the writing of novels on social life with the unsuccessful "Precaution." Lowell refers to this fact in the "Fable for Critics":

> There is one thing in Cooper I like, too, and that is
> That on manners he lectures his countrymen gratis:
> Not precisely so either, because, for a rarity,
> He is paid for his tickets in unpopularity.
> Now he may overcharge his American pictures,
> But you'll grant there's a good deal of truth in his strictures;
> And I honor the man who is willing to sink
> Half his present repute for the freedom to think,
> And, when he has thought, be his cause strong or weak,
> Will risk t'other half for the freedom to speak,
> Caring naught for what vengeance the mob has in store,
> Let that mob be the upper ten thousand or lower.

In 1826 Cooper went abroad with his family, staying on the other side for nearly six and a half years. His reputation was well established, and he left with the best wishes of his countrymen and the respect of the many foreigners who knew him through his books. He was an ardent believer in his own land and in the theory of its government, and at the same time he was an admirer, as he had been taught to be, of the dignity and the traditions of the Old World. It was to be expected that he would grow wiser with travel and that his later works, while retaining all their interest as stories, would be enriched by a deeper and mellower feeling for humankind. But he had already displayed one weakness which was destined to increase in him until it almost wholly offset his virtues with his readers. He was positive to the last degree in the opinions he held, and brutally untactful in expressing them. If he had ever heard of the soft answer that turneth away wrath, he felt contempt for it. Thus, for example, in the preface to " The Pioneers " he referred to the least of authors' ills, the contradiction among critics : "There I am, left like an ass between two locks of hay ; so that I have determined to relinquish my animate nature, and remain stationary, like a lock of hay between two asses." The fruit of travel was naturally a more vivid sense of the differences between American and European ways, a fertile crop of opinions, a belligerent assertion of them, and an unhappy series of quarrels with all sorts of Americans — business men, editors, naval officers, congressmen, and the majority of his readers, a vast army of representatives of the upper ten thousand and the lower.

During the first three years abroad he went on, under the headway gained at home, with three novels of American themes — one in the " Leatherstocking " series, one on Puritan life in New England, and one sea story. Then he went off on a side issue and sacrificed the next ten years to controversial books which are very interesting side lights on literary history but very defective novels. The whole sequence started with Cooper's resentment at the " certain condescension in foreigners " which was to make Lowell smart nearly forty years later. To meet this, and particularly the condescension of the English, he left the field of fiction to write " Notions of the Americans ; Picked up by a Traveling Bachelor." It failed of its purpose because it was too complacent about America and now and then too offensive about England, but the underlying trouble with it was its aggressive tone. A man could hardly make friends for America when he was in the temper to write of Englishmen, "We have good reason to believe, there exists a certain querulous class of readers who consider even the most delicate and reserved commendations of this western world as so much praise unreasonably and dishonestly abstracted from themselves." Cooper never could refrain from "the retort of abuse" against which Irving had advised in "The Sketch Book." Then followed three novels located in Venice, Switzerland, and Germany, — "The Bravo," "The Headsman," and "The Heidenmauer," — all designed to show how charming was Old World tradition and how mistaken was its undemocratic scheme of life. They were failures, like "Precaution," because Cooper could not write an effective novel which attempted to prove anything. It was his gift to tell a good story well and to build it out of the material in the midst of which he had grown up.

By the time he was ready to come back to America he had become kinked and querulous. The story of his controversies is too long for detailing in this chapter. The chief literary result of it is the pair of stories "Homeward Bound" and "Home as Found." The point of them, for they again were written to prove something, was to expose the crudities of a commercialized America. There is no question that the country was crude and raw (see pp. 111–114). A period of such rapid development was bound to produce for the time poor architecture, bad manners, shifty business, superficial learning, and questionable politics. Many other critics, home and foreign, were telling the truth about America to its great discomfort. Cooper's picture of Aristabulus Bragg was probably not unfair to hundreds of his contemporaries :

This man is an epitome of all that is good and all that is bad, in a very large class of his fellow citizens. He is quick-witted, prompt in action, enterprising in all things in which he has nothing to lose, but wary and cautious in all things in which he has a real stake, and ready to turn not only his hand, but his heart and his principles, to anything ᵗhat offers an advantage. With him, literally, " Nothing is too high to be aspired to, nothing too low to be done." He will run for governor or for town clerk, just as opportunities occur, is expert in all the practices of his profession, has had a quarter's dancing, with three years in the classics, and turned his attention toward medicine and divinity, before he finally settled down to law. Such a compound of shrewdness, impudence, common-sense, pretension, humility, cleverness, vulgarity, kind-heartedness, duplicity, selfishness, law-honesty, moral fraud, and mother wit, mixed up with a smattering of learning and much penetration in practical things, can hardly be described, as any one of his prominent qualities is certain to be met by another quite as obvious that is almost its converse. Mr. Bragg, in short, is purely a creature of circumstances.

The weakness of Cooper's criticisms on America is not that they were unjust, but that they were so evidently ill-tempered and bad-mannered. He made the utter mistake of locating the returning Europeans, the accusers of America, in Templeton Hall, which was the name of his own country place. He involved them in his own quarrel with the villagers over the use of a picnic ground belonging to him, and thus loaded on himself all the priggishness which he ascribed to them. The public was only too ready to take it as a personal utterance when he made one of them say :

I should prefer the cold, dogged domination of English law, with its fruits, the heartlessness of a sophistication without parallel, to being trampled on by every arrant blackguard that may happen to traverse this valley in his wanderings after dollars.

It is a misfortune that most men and women who are willing to risk repute for the freedom to think and speak are eccentric in other respects. They are unusual first of all in having minds so independent that they presume to disagree with the majority even in silence. They are more unusual still in having the courage to disagree aloud. When they have said their say, however, their neighbors begin to carp at them, respectable

people to pass by on the other side, and the newspapers to dis-
tort what they have said and then abuse them for what they
never uttered. The honest and truly reckless talkers, stung to
the quick, feel injured and innocent, talk extravagantly, rely
more and more on their own judgments and less and less on
the facts, and sooner or later lose their influence, if they do not
become outcasts. In the end they have the courage and honesty
with which they started, a few deploring friends, and a thousand enemies who hate them with an honest and totally
unjustified hatred. It is a tragic round which all but the most
extraordinary of free speakers seem doomed to travel. And
Cooper did not escape it. Yet he did have the remarkable
strength and good fortune to pass out of this vale of controversy toward the end of his life. With 1842 his campaign
against the public ceased — and theirs against him. He spent
his last years happily at Cooperstown and slowly returned into
an era of good feeling. It was in these later years that Lowell
paid him the well-deserved tribute quoted above. He was
really a great patriot. If his love of America led him into this
sea of troubles, it was the same love that made him the successful writer of a masterly series of American stories. It is
the native character of the man that is worth remembering,
and the native quality of his books that earned him a wide
and lasting fame.

BOOK LIST

Individual Author

James Fenimore Cooper. Collected Works. New York. 1854.
33 vols. These have appeared in many later collected and individual
editions in America, England, and many other lands and languages.
The chief works appeared originally as follows: Precaution, 1820;
The Spy, 1821; The Pioneers, 1823; The Pilot, 1823; Lionel
Lincoln, 1825; The Last of the Mohicans, 1826; The Prairie,
1827; The Red Rover, 1828; Notions of the Americans, 1828; The
Wept of Wish-ton-Wish, 1829; The Water-Witch, 1831; The Bravo,
1831; The Heidenmauer, 1832; The Headsman, 1833; The Moni-
kins, 1835; Homeward Bound, 1838; Home as Found, 1838; **The**

Pathfinder, 1840; Mercedes of Castile, 1840; The Deerslayer, 1841; The Two Admirals, 1842; Wing and Wing, 1842; Wyandotte, 1843; Ned Myers, 1843; Afloat and Ashore, 1844; Satanstoe, 1845; The Chain Bearer, 1845; The Redskins, 1846; The Crater, 1847; Jack Tier, 1848; The Oak Openings, 1848; The Sea Lions, 1849; The Ways of the Hour, 1850.

Bibliographies

Good bibliographies in Lounsbury's Life (see below), and Cambridge History of American Literature, Vol. I, pp. 532–534.

Biography and Criticism

There is no official biography, Cooper having opposed such a publication. The best single volume is by T. R. Lounsbury (*A. M. L. Series*).

BROWNELL, W. C. Cooper. *Scribner's Magazine*, April, 1906. Also in *American Prose Masters*. 1909.

BRYANT, W. C. A Discourse on the Life and Genius of James Fenimore Cooper. 1852.

CLEMENS, S. L. (Mark Twain). Fenimore Cooper's Literary Offenses. *North American Review*, July, 1895. Also in *How to tell a Story and Other Essays*. 1897.

ERSKINE, JOHN. Leading American Novelists. 1910.

HILLARD, G. S. Fenimore Cooper. *Atlantic Monthly*, January, 1862.

HOWE, M. A. DEW. James Fenimore Cooper. *The Bookman*, March, 1897. Also in *American Bookmen*. 1898.

HOWELLS, W. D. Heroines of Fiction. 1901.

MATTHEWS, B. Fenimore Cooper. *Atlantic Monthly*, September, 1907. Also in *Gateways to Literature*. 1912.

PHILLIPS, MARY E. James Fenimore Cooper. 1913.

SIMMS, W. G. The Writings of J. Fenimore Cooper. *Views and Reviews*. 1845. *Ser. 1*.

STEDMAN, E. C. Poe, Cooper, and the Hall of Fame. *North American Review*, August, 1907.

TUCKERMAN, H. T. James Fenimore Cooper. *North American Review*, October, 1859.

VAN DOREN, CARL. Cambridge History of American Literature. Vol. I, Bk. II, in chap. vi.

VINCENT, L. H. American Literary Masters. 1906.

WILSON, J. G. Cooper Memorials and Memories. *The Independent*, January 31, 1901.

TOPICS AND PROBLEMS

Read Brownell's defense of Cooper's Indian characters in his "Masters of American Prose" and check his statements by your own observations in a selected novel.

Read the comments of Brownell in "American Prose Masters," and of Lounsbury in the *A. M. L. Series*, on Cooper's women, and then arrive at your own conclusions from the reading of a selected novel.

If you have read two or three of Cooper's novels, see if he has introduced his usual polished gentleman and his bore or pedant in each, and see how nearly these characters correspond in themselves and in their story value.

Make a study of the actual plot and its development in any selected novel of Cooper's.

Read Mark Twain's essay on "Fenimore Cooper's Literary Offenses" and decide on how far it is fair and how far it was dictated by Mark Twain's hostility to romantic fiction.

Read Cooper's prefaces to a half-dozen or more novels for the light they will throw on his belligerency of temper.

Read "Home as Found" for comparison of the topics treated with those in the "Salmagundi" and "Croaker" papers, for observation on the variety of American weaknesses presented, for a decision as to how fundamental or how superficial these weaknesses were, and for a conclusion as to the amount of evident ill temper in the book.

CHAPTER XI
WILLIAM CULLEN BRYANT

The mention of Irving, Cooper, and Bryant as representatives of New York in the early nineteenth century is likely to mislead students into thinking of them as literary associates. As a matter of fact they seem not to have had any more contact than any other three educated residents of the city. They were not unsociable men, but each went his own social way. Until his period of controversy Cooper was leading member of a literary club of which he had been the founder. Irving, without going to the pains of organizing a group, was the natural center of one which delighted in his company and emulated his ways of thinking and writing. Bryant, instead of being drawn after either of these older men, stepped into journalism, becoming a friend of the great editors and the political leaders. Irving was the only one of the three who was born and bred in town. Cooper and Bryant were not sons of New York; they were among the first of its long list of eminent adopted children.

Bryant (1794–1878) was born at Cummington, Massachusetts. His descent can be traced to the earliest Plymouth families, and, on his mother's side, to Priscilla Alden. His father was a much-loved country doctor, the third of the family in recent generations to follow this budding profession. He was a man of dignities in his town, a state representative and senator, and a welcome friend of the Boston book-lovers. His services were so freely given, however, that he had little money to spend on his boy's education. This was carried on, according to a common custom, under charge of clergymen, though not the least important teaching came direct from the father's guidance of his reading and criticism of his writing. Bryant's talents began to show promise while he was still a boy, for he read eagerly, and in his early 'teens wrote a number of "pieces" which were more or less widely circulated in print. One of these, "The Embargo," a political satire addressed to President Jefferson, ran to two editions and roused so much doubt as to its authorship that his father's friends soberly certified to it as the work of a boy of thirteen. In these years Bryant made Alexander Pope his adored model, and for so young an imitator he succeeded remarkably well. A little later he fell under the influence of a group of minor Englishmen who have rather wickedly been nicknamed the "Graveyard Poets" because of the persistency with which they versified on death, the grave, and the after-life. "Thanatopsis," written before he was eighteen, was a reflection of and a response to certain lines of Kirke White, who had deeply stirred his imagination.

Once again it was hard to persuade the literary world that young Bryant was the actual author. "Thanatopsis" and the "Inscription for the Entrance to a Wood" were published in the *North American Review* without signature, according to the usual custom. The editors had requested contributions from the elder Bryant, and he had found these verses unfinished at home and had sent them on after copying them in his own handwriting. The more famous poem so impressed the editors that, far from believing it the work of an American boy, Richard H. Dana, on hearing it read aloud, said to his colleague, "Ah, Phillips, you have been imposed upon; no one on this side the Atlantic is capable of writing such verses." In the meantime Bryant had been admitted at fifteen to the sophomore class at Williams College, had withdrawn at the end of a year intending to enter Yale the next autumn, had been unable to carry out the plan through lack of funds, and had studied law and been admitted to the bar. While still in doubt as to his choice of profession he had written the "Lines to a Waterfowl," which were later published in the *North American*, following the acceptance of "Thanatopsis." He became a lawyer not through any love of the profession but because it seemed a reasonable way to earn a living in a period when one could not hope for support from his pen. He practiced for nine years, never with any real enthusiasm, describing himself in the midst of these years as

> forced to drudge for the dregs of men,
> And scrawl strange words with the barbarous pen,
> And mingle among the jostling crowd,
> Where the sons of strife are subtle and loud.

His discontent was increased by the applause which came with his magazine poems and by the compliment of an invitation to deliver the Phi Beta Kappa poem at Harvard in 1821. Finally, in 1825, he went down to New York in the hope of making a success of a new periodical there. In spite of his associate editorship *The New York Review and Athenæum Magazine* was as shortlived as scores of others. It was a bad time in America for such a venture. The country was flooded with English publications and American pirated editions of English works. The public was not educated to the idea of magazines, nor the publishers to the methods of financing them. They were unattractive in form and as heavy in contents as the labored name of Bryant's ill-fated experiment. After the collapse he returned for a short time to the practice of law, but in 1826 he accepted the assistant editorship of the New York *Evening Post*, three years later became editor, and continued with it until his death in 1878. He was the first nineteenth-century man of letters to enter the field of American journalism, and he played a highly distinguished part in its history.

When Bryant became editor in chief of the New York *Evening Post* he was thirty-five years old. He had written about one third of the poetry saved in the collected editions and about one half of the better-known poems on which his reputation rests. This much is worth considering by itself, because it has a character of its own and is quite different from the output of the latter fifty years. In the first place it was consciously religious in tone. Bryant came from Puritan ancestry. He was brought up to believe in a stern God who had doomed all mankind to eternal destruction and who ruled them relentlessly, sometimes in sorrow but more often in anger. To the Puritans life on earth was a prelude to eternity, and eternity was to be spent possibly in bliss, but probably in torment. They were truly a people " whose minds had derived a peculiar character from the daily contemplation of superior beings and eternal interests." His mind and imagination were therefore wide open to the influence of Kirke White and the other " Graveyard Poets." " Thanatopsis," or " a glimpse of death," was composed under the eye of God as Bryant knew him. In setting down " When thoughts of the last bitter hour come like a blight over thy spirit," he was not indulging in any far-fetched fancy; he was alluding to what the minister brought home to him in two sermons every Sunday and to the unfailing subject of discussion at the mid-week prayer meeting. And when he wrote of approaching the grave " sustained and soothed by an unfaltering trust," he was writing of a trust which needed to be especially strong to face the thought of possible damnation.

In a broad sense all true poetry is religious, for it deals with truths that lie beneath life and leads to higher thinking and better living, but the religion of the youthful Bryant was specialized to a single creed. The point is strikingly illustrated by the " Hymn to Death." The first four fifths of this poem were written when he was twenty-five years old, a meditation based on Puritan theology. All men die, he said, even those one loves; but death is really God's instrument to punish the wicked. Oppressors, idolaters, atheists, perjurers, revelers, slanderers, the sons of violence and fraud are struck down.

> Thus, from the first of time, hast thou been found
> On virtue's side; the wicked, but for thee,
> Had been too strong for the good; the great of earth
> Had crushed the weak for ever.

Then, with the poem left at this stage, Bryant's father died while still in the height of his powers and as the result of exposure in meeting his duties as a country doctor. In the face of this calamity the young poet's verses seemed to him a bitter mockery:

> Shuddering I look
> On what is written, yet I blot not out
> The desultory numbers; let them stand,
> The record of an idle revery.

This leads to the second characteristic of Bryant's earlier verse — more often than not it was self-conscious and self-applied. He wrote to "The Yellow Violet" and devoted five stanzas to it, but ended with three more of self-analysis. The stanzas "To a Waterfowl" have a general and beautiful application, but they were pointed in his mind by the thought that he needed aid to "lead my steps aright" in the choice of his life's vocation. Even the modest autumn flower, the "Fringed Gentian," reminded him of the autumn of his own life and the hope that he might do as the flower, and look to heaven when the hour of death drew near. This was the voice of youth which takes life as a personal matter and assumes, out of sheer inexperience, that to his concrete wants "the converging objects of the universe perpetually flow." Maturity makes the wise man lift his eyes unto the hills whence cometh his help, instead of continually brooding on his own hopes and fears. But this habit of self-examination was natural not only to the young Puritan, vaguely dissatisfied with the barren existence of a country lawyer; it was closely akin to the sentimentalism

of the age (see pp. 125 and 148). Bryant was like many of
the late eighteenth-century poets, dramatists, and novelists in
his belief that quickness of emotion was admirable in itself
and that the tenderer emotions were marks of refinement.
After he had settled in the city he looked back with a glance
of approval to the days when the springs of feeling were filled
to the brim.

> I cannot forget with what fervid devotion
> I worshipped the visions of verse and of fame;
> Each gaze at the glories of earth, sky, and ocean,
> To my kindled emotions was wind over flame.
>
> And deep were my musings in life's early blossom,
> Mid the twilight of mountain-groves wandering long;
> How thrilled my young veins, and how throbbed my full bosom,
> When o'er me descended the spirit of song.

There is a slight touch of self-commendation in his continual
references to his thrills and awes and adorations and in the
"pleasurable melancholy," as Poe called it, with which he
enjoyed life, but we shall see that life in the city changed
this for something more positive.

Before turning away from this period, however, the student
should take heed of its poetic form. The remarkable thing
about "Thanatopsis" was not that Bryant should have entertained the thoughts it contains or that he should have aspired
to write them, but that he expressed them in verses that were
so beautiful and so different from anything ever written before
in America. It was their form at which Dana exclaimed in
his much-quoted remark to Phillips in the *North American
Review* office. When Bryant was a boy our native writers
were, all but Freneau, in the habit of imitating the English
poets and essayists who had set the style a full hundred years
before. The young American who felt a drawing to literature
saturated himself in the writings of Addison, Pope, Goldsmith,
Johnson, and their followers (see pp. 70, 93, 116, etc.). The

verses of these men were neat, clean-cut, and orderly, and filed down their pages like regiments of soldiers on dress parade. They went along in rimed pairs, with a place to draw breath near the middle of each line, a slight pause at the end of the first, and a full stop at the end of the second. As a fashion, to be sure, it was no more natural than the high, powdered headdresses and hoop skirts which prevailed with the ladies at the same time, but it was a courtly literary convention, and it could be acquired by any writer who was patient and pains-taking. In 1785 the best that John Trumbull could hope for America was that it might produce copyists of these English-men, and he expressed his hope in the usual set style — like a boy scout in uniform dreaming of the day when he and his fellows may develop into Leonard Woodses and Pershings (see p. 70). And Joseph Rodman Drake, writing in one of the years when "Thanatopsis" was lying unpublished in Dr. Bryant's desk, put his desire into an even more com-plex measure, a modification of the Spenserian stanza (see p. 136).

Bryant, it will be remembered, made his first poetic flights in the style of Pope, and he did well enough to be apparently on the highroad of old-fashioned imitation. Then suddenly, while still a boy, he lifted himself out of the rut of rime and began writing a free, fluent "blank verse." It is the same five-stressed measure which Pope used, — the measure of Shakespeare too, "If *mu*sic *be* the *food* of *love*, play *on*," — but it is without rime, and the pauses come where the sense demands instead of where the versification dictates. In the passages just cited from Trumbull and Drake there is only one line where the sense runs on without a slight pause, — the sense is forced to conform to the rhythm; but in "Thanatopsis," although the rhythm is quite regular, the pauses occur at all sorts of places, and seldom at the line-ends. As Bryant set down the first seven and four-fifth lines, for example, they read:

> To him who in the love of Nature holds
> Communion with her visible forms, she speaks
> A various language; for his gayer hours
> She has a voice of gladness, and a smile
> And eloquence of beauty, and she glides
> Into his darker musings, with a mild
> And healing sympathy, that steals away
> Their sharpness, ere he is aware;

but broken into groups, as one would read them, they fall:

> To him who in the love of Nature
> Holds communion with her visible forms,
> She speaks a various language;
> For his gayer hours she has a voice of gladness,
> And a smile and eloquence of beauty,
> And she glides into his darker musings,
> With a mild and healing sympathy,
> That steals away their sharpness, ere he is aware.

This was nothing new in poetry. Shakespeare had written his plays almost entirely in this way, and Milton all of "Paradise Lost" and "Paradise Regained," and the later English poets, most notably Wordsworth, had just returned to it; but in America it was as unfamiliar as the "free verse" which is puzzling a good many readers to-day partly because it is printed in units of meaning instead of units of measure. No wonder that Dana was surprised, "on this side the Atlantic."

When Bryant went down into the crowded activity of New York City the general tone of his work began to change. The things that he was doing interested him as the practice of law never had done. The editorship of the *Evening Post* made him not merely a news vender but a molder of public thought, and his entrance into the world of opinion gave him more of an interest in life itself and less in his own emotions. Very soon he wrote the "Hymn of the City" to record his discovery that God lived in the town as well as in the country and that he was the God of life quite as much as the God of death.

> Thy Spirit is around,
> Quickening the restless mass that sweeps along;
> And this eternal sound —
> Voices and footfalls of the numberless throng —
> Like the resounding sea,
> Or like the rainy tempest, speaks of Thee.

Then in "The Battle Field" (1837) and "The Antiquity of Freedom" (1842) he moved on to what was a new thought in his verse. He was still interested in beauty, whether it were the beauty of nature or the beauty of holiness; but as a man who had plunged into the thick of things he became for the first time wide-awake to the idea that as the world grows older it grows wiser and that the well-rounded life cannot be content simply to contemplate the beauties of June, for it must also have some part in the struggle for justice. He had grown into nothing less than a new idea of God. As a young Puritan he had felt Him to be a power outside, who managed things. He had been content to pray, "Thy will be done on earth as it is in heaven," and then he had turned his back on earth and meditated about heaven. But now he aspired to do with heaven what Addison had attempted to do with "philosophy," and bring it down from the clouds into the hearts of men. When he wrote, in "The Battle Field," "Truth crushed to earth shall rise again," he meant, as the rest of the poem shows, not the old truth of centuries but the unfamiliar truth which the new age must set on its throne.

There is perhaps no more striking illustration of the adoption of so-called new truth than in the world's attitude toward the holding of property in human life. Up to the time of Bryant's birth slaveholding had been practiced in all the United States, by the Puritans of New England as well as by the Cavaliers of the South. During the colonial days in both regions

the Bible had been accepted as final authority. What it counseled and what it did not prohibit was right, and what it
condemned was wrong; and, judged on these grounds, slavery
was apparently sanctioned in the Bible. In spite of this, many
leaders, both North and South, protested against the practice
before 1800. As time went on, largely on account of the climate
and the nature of the industries, slavery waned in the North and
thrived in the South. Then in New England the great agita-
tion arose; but still, in Massachusetts as well as in Virginia,
the men whose bank accounts were involved defended human
bondage on Scriptural grounds, protesting violently against

> creeds that dare to teach
> What Christ and Paul refrained to preach.

Yet in the end the principle for which the Revolution was
fought was reaffirmed in behalf of the slaves who were serving
the sons of the Revolution.

Bryant became painfully conscious of the many issues to be
fought out in the cause of liberty, and in " The Antiquity of
Freedom " he wrote of the eternal vigilance and the eternal
conflict needed to maintain it.

> Oh! not yet
> May'st thou unbrace thy corslet, nor lay by
> Thy sword; nor yet, O Freedom! close thy lids
> In slumber; for thine enemy never sleeps,
> And thou must watch and combat till the day
> Of the new earth and heaven.

That combat is still on; the right of the subject — including
woman — to a voice in the government, the right of the laborer
to a fair return on his work, and the right of the smaller nation
to undisturbed independence are among the uppermost problems that occupy the mind of the world to-day.

Like many of his thoughtful countrymen Bryant founded his
loyalty to America on the hope that in this new land the seed

of new truth would fall on fertile soil. In "Earth," composed
when he was in Italy, he wrote :

> O thou,
> Who sittest far beyond the Atlantic deep,
> Among the sources of thy glorious streams,
> My native Land of Groves ! a newer page
> In the great record of the world is thine ;
> Shall it be fairer ? Fear, and friendly Hope,
> And Envy, watch the issue, while the lines
> By which thou shalt be judged, are written down.

The number and bulk of his poems dedicated to America
are not so great as those by Freneau or Whittier and Lowell
or Timrod and Lanier, but his smaller group are as distinguished and as representative as an equal number by any of
the others except, possibly, Lowell. In "O Mother of a
Mighty Race " he alluded again to the envy and unfriendliness of the older nations, which disturbed him as it did Irving
and Cooper. In the face of it he tried, with less success than
Irving, to keep his own temper, taking comfort in the thought
that the downtrodden and oppressed of Europe could find
shelter here and a chance to live. As a journalist he was a
strong champion of Abraham Lincoln long before the conservative East had given him unreserved support ; and when the
Civil War came on he sounded "Our Country's Call" and
encouraged all within sound of his voice in "the grim resolve
to guard it well." During the war he wrote from time to time
verses that were full of devotion to the right and quite free
from the note of hate that poisons most war poetry ; and at
the end he mourned the death of Lincoln no less fervently
than he rejoiced at "The Death of Slavery."

Aside from these poems and others of their kind, which
make the connection between Bryant the editor and Bryant the
poet, he continued to write on his old themes — nature and
the individual life. There was no complete reversal of attitude ; some of the later poems were reminders of some of the

earlier ones. Yet a real change came after he had mixed with the world. At first he was inclined to lament the loss of the old life, seeming to forget how irksome it had been when he was in the midst of it. In such personal verses as " I cannot forget with what fervid devotion" and "I broke the spell that held me long" he was indulging in the luxury of mild self-pity. " In my younger days I had lots of time, but no money and few friends. Now I have friends and an income, but alas, I have no time." This was but a temporary mood, however. It is quite clear from his later poems that he enjoyed life more in town than in country. This is proven by the fact that nature did not continue to suggest mournful thoughts. "The Planting of the Apple Tree" is serenely recorded in "quaint old rhymes." Instead of saying, as in his earlier manner : " We plant this apple tree, but we plant it only for a few short years. Then it will die, like all mankind. Perhaps I may be buried beneath its shade," he said : " Come, let us plant it. It will blossom and bear fruit which will be eaten in cottage and palace, here and abroad. And when it is old, perhaps its aged branches will throw thin shadows on a better world than this is now. Who knows ? " The stanzas on "Robert of Lincoln" are not merely free from sadness ; they are positively jolly.

In the last years of his long career — he lived to be eighty-four — he seems at first glance to have gone back to his youthful sadness ; but this is not really the case, for thoughts which are premature or affected in youth are natural to old age. At eighty-two, in " A Lifetime " and " The Flood of Years " he actually looked back over many bereavements and forward but a very short way to the life after death. The two poems taken together are an old man's farewell to the world. Like the poem with which he won his first fame, they present another glimpse of death, but this time it is a fair prospect of

> A present in whose reign no grief shall gnaw
> The Heart, and never shall a tender tie
> Be broken.

When Bryant came to his seventieth birthday there was a notable celebration at the Century Club in New York City. At that time three poems were read by three of his fellow-poets — Holmes, Lowell, and Whittier. What they said throws a great deal of light on Bryant's part in American life and literature. Holmes sang his praises as a poet of nature, a journalist of high ideals, a writer of solemn and majestic verse whose later works fulfilled the promise of his first great poem. Lowell went a step farther in paying his tribute to Bryant as a poet of faith and freedom and as a citizen who gave life and courage to the nation during the crisis of the Civil War. In this respect the author of "The Battle Field" was quite as much of a pioneer as in his poems about birds and flowers. He was far ahead of most of his countrymen in his feeling for America as a nation among nations — not merely in the slightly indignant mood of "O Mother of a Mighty Race," but better in his feeling that new occasions bring new duties. Finally, Whittier revered Bryant as a man. With all admiration for his art,

> His life is now his noblest strain,
> His manhood better than his verse!

In his later years Bryant was one of the best citizens of New York. His striking presence on the streets, with his white hair and beard and his fine vigor, made poetry real to the crowds who were inclined to think of it as something impersonal that existed only in books. On account of his powers as a public speaker and his place in literature he was often called on to deliver memorial addresses, and was affectionately named "the old man eloquent." His orations on Cooper and Irving were among the first of these. His last was in 1878, at the unveiling of a statue to the Italian patriot Mazzini. As he was returning into his home he fell, receiving injuries from which he died shortly after. It was fitting that his last words should have been in praise of a champion of freedom and that he should have died with the echoes of his countrymen's applause still ringing in his ears.

BOOK LIST

Individual Author

WILLIAM CULLEN BRYANT. The Life and Works of. Parke Godwin, editor. 6 vols. Vols. I and II, Biography, 1883; Vols. III and IV, Poetical Works, 1883; Vols. V and VI, Prose Writings, 1884-1889. Best single-volume edition is The Household, 1909, and The Roslyn, 1910. His poems appeared originally as follows: The Embargo, 1808; Poems, 1821, 1832, 1834, 1836, 1839, 1840; The Fountain and Other Poems, 1842; The White-Footed Deer and Other Poems, 1844; Poems, 1847, 1848, 1849, 1850, 1854, 1855, 1856, 1857. A Forest Hymn [1860]; In the Woods, 1863; Thirty Poems, 1864; Hymns [1864]; Voices of Nature, 1865; The Song of the Sower, 1871; The Story of the Fountain, 1872; The Little People of the Snow, 1873; Among the Trees [1874]; The Flood of Years, 1878; Unpublished Poems of Bryant and Thoreau, 1907.

Bibliography

STURGES, H. C. Prefixed to the Roslyn edition of Bryant and also published separately. Also Cambridge History of American Literature, Vol. I, pp. 517-521.

Biography and Criticism

The standard life is by Parke Godwin. Vols. I and II of the Life and Works in 6 vols.

BIGELOW, J. William Cullen Bryant. 1890.

BRADLEY, W. A. William Cullen Bryant (*E. M. L. Series*). 1905.

COLLINS, CHURTON. Poets and Poetry of America.

CURTIS, G. W. The Life, Character, and Writings of William Cullen Bryant. 1879.

LEONARD, W. E. Cambridge History of American Literature, Vol. I, Bk. II, in chap. v.

PALMER, G. H. Atlas Essays.

POE, E. A. William Cullen Bryant. Complete Works. Vol. VIII. 1902.

STEDMAN, E. C. Genius and Other Essays. 1911.

STEDMAN, E. C. Poets of America. 1885.

TAYLOR, B. Critical Essays and Literary Notes. 1880.

VAN DOREN, CARL. Growth of Thanatopsis. *Nation*, Vol. CI, p. 432.

WILKINSON, W. C. A Free Lance in the Field of Life and Letters. 1874.

WILSON, J. G. Bryant and his Friends. 1886.

WOODBERRY, G. E. America in Literature. 1903.

TOPICS AND PROBLEMS

Read the early poems of Bryant with reference to the prevalence of death in them and particularly to the unexpected appearance of this idea.

Read them again with reference to the sentimentalism in them.

Read "A Forest Hymn" and the "Hymn to Death" for a comparison of the blank verse with that in "Thanatopsis."

Read "The Battle Field" and Wordsworth's sonnet "Written above Westminster Abbey" for the different but sympathetic developments of the same idea.

Compare Bryant's "Robert of Lincoln" and "The Planting of the Apple Tree" with Freneau's "The Wild Honeysuckle" and "To a Caty-did."

Read Bryant's "Song of the Sower," Lanier's "Corn," and Timrod's "The Cotton Boll" for evident points of likeness and difference.

Note in detail the relation between Bryant's journalistic career and the turn of his mind in the poetry of the journalistic period.

Bryant wrote no journalistic poetry in the sense in which Freneau did, or Whittier, or Lowell. For an explanation see his verses on "The Poet."

CHAPTER XII

EDGAR ALLAN POE

Edgar Allan Poe (1809–1849) is one of the two American poets regarded with greatest respect by authors and critics in England and on the Continent. To Whitman respect is paid because he is so essentially American in his subject matter and point of view; it is yielded to Poe because his subject matter is so universal — located out of space and out of time — and because he was such a master craftsman in his art. Whitman was intensely national and local, looking on life, however broadly he may have seen it, always from his American vantage point. Poe was utterly detached in his creative writing, deriving his maturer tales and poems neither from past nor present, neither from books nor life, but evolving them out of his perfervid imagination and casting the best of them into incomparable form. Poe is therefore sometimes said to have been in no way related to the course of American literature; but this judgment mistakenly overlooks his unhappily varied career as a magazine contributor and editor. He has a larger place in the history of periodicals than any other American man of letters. His connection with at least four is the most distinguished fact that can now be adduced in their favor; and his frustrated ambition to found and conduct a monthly in "the cause of a Pure Taste" was a dream for a thing which his country sorely needed.

Poe was born in Boston, January 19, 1809. His parents were actors — his father a somewhat colorless professionalized amateur, his mother brought up as the daughter of an actress and moderately successful in light and charming rôles. By 1811 the future poet, a brother two years older, and a sister a year younger were orphans. Each was adopted into a different home — Edgar into that of Mr. John Allan, a well-to-do Richmond merchant, to whom he owed, more permanently than any other gift, his middle name. The boy was given the generous attention of an only child. From 1815 to 1820, while his foster father's business held him in residence across the Atlantic, he was in English schools. Then for five years he was in a Richmond academy, and during 1825 apparently studied under private tutors. Up to the time of his admission to the University of Virginia he was handsome, charming, active-minded, and perhaps somewhat " spoiled." Although only seventeen he had passed through a love affair culminating in an engagement, which was very naturally broken by the father of the other contracting party.

With his year at the university Poe entered on the unfortunate succession of eccentricities that blighted all the rest of his tumultuous career and hastened him to an early and tragic death. He did everything intensely, though he was methodical and industrious ; but his method was not equal to his intensity, and from time to time, with increasing frequency, unreasoned or foolish or mad impulses carried him off his balance and into all sorts of trouble. Thus, at the university he stood well in his classes, but he drank to excess (and he was so constituted that a very little was too much) and he played cards recklessly and very badly, so that at the year's end his " debts of honor " amounted to over two thousand dollars. Thus again, after a creditable year and a half in the army he had earned the office of sergeant major and had secured honorable discharge and admission to West Point, but in this coveted academy he neglected his duties and courted the dismissal which came to him within six months. Thus in one editorial position after another he met his obligations well and brilliantly until he came to the inevitable breaking point with his less talented employers. And thus, finally, in the succession of love affairs which preceded and followed his married life the violence of his feelings made him irresponsible and intolerable. Again and again just at the times when he most needed full control of himself he became intoxicated ; yet he was not an habitual drinker, and in the long intervals between his lapses he doubtless deserved from many another the famous testimony of Nathaniel Parker Willis :

With the highest admiration for his genius, and a willingness to let it atone for more than ordinary irregularity, we were led by common report to expect a very capricious attention to his duties, and occasionally a scene of violence and difficulty. Time went on, however, and he was invariably punctual and industrious. With his pale, beautiful and intellectual face, as a reminder of what genius was in him, it was impossible, of course, not to treat him with deferential courtesy, and, to our occasional request that he would not probe too deep in a criticism, or that he would erase a passage colored too highly with his resentments against society and mankind, he readily and courteously assented — far more yielding than most men, we thought, on points so excusably sensitive.

Willis, however, was more considerate and far more intelligent than others, giving Poe no new ground for the " resentments against society and mankind " which he cherished against all too many with whom he had differed. On the whole he was a victim not of friends or foes or " circumstances over which he had no control " but of the erratic temperament with which fate had endowed him. He was like Byron and Shelley in his youthful enjoyment of privilege and good fortune, in his violent rejection of conventional ease and comfort, in his unhappy life and his early death. It is impossible to conceive that any devisable set of conditions would in the end have served Poe better. He was one of the very few who have been truly burdened with " the eccentricities of genius."

The first milestone in his literary career was in 1827. Mr. Allan's refusal to honor his gambling debts resulted in withdrawal from the university and the first clear-cut break with his patron. Shortly after appeared " Tamerlane and Other Poems. By a Bostonian. Boston : Calvin F. S. Thomas . . .

Printer, 1827, pp. 40." It was a little book in which the
passion and the pathos of his whole life were foreshadowed
in the early couplet,

> Know thou the secret of a spirit
> Bowed from its wild pride into shame.

"Tamerlane," the title poem, was a Byronic effusion without
either structure or a rational theme, but with a kind of fire
glowing through in occasional gleams of poetry and flashes
of power. It was the sort of thing that had already been done
by the youthful Drake in "Leon" and that Timrod was to
attempt in "A Vision of Poesy," but though all three were
boyishly imitative, Poe's was the most genuine as a piece of
self-revelation. This volume was followed by "Al Aaraaf,
Tamerlane, and Minor Poems" in 1829, shortly before his
admission to West Point, and by the "Poems" of 1831 just
after his dismissal, each largely inclusive of what had appeared
before, with omissions, changes, and some new poems but no
distinctively new promise.

Then for a while he settled in Richmond, receiving an allowance from Mr. Allan, with whom he had experienced two
estrangements and two reconciliations. In 1832 five of his
prose tales were printed in the *Philadelphia Saturday Courier.*
The fruits of his unwearying devotion to authorship began to
mature in 1833, when he was awarded a hundred-dollar prize
for a short story in the Baltimore *Saturday Visiter*, and when
the first prize for a poem in the same competition was withheld
from him only because of his success with the "MS. Found in
a Bottle." From then on his literary activities were interwoven
with the development of American journalism. His poems,
tales, and critical articles appeared in no less than forty-seven
American periodicals, from dailies to annuals, and he served
in the editorial offices of five.

First of these was the *Southern Literary Messenger*, with
which he was connected in Richmond, Virginia, from July, 1835,

till January, 1837. This monthly had already printed some fifteen poems and stories by Poe, and during his editorship included eleven more; but in that year and a half he discovered and developed his powers as a critic — powers which, though of secondary value, had more to do with advancing his reputation and building up the *Messenger* circulation than his creative verse and prose. He was writing in a period when abject deference to English superiority was giving way to a spirit of provincial puffery. In April, 1836, he wrote:

We are becoming boisterous and arrogant in the pride of a too speedily assumed literary freedom. We throw off with the most presumptuous and unmeaning hauteur *all* deference whatever to foreign opinion . . . we get up a hue and cry about the necessity of encouraging native writers of merit — we blindly fancy that we can accomplish this by indiscriminate puffing of good, bad, and indifferent, without taking the trouble to consider that what we choose to denominate encouragement is thus, by its general application, precisely the reverse. In a word, so far from being ashamed of the many disgraceful literary failures to which our own inordinate vanities and misapplied patriotism have lately given birth, and so far from deeply lamenting that these daily puerilities are of home manufacture, we adhere pertinaciously to our original blindly conceived idea, and thus often find ourselves involved in the gross paradox of liking a stupid book the better because, sure enough, its stupidity is American.

The fresh honesty of this point of view was doubtless reënforced by the local gratification which Poe afforded a body of Southern readers in laying low the New York Knickerbockers and worrying the complacent New Englanders. At all events, the circulation of the *Messenger* rose from seven hundred to five thousand during his editorship.

After his break with the proprietor, which came suddenly and unaccountably, there was a lapse of a year and a half before he took up his duties with *Burton's Gentleman's Magazine*, continuing in a perfunctory way for about a year (July, 1839–June, 1840) when, with much bitter feeling, the connection was severed. In the following April *Burton's* was bought out and combined with Graham's feeble monthly, *The Casket*, as *Graham's Magazine*, and Poe gave over his own design to found the *Penn Magazine* to join forces with a new employer. In the year that ensued he wrote and published several analytical tales and continued his aggressive criticism, while the magazine, under good management, ran its circulation up from eight to forty thousand. Then suddenly, in May, 1842, he was a free lance once more, facing this time two years of duress before he secured another salaried position, now with the *Evening Mirror* and the tactful Willis, as a "mechanical paragraphist." The months of quiet routine with this combination daily-weekly were marked by one overshadowing event, the burst of applause with which "The Raven" was greeted. It was the literary sensation of the day, it was supplemented by the chance publication in the same month of a tale in *Godey's* and a biographical sketch in *Graham's*, and it was reprinted in scores of papers. Such general approval, dear to the heart of any artist, seems for the moment to have lifted Poe out of his usual saturnine mood. "I send you an early number of the *B. Journal*," he wrote to his friend F. W. Thomas, "containing my 'Raven.' It was copied by Briggs, my associate, before I joined the paper. The 'Raven' has had a great run' . . . — but I wrote it for the express purpose of running — just as I did the 'Gold Bug,' you know. The bird has beat the bug, though, all hollow."

The reference to his new associate records another editorial shift. Poe's position on the *Mirror* had been too frankly subordinate to last long, and with the best of good feelings he changed to an associate editorship of the *Broadway Journal* in February, 1845. With the next October he had realized his long-cherished ambition by obtaining full control; yet before the year was out, for lack of money and of business capacity, his house of cards had fallen and the *Journal* was a thing of the past. One more magazine contribution of major importance remained for him. This was the publication in *Godey's*, from May to

October, 1846, of "The Literati," a series of comments on thirty-eight New York authors, done in his then well-known critical manner. His story-writing was nearly over ; "The Cask of Amontillado " was the only important one of the last half dozen, but of the twelve poems later than the "Raven," four — "Ulalume," "To Helen," "Annabel Lee," and "The Bells " — are among his best known.

The personal side of Poe's life after his last breach with Mr. Allan, in 1834, is largely clouded by poverty and bitterness and a relaxing grip on his own powers. His marriage to his cousin, Virginia Clemm, in 1836 was unqualifiedly happy only until the undermining of her health, three years later, and from then on was the cause of a shattering succession of hopes and fears ending with her death in 1847. His relations to most other men and women were complicated by his erratic, jealous, and too often abusive behavior. Only those friendships endured which were built on the magnanimous tolerance or the insuperable amiability of his friends and associates. His nature, which was self-centered and excitable to begin with, became perverted by mishaps of his own making until the characterization of his latest colleague was wholly justified. Said C. F. Briggs to James Russell Lowell :

He cannot conceive of anybody's doing anything, except for his own personal advantage ; and he says, with perfect sincerity, and entire unconsciousness of the exposition which it makes of his own mind and heart, that he looks upon all reformers as madmen ; and it is for this reason that he is so great an egoist. . . . Therefore, he attributes all the favor which Longfellow, yourself, or anybody else receives from the world as an evidence of the ignorance of the world, and the lack of that favor in himself he attributes to the world's malignity.

Under the accumulating distresses of his last two years the decline of will-power and self-control terminated with his tragic death in Baltimore in 1849. The gossip which pursued him all his life has continued relentlessly, even to the point of coloring the prejudices of his biographers, — commonly classified as

"malignants" and "amiables," — but only such facts and reports have been mentioned here as have some legitimate bearing
on his habits of mind as an author.

Poe was first a writer of poems, then of prose tales, and then
of analytical criticisms, and one may take a cue from his famous
discussion of the "Raven" by considering them in reverse
order. His theory of art can be derived from the seventy-odd
articles on his contemporaries which he printed and reprinted,
from the days of the *Southern Literary Messenger* to those of
Godey's, and from the summarized essays which he formulated
in the three latest years. "The Philosophy of Composition"
and "The Poetic Principle" are equally well illustrated by his
own poems and his comments on the poems of others. He
accepts the division of the world of mind into Intellect, which
concerns itself with Truth; Taste, which informs us of the
Beautiful; and the Moral Sense, which is regardful of Duty.
He defines poetry of words as "The Rhythmical Creation of
Beauty. Its sole arbiter is Taste. With the Intellect or with the
Conscience it has only collateral relations. Unless incidentally,
it has no concern whatever either with Duty or with Truth."
In the moods aroused by the contemplation of beauty man's
soul is elevated most nearly to the level of God; and the privilege of Poetry — one refrains from using such a word as "func-
tion" — is to achieve an elevation of soul which springs from
thought, feeling, and will, but which is above them all.

For the composition of poetry, thus limited in its province,
he developed a fairly rigid formula, a Procrustes bed on
which he laid out his several contemporaries. Poems, he said,
should be brief; they should start with the adoption of a novel
and vivid effect; they should be pitched in a tone of sadness;
they should avail themselves of fitting refrains; they should
be presented, in point of setting, within a circumscribed space;
and always they should be scrupulously regardful of conventional poetic rhythms. These artistic canons are largely observed
in his poems and severely insisted on in his criticisms. He

was immensely interested in detail effects, and hardly less so in the isolated details themselves. All the fallacious and inconsistent metaphors of Drake's "Culprit Fay," for example, by which the reader is distracted, he assembled into a final indictment of that hasty poem; and in the works of Elizabeth Barrett, of whom he was one of the earliest champions, he discussed diction, syntax, prosody, and lines of distinguished merit in the minutest detail. Seldom in these critiques does he rise to the task of expounding principles, and more seldom still does he discuss any principles of life. Always it is the cameo, the gold filigree, the miniature on ivory under the microscope.

It is not unfair to apply his own method to him, with reference, for instance, to poetic passages he most admired, by quoting a few of his quotations. From Anna Cora Mowatt:

> Thine orbs are lustrous with a light
> Which ne'er illumes the eye
> Till heaven is bursting on the sight
> And earth is fleeting by.

From Fitz-Greene Halleck:

> They were born of a race of funeral flowers
> That garlanded in long-gone hours,
> A Templar's knightly tomb.

From Bayard Taylor:

> In the red desert moulders Babylon
> And the wild serpent's hiss
> Echoes in Petra's palaces of stone
> And waste Persepolis.

From William Wallace:

> The very dead astir within their coffined deeps.

From Estelle Anna Lewis:

> Ætna's lava tears —
> Ruins and wrecks and nameless sepulchres.

And from Bryant the concluding familiar lines of "Thana-topsis." These are the natural selections of the mind which evolved "The Masque of the Red Death" and "The Cask of Amontillado" and "The Fall of the House of Usher." His readiness to indulge in a "pleasurable melancholy" led him to delight chiefly in the mortuary beauties of his fellow-poets.

At times, to be sure, he responded to the beauties of entire compositions. "Thanatopsis," "To a Waterfowl," "June," all appealed to him for the "elevation of soul" on which he laid critical stress, and so did poems hither and yon by others than Bryant. But for the most part even those productions which stirred or pleased him resulted in detailed technical comments on defects of unity or structure or style, and for the most part what he commended was not so much ideas as poetic concepts. He could lose himself in the chromatic tints from one facet of a diamond to the extent of quite forgetting the stone in its entirety. Hence it was that Poe was a poet in the limited sense of one who is highly and consciously skilled in the achievement of poetic effects, but by his own definition of poetry wholly uninspired toward the presentation of poetic truth. If the creative gift is "to see life steadily and to see it whole," Poe was as far from fulfilling the equation as mortal could be — as far, let us say, as William Blake was.

This is not to say that Poe failed to appreciate or to write the kind of poetry in which he believed. It is an estimate of his own sense of values rather than for the moment of his performance. A letter to Lowell written in 1844 presents the negative background against which his theory and practice are thrown into relief.

I really perceive that vanity about which most men merely prate, — the vanity of the human or temporal life. I live continually in a reverie of the future. I have no faith in human perfectibility. I think that human exertion will have no appreciable effect on humanity. . . . I cannot agree to lose sight of man the individual in man the mass. — I have no belief in spirituality. I think the word a *mere* word. . . .

You speak of "an estimate of my life,"— and, from what I have already said, you will see that I have none to give. I have been too deeply conscious of the mutability and evanescence of temporal things to give any continuous effort to anything — to be consistent in anything. My life has been *whim* — impulse — passion — a longing for solitude — a scorn of all things present, in an earnest desire for the future.

An estimate of his own plays and poems can be fairly made only in the light of this thing that he set out to do, a fairness of treatment, by the way, which he often withheld from the objects of his criticism. Not to paraphrase Poe's minute analysis of "The Raven," we may select the "Ulalume" of a year or two later as a production which satisfies the formula of "The Philosophy of Composition" and which is richer in meaning and in self-revelation than any other. In length and tone and subject and treatment it is according to rule. In ninety-four lines of increasing tension the ballad of the bereaved lover is told. The effect toward which it moves is the shocked moment of discovery that grief for the lost love is not yet "pleasurable," but on this anniversary night is still a source of poignant bitterness. It is built around a series of unheeded warnings — as "The Cask of Amontillado" is — which fall with accumulated weight when the lover's cry explains at last the mistrusts and agonies and scruples of the pacified Psyche. The effect is intensified by use of the whole ominous first stanza in a complex of refrains throughout the rest of the ballad. The employment of onomatopœia, or "sound-sense" words, is more subtle and more effective than in "The Bells" or "The Raven"; and the event occurs in the usual circum-scribed space — the cypress-lined alley which is blocked by the door of the tomb.

These, however, are the mere externals of the poem; the amount of discussion to which it has been subjected shows that, as a poem of any depth should, it contains more than meets the eye. It is a bit of life history, for it refers to Poe's own bereavement, but it is, furthermore, a piece of analysis with a general as well as a personal application. The " I " of the ballad is one half of a divided personality, what, for want of a better term, may be called the masculine element. He is self-confident, blundering, slow to perceive, perfectly brave, in his blindness to any cause for fear. Psyche, the soul, is the complementary, or feminine, element in human nature — intuitive, timid, eager for the reassurance that loquacious male stupidity can afford her. They are the elements incarnate in Macbeth and Lady Macbeth in the early half of the play, and the story in " Ulalume " is parallel to the story of Macbeth up to the time of the murder. Yet, and here is the defect in Poe, true as the analysis may be, in Poe's hands it becomes nothing more than that. It is like a stage setting by Gordon Craig or Leon Bakst — very somber, very suggestive, very artistic, but so complete an artifice that it could never be mistaken for anything but an analogy to life. It is, in a word, the product of one whose " life has been *whim* — impulse — passion — a longing for solitude — a scorn of all things present."

Poe's briefer lyrics are written to a simpler formula, modified from that for the narratives. The resemblance is mainly to be found in the scrupulous care and nicety of measure, in the adjustment of diction to content, and in the heightened dream tone prevailing in them. As they are not attached to any scenic background, the appeals to the mind's eye are unencumbered by any obligations to continuity. Poe's technique in some of the best is quite in the manner of the twentieth-century imagists, and no less effective than in the best of these poets at their best. The earlier of the two poems entitled " To Helen " is quite matchless in its beauty of sound and of suggestion, but it is utterly vulnerable before the kind of searching analysis to which he subjected the verse of the luckless contemporary who stirred his critical disapproval. One has not the slightest objective conception of what " those Nicéan barks " may have been nor why the beauty which attracts a wanderer homeward should be likened to a ship which bears him to his native shore. The two fine lines from Byron in the second stanza reverberate splendidly in their new setting, but again they seem to have small likeness to the beauty of Helen. And the last pair of lovely lines are altogether beyond understanding. Read in the dream mood, however, which is utterly unreasonable but utterly unexacting, " To Helen " is as captivating as the sound of a distant melody.

Poe's tales are of two very different sorts : those that are in the likeness of his poetry and those that were done in the analytical spirit of his criticism. " Ligeia " is an example of the poet's work and, indeed, includes, as some others do, one of his own lyrics, " The Conqueror Worm." This is cast in the misty mid-region between life and death, with none of the pleasures of the one except as foils to the reduplicated horrors of the other. In all the laws of construction it is one with " The Raven " and " Ulalume," as it is also in general effect. Like the poems, too, these narratives contain no human interest, unless this is derived from the consciousness that the " I " narrator is made in the image of Poe and hence is partly his spokesman, — a claim on the attention to which the stories, if considered as works of art, have no title. Once again these tales and poems are of the same family in the degree to which they subordinate any kind of event to the dominant mood and in the painstaking use of every accessory that will contribute to a sense of shivery horror.

Perhaps, to indulge in the type of classification that is after the manner of Poe, a connecting group should be mentioned between the two extreme types. This includes the kind of story that substitutes the horrors of crime and its consequences for the horrors of death, giving over any elevation of soul for the thrill derived from the malignance of fear or hatred. They deal with crime as quite distinct from sin, and when they involve conscience at all, introduce the conscience that doth make cowards of us, rather than the voice of guidance or correction. Of this sort are " The Imp of the Perverse " — less a tale than an essaylet with an illustrative anecdote — and "The Black Cat" and "The Cask of Amontillado." In some ways this story of cold-blooded vengeance comes nearer than any other of Poe's tales to completely representing its author's artistic designs. In the matter of its contrivance it is cut on the pattern of "The Raven." One can apply "The Philosophy of Composition" by replacing each allusion to the poem with a parallel from the story. Montresor, the avenger, is an incarnate devil; Fortunato, the victim, is a piece of walking vanity not worth bothering to destroy. The slow murder is conceived during "the supreme madness of the carnival season," is pursued in a tone of grim mockery, and concluded with ironic laughter and the jingling of the fool's-cap bells. And finally, to free the tale from any least relation to life, the assassination does "trammel up the consequence, and catch with his surcease, success."

The stories that show the mind of the critic — and the greatest of them come in his later career — are in different fashions riddle-solutions, the most famous being "The Murders in the Rue Morgue," "The Mystery of Marie Roget," "The Gold Bug," and "The Purloined Letter," pioneers in the field of the detective story. In the elaboration of these Poe combined his gift as a narrator with the powers which appeared equally in deciphering codes, discrediting Maelzel's chess player, dealing with the complications of "Three Sundays in a Week," or foreseeing the outcome of "Barnaby Rudge" from the opening chapter. Still, as in the earlier types, they are composed of the things that life is made of, but themselves are uninformed with the breath of life. It has been well said by a recent critic that the detective story is in a way a concession to the moral sense of the reading public, following the paths of the older romance of roguery, but pursuing the wrongdoer to the prison or the gallows instead of sharing in his defiance of the social order. But this concession is one in which Poe had no hand. For him detection is an end in itself; he is like the sportsman who is stirred by the zest of the hunt and shoots to kill, but at the day's end, with fine disregard, hands over his bag to the gamekeeper. It should be said as a last word in the classification of Poe's stories that the best work in the threescore and ten can be found in one fourth of that number, that the remainder are in varying degrees overburdened by exposition, and that the least successful, unredeemed by technical excellence and unanimated by any vital meaning, trail off into "sound and fury, signifying nothing."

As a contemporary figure, to summarize, Poe was a vigorous agent in the upbuilding of the American magazine, a stimulator of honest critical judgment, a writer of a few poems and a few tales of the finest but the most attenuated art. At his lowest he is a purveyor of thrills to readers of literary inexperience, people with just a shade more maturity than the habitual matinée-goer; and at the other end of the scale he serves as a stimulant to the decadents who are weary of actual life and real romance, whose minds are furnished like the apartment in "The Assignation," in the embellishment of which "the evident design had been to dazzle and astound." At his highest, however, he has exerted an extraordinary influence not only on those who have fallen completely into his ways but on several prose writers of distinction who have bettered their instructions. Wilkie Collins, Conan Doyle, Stevenson, Chesterton, are only the beginning of a list, and in only one language, who have taken up the detective story where Poe laid it down. Wells and Jules Verne have developed the scientific wonder-tales. Bierce, Stevenson, Kipling, Hardy, have written stories of horror and fantasy; and the touch of his art is suggested by many who have absorbed something from it without becoming disciples or imitators of it or refiners upon it.

BOOK LIST

Individual Author

EDGAR ALLAN POE. Works. Virginia edition. J. A. Harrison, editor. 1902. 17 vols. Another edition. E. C. Stedman and G. E. Woodberry, editors, 1894–1895. 10 vols. Best single-volume editions are : J. H. Whitty, editor, 1911, and Killis Campbell, editor, 1917. Poe's chief works appeared originally in book form as follows : Tamerlane and Other Poems, 1827; Al Aaraaf, Tamerlane, and Minor Poems, 1829; Poems, 1831; Narrative of Arthur Gordon Pym, 1838; The Conchologist's First Book, 1839; Tales of the Grotesque and Arabesque, 1840; The Raven, and Other Poems, 1845; Tales, 1845; Eureka: a Prose Poem, 1848; The Literati, 1850.

Bibliography

The best is by Killis Campbell in the Cambridge History of American Literature, Vol. II, pp. 452–468. See also Vol. X, Stedman-Woodberry edition, and Vol. XVI, J. A. Harrison edition.

Biography and Criticism

The standard life of Poe is by George E. Woodberry. 1884.

BASKERVILL, W. M. Southern Writers.

BEAUDELAIRE, CHARLES. Edgar Poe, sa vie et ses œuvres. 1856.

BROWNELL, W. C. American Prose Masters. 1909.

CAMPBELL, KILLIS. Edgar Allan Poe. Cambridge History of American Literature, Vol. II, Bk. II, chap. xiv.

CAMPBELL, KILLIS. Introduction to Edition of Poems. 1917.

COLLINS, J. C. The Poetry and Poets of America.

FRANCE, ANATOLE. La vie littéraire, Vol. IV.

GATES, L. E. Studies and Appreciations. 1900.

GRISWOLD, R. W. Memoir of Poe (with Poe's works). 1850–1856.

HARRISON, J. A. Life and Letters of Poe. 1902.

HUTTON, R. H. Contemporary Thought and Thinkers. 1900.

INGRAM, J. H. Life, Letters, and Opinions of Poe. 1880.

KENT, C. W. Poe the Poet (in Vol. VII, Virginia edition). 1902.

LANG, ANDREW. Letters to Dead Authors. 1886.

LAUVRIÈRE, E. Edgar Poe: sa vie et son œuvre. 1904.

MACY, JOHN. Poe. (Beacon Biographies.) 1907.

MALLARMÉ, S. Divagations, and Poèmes de Edgar Allan Poe. 1888.

MINOR, B. B. The Southern Literary Messenger, 1834–1864. 1905.

MORE, P. E. Shelburne Essays. Ser. 1. 1907.

MOSES, M. J. Literature of the South. 1910.

RICHARDSON, C. F. American Literature, Vol. III, chap. iv. 1889.

ROBERTSON, J. M. New Essays towards a Critical Method. 1897.

STEDMAN, E. C. Poets of America. 1885 and 1898.

STEPHEN, LESLIE. Hours in a Library. Ser. 1.

SWINBURNE, A. C. Under the Microscope. 1872.

TRENT, W. P. Edgar Allan Poe (announced in *E. M. L. Ser.*).
WENDELL, BARRETT. Stelligeri and Other Essays. 1893.
WHITTY, J. H. Memoir in edition of Poe's Poems. 1911.
WOODBERRY, G. E. America in Literature, chap. iv. 1908.

TOPICS AND PROBLEMS

Read " The Purloined Letter " and compare it as a detective story with any one of Conan Doyle's detections of theft.

Read the introductions of ten or twelve stories for Poe's method of establishing the dominant mood.

Apply the formula presented in " The Philosophy of Composition " to " Annabel Lee " and to any of Poe's best-known prose tales.

No intelligent estimate of Poe can be reached without reading his two analytical essays, " The Philosophy of Composition " and " The Poetic Principle."

Compare the " I " in Poe with the " I " in Whitman. Read " William Wilson " and " The Man in the Crowd," which are felt to have more of autobiography in them than any others.

For the influence of Byron on Poe and on various other impressionable Americans see the index to this volume, and note the variety of ways in which it was recorded.

Light will be thrown on Poe's relationship to the periodicals through a reading of passages on the magazines with which he was connected in " The Magazine in America," by Algernon Tassin. See also the volume called " The Southern Literary Messenger," by B. B. Minor.

CHAPTER XIII

THE TRANSCENDENTALISTS

With the passing of Irving, Cooper, and Bryant the leadership in American letters was lost to New York. Indeed, by 1850, while all this trio were living, four men in eastern Massachusetts were in full career, — Emerson, Longfellow, Lowell, and Whittier; and before the death of Irving, in 1859, Hawthorne, Thoreau, and Holmes came into their full powers. The New Yorkers had done a very distinguished work. The two prose writers in particular had shown talents of which their countrymen could be proud and had introduced the New World to the Old. Yet, though their fame was destined to live, their influence on other authors was bound to die with them because they both were looking backward. The roots of these men were struck deep in the eighteenth century. Cooper's strength lay in his ability to write stories of the romantic past. Even when he brought them up to date, as in " The Pioneers " and " The Prairie," he presented the decline of a passing type of American life. When he wrote of the present pointing to the future, as in " Homeward Bound " and " Home as Found," he was filled with distress and alarm. He was bred in the traditions of aristocracy; he believed in the theories of democracy, but he was very much afraid that they would not turn out well in practice. Irving was a gentleman of the old school. He was loyal to the ideals of his country and confident of its future, but he was fascinated by the traditions of England and Europe. When he wrote of the weaknesses of his city and his fellow-citizens he cast his gentle satires into the form made popular by two Englishmen of a bygone day, and limited himself, as they had done, to commenting on customs, manners, recreations — the external habits of daily life. Of the three Bryant was the only modern man. His later life was finely admirable; but, though his thinking was wise and just, he influenced men less as a thinker than as a stalwart citizen. The New Yorkers, in a word, all wrote as men who were educated in the world of action; they were almost untouched by the deeper currents of human thought which in the nineteenth century were to make great changes in the world.

In 1821, the year of the fifth edition of " The Sketch Book " and " The Spy " and Bryant's first volume, there was growing up in the quieter surroundings of Boston a generation of New England boys with a different training. They all went to and through college, most of them to Harvard, and after college they set to reading philosophy. Many of them came from a long line of Puritan ancestry, as Bryant did. Unlike Bryant several of them felt a distrust and dislike for the sternness of the old creeds. Yet they had the strength of Puritan character in them and the born habit of thinking deeply on " the things that are not seen and eternal." What was new in them was that they were prepared to think independently and to come to their own conclusions. The reading of these boys was no longer chiefly in Pope, Addison, and Goldsmith. It was in the great English writers who were just arriving at fame — Wordsworth, Coleridge, and Carlyle — or in the French and German philosophers.

In the Concord group — Emerson, Thoreau, and Hawthorne — the contrast with the New Yorkers is particularly striking. They were anything but men of the world. When they began to write they stayed in the seclusion of little villages and waited patiently. They matured slowly. Emerson was past middle life before America heeded him ; Hawthorne was forty-six at the time of his first marked success ; Thoreau's fame did not come till after his death. They were not " team workers." Emerson was a clergyman for a short while, but retired in the very year

when Bryant began his long service with the *Evening Post*;
Hawthorne was a recluse for fourteen years after college and
then held positions reluctantly for only half of his remaining
life ; Thoreau never put on the harness. They were not swept
into the current of city life, — "warped out of their own orbits," —
but, instead, they made Concord, whose "chief product" was
literature, more famous than any center of shipping or banking
or manufacture.

"Concord is a little town," Emerson wrote in his Journal,
"and yet has its honors. We get our handful of every ton
that comes to the city." In his address at the two hundredth
anniversary he dwelt on his pride in its history and character.
He traced the earliest settlement, the partitioning of the land,
the events leading up to the Revolution, and, in the presence
of some of the aged survivors, the firing by the embattled
farmers of "the shot heard round the world" in 1775. The
institution in Concord that most appealed to him was the town
meeting, where the whole body of voters met to transact the
public business. The meetings of those two hundred years
had witnessed much that was petty, but on the whole they had
made for good.

It is the consequence of this institution that not a school-house, a
public pew, a bridge, a pound, a mill-dam hath been set up, or pulled
down, or altered, or bought, or sold, without the whole population of
this town having a voice in the affair. A general contentment is the
result. And the people truly feel that they are lords of the soil. In
every winding road, in every stone fence, in the smokes of the poor-
house chimney, in the clock on the church, they read their own power,
and consider at leisure the wisdom and error of their judgments.

Emerson noted that the English government had recently
given to certain American libraries copies of a splendid edition
of the "Domesday Book" and other ancient public records of
England. A suitable return gift, he thought, would be the
printed records of Concord, not simply because Concord was
Concord but because Concord was America. "Tell them the

Union has twenty-four states, and Massachusetts is one. Tell them that Massachusetts has three-hundred towns, and Concord is one ; that in Concord are five hundred rateable polls [that is, taxable voters] and every one has an equal vote." In closing his address Emerson gave his reason for choosing when thirty-one years old to come back to "the fields of his fathers" and spend his life there.

I believe this town to have been the dwelling place at all times since its planting of pious and excellent persons, who walked meekly through the paths of common life, who served God, and loved man, and never let go the hope of immortality. The benediction of their prayers, and of their principles lingers around us.

In the Journal he carries this general indorsement down to particulars that would have been out of place in a public memorial address.

Perhaps in the village we have manners to paint which the city life does not know. Here we have Mr. S., who is man enough to turn away the butcher, who cheats in weight, and introduces another into town. The other neighbors could n't take such a step. . . . There is the hero who will not subscribe to the flag-staff, or the engine, though all say it is mean. There is the man who gives his dollar, but refuses to give his name, though all other contributors are set down. There is Mr. H., who never loses his spirits, though always in the minority. . . . Here is Mr. C., who says " honor bright," and keeps it so. Here is Mr. S., who warmly assents to whatever proposition you please to make, and Mr. M., who roundly tells you he will have nothing to do with the thing. Here, too, are not to be forgotten our two companies, the Light Infantry and the Artillery, who brought up one the Brigade Band and one the Brass Band from Boston, set the musicians side by side under the great tree on the Common, and let them play two tunes and jangle and drown each other, and presently got the companies into active hustling and kicking.

Thus Concord was a little community with a noble and dignified past and at the same time with the homely virtues, oddities, and weaknesses of a New England village. In these respects it was a fit dwelling place for the man who made it famous, for they were like the town in being both finely idealistic and very human. The contrast with the New York of these same years is vivid (see pp. 110, 113, 190 et al.):

Centering about Concord, but by no means located within it, was a "Transcendental Movement" of which Emerson is considered the chief exponent. When the proper nouns "Transcendentalist" and "Transcendentalism" are used they are made to refer to this movement in eastern Massachusetts. In any critical sense, however, the thing that they stood for was only an expression of world thought and was one of the many outcroppings of the movement toward independence of spirit which had been developing for generations. The refusal of the nineteenth-century mind to submit to a philosophy which limited man's faith to the knowledge derived through the senses had already brought about in Germany, France, and England a reaction which insisted on the right of man to believe much which he could not prove. Thus developed transcendentalism, a system of thought "based on the assumption of certain fundamental truths not derived from experience, not susceptible of proof, which transcend human life, and are perceived directly and intuitively by the human mind."

This stood in complete contrast with the faith of the Puritans and yet in strong resemblance to it. Like the Calvinists the Transcendentalists proceeded from a set of assumptions rather than a set of facts, but unlike the Calvinists the Transcendentalists drew these assumptions from their own inner conviction instead of from a set of dogmas which had been distorted out of the Scriptures. They believed in God, and they found his clearest expression in the spirit of man and in the natural surroundings in which God had placed him. They believed that in each man was a spark of divinity. They were assailed because they did not acknowledge an utter difference between Jesus Christ and the average man, though their sin lay not in degrading Christ to the level of man, but in exalting man potentially to the level of Christ. They insisted that it was the duty of each individual to develop the best that was in him on earth, thinking more of the life here than of the life hereafter. They were inspired by the love of God rather than threatened by his wrath, and so they "substituted for a dogmatic dread an illimitable hope."

Fortunately for the influence of this group they inherited the sound qualities of Puritan character. They therefore did not lay themselves open to attack on account of any wild vagaries of conduct. Emerson was a saint, Thoreau an ascetic, Bronson Alcott a pure philosopher, Theodore Parker a great preacher and reformer, Margaret Fuller a high-minded woman of letters, and the scores of their associates just as devoted to a high religious ideal as any equal number of the early Pilgrims.

Two undertakings chiefly focused the group activity of the Transcendentalists. The first of these was the *Dial*, a quarterly publication which ran for sixteen numbers, 1840–1844. The so-called Transcendental Club, an informal group of kindred spirits, came toward the end of the thirties to the point where they felt the need of an "organ" of their own. After much discussion they undertook the publication of this journal of one hundred and twenty-eight pages to an issue. For the first two years it was under the editorship of Margaret Fuller. When her strength failed under this extra voluntary task, Emerson, with the help of Thoreau, took charge for the remaining two years. Its paid circulation was very small, never reaching two hundred and fifty, and finally, when in the hands of its third set of publishers, it had to be discontinued, Emerson personally meeting the final small deficit. It contained chiefly essays of a philosophical nature, but included in every issue a rather rare body of verse. The essays reflected and expounded German thought and literature and oriental thought, and discussed problems of art, literature, and philosophy. The section given to critical reviews is extremely interesting for its quick response to the new writings which later years have proved and accepted.

Possibly the nearest analogy of to-day to the old *Dial* is the *Hibbert Journal*, — the first journal of its kind to achieve an international circulation and self-support. *The Dial* is in a way the literary journal or diary of the Transcendental Movement in America from 1840 to 1844.

The other undertaking associated with the Transcendentalists is less formally their own venture. This was the Brook Farm Institute of Agriculture and Education in West Roxbury, nine miles out from Boston. It was financially the undertaking of a small group of stockholders of whom the Reverend George Ripley was the chief and Nathaniel Hawthorne the man of widest later fame. It was an attempt at the start to combine "plain living and high thinking," the theory being that the group could do their own work and pursue their own intellectual life. During the first three years, from 1841 to 1844, it was carried on as a quiet assembling of idealists who were withdrawing slightly from the hubbub of the world. Agriculture was supplemented by several other simple industries, a school was successfully maintained, and the people who lived there were viewed and visited with interest by many who looked on in sympathetic amusement. The number of actual residents never exceeded one hundred and fifty. Of the leading Transcendentalists Margaret Fuller was the only one to settle. Parker was occupied with his multitudinous duties at Boston; Thoreau attempted his own solution at Walden; Alcott was at his short-lived and ill-fated Fruitlands; and Emerson stayed in Concord with the comment: "I do not wish to remove from my present prison to a prison a little larger. . . . I have not yet conquered my own house. It irks and repents me. Shall I raise the siege of this hen coop, and march baffled away to a pretended siege of Babylon?" In the latter half of its life Brook Farm was drawn into the communistic movement which the French philosopher Charles Fourier had elaborated, and was made the first "phalanx" in America. With this movement its whole nature changed, as it became a part of a great social project with a mission to transform the world. An ambitious central building was erected in 1846, and by an irony of fate the uninsured "phalanstery" was burned down at the very moment when its completion was being celebrated. This last financial burden broke the back of the enterprise, which was discontinued in 1847. It is significant of Brook Farm that however unqualified a material failure it was, it served as a gathering spot for a group of idealists who never ceased to recall their life on the Farm as a happy and fruitful experience.

BOOK LIST

General References
Bibliography

In GODDARD, H. C. Studies in New England Transcendentalism. 1908. See also Cambridge History of American Literature, Vol. I, pp. 546–549.

History and Criticism

COOKE, G. W. Poets of Transcendentalism: an Anthology with Introductory Essay. 1903.

EMERSON, R. W. The Transcendentalist, in *Nature, Addresses and Lectures.*

FROTHINGHAM, O. B. Transcendentalism in New England, a History. 1876.

GODDARD, H. C. Studies in New England Transcendentalism. 1908.

PARKER, THEODORE. Transcendentalism: a Lecture. 1876.

Special Biographies
Alcott, A. B.

SANBORN, F. B. Bronson Alcott at Alcott House, England, and Fruitlands, New England, 1842–1844. 1908.

SANBORN, F. B. and HARRIS, WM. T. A. Bronson Alcott: his Life and Philosophy. 1893. 2 vols.

Emerson, R. W.

See Book List, chap. xiv.

Fuller, Margaret

EMERSON, R. W., CHANNING, W. H., and CLARKE, J. F. Memoirs of Margaret Fuller Ossoli. 1852. 2 vols.

HIGGINSON, T. W. Margaret Fuller Ossoli. 1884.

HOWE, JULIA WARD. Margaret Fuller (Marchesa Ossoli). 1883.

Parker, Theodore

FROTHINGHAM, O. B. Theodore Parker: a Biography. 1874.

WEISS, JOHN. Life and Correspondence of Theodore Parker. 1864. 2 vols.

Ripley, George
> Frothingham, O. B. George Ripley. (*A. M. L. Ser.*) 1882.

Thoreau, Henry David
> See Book List, chap. xiv.

The Dial

> The standard work is by G. W. Cooke. An Historical and Biographical Introduction to accompany *The Dial* as reprinted in Numbers for the Rowfant Club, Cleveland. 1902. 2 vols.
> *The Dial:* a Magazine for Literature, Philosophy, and Religion, Vols. I–IV. 1840–1844. Reprinted by the Rowfant Club of Cleveland, 1900–1903.

Brook Farm

> The standard work is by Lindsay Swift. Brook Farm: its Members, Scholars, and Visitors. 1900. (Contains bibliography.)
> Codman, J. T. Brook Farm: Historic and Personal Memoirs. 1894.
> Cooke, G. W. John Sullivan Dwight, Brook-Farmer, Editor, and Critic of Music. 1898.
> Frothingham, O. B. George Ripley. 1882. (*A. M. L. Ser.*)
> Hawthorne, Nathaniel. The Blithedale Romance. 1852.
> Hawthorne, Nathaniel. Passages from the American Notebooks. 1868. 2 vols.

CHAPTER XIV

RALPH WALDO EMERSON

Ralph Waldo Emerson (1803–1882) was born in Boston. He came from old Puritan stock, several of his direct ancestors being clergymen. He was one of eight children, of whom six were living when his father, the Reverend William Emerson, died in 1811. Mr. Emerson had been so beloved by his parishioners that they continued to pay his salary for seven years, and for three years gave the use of the parish house to the family. The nature of these years is presented in the essay on " Domestic Life " :

Who has not seen, and who can see unmoved, under a low roof, the eager, blushing boys discharging as they can their household chores, and hastening into the sitting-room to the study of to-morrow's merciless lesson, yet stealing time to read one chapter more of the novel hardly smuggled into the tolerance of father and mother — atoning for the same by some passages of Plutarch or Goldsmith ; the warm sympathy with which they kindle each other in school-yard, or barn, or wood-shed, with scraps of poetry or song, with phrases of the last oration or mimicry of the orator ; the youthful criticism, on Sunday, of the sermons ; the school declamation, faithfully rehearsed at home. . . . Ah, short-sighted students of books, of nature, and of man, too happy could they know their advantages, they pine for freedom from that mild parental yoke ; they sigh for fine clothes, for rides, for the theatre, and premature freedom and dissipation which others possess. Woe to them if their wishes were crowned. The angels that dwell with them, and are weaving laurels of life for their youthful brows, are Toil, and Want, and Truth, and Mutual Faith.

There was a great deal of work for the young Emersons in the day, but the spirit of play and playfulness survived it all, as this bit of verse shows. It was written by Ralph to his brother Edward.

> So erst two brethren climb'd the cloud-capp'd hill,
> Ill-fated Jack, and long-lamented Jill,
> Snatched from the crystal font its lucid store,
> And in full pails the precious treasure bore.
> But ah, by dull forgetfulness oppress'd
> (Forgive me, Edward) I 've forgot the rest.

In due time Emerson went to Harvard, entering the class of 1821. Here he earned part of his expenses and profited by scholarships, which must have been given him more on account of his character than because of his actual performance as a student, for he stood only in the middle of his class. He was almost hopelessly weak in mathematics, but he won three prizes in essay-writing and declamation. He was a regular member of one of the debating societies, crossing swords with his opponents on the vague and impossible subjects which lure the minds of youth. His appointment as class poet at graduation argues no special distinction, for it was conferred on him after seven others had refused it. All the while, however, his mind had been active, and he came out from college with the fruits of a great amount of good reading which had doubtless somewhat distracted him from the assigned work. Emerson's experience at college should not be confused with that of many budding geniuses who showed their originality by mere eccentricity. With Emerson, as with Hawthorne and Thoreau too, the independence appeared simply in his choosing the things at which he should do his hardest work. He was full of ambition. An entry in the Journal of 1822 proves that at this age he was more like the Puritan Milton than the care-free Cooper: "In twelve days I shall be nineteen years old, which I count a miserable thing. Has any other educated person lived so many years and lost so many days?" He blamed himself for dreaming of greatness and doing little to

achieve it, but he decided not yet to give up hope of belonging to the "family of giant minds." Already, too, he was in
thought joining his own future with the future of the country
in such jottings as these. "Let those who would pluck the
lot of immortality from Fate's urn, look well to the future of
America." "To America, therefore, monarchs look with
apprehension and the people with hope." If his countrymen
could boast no great accomplishment in the arts, "We have
a government and a national spirit that is better than persons
or histories." The judges of his own future utterances were
to be a nation of free minds, "for in America we have
plucked down Fortune and set up Nature in his room."
These comments, of course, reveal the sentiment and the
lofty rhetoric of the commencement orator, for they were all
written before he was twenty-two. In later years he wrote
more simply and less excitedly, but he never forgot that his
own life was always part of the life of the nation.

The five years just after graduation were not encouraging.
He taught in his brother's school for a while, but loathed it
because he taught so badly. Ill-health harassed him. While
he was studying in the Divinity School his eyes failed him,
so that he was excused from the regular examinations at the
end. And a month after he was admitted to the ministry his
doctor advised him to spend the winter in the South. It was
not until 1829, when he was twenty-six years old, that he
was settled in a pastorate. Then the future seemed assured
for him. The church was an old and respected one, the
congregation made up of "desirable" people. If the young
preacher was able to prepare acceptable sermons and make
friends among his parishioners, he could be sure of a permanent and dignified position in his native city. But although
the flock were perfectly satisfied with their shepherd, in three
years he resigned. He had found that certain of the forms
of church worship embarrassed him because he could not
always enter into the spirit of them. Sometimes when the

moment for the "long prayer" came, he did not feel moved
to utter it, and he felt that to "deliver" it as a piece of
elocution was dishonest and irreverent. Administering the
holy communion troubled him still more, because he felt
afraid that to the literal Yankee mind this symbolical ceremony
was either meaningless or tinged with superstition. So he expressed his honest doubts to his congregation, explaining that
if these features of worship were necessary he could no longer
continue to be their pastor, and they reluctantly let him go.

Two years were yet to pass in the preparatory stage of
Emerson's life. For the first seven months of 1833 he was
abroad, traveling slowly from Italy up to England. In reading
his daily comments on what he saw, one finds no trace of the
eager zest for the novelties of travel enjoyed by Irving and
Cooper; he seems rather to have gone through with the tour
as a sober and conscientious process of education. His most
vivid experiences were not in seeing places but in meeting
English authors, and with one of these, Thomas Carlyle, he
made the beginning of a lifelong friendship. It was like
Emerson to be especially attracted to Carlyle, who was almost
unknown at the time, to seek him out on his lonely Scotch
farm, and to feel a deeper sympathy and admiration for him
than for famous men like Wordsworth and Coleridge and
De Quincey. No single man and no amount of public opinion
ever made up this young American's mind for him. When,
after a year of preaching and lecturing in America he went
late in 1834 to settle in Concord, the richest memory he
treasured from his travel was the founding of this new companionship. In the fabric of the long life that remained to
him no two threads are more important than those of Concord
and Carlyle — the place he loved most and the greatest of
his friends.

Rightly considered, these thirty-one years are a piece not
only of Emerson's life; they are a piece of American history.
They exhibit the life in Boston of a boy and young man with

a fine Puritan inheritance. Among all the traits which came
down to him from the past, none were more dominant than
his rectitude and his independence. Like the boys of earliest
Pilgrim families, he was trained at home in "the uses of
adversity," given a careful schooling, and sent to college
to be prepared for the ministry. His mind, like that of his
ancestors, "derived a peculiar character from the daily contemplation of superior beings and eternal interests"; but like
some of the strongest of these — like Roger Williams, for
example (p. 11), he was bent on arriving at his own conclusions.
Fortunately men were no longer persecuted for their religious
beliefs in the old savage ways. Emerson's withdrawal from the
pulpit did not forfeit him the love of the people whom he had
been serving. Though men could still feel bitterly on the subject of religious differences, the new century was more generous
than the old had been. Travel along the Atlantic seaboard and
in Europe enriched his knowledge of the world, but only deepened his love of the home region; and here as a full-grown man
he settled down with his books and among an increasing circle
of congenial friends to think about life and to record what he
had thought.

It was therefore no accident that in three successive years
— 1836, 1837, and 1838 — Emerson made three statements in
summary of his chief ideas on men and things. In all of
them there was a central thought — that life had become too
much a matter of unconsidered routine and that people must
stop long enough to make up their minds what it was all
about. He offered no "system." He pleaded only that people
begin to think again, so that if they followed in the footsteps
of their fathers they should do so with their eyes open, or
if they decided to strike off into new paths they should not
be blind men led by the blind.

The first of the trio [1] was the essay on "Nature," published
as a slender little book in 1836. He opened with an appeal

1 Found in the volume " Nature, Addresses and Lectures."

for his readers to look at the wonders around them. "If the stars should appear but one night in a thousand years, how would men believe and adore; and preserve for many generations the remembrance of the city of God which had been shown." He went on to discuss nature as Commodity, or source of all the things man may use or own; as Beauty, or source of delight to body, spirit, and mind; as Language, or source of the images and comparisons by means of which man attempts to express abstract ideas; and as a Discipline, or source of training to the intellect in understanding nature's laws and to the moral sense in obeying and interpreting them. In all these respects he contended that the man who will truly understand nature must combine the exactness of observation which belongs to science with the reverence of feeling which is the basis of religion.

No man ever prayed heartily without learning something. But when a faithful thinker, resolute to detach every object from personal relations, and see it in the light of thought, shall, at the same time, kindle science with the fire of the holiest affections, then will God go forth anew into the creation. . . . So shall we come to look at the world with new eyes. . . . The kingdom of man over nature, which cometh not with observation, — a dominion such as now is beyond his dream of God, — he shall enter into without more wonder than the blind man feels who is gradually restored to perfect sight.

Such was Emerson's gospel of beauty. It did not attract any wide attention; but across the sea it was hailed with admiration by Carlyle, who showed it to his friends, and it attracted the attention of Harvard College, so that Emerson was invited to speak before the Phi Beta Kappa society in the following summer.

The result of this invitation was his famous address on "The American Scholar." It was an appeal this time for independence in the realm of the intellect. It has frequently been described as the American Declaration of Intellectual Independence; and the comparison to Jefferson's document

stands in the fact that it did not contain a new idea in America,
but that it stated memorably what had been uttered again and
again by other Americans. "Our day of dependence, our
long apprenticeship to the learning of other lands, draws to
a close. The millions that around us are rushing into life,
cannot always be fed on the sere remains of foreign harvests."
To make his point, Emerson held that the American scholar
must not continue to be "a delegated intellect" but must
become *Man Thinking*. Unlike most of the later essays the
address is clear and orderly in structure. After a brief introduction the scholar is discussed in terms of the chief influences
which surround him. The first is nature, and this section is
brief because of its full treatment in the essay of the preceding
year. The second is the spirit of the past as it is best
recorded in books. Emerson accepted without qualification
the books which contain the story of history and the explanation of exact science. Yet, as science is ever advancing and
the interpretations of history are continually changing, he
might have said of these what he said of books which attempt
to explain life : "Each age, it is found, must write its own
books; or rather, each generation for the next succeeding.
The books of an older period will not fit this." The third
great influence on the scholar is participation in life.

Only so much do I know as I have lived. . . . If it were only for
a vocabulary, the scholar would be covetous of action. Life is our
dictionary. Years are well spent in country labors; in town; in the
insight into trades and manufactures ; in frank intercourse with many
men and women ; in science ; in art; to the one end of mastering in
all their facts a language by which to illustrate and embody our
perceptions. . . . Life lies behind us as the quarry from whence we
get tiles and copestones for the masonry of to-day.

With these influences affecting him the scholar must perform
his duties without thought of reward in money or praise. He
must feel all confidence in himself. "Let him not quit his
belief that a popgun is a popgun, though the ancient and

honorable of the earth affirm it to be the crack of doom."
Signs of the interest that the scholar is showing in life
(as a combination of all sorts of people with common interests
but diverse fortunes) comfort Emerson. These *will redeem*
scholarship. And so he concludes to the young college men:

> We will walk on our own feet; we will work with our own hands;
> we will speak our own minds. The study of letters shall be no longer
> a name for pity, for doubt, and for sensual indulgence. The dread of
> man and the love of man shall be a wall of defence and a wreath of joy
> around all. A nation of men will for the first time exist, because each
> believes himself inspired by the divine soul which also inspires all men.

This address was inspiring to all who heard it. The young
scholars went out with a new feeling for the dignity of learning as an equipment toward leadership, and the older Harvard
professors felt in Emerson's words some reward for a college
that had helped to produce such a man as he. An immediate
consequence of the address was a further invitation to speak
the next year before the students of the Divinity School; and
in 1838 he talked in a similar vein to the budding clergymen.
This address in a way rounded out his "philosophy" by applying
the rule of self-reliance to the third aspect of man's life; after
beauty in "Nature" and truth in "The American Scholar"
came the moral sense in "The Divinity School Address." He
started, as in the former two, with a kind of prose poem on
the wonder of life. He went on to speak of the need of religion that was fresh, vivid, and personal. Then he referred to
the defects of "historical Christianity," which was his name
for the church embodiment of Christ's teaching. These, in his
opinion, were two: that modern Christianity was a system of
belief very different from the simple teachings of Jesus and
that this system was dangerous because it had become fixed.
"Men have come to speak of the revelation as somewhat long
ago given and done, as if God were dead." The remedy for
these defects was the same as for the deadened attitude toward

Nature and Truth — that man should be self-reliant. To the young divinity student he declared, "Yourself a newborn bard of the Holy Ghost, cast behind you all conformity, and acquaint men at first hand with Deity." Christianity has given mankind two great gifts : the Sabbath and the institution of preaching. What hinders that now, everywhere, in pulpits, in lecture-rooms, in houses, in fields, wherever the invitation of men or your own occasions lead you, you speak the very truth, as your life and conscience teach it, and cheer the waiting, fainting hearts of men with new hope and revelation?

Although the Harvard authorities might have foreseen that he would speak as frankly as this, they were shocked when he presumed to advocate independence in religion. Two hundred years earlier he would have been banished from Massachusetts for saying less. As it was, however, Harvard closed its lecture rooms to him for nearly thirty years, and the conservative clergy expressed their outraged feelings in speech and print. Emerson was undisturbed. To one of them, his friend the Reverend Henry Ware, he wrote a seldom-quoted letter that completely represents him. It deserves careful study.

Concord, October 8, 1838.

My dear Sir : —

I ought sooner to have acknowledged your kind letter of last week, and the Sermon it accompanied. The letter was right manly and noble. The Sermon, too, I have read with great attention. If it assails any doctrines of mine — perhaps I am not so quick to see it as writers generally — certainly I did not feel any disposition to depart from my habitual contentment, that you should say your thought, whilst I say mine.

I believe I must tell you what I think of my new position. It strikes me very oddly, that good and wise men at Cambridge and Boston should think of raising me into an object of criticism. I have always been — from my very incapacity of methodical writing — "a chartered libertine" free to worship and free to rail, — lucky when I could make myself understood, but never esteemed near enough to the institution and mind of society to deserve the notice of the masters of literature and religion. I have appreciated fully the advantages of my position; for I well know, that there is no scholar less willing or less able to be a polemic. I could not give account of myself, if challenged. I could not possibly give you one of the "arguments" you cruelly hint at, on which any doctrine of mine stands. For I do not know what arguments mean, in reference to any expression of thought. I delight in telling what I think; but if you ask me how I dare say so, or, why it is so, I am the most helpless of mortal men. I do not even see, that either of these questions admits of an answer. So that, in the present droll posture of my affairs, when I see myself suddenly raised into the importance of a heretic, I am very uneasy when I advert to the supposed duties of such a personage, who is to make good his thesis against all comers.

I certainly shall do no such thing. I shall read what you and other good men write, as I have always done, — glad when you speak my thoughts, and skipping the page that has nothing for me. I shall go on, just as before, seeing whatever I can, and telling what I see; and, I suppose, with the same fortune that has hitherto attended me; the joy of finding, that my abler and better brothers, who work with the sympathy of society, loving and beloved, do now and then unexpectedly confirm my perceptions, and find my nonsense is only their own thought in motley.

And so I am,

Your affectionate servant,

Ralph Waldo Emerson.

Thus far it is clear that Emerson's message to the world was almost unqualifiedly personal: an attempt to shake men out of their lazy ways of drifting with the current into active swimming — with the current if they thought best, but usually against it. The whole problem was summarized in his single defiant essay on " Self-Reliance," [1] — defiant because in this protest he was almost entirely concerned with telling men what they should *not* do. They should not pray, not be consistent, not travel, not imitate, not conform to society; but should be Godlike, independent, searching their own hearts, and behaving in accord with the truth they found there. It is an anarchy he

---

[1] " Self-Reliance " Essays, First Series.

was preaching, an elevated lawlessness. And the first reaction to such teaching is to ask with shocked disapproval, "What would happen to the world if all men followed his advice?" There are two very simple answers. The first is that if all men followed Emerson's advice, completely as he gave it, the world would be peopled with saints, for what he asked was that men should disregard the laws of society only that they might better observe the laws of God. And the second answer is that such a query sets an impossible condition, for the pressure of custom is so strong and the human inclination to do as others do is so prevailing that counsel like Emerson's will never be adopted, at the most, by more than a very small and courageous minority.

One fact to keep in mind in reading all Emerson is that he regularly expresses himself in emphatic terms. In consequence, what he says in one mood he is likely in another to gainsay, and in a third, though without any deliberate intention to defend himself, he may reconcile the apparent contradiction. He simply follows out his own ideas on consistency.

But why should you keep your head over your shoulder? Why drag about this corpse of your memory, lest you contradict somewhat you have stated in this or that public place? Suppose you should contradict yourself; what then? . . . A foolish consistency is the hobgoblin of little minds, adored by little statesmen and philosophers and divines.

This sort of balancing of his views of independence is to be found in an essay of thirty years later on "Society and Solitude." The first two thirds of this seem to be quite as unqualified as anything in the early declarations. He quotes Swedenborg: "There are angels who do not live consociated, but separate, house and house; these dwell in the midst of heaven, because they are the best of angels." He says for himself: "We pray to be conventional. But the wary Heaven takes care you shall not be, if there is anything good in you." "We sit and muse, and are serene and complete; but the moment we meet with anybody, each becomes a fraction." Then, however, comes the corrective note : " But this banishment to the rocks and echoes no metaphysics can make right or tolerable. This result is so against nature, such a half view, that it must be corrected by a common sense and experience." In the earlier essays and addresses Emerson had said repeatedly that a man's education could not be complete unless it included contact with people, and in this essay he came round to the reverse of the medal, that no man could fully express himself who was not useful to his fellows. "Society cannot do without cultivated men." This idea was, of course, always in Emerson's mind, but it was in the later years, after he himself had seen more and more of life, that he expressed it in definite assertions instead of taking it for granted as something the wise man would assume. The concluding paragraph in this essay not only sums up Emerson's views on society and solitude but illustrates the kind of balance which he often strikes between statements which little minds could erect into hobgoblins of inconsistency :

Here again, as so often, Nature delights to put us between extreme antagonisms, and our safety is in the skill with which we keep the diagonal line. Solitude is impracticable, and society fatal. We must keep our head in the one and our hands in the other. The conditions are met, if we keep our independence, yet do not lose our sympathy. These wonderful horses need to be driven by fine hands. We require such a solitude as shall hold us to its revelations when we are in the street and in palaces; for most men are cowed in society, and say good things to you in private, but will not stand to them in public. But let us not be the victims of words. Society and solitude are deceptive names. It is not the circumstance of seeing more or fewer people, but the readiness of sympathy that imports; and a sound mind will derive its principles from insight, with ever a purer ascent to the sufficient and absolute right, and will accept society as the natural element in which they are to be applied.

Throughout the most fruitful years of Emerson's life he lived quietly in Concord, writing without hurry in the mornings, walking and talking with his friends who lived there and with the increasing number of more and less distinguished men who came to receive his inspiration. But three winter months of each year he gave to lecturing, giving frequent series in New York and Boston and going out into the West as far as Wisconsin and Missouri. In these months, as a combined prophet and man of business, he earned a fair share of his income and exerted his widest influence. What he meant to his auditors has been best said by Lowell in his brief essay on " Emerson the Lecturer." Recalling the days when he was a college student, sixteen years younger than Emerson, Lowell wrote :

We used to walk in from the country [Cambridge, four miles out from Boston] to the Masonic Temple (I think it was) through the crisp winter night, and listen to that thrilling voice of his, so charged with subtle meaning and subtle music, as shipwrecked men on a raft to the hail of a ship that came with unhoped-for food and rescue. . . . And who that saw the audience will ever forget it, where everyone still capable of fire, or longing to renew in himself the half-forgotten sense of it, was gathered ? . . . I hear again that rustle of sensation, as they turned to exchange glances over some pithier thought, some keener flash of that humor which always played about the horizon of his mind like heat-lightning. . . . To some of us that long-past experience remains as the most marvellous and fruitful we have ever had. . . . Did they say he was disconnected ? So were the stars, that seemed larger to our eyes, as we walked homeward with prouder stride over the creaking snow. And were not *they* knit together by a higher logic than our mere senses could master ? Were we enthusiasts ? I hope and believe we were, and am thankful to the man who made us worth something for once in our lives. If asked what was left ? what we carried home ? we should not have been careful for an answer. It would have been enough if we had said that something beautiful had passed that way.

If people were puzzled to follow the drift of Emerson's lectures — and they often were — it was because most of them were so vague in outline. They literally did drift. There were two or three explanations for this defect. One was that

Emerson seldom set himself the task of "composing" a complete essay. His method of writing was to put down in his morning hours at the desk the ideas that came to him. As thoughts on subjects dear to him flitted through his mind he captured some of them as they passed. These were related, — like the moon and the tides and the best times for digging clams, — but when he assembled various paragraphs into a lecture he took no pains to establish "theme coherence" by explaining the connections that were quite clear in his own mind. It happened further, as the years went on, that in making up a new discourse he would select paragraphs from earlier manuscripts, relying on them to hang together with a confidence that was sometimes misplaced. And auditors of his lectures in the last years recall how, as he passed from one page to the next, a look of doubt and slight amusement would sometimes confess without apology to an utter lack of connection even between the parts of a sentence.

In his sentences and his choice of words, however, there were perfect simplicity and clearness. Here is a passage to illustrate, drawn by the simplest of methods — opening the first volume of Emerson at hand and taking the first paragraph. It happens to be in the essay on "Compensation."

Commit a crime, and the earth is made of glass. Commit a crime, and it seems as if a coat of snow fell on the ground, such as reveals in the wood the track of every partridge and fox and squirrel and mole. You cannot recall the spoken word, you cannot wipe out the foot-track, you cannot draw up the ladder, so as to leave no inlet or clew. Some damning circumstance always transpires. The laws and substances of nature — water, snow, wind, gravitation — become penalties to the thief.

In this passage of ninety words more than seventy are words of one syllable, and only one of the other eighteen — *transpires* — can baffle the reader or listener even for a moment. The general idea in Emerson's mind is expressed by a series of definite and picturesque comparisons. "Be sure your sin will find you out," he said. "You commit the wicked deed, creep, dodge, run away, come to your hiding place, climb the ladder, and hope for escape. But nature or God — has laid a trap for you. Your footprints are on the new-fallen snow ; human eyes follow them to the tell-tale ladder leading to your window ; and you are caught. The laws of the universe have combined against you in the snowfall, the impress of your feet, and the weight of the ladder which you could not raise."

There is, perhaps, no great difference in the language used by Emerson and that in the paraphrase, but in the way the sentences are put together Emerson's method of composing is once more illustrated. Emerson suggests ; the paraphrase explains. Emerson assumes that the reader is alert and knowing ; the paraphraser, that he is a little inattentive and a little dull. Lowell again has summed up the whole matter : " A diction at once so rich and homely as his I know not where to match·in these days of writing by the page ; it is like homespun cloth-of-gold. The many cannot miss the meaning, and only the few can find it." This is another way of saying, " Anybody can understand him sentence by sentence, but the wiser the reader the more he can understand of the meaning as a whole." What is said of his prose applies in still greater degree to his poetry, as it does to all real poetry.

About his poetry, however, because common agreement has made poetry so much more dependent upon form and structure than prose, there has been wide disagreement, swinging all the way from the strictures of Matthew Arnold to the unqualified praise of George Edward Woodberry. On the whole, a good deal of the argument has been beside the mark because it has been a condemnation of Emerson for writing in an unusual fashion rather than an appraisal of the actual value of his verse. In " Merlin " Emerson stated his poetic thesis and in a measure threw out his challenge :

> Thy trivial harp will never please
> Or fill my craving ear ;
> Its chords should ring as blows the breeze,
> Free, peremptory, clear.

No jingling serenader's art,
Nor tinkle of piano strings,
Can make the wild blood start
In its mystic springs.
The kingly bard
Must smite the chords rudely and hard,
As with hammer or with mace. . . .

The natural result was that there is the closest of resemblances between much of Emerson's verse and some of his most elevated prose. His prose frequently contains poetic flashes; his verse not seldom is spirited prose both in form and substance. In his Journal he sometimes wrote in prose form what with a very few changes he transcribed into verse, and in his essays there are many passages which are closely paralleled in his poems.[1] They are the poems of a philosopher whose first concern is with truth and whose truth is all-embracing. Emerson wrote no narratives, no dramatic poems, no formal odes, almost no poems for special occasions, and when he did write such as the " Concord Hymn " he made the occasion radiate out into all time and space when the embattled farmers " fired the shot heard round the world." The utter compactness and simplicity of his verse made it at times not only rugged but difficult of understanding. " Brahma," which bewildered many of its first readers, is hard to understand only so long as one fails to realize that God is the speaker of the stanzas. The poems are like Bacon's essays in their meatiness and unadornment. Had they been more strikingly different from the ordinary measures they would probably have been both blamed

[1] Such abstruse poems as the following are really expounded in corresponding essays: " Written in Naples " and " Written in Rome "— the essay on " History "; " Each and All "—the essay on " Compensation "; " The Problem "— the essays on " Art " and " Compensation "; " Merlin "— the essay on " The Poet "; " The World-Soul " — the essays on " Nominalist and Realist " and " The Over-Soul "; " Hamatreya "— the essay on " Compensation "; " Musketaquid "— the essay on " Nature "; " Étienne de la Boéce "— the essay on " Friendship "; " Brahma "— the essays on " Circles " and " The Over-Soul."

and praised more widely. Few of his poems have passed into
wide currency, but many of his brief passages are quoted by
speakers who have little idea as to their source.

> Not for all his faith can see
> Would I that cowled churchman be.

> Wrought in a sad sincerity.

> Earth proudly wears the Parthenon
> As the best gem upon her zone.

> . . . if eyes were made for seeing,
> Then Beauty is its own excuse for being.

> Oh, tenderly the haughty day
> Fills his blue urn with fire !

Those who are fortunate enough to have known him — he
died in 1882 — all agree that the real Emerson can be known
only in part through his printed pages. His life was after all
his greatest work. He was serene, noble, dignified. His portraits, at whatever age, testify to his fine loftiness. Every hearer
speaks of the music of his voice. Withal he was friendly, full
of humor, a good neighbor, a loyal townsman, and an engaging
host to those who were worthy of his hospitality. Charles
Eliot Norton, returning from Europe with him in 1873, when
Emerson was sixty-nine years old, wrote in his journal :
" Emerson was the greatest talker in the ship's company.
He talked with all men, yet was fresh and zealous for talk at
night. His serene sweetness, the pure whiteness of his soul,
the reflection of his soul in his face, were never more apparent
to me." No single quotation nor any group of them can make
real to the young student that quiet refrain of reverent affection
which is sounded in the recollections of scores and hundreds
who knew him.

This almost unparalleled beauty of character is the final
guarantee of the line upon line of his poetry and the precept
upon precept of his prose. What he taught must be understood

partly in the light of himself and partly in the light of the years in which he was teaching. Let us take, for example, his two chief contentions. First, his insistence that the truth can be found only by searching one's own mind and conscience. Testing this doctrine by an examination of the man who preached it, one sees that he inherited a power to think from generations of educated ancestry. He had an "inquiring mind" and an inclination to use it. Furthermore, he inherited from this same ancestry a complete balance of character. He did not tend to selfishness or self-indulgence, and was free from thinking that the "voice of God" counseled him to ignoble courses. Puritan restraint was so ingrained in him that he needed no outward discipline and did not see the need of it for others. Freedom for him was always liberty under the law of right; and this freedom he championed in a period and among a people who for two centuries had been accepting without thought what the clergy had been telling them to believe. It had been for them to do what they were told, rather than to think what they should do. Now in Emerson's day there was a general restlessness. The domination of the old church was relaxed, and all sorts of new creeds were being propounded. The theory of democratic government was on trial, and no man was quite certain of its outcome. The expansion of Western territory and the development of the factory system were making many quick fortunes and creating discontent with quiet and settled frugality. Men needed to be told to keep their heads, to combine wisely between the old and the new, and to accept no man's judgment but their own. The "standpatter" would be left hopelessly behind the current of human thought; the wild enthusiast would just as certainly run on a snag or be cast up on the shore.

This led to the second of Emerson's leading ideas — that a man should not be "warped clean out of his own orbit." Reasoning from the evident working of a natural law in the universe, he was convinced that there was a spiritual law which controlled human affairs. He was certain that in the end all would be well with the world. It was his duty and every other man's to be virtuous and to encourage virtue, but as the times were "in God's hand" no man need actively fight the forces of evil. It was the "manifest destiny" theory cropping out again, a belief easy to foster in a new country like America, where wickedness could be explained on the ground that in a period of national youth temporary mistakes were sure to be committed, — and equally sure to be rectified. "My whole philosophy," he said, "is compounded of acquiescence and optimism." Hence there was more of sympathy than coöperation in Emerson's attitude toward life. Like Matthew Arnold in these same years, he distrusted all machinery, even the "machinery" of social reform.

To some of his younger friends, and particularly to those who were more familiar than he with the unhappy conditions in the older European nations, Emerson's "acquiescence and optimism" seemed wholly mistaken. We may return to Norton's comment (p. 215), which was unfairly interrupted: "But never before in intercourse with him had I been so impressed with the limits of his mind. . . . His optimism becomes a bigotry, and though of a nobler type than the common American conceit of the preëminent excellence of American things as they are, had hardly less of the quality of fatalism. To him this is the best of all possible worlds, and the best of all possible times. He refuses to believe in disorder or evil." This comment is not utterly fair to Emerson, but it represents the view of the practical idealist who feels that for all Emerson's insistence on the value of learning from life, he had drawn more from solitude than from society. One may quote with caution what the pragmatic Andrew D. White said of Tolstoi:

He has had little opportunity to take part in any real discussion of leading topics; and the result is that his opinions have been developed without modification by any rational interchange of thought with other men. Under such circumstances any man, no matter how noble or gifted, having given birth to striking ideas, coddles and pets them until they become the full-grown, spoiled children of his brain. He can see neither spot nor blemish in them, and comes virtually to believe himself infallible.

Those who most admire Emerson to-day have perhaps as much optimism as he but very much less acquiescence. For certain vital things have happened since he did his work. Time, — Emerson's " little gray man," — who could perform the miracle of continual change in life, has done nothing more miraculous than making men share the burden of creating a better world. Millions are now trying to follow Emerson's instruction to retain their independence and not to lose their sympathy, but they are going farther than he in expressing their sympathy by work. They are fighting every sort of social abuse, as Emerson's Puritan ancestors fought the devil; they are adopting Emerson's principles and Bryant's tactics; they are subscribing to Whittier's line:

O prayer and action, ye are one.

BOOK LIST

RALPH WALDO EMERSON. Centenary Edition. The Complete Works of Ralph Waldo Emerson. 1903–1904. 12 vols. Uncollected Writings. Essays, Addresses, Poems, Reviews, and Letters, by Ralph Waldo Emerson. 1912. The chief works appeared in book form originally as follows: Nature, 1836; The American Scholar, 1837; An Address delivered before the Senior Class in Divinity College, Cambridge, 1838; Essays, 1841; ·Essays, Second Series, 1844; Poems, 1847; Nature, Addresses, and Lectures, 1849; Representative Men, 1850; English Traits, 1856; The Conduct of Life, 1860; May-Day and Other Pieces, 1867; Society and Solitude, 1870; Letters and Social Aims, 1876; The Correspondence of Thomas Carlyle and Ralph Waldo Emerson, 1883; Lectures and Biographical Sketches, 1884; Natural History of Intellect and Other Papers, 1893; Journals of Ralph Waldo Emerson, with Annotations, 1909–1914.

Bibliography

A volume compiled by G. W. Cooke. 1908. Cambridge History of American Literature, Vol. I, pp. 551–566.

Biography and Criticism

The standard life is by James Elliot Cabot. A Memoir of Ralph Waldo Emerson. 1887. 2 vols.

BOYNTON, PERCY H. Democracy in Emerson's Journals. *New Republic*, Vol. I, No. 4, pp. 25–26.

BOYNTON, PERCY H. Emerson's Feeling toward Reform. *New Republic*, Vol. I, No. 13, pp. 16–18.

BOYNTON, PERCY H. Emerson's Solitude. *New Republic*, Vol. III, pp. 68–70.

BROWNELL, WILLIAM C. Emerson, in *American Prose Masters*. 1909.

BURROUGHS, JOHN. Emerson. Birds and Poets. 1877.

CHAPMAN, J. J. Emerson, Sixty Years After, in *Emerson and Other Essays*. 1898.

Concord School of Philosophy. The Genius and Character of Emerson. Lectures at the Concord School of Philosophy. F. B. Sanborn, editor. 1885.

EMERSON, EDWARD WALDO. Emerson in Concord. A Memoir. 1889.

FIRKINS, O. W. Ralph Waldo Emerson. 1915.

GARNETT, RICHARD. Life of Ralph Waldo Emerson. 1888.

HIGGINSON, T. W. Ralph Waldo Emerson, in *Contemporaries*. 1899.

HOLMES, OLIVER WENDELL. Ralph Waldo Emerson. 1885. (*A. M. L. Ser.*)

JAMES, HENRY. Emerson. Partial Portraits. 1888.

LOWELL, J. R. Mr. Emerson's New Course of Lectures, in *My Study Windows*. 1871.

MAETERLINCK, MAURICE. Emerson, in *Sept Essais d'Emerson*. 1894.

MORE, PAUL ELMER. The Influence of Emerson, in *Shelburne Essays*. Ser. 1. 1904. Cambridge History of American Literature, Vol. I, Bk. II, chap. ix.

PAYNE, W. M. Ralph Waldo Emerson, in *Leading American Essayists*. 1910.

SANBORN, F. B. Ralph Waldo Emerson. (Beacon Biographies.) 1901.

SANBORN, F. B. The Personality of Emerson. 1903.

STEDMAN, E. C. Ralph Waldo Emerson, in *Poets of America*. 1885.

STEPHEN, LESLIE. Emerson, in *Studies of a Biographer. Ser. 2*. 1902.

WHIPPLE, E. P. Recollections of Eminent Men and Other Papers. 1887.

WILLIS, N. P. Emerson. Second Look at Emerson, in *Hurry-Graphs*. 1851.

WOODBERRY, G. E. Ralph Waldo Emerson. 1907. (*E. M. L. Ser.*)

TOPICS AND PROBLEMS

Read the introductions and conclusions of the essays of 1836, 1837, and 1838 and note the poetical setting into which the essays are cast. With these in mind read the foregoing comments on Emerson's poetry (pp. 213–215).

Compare the Emerson and Lowell essays on Shakespeare.

Compare any corresponding sections in Emerson's " Representative Men " and Carlyle's " Heroes and Hero Worship."

Read Emerson's " English Traits " and Hawthorne's " Our Old Home " for a comparison in the points of view of the two Americans.

Read any two or three essays for the nature element in them, the kind of things alluded to, and the kind of significances derived from them.

Read any one or two essays for Emerson's allusions to science and to the sciences, the kinds of allusions made, and the kind of significances derived from them.

Follow the footnote on page 214 for a comparison of Emerson's treatments of the same theme in prose and verse. Read also his poem " Threnody " and the corresponding passage in the Journal for the winter of 1842.

Read the essay on Goethe and see whether in Emerson's judgment of Goethe as a German national character he agrees with or dissents from the judgment of the twentieth century. Compare with Santayana's estimate of Goethe in " Three Philosophical Poets."

A sense of the ecclesiastical and theological unrest in Emerson's day can be secured through the reading of Mrs. Stowe's " Oldtown Folks," Charles Kingsley's " Yeast," Anthony Trollope's " Barchester Towers "; or in poetry, in the poems of doubt of Arnold and Clough and Tennyson's " In Memoriam."

Read " The American Scholar " with reference to the three influences surrounding the scholar, and then read Wells's " The Education of Joan and Peter." Are there any points in common? Compare the section on Beauty in Emerson's " Nature " and Poe's discussion of beauty in " The Poetic Principle " and " The Philosophy of Composition."

CHAPTER XV

HENRY DAVID THOREAU

Henry D. Thoreau was born in Concord, Massachusetts, in 1817. His grandfather, John Thoreau, a Frenchman, had crossed to America in 1773 and had married a woman of Scotch birth in 1781. His mother came from a Connecticut family of much earlier settlement in America, but his more striking traits seem to have passed to him from the father's side. He was a normal, out-of-door, fun-loving boy, though with more than average fondness for books. At Harvard, where he was a graduate in 1837, he was able but unconventional. He was more or less out of patience with the narrow limits of the course of study and the spirit of rivalry among the boys which made them work quite as much for class ranking as for the value of what they learned. Toward the end of senior year this contempt for college honors came to a head. He had been ill, and on his return, as the wise President Quincy put it, revealed " some notions concerning emulation and college rank, which had a natural tendency to diminish his zeal, if not his exertions." When the faculty resented this, even to the extent of planning to withdraw scholarship support, the president took up his cause and backed him for his character rather than for his performance. It was appropriate that Emerson should have written in his young townsman's behalf, for his own experience had not been altogether different.

The story of Thoreau's remaining years is quickly told. He lived, unmarried, a kind of care-free, independent life that in an uneducated laboring man would be called shiftless. Many of his townsmen disapproved of his eccentricities — his brusque manners, abrupt speech, and radical opinions, and his unwillingness to work for money unless he had an immediate need for it. Yet he was less irregular than he was reputed to be. From 1838 to 1841 he conducted a very successful school in Concord with his brother John, giving it up only with the failure of John's health, and — in spite of Emerson's statement to the contrary — he had throughout his life a hand in the family business first of pencil-making and later of preparing fine plumbago for electrotyping. However, he was not an ordinary routine man. Like Crèvecœur, whom he variously suggests, he was a surveyor and a handy man with all sorts of tools. Ten years after graduation he wrote to the secretary of his college class:

> I don't know whether mine is a profession, or a trade, or what not. . . . I am a schoolmaster, a private Tutor, a Surveyor, a Gardener, a Farmer, a Painter (I mean a House Painter), a Carpenter, a Mason, a Day-laborer, a Pencil-maker, a Glass-paper-maker, a Writer, and sometimes a Poetaster.

So as he was able to turn an honest penny whenever he needed one, and as his needs were few, he worked at intervals and betweenwhiles shocked many of his industrious townsfolk by spending long days talking with his neighbors, studying the ways of plants and animals in the near-by woods and waters, and occasionally leaving the village for trips to the wilds of Canada, to the Maine woods, to Cape Cod, to Connecticut, and, once or twice on business, to New York City. After college he became a devoted disciple and friend of Emerson. From the outset Emerson delighted in his "free and erect mind, which was capable of making an else solitary afternoon sunny with his simplicity and clear perception." They differed as good friends should, Emerson acquiescing in laws and practices which he could not approve, and Thoreau defying them. The stock illustration is on the issue of tax-paying. Emerson, as a property-holder, paid about two hundred dollars and refused to protest at what was probably an undue assessment. Thoreau, outraged at the national policy in connection with the Mexican

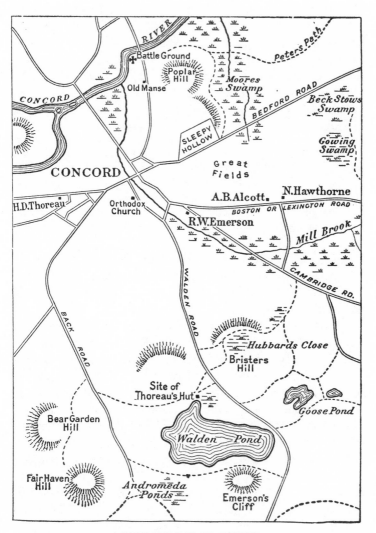

A LITERARY MAP OF CONCORD

War, refused on principle to pay his few dollars for poll tax and had to be shut up by his good friend, Sam Staples, collector, deputy sheriff, and jailer, who tried in vain to lend him the money. Emerson visited him at the jail, where ensued the historic exchange of questions : " Henry, why are you here ? " " Waldo, why are you not here ? "

The records of the rambles of the two men are many. In his memorial essay on Thoreau, Emerson wrote :

> It was a pleasure and a privilege to walk with him. He knew the country like a fox or a bird, and passed through it as freely by paths of his own. He knew every track in the snow or on the ground, and what creature had taken this path before him. . . . On the day I speak of he looked for the Menyanthes, detected it across the wide pool, and on examination of its florets, decided it had been in flower five days.

Emerson's records after walks with Thoreau are full of wood lore. He may have recognized the plants himself, but he seldom recorded them except when he had been with his more expert friend.

In 1839 Thoreau, in company with his brother, spent " A Week on the Concord and Merrimac Rivers," from which he drew the material published ten years later in a volume with that title. It is a meandering record of the things he saw during the seven days and the thoughts suggested by them. In his lifetime the book was so complete a commercial failure that after some years he took back seven hundred of the thousand copies printed. In the meanwhile, from 1845 to 1847, he indulged in his best-known experience — his " hermitage " at Walden Pond, a little way out from Concord. This gave him the subject matter for his most famous book, " Walden," published in 1854 and much more successful in point of sales. These two volumes, together with a few prose essays and a modest number of poems, were all that was given to the public during his lifetime. Since his death a large amount of the manuscript he left has been published, as shown in the list at the end of this chapter.

"Walden" is externally an account of the two years and two months of his residence at the lakeside, but it is really, like his sojourn there, a commentary and criticism on life. In the chapter on "Where I lived and What I lived for" he wrote :

I went to the woods because I wished to live deliberately, to front only the essential facts of life, and see if I could not learn what it had to teach, and not, when I came to die, discover that I had not lived. . . . I wanted to live deep and suck out all the marrow of life, to live so sturdily and Spartan-like as to put to rout all that was not life, to cut a broad swath and shave close, to drive life into a corner, and reduce it to its lowest terms, and, if it proved to be mean, why then, to get the whole and genuine meanness of it, and publish its meanness to the world ; or if it were sublime, to know it by experience, and be able to give a true account of it in my next excursion.

The actual report of his days by the lakeside can be separated from his decision as to what they were worth. He went out near the end of March, 1845, to a piece of land owned by Emerson on the shore of the pond. He cut his own timber, bought a laborer's shanty for the boards and nails, during the summer put up a brick chimney, and counting sundry minor expenses secured a tight and dry — and very homely — four walls and ceiling for a total cost of $28.12½. Fuel he was able to cut. Food he largely raised. His clothing bill was slight. So that his account for the first year runs as follows :

House	$28.12½
Farm, one year	14.72½
Food, eight months	8.74
Clothing, etc., eight months	8.40¾
Oil, etc., eight months	2.00
	$61.99¾

To offset these expenses he recorded :

Farm produce sold	$23.44
Earned by day labor	13.34
	$36.78

leaving $25.21¾, which was about the cash in hand with which he started. The expense of the second year did not, of course, include the heaviest of the first-year items — the cost of the house.

I learned from my two years' experience that it would cost incredibly little trouble to obtain one's necessary food, even in this latitude. . . . In short, I am convinced, both by faith and experience, that to maintain oneself on this earth is not a hardship but a pastime, if we will live simply and wisely ; as the pursuits of the simpler nations are still the sports of the more artificial. It is not necessary that a man should earn his living by the sweat of his brow, unless he sweats easier than I do.

So much for the external account of the Walden years. The last words of the quotation give a cue to the criticism with which he accompanies the bare statement. This is contained chiefly in chapters I, " Economy " (the longest, amounting to one fourth of the book) ; II, " Where I lived and What I lived for"; V, "Solitude"; VIII, "The Village"; and XVIII, "Conclusion." He contended that life had been made complex and burdensome because of the mistaken notion that property was much to be desired. This idea had led men to buy land and build houses, go into trade, construct railways and ships, and to set up government and rival governments, in order to protect the things men owned and those they were buying and selling. Being who he was, he asserted boldly and sometimes savagely a large number of charges against organized society and the men who submitted to it. " The laboring man has not leisure for a true integrity." " The civilized man's pursuits are not worthier than the savage's." " The college student obtains an ignoble and unprofitable leisure, defrauding himself." " Thank God, I can sit and I can stand without the aid of a furniture warehouse." " Men say a stitch in time saves nine, so they take a thousand stitches to-day to save nine to-morrow." " Society is commonly too cheap." " Wherever a man goes, men will pursue and paw him with their dirty institutions, and, if they can, constrain him to belong to their desperate, odd-fellow society." At this point he challenges comparison again with Crèvecœur (see p. 60). To the hearty immigrant of the eighteenth century the common right to own the soil and to enjoy the fruits of labor seemed almost millennial in view of the Old World conditions which denied these privileges to the masses. To the New England townsman the ownership of property was oppressive in view of the aboriginal right to traverse field and forest without any obligation to maintain an establishment or "improve" an acreage. In Crèvecœur's France, where for centuries the people had lived on sufferance, tenure of the land seemed an inestimable privilege. Thoreau's America seemed so illimitable that he apparently supposed land would always be "dirt cheap." Yet though one prized property and the other despised it, they were alike in not foreseeing the economic changes that the nineteenth century was to produce.

The more positive side of Thoreau's criticism lies in the passages in which he told how excellent was his way of living, how full of freedom and leisure and how blest with solitude. There is no question that he did live cheaply, easily, happily, and independently, nor is there any question that the love of money and what it represents has made life more of a burden than a joy for millions of people; but there is this immense difference between the independence of Thoreau and the independence of Emerson — that Emerson discharged his duties in the family and in the state and that Thoreau protested at his obligations to the group even while he was reaping the benefits of other men's industry. At Walden he lived on land owned by Emerson, who bought it and paid the taxes on it. The bricks and glass and nails in his shanty and the tools he borrowed to build it with were the products of mines and factories and kilns brought to him on the railroads and handled by the shopkeepers whom he scorned. He was therefore in the ungraceful position of being a beneficiary of society while he was carrying on a kind of guerrilla warfare against it.

As a citizen and as a critic of society Thoreau lacked the sturdy Puritan conscience which is the bone and sinew of Emerson's character, and he lacked the "high seriousness" of his greater townsman. In consequence, instead of being serenely self-reliant he was often petulant; and instead of being nobly dignified he was nervously on guard against deserved rebuke. Emerson frequently uttered and wrote striking sentences which surprise one into pleased attention. Thoreau came out with smart and clever sayings like an eager and half-naughty boy who is trying to shock his elders. Almost the only rejoinder that his protests called forth must have been disturbing to him, because Oliver Wendell Holmes was so unruffled as he wrote his "Contentment."

"This is an interesting argument from a well-meaning young man," Holmes seems to have said:

Little *I* ask, *my* wants are few;

and then in playful satire he told about the hut — of stone — on Beacon Street that fronts the sun, where he too could live content with a well-set table, the best of clothes, furniture, jewelry, paintings, and a fast horse when he chose to take an airing. This was the attitude of many good-humored men and women of the world who were inclined to smile indulgently at whatever came out of Concord.

However, a fair estimate of Thoreau and his case against the world should steer the wise course between taking him too seriously and literally and not taking him seriously at all, between Stevenson's scathing attack in "Familiar Portraits" and Holmes's supercilious "Contentment." If one elects to act as a prosecuting attorney, one can say of him what Thoreau quotes a friend as saying of Carlyle, that he "is so ready to obey his humour that he makes the least vestige of truth the foundation of any superstructure, not keeping faith with his better genius nor truest readers." But if one choose to value him as a friend might, one can exonerate him in the light of a warning and a confession of his own: "I trust that you realize what an exaggerator I am, — that I lay myself out to exaggerate whenever I have an opportunity, — pile Pelion upon Ossa, to reach heaven so." This is the very point of his title-page inscription to "Walden": "I do not propose to write an ode to dejection, but to brag as lustily as chanticleer in the morning, standing on his roost, if only to wake my neighbors up." It is easy to compare Emerson and Thoreau to the disadvantage of the younger man. But at one point they were quite alike, and that is in the fact that both were more social in their lives than in their writings. Thoreau was not an unmitigated anarchist, or hermit, or loafer. He was more capable and industrious than he admits; he was devoted to his family and a loyal friend. In his protest at the ways of the world he was, in a manner, "whistling to keep his courage up," and often his whistling became rather shrill.

The greater part of "Walden" and, indeed, of his writing as a whole is the work of a naturalist — the work included in such chapters as "Sounds," "The Ponds," "Brute Neighbors," "Former Inhabitants," and "Winter Visitors," "Winter Animals," and "The Pond in Winter." In the two generations since Crèvecœur's "Letters from an American Farmer," no one on this side the Atlantic had written about the out of doors with such fullness and intimate knowledge. In this respect, moreover, Thoreau, instead of being a student or imitator of Emerson, was his guide and instructor. Although modern science owes little to him and has corrected many of his findings, it recalls his help to Agassiz in collecting specimens; and modern literature has produced only one or two men, like John Burroughs and John Muir, who write of nature with the same sympathy and beauty. The title of his friend Channing's book "Thoreau: the Poet-Naturalist" tells the whole story. He was fascinated by growing things. He could not learn enough about their ways. The life in Concord's rivers, ponds, fields, and woods by day and night and during the changing seasons was an endless study and pleasure. In his journal he kept a detailed record of the pageant of the year, which after his death was assembled in the four volumes "Spring in Massachusetts," "Summer," "Autumn," and "Winter." When he went to other parts of the country he carried his knowledge of Concord as a sort of reference book. From Staten Island he wrote : " The woods are now full of a large honeysuckle in full bloom, which differs from ours. . . . Things are very forward here compared with Concord." In the Maine woods he recognized his old familiars but in more massively primitive surroundings than those at home. The sandy aridity of Cape Cod furnished him daily with fascinating contrasts, in natural surroundings and in their effect on the residents. On his trip to Mount Washington he found forty-two of the forty-six plants he expected, adding one to his list when, after falling and spraining his ankle, he limped a few steps and said, " Here is the arnica, anyhow," reaching for an *arnica mollis*, which he had not found before. And when he chose to put into essay form some of the information he had gleaned, he was exact without being technical and never for long repressed his lively spirits.

The poet in him brought him back continually to the beauty in what he saw. He did not particularly incline to philosophize about creation like Emerson, the sheer facts of it meant so much more to him. Nor did he care to expound the beauties of nature ; he simply held them up to view. Take, for example, this bit from " The Pond in Winter," in which the last twelve words are quite as beautiful as the thing they describe :

Standing on the snow-covered plain, as if in a pasture amid the hills, I cut my way first through a foot of snow, and then a foot of ice, and open a window under my feet, where, kneeling to drink, I look down into the quiet parlor of fishes, pervaded by a softened light as through a window of ground glass, with its bright sanded floor the same as in summer ; there a perennial waveless serenity reigns as in the amber, twilight sky.

Or, again, this prose poem quoted in Channing's book:

One more confiding heifer, the fairest of the herd, did by degrees approach as if to take some morsel from our hands, while our hearts leaped to our mouths with expectation and delight. She by degrees drew near with her fair limbs (progressive), making pretence of browsing; nearer and nearer, till there was wafted to us the bovine fragrance, — cream of all the dairies that ever were or will be: and then she raised her gentle muzzle toward us, and snuffed an honest recognition within hand's reach. I saw it was possible for his herd to inspire with love the herdsman. She was as delicately featured as a hind. Her hide was mingled white and fawn-color, and on her muzzle's tip there was a white spot not bigger than a daisy; and on her side turned toward me, the map of Asia plain to see.

The following passages fulfill the main tenets of the contemporary Imagists:

I am no more lonely than the loon in the pond that laughs so loud, or than Walden pond itself. What company has that lonely lake, I pray? . . . I am no more lonely than a single mullein or dandelion in a pasture, or a bean-leaf, or sorrel, or a horse-fly, or a bumble-bee. I am no more lonely than the Mill Brook, or a weather-cock, or the north star, or the south wind, or an April shower, or a January thaw, or the first spider in a new house.

The wind has gently murmured through the blinds, or puffed with feathery softness against the windows, and occasionally sighed like a summer zephyr, lifting the leaves along, the livelong night. The meadow-mouse has slept in his snug gallery in the sod, the owl has sat in a hollow tree in the depth of the swamp; the rabbit, the squirrel and the fox have all been housed. The watch-dog has lain quiet on the hearth, and the cattle have stood silent in their stalls. . . . But while the earth has slumbered, all the air has been alive with feathery flakes descending, as if some northern Ceres reigned, showering her silvery grain over all the fields.

No yard; but unfenced Nature reaching to your very sills. A young forest growing up under your windows, and wild sumachs and blackberry vines breaking through into your cellar; sturdy pitch-pines rubbing and creaking against the shingles for want of room, their roots reaching quite under the house. Instead of a scuttle or a blind blown off in the gale, — a pine tree torn up by the roots behind your house for fuel. Instead of no path to the front-yard gate in the Great Snow, — no gate — no front yard, and no path to the civilized world.

His manner of writing was so like Emerson's that the comments on the style of the elder man (see pp. 212–215) apply for the most part to that of the younger.

From the year of "Walden's" appearance to the end of Thoreau's life, in 1862, three matters are specially worthy of record. The first is that recognition began at last to come. This probably did not hasten his writing, but it released some of the great accumulation of manuscript in his possession. Several of the magazines accepted his papers, notably *The Atlantic Monthly*, which took eight of his articles, although seven of them were not published until the two years just after his death. The second is his eager friendship for two of the most strikingly unconventional men of his day — Walt Whitman and John Brown "of Harper's Ferry." Of Whitman he wrote, when few were reading him and few of these approving :

I have just read his second edition (which he gave me), and it has done me more good than any reading for a long time. . . . I have found his poems exhilarating, encouraging. . . . We ought to rejoice greatly in him. He occasionally suggests something a little more than human. You can't confound him with the other inhabitants of Brooklyn or New York. How they must shudder when they read him ! . . . Since I have seen him, I find I am not disturbed by any brag or egoism in his book. He may turn out the least of a braggart of all, having a better right to be confident.

John Brown he had met in Concord only a few weeks before the Harper's Ferry raid. Two weeks after the capture of Brown he delivered an address on the issues, first in Concord and later in Worcester and in Boston, defying his friends who advised him to silence. And after the execution of the old Kansan he arranged funeral services in Concord.

It turns what sweetness I have to gall, to hear, or hear of, the remarks of some of my neighbors. When we heard at first that he was dead, one of my townsmen observed that " he died as the fool dieth "; which, pardon me, for an instant suggested a likeness in him dying to my neighbor living. . . . This event advertises me that there is such a fact as death, — the possibility of a man's dying. It seems as if no man had ever lived before; for in order to die you must first have lived. . . . I hear a good many pretend that they are going to die; or that they have died, for aught that I know. Nonsense! I 'll defy them to do it. They have n't got life enough in them. They 'll deliquesce like fungi; and keep a hundred eulogists mopping the spot where they left off. Only a half a dozen or so have died since the world began.

The final fact of these later years is the breakdown of his own health. In spite of the moderation and sanity of his out-of-door habits his strength began to fail him before he had reached what should be the prime of life. From the ages of thirty-eight to forty he had to exercise the greatest care, avoiding any heavy exertion. A severe cold caught in 1860 developed soon into consumption, which carried him off in the spring of 1862 at the age of forty-five

BOOK LIST

HENRY DAVID THOREAU. Works. The Riverside Edition. 1894. 10 vols. Walden Edition. 1906. 20 vols. (Of these volumes the last fourteen are the complete Journal, which includes in its original form what stands in Vols. V–VIII of the Riverside Edition, as Early Spring in Massachusetts, Summer, Autumn, Winter.) His works appeared in book form originally as follows: A Week on the Concord and Merrimack Rivers, 1849; Walden, 1854; Excursions, 1863; The Maine Woods, 1864; Cape Cod, 1865; Letters to Various Persons, 1865; A Yankee in Canada, 1866; Early Spring in Massachusetts, 1881; Summer, 1884; Winter, 1888; Anti-Slavery and Reform Papers, 1890; Essays and Other Writings, 1891; Autumn, 1892; Miscellanies, 1893; Familiar Letters, 1894; Poems, 1895.

Bibliography

A volume compiled by Francis H. Allen. 1908. Also Cambridge History of American Literature, Vol. II, pp. 411–415.

Biography and Criticism

The standard life is by Frank B. Sanborn. 1917.

BENTON, JOEL. The Poetry of Thoreau. *Lippincott's*, May, 1886.

BURROUGHS, JOHN. Indoor Studies. 1889.

CHANNING, W. E. Thoreau, the Poet-Naturalist. 1873.

EMERSON, R. W. Lectures and Biographical Sketches. Centenary Edition. 1903.

FOERSTER, NORMAN. Humanism of Thoreau. *Nation*, Vol. CV, pp. 9–12.

LOWELL, J. R. My Study Windows. 1871.

MACMECHAN, ARCHIBALD. Cambridge History of American Literature, Vol. II, Bk. II, chap. x.

MARBLE, A. R. Thoreau: his Home, Friends, and Books. 1902.

MORE, P. E. Shelburne Essays. *Ser. 1.* 1904.

PATTEE, F. L. American Literature since 1870, chap. viii, sec. 1. 1915.

RICHARDSON, C. F. American Literature, Vol. I. 1887.

SALT, H. S. Life of Thoreau. 1890.

SALT, H. S. Literary Sketches. 1888.

SANBORN, F. B. Life of Thoreau. 1882. (*A. M. L. Ser.*)

SANBORN, F. B. Personality of Thoreau. 1901.

STEVENSON, R. L. Familiar Studies of Men and Books. 1882.

TORREY, BRADFORD. Friends on the Shelf. 1906.

TRENT, W. P. American Literature. 1903.

VAN DOREN, MARK. Henry David Thoreau: a Critical Study. 1916.

Pertaining to Thoreau. S. A. Jones, editor. 1901. (Contains ten reprinted magazine articles on Thoreau.)

TOPICS AND PROBLEMS

Read Emerson's " Woodnotes," Vol. I, pp. 2 and 3, for a passage which admirably characterizes Thoreau, though it is said to have been written without specific regard to him.

Read " A Week on the Concord and Merrimack Rivers," noting chiefly either the passages on literature and men of letters or the passages of a sociological interest. Is there a connecting unity in these passages?

Read " Economy " in " Walden " and the second and third of Crèvecœur's " Letters from an American Farmer " for the contrast in ideas on property or for the contrast in ideas on the privileges and the obligations of citizenship.

Read in " Walden " or " The Maine Woods " or " Cape Cod " or " A Yankee in Canada " or " Excursions " for examples of exaggeration and of aggressive self-consciousness. Is there any real likeness between Thoreau and Whitman in these respects?

Read the characterizations of Thoreau in the essays by Robert Louis Stevenson and James Russell Lowell and decide in which points they should be modified.

Read any one or two essays for Thoreau's allusions to science and to the sciences, the kind of allusions made, and the kind of significances derived from them.

Read any two or three essays for the nature element in them, the kind of things alluded to, and the kind of significances derived from them.

CHAPTER XVI

NATHANIEL HAWTHORNE

The thought of Hawthorne (1804–1864) as a member of the "Concord group" should be made with a mental reservation. He did not belong to Concord in any literal or figurative sense, he was not an intimate of those who did, he lived there for only seven years at two different periods in his career, and, wherever he lived, he was in thought and conduct anything but a group man. Yet he was a resident there for the first three years after his marriage (1842–1846), and he developed enough of a liking for the town to return to it for the closing four years of his life. What the town was by tradition and what it had become through Emerson's influence made it the most congenial spot in America for Hawthorne.

On the other hand, he lived far longer in Salem — all but twelve out of his first forty-six years — and he belonged to the town of his heritage both far more and far less. Through instinctive feelings which were quite beyond his control he belonged to Salem from the bottom of his heart.

This old town of Salem — my native place, though I have dwelt much away from it, both in boyhood and maturer years — possesses, or did possess, a hold on my affections, the force of which I have never realized during my seasons of actual residence here. . . . And yet, though invariably happiest elsewhere, there is within me a feeling for old Salem, which, in lack of a better phrase, I must be content to call affection. The sentiment is probably assignable to the deep and aged roots which my family has struck into the soil. It is now nearly two centuries and a quarter since the original Briton, the earliest emigrant of my name, made his appearance in the wild and forest-bordered settlement, which has since become a city. And here his descendants have been born and died, and have mingled their earthy

substance with the soil; until no small portion of it must necessarily be akin to the mortal frame wherewith, for a little while, I
walk the streets. In part, therefore, the attachment which I speak of
is the mere sensuous sympathy of dust for dust. Few of my countrymen can know what it is; nor, as frequent transplantation is perhaps
better for the stock, need they consider it desirable to know.

Yet, strong as this unreasoned feeling was, to his mind
the traditions of Salem were repellent, and it offered him no
attractions as a place to live in.

But the sentiment has likewise its moral quality. The figure of
that first ancestor, invested by family tradition with a dim and dusky
grandeur, was present to my boyish imagination, as far back as I can
remember. It still haunts me, and induces a sort of home feeling for
the past, which I scarcely claim in reference to the present phase
of the town. I seem to have a stronger claim to a residence here
on account of this grave, bearded, sable-cloaked and steeple-crowned
progenitor . . . than for myself, whose name is seldom heard and my
face hardly known. He was a soldier, legislator, judge; he was a ruler
in the Church; he had all the Puritanic traits, both good and evil.
He was likewise a better persecutor. . . . His son, too, inherited the
persecuting spirit. . . . I know not whether these ancestors of mine
bethought themselves to repent, and ask pardon of heaven for their
cruelties; or whether they are now groaning under the heavy consequences of them, in another state of being. At all events, I, the present writer, as their representative, hereby take shame upon myself for
their sakes, and pray that any curse incurred by them — as I have
heard, and as the dreary and unprosperous condition of the race, for
many a long year back, would argue to exist — may be now and
henceforth removed.

On this side Hawthorne's attitude toward Salem — but really
toward New England and all America — was like that of a man
who has inherited debts of honor which he feels bound to discharge, though he never would have incurred them himself.

Hawthorne was born in this town of his affection and his
distrust on the Fourth of July, 1804. When he was four
years old his father, a shipmaster, died during a foreign

voyage. The sobering effect of this loss was increased by the way in which Mrs. Hawthorne solemnized it, for she dedicated her life to mourning, not only withdrawing from the outer world but even taking all her meals apart from her little daughters and her son. An accident to the boy when he was nine years old robbed him of healthy companionship with playmates by keeping him out of active sports for the next three years. So he developed, a bookish child in a muffled household. At this time he was reading Shakespeare, Milton, and the eighteenth-century poets ; later he was to transfer allegiance to the romantic novelists. In his fifteenth year the family lived together for several months at Raymond, Maine, a "town" of a half-dozen houses on the shore of Sebago Lake. "There," he told his publisher, James T. Fields, late in life, "I lived . . . like a bird of the air, so perfect was the freedom I enjoyed. But it was there I first got my cursed habits of solitude." The need of proper tutoring for college preparation caused his reluctant return to Salem, and he was glad to escape from it again when he went back in Maine to Bowdoin College at the age of seventeen. He was not at all eager for college, but regarded it as an unavoidable step in his training. At the same time he rejected the prospect of entering the church, the law, or the practice of medicine, and even as a freshman he wrote to his mother, "What do you think of my becoming an author, and relying for support upon my pen ?" With such a point of view he did no better work than could have been expected. He was more interested in the reading of his own choice than in the assigned studies. He was somewhat frivolous, and even incurred discipline for minor offenses concerning which he wrote to his mother with amused and amusing frankness. He finished a shade below the middle of his class, and left Bowdoin with no more college interest than he had brought to it.

Hawthorne's life for the twelve years which followed graduation explains why he later referred so bitterly to his "cursed habits of solitude." The household to which he returned from Bowdoin was almost utterly unsocial. His mother's way of life had been adopted by his two sisters as well. The four members of the family — one is tempted to refer to them as "inmates" — saw very little of each other as the days went on. The young author neither gave nor received open sympathy. His writing, done in solitude, was not read to the rest. Conditions would have been sufficiently abnormal if he had daily come back to this sort of negative family experience from busy activity in the outer world, but of the outer world he knew nothing. Not twenty people in all Salem, he said, were even aware of his existence. If he left the house during sunlight hours, it was to take long walks in the country. He swam in the near-by sea before the town was stirring; he walked the streets in the shadows of evening. His vital energy was drawn from reading and was vented on his own manuscripts.

His writing during these years was done with patient persistence and without any reward of applause from the public. His first novel, "Fanshawe," was published in 1828 at his expense, was a failure, and was subsequently suppressed — as far as the discouraged author could recover the copies issued. From 1829 to 1836 *The Token*, an annual put out by S. G. Goodrich of Boston, was his main channel of publication, taking in these years about twenty-five stories and sketches. Through Goodrich he had also found a market for his wares in the *New England Magazine*, and toward the end of the period in the *American Monthly Magazine* of New York, and, best of all, with the *Knickerbocker Magazine*, which was the periodical embodiment of the Irving tradition and point of view. But though he was not unsuccessful in getting his work into print, he enjoyed no reputation from it, for only a few discriminating critics took any notice of it, and none of these was fully aware of the author's output, since he wrote not under one but under several pseudonyms. The lack of wholesome human contact either at home or abroad told inevitably on

Hawthorne's nerves and temper — he had become abnormally thin-skinned — and resulted in the touch of querulousness which the student finds from time to time in his accounts of himself. And it also resulted in the deep self-distrust and discouragement which grew steadily on him. "I have made a captive of myself," he wrote finally to his old college classmate, Longfellow, "and put me into a dungeon, and now I cannot find the key to let myself out, — and if the door were open, I should be almost afraid to come out. You tell me that you have met with troubles and changes. I know not what these may have been, but I can assure you that trouble is the next best thing to enjoyment, and that there is no fate in this world so horrible as to have no share in either its joys or sorrows."

With 1837 the friendship of two college associates, Horatio Bridge, a man of political influence and a large heart, and Franklin Pierce, soon to be the president of the country, began to assert itself. Through Bridge the publication of "Twice-Told Tales" was effected in 1837. Through the influence these men were able to exert, Hawthorne was appointed weigher and gauger in the Boston Customhouse. With this post Hawthorne for the first time entered into active life, yet when he lost it as a result of a change of administration in 1841 he was somewhat relieved at the hardship. His engagement to Sophia Peabody led him next to attempt a living solution through residence and partnership in the Brook Farm enterprise during 1841. Again he was oppressed by having the world too much with him, and in 1842, on his marriage, he settled in the seclusion of Concord for his first residence of something over three years. At the end of this time the needs of his growing family made an assured income imperative, and once more through the political influence at his command he was given a federal office, this time as head of the customhouse at Salem. He held this position, like the one at Boston, until a political reverse took it away from him in 1849.

Hawthorne was now nearly forty-six years of age. For the twelve years following the publication of " Twice-Told Tales " he had accomplished almost nothing in creative authorship. The human sympathy and companionship of his marriage, much as it meant to him, was offset as far as authorship went by the distracting need for money. With the loss of the post at Salem the outlook was almost desperate. In the dark hour, however, it appeared that his wife had saved a little from his slender earnings, and in the following months he wrote what appeared, through the friendly insistence of James T. Fields, as his first widely recognized work — " The Scarlet Letter." The first edition of this was exhausted in two weeks. The stimulus of popular attention encouraged him to a rapidity of production wholly out of proportion to anything in his earlier experience. In 1851 " The House of the Seven Gables " was issued; in 1852 " The Blithedale Romance "; and in the meanwhile various lesser narratives were produced. At this stage his political friendships once more proved of value, and through the influence of Pierce, now president, he was enabled to go abroad in the consular service, first to Liverpool and then to Rome. His foreign residence continued until 1860 and resulted, in authorship, in the last of his great romances, "The Marble Faun," the book of English reminiscences, " Our Old Home," and the " Italian Notebooks." With his return to America he went back to Concord, but though he was quite free and undistracted by financial worries, his major period as an author was over, and he died in 1864, leaving behind him only the unimportant stories " Doctor Grimshaw's Secret," " Septimius Felton," and the uncompleted "Dolliver Romance."

In all the most obvious ways Hawthorne's literary output was a fruit of his peculiar heritage and surroundings and his consequent manner of life. A reading of his "American Note-books," the product of the late 30's and the 40's, reveals how definite was the preparation for the harvest to come. It was the gift of Hawthorne's imagination to shroud with a kind of unreality characters and backgrounds that were drawn from close observation. His interpretation made them his own, though they were evidently derived from the life about him. This process is in utter contrast, for example, with the invention of Poe. There never were such individuals as Arthur Gordon Pym or Monsieur Dupin or Fortunato or Roderick Usher. They are essentially human, but they belong to no time or place. But Arthur Dimmesdale, Jaffrey Pyncheon, Hollingsworth and Kenyon, Hester, Phœbe, Zenobia, and Miriam were portraits, made in the image of people who had walked the streets familiar to Hawthorne. Poe's settings are convincingly real. One can visualize every detail of the City in the Sea or the ghoul-haunted woodland of Weir, although one realizes that they never existed in fact; but Boston, Salem, Brook Farm, and Rome supply actual backgrounds for Hawthorne. Had the Puritans builded as securely as the Romans, "The Scarlet Letter," "The House of the Seven Gables," and "The Blithedale Romance" could be illustrated — as "The Marble Faun" often has been — from photographs of surviving structures. Again, these actual scenes and people were put into stories for which there were historical bases, and the symbols around which they were constructed — like the letter of scarlet and the many-gabled house — had been seen and touched by the author. The Maypole of Merry Mount once stood on the Wollaston hilltop, the great stone face is not yet weathered beyond all recognition, and the legends of the Province House are amply documented.

In the Notebooks, particularly for 1835–1845, there is abundant record of how Hawthorne's fancy was continually at play with the material within his reach. He made definite entries as to past events and vital associations of old buildings. He made detailed studies of odd characters seen in his occasional little journeys into the world. He even saved proper names, phrases, similes, epigrams which some day might be of use: " Miss Asphyxia Davis," "A lament for life's wasted sunshine,"

" A scold and a blockhead, — brimstone and wood, — a good match," " Men of cold passions have quick eyes." But far more significant than these explicit items are the many which are suggestive of whole sketches or stories later to be written. Among these the following may easily be identified: " To make one's own reflection in a mirror the subject of a story"; " A snake taken into a man's stomach and nourished there from fifteen years to thirty-five, tormenting him most horribly. A type of envy or some other evil passion." " A person to be in the possession of something as perfect as mortal man has a right to demand; he tries to make it better, and ruins it entirely." " Some very famous jewel or other thing, much talked of all over the world. Some person to meet with it, and get possession of it in some unexpected manner, amid homely circumstances." " The influence of a peculiar mind, in close communion with another, to drive the latter to insanity." " Pandora's Box for a child's story." " A person to be the death of his beloved in trying to raise her to more than mortal perfection; yet this should be a comfort to him for having aimed so highly and holily." " To make a story out of a scarecrow, giving it odd attributes. . . ." " A phantom of the old royal governors, or some such shadowy pageant, on the night of the evacuation of Boston by the British." What Hawthorne attempted was essentially what Wordsworth did: to lift the material of everyday life out of the realm of the commonplace.

In another and more important way Hawthorne's writings show the effect of these long years of preparation, and that is in the self-reflection in the majority of them, and especially in the four major romances. In the quarter century between his graduation from Bowdoin and the publication of " The Marble Faun," the most striking and the most dangerous feature had been his long isolation and the resultant effects of it. He had not withdrawn from the world in contempt; he had insensibly drifted out of it. He was by no means indifferent to it; on the contrary, he was increasingly sensitive to it. He needed to fill his purse and he needed encouragement to write. Yet when he went out into the market place he was cruelly ignored by many and shouldered about by the hustling crowds, who were so used to their own rude ways that they were often quite innocent of the affronts they put upon him. It is a consequence of this unhappy experience that in the famous romances and in many of the shorter sketches the narrative is woven around two types — a shrinking, hypersensitive character and a rude or insidious but always malevolent man who stands for the incarnation of the outer world. For Hester and for Arthur Dimmesdale, for Hepzibah and Clifford Pyncheon, for Priscilla and for Donatello, no complete isolation is possible. No deed which involves them, whether committed by themselves or by others, can be committed without regard to the future. Always there is a knocking at the gate, as the outer world insists on obtruding itself into the holiest of holies. And this invasion is the more cruel as it is the less deserved. Chillingworth's malign and subtle revenge on Arthur Dimmesdale is an exercise of poetic justice. It is a horrible but not undeserved visitation. But Priscilla, Donatello, and the two pitiful Pyncheons are innocent victims. Hepzibah and Clifford are hounded out of life by a bland representative of the law and the church, a wolf in the sheep's clothing of respectability. Priscilla falls in love with a reformer, one of the type who Thoreau complained pursued and pawed him with their "dirty institutions" and tried to constrain him into their "desperate, odd-fellow society"; she wilts at his touch. Donatello, the embodiment of innocent happiness, is enmeshed in the web of society and destroyed by the fell spirit at its center. Hawthorne never could have presented this view in its repeated tableaux if he had not for years seen the concourse of life rush by him, and for years made his successive efforts to reënter its currents.

The whole situation is summarized in Hawthorne's introduction of Septimius Felton, hero of the last work of his pen. "I am dissevered from it," he says in the opening scene.

"It is my doom to be only a spectator of life; to look on as one apart from it. Is it not well, therefore, that, sharing none of its pleasures and happiness, I should be free of its fatalities, its brevity? How cold I am now, while this whirlpool is eddying all around me." Yet, a moment later he snatches a gun and rushes out of the house to where he can see the British redcoats passing the Concord house. He refrains from shooting, only to be seen by a flanking party, and against his will is forced to fire a deadly bullet. "I have seen and done such things," he says an hour later, "as change a man in a moment. . . . I have done a terrible thing for once . . . one that might well trace a dark line through all my future life." To this degree, then, Hawthorne's surroundings and his own unfolding experience had supplied him with themes and materials.

Much of the remainder of his work had its source in his Puritan inheritance. To this the already quoted passage on old Salem (p. 237) bears witness. To this heritage is due in large measure the essential gravity of his nature, which has been unfairly but suggestively described as a compound of " seven eighths conscience and the rest remorse "; and to this is partly attributable his absorption with the presence and the problem of sin in the world. " The Scarlet Letter " deals with its immediate effect on the transgressor; " The House of the Seven Gables," with its effect on succeeding generations; " The Blithedale Romance," with its blighting effect on the reformer, who is selfish and heartless even in his fight against social wrong; " The Marble Faun," with the basic reasons for the existence of evil. Yet though the Puritan strain in him could determine the direction of his thoughts, it could not determine their goal, for Hawthorne recoiled from the Puritan acceptance of sin as a devil's wile to be atoned for only through the sufferings of a mediator or the tortures of the damned. He rejected the Calvinistic fear of eternal punishment for the Miltonic conclusion that the mind is its own place, and of itself can make a heaven of hell; at which point he was at one with the Transcendentalists in substituting "for a dogmatic dread, an illimitable hope." His indictment of the Puritans themselves was more insistent than his charges against their theology. He condemned them for their cruel intolerance and for the arid bleakness of their lives. So he was at once a product of his ancestry and a living protest against it.

But Hawthorne was more than a Puritan apostate; he was in accord with most of the rising individualism of his day. He felt that as the result of multitudinous changes in government, church, and industry, the world had for the moment "gone distracted through a morbid activity" and needed above all things a period of quiet in which to recover its balance of judgment. So he distrusted the schemes of "young visionaries," "gray-headed theorists," "uncertain, troubled, earnest wanderers through the midnight of the moral world." Yet he acknowledged that as long as the world could not be put to sleep, restlessness was better than inertia. The radical Holgrave, in "The House of the Seven Gables," is his most sympathetic portrait of young America. A colloquy with Phœbe Pyncheon represents him as spokesman for the future, and Phœbe as the voice of the placidly thoughtless present. Her remarks, though brief, are quite as significant as his.

" 'Just think a moment [he exclaims] and it will startle you to see what slaves we are to bygone times, — to Death, if we give the matter the right word!'

" 'But I do not see it,' observed Phœbe.

" 'For example then,' continued Holgrave, 'a dead man, if he happen to have made a will, disposes of wealth no longer his own; or, if he die intestate, it is distributed in accordance with the notions of men much longer dead than he. A dead man sits on all our judgment seats; and living judges do but search out and repeat his decisions. We read in dead men's books! We laugh at dead men's jokes, and cry at dead men's pathos! — We are sick of dead men's diseases, physical and moral, and die of the same remedies with which dead doctors killed their patients! We worship the living deity according to dead men's forms and creeds. Whatever we seek to do, of our own free motion, a dead man's icy hand obstructs us. Turn our eyes to what point we may, a dead man's white immitigable face encounters them, and freezes our very heart! And we must be dead ourselves before we can begin to have our proper influence on our own world, which will then be no longer our world, but the world of another generation with which we shall have no shadow of a right to interfere. I ought to have said, too, that we live in dead men's houses; as, for instance, this of the Seven Gables.'

"'And why not?' said Phœbe, 'so long as we can be comfortable in them.'"

Properly interpreted, this conversation implies vigorous criticism of both the youthful speakers. Holgrave's sweeping protests are too drastic, but Phœbe's placid acquiescence is deadening. As if Hawthorne were afraid his sympathy with Holgrave would not appear, he goes on to say that in the course of time the youth will have to conform his faith to the facts without losing his hopes for the future, "discerning that man's best directed effort accomplishes a kind of dream, while God is the sole worker of realities."

It was this breadth of view, combined with his technical gifts as a teller of tales, that made Hawthorne a great artist; for no degree of skill or cleverness can give lasting significance to the work of a man who has not in spirit been taken up to a high mountain and shown the uttermost kingdoms of the world. Granted a "philosophy of life" which inspires a man to high endeavor and enables him to see the relation between the things that are seen and are temporal and the things that are not seen and are eternal, the creative artist need not be always preaching a moral or adorning a tale. The implications that he finds in his material and the abiding convictions he has about life and death need no labeling. They appear as a man's character does, from his daily talk and conduct. Let the romancer state this in his own words :

When romances really do teach anything, or produce any effective operation, it is usually through a far more subtile process than the ostensible one. The author has considered it hardly worth his while, therefore, relentlessly to impale the story with its moral, as with an iron rod, — or, rather, as by sticking a pin through a butterfly, — thus at once depriving it of life, and causing it to stiffen in an ungainly and unnatural attitude. A high truth, indeed, fairly, finely, and skilfully wrought out, brightening at every step, and crowning the final development of a work of fiction, may add an artistic glory, but is never any truer, and seldom any more evident, at the last page than at the first.

Now and again Hawthorne forgot this, and stopped to expound and explain, which was unnecessary. And now and again he used his powers to vent his feelings by contemptuous portrayal of living people, holding them up to scorn, which was unworthy. But even though he lacked the Olympian serenity of the supreme story-tellers, he wrote as a wise man, and he wrote surpassingly well. It remains, then, to speak of his workmanship.

In the preface to " The House of the Seven Gables," from which the above passage is quoted, Hawthorne discusses his methods as a romancer : how he combines materials at hand, but makes them present the truth of the human heart not as the realist but under circumstances of his own choosing and with a " slight, delicate and evanescent flavor" of the marvelous. And this shadowy unreality, he points out, comes from the connection of " a bygone time with the very present that is flitting away from us. It is a legend, prolonging itself, from an epoch now gray in the distance, down into our own broad daylight, and bringing along with it some of its legendary mist." It is a cue to every one of the longer tales and to most of the short ones. Always the outreaching hand of the past plucking at the garments of the present, — the traditions of an elder day or the consequences of a deed committed before the opening of the story.

In a misty, twilight atmosphere, starting where stories frequently end, — with a momentous act already performed, — Hawthorne's romances proceed almost by formula. Each is dominated by a physical symbol, itself a suggestion of some connection with the past, continually recurrent, always half mysterious. Each is told in terms of a very small group of characters, of whom three usually emerge farthest from the shadows. The best of his longer works are not put into the " well-made plot " strait-jacket; and on this point Mrs. Hawthorne's testimony is on record that the plots grew out of the people instead of being imposed upon them. Each is made up mostly of analytic interpretation of moods, and each is garnished with many a meditative commentary on the story-text. Finally, each and all of Hawthorne's writings are characterized by a scrupulous nicety of style, a leisureliness of sentence, a precision of diction that become the courtly manners of the old régime. He was as simple as formality will allow, as formal as simplicity will permit. If we are to liken him to other writers, it will not be to any contemporaries, not even to Mr. Howells. The comparison will take us back to Goldsmith or Jane Austen or to those passages in Thackeray which are most reminiscent of the elder day. Moreover, the book style of Hawthorne was something quite apart from his letter writing, which had a masculine directness and vigor. He was a late member of Irving's generation. When he wrote he " took his pen in hand " to address " the gentle reader." All such literary amenities are now the oldest of old fashions ; but when they were the vogue Hawthorne was a master of them.

BOOK LIST

NATHANIEL HAWTHORNE. Works. There have been eighteen editions of Hawthorne's Collected Works between 1871 and 1904 in from 6 to 18 vols. These appeared in book form originally as follows: Fanshawe, 1828 ; Twice-Told Tales, 1837 ; Grandfather's Chair, 1841 ; Famous Old People, 1841 ; Biographical Stories for Children,

1842; Mosses from an Old Manse, 1846; The Scarlet Letter, 1850; True Stories, 1851; The House of the Seven Gables, 1851; A Wonder Book, 1851; The Blithedale Romance, 1852; Tanglewood Tales, 1853; The Marble Faun, 1860; Our Old Home, 1863; American Notebooks, 1868; English Notebooks, 1870; French and Italian Notebooks, 1871; Septimius Felton, 1871; The Dolliver Romance, 1876; Doctor Grimshawe's Secret, 1883.

Bibliography

A volume compiled by Nina E. Browne. 1905. Also Cambridge History of American Literature, Vol. II, pp. 415–424.

Biography and Criticism

BRIDGE, HORATIO. Personal Recollections of Nathaniel Hawthorne. 1893. (Based on three papers in *Harper's Magazine*, January–March, 1892.)

BROWNELL, W. C. American Prose Masters. 1909.

CONWAY, M. D. Life of Nathaniel Hawthorne. 1890.

ERSKINE, JOHN. Leading American Novelists. 1910. Cambridge History of American Literature, Vol. II, Bk. II, chap. xi.

FIELDS, J. T. Hawthorne. 1876.

FIELDS, MRS. ANNIE. Nathaniel Hawthorne. 1899.

HAWTHORNE, JULIAN. Hawthorne and his Circle. 1903.

HAWTHORNE, JULIAN. Nathaniel Hawthorne and his Wife. 1885.

HAWTHORNE, NATHANIEL. American Notebooks.

HAWTHORNE, NATHANIEL. English Notebooks.

HAWTHORNE, NATHANIEL. French and Italian Notebooks.

JAMES, HENRY. Nathaniel Hawthorne. 1879. (*E. M. L. Ser.*)

LATHROP, GEORGE P. A Study of Hawthorne. 1876.

LATHROP, ROSE HAWTHORNE. Memories of Hawthorne. 1897.

TICKNOR, CAROLINE. Hawthorne and his Publisher. 1913.

WOODBERRY, G. E. Nathaniel Hawthorne. 1902. (*A. M. L. Ser.*)

TOPICS AND PROBLEMS

Read the title essay in " Mosses from an Old Manse " and " The Custom-House " prefatory to " The Scarlet Letter " for Hawthorne's analysis of his feeling for the Puritan heritage.

With these in mind read " Young Goodman Brown," " Governor Endicott and the Red Cross," and " The May-Pole of Merry Mount."

Survey the " Mosses from an Old Manse " or " Twice-Told Tales " for the proportion of stories which are written against evident New England background.

Identify the passages from " The American Notebooks," cited on page 243, with the complete works for which they furnished cues.

Read " The House of the Seven Gables " for the light it throws on the history of the Hawthorne family in the earlier generations.

Read any one of the four great romances or the three later ones with reference to the constant recurrence of sin as a theme.

Compare this treatment of sin in Hawthorne with the treatment of crime in Poe.

Hawthorne is chiefly interested in individual experience. Read one of his romances for clear evidence of his social consciousness.

Discuss his success in any given story in connecting " a bygone time with the very present that is flitting away from us."

The use of symbols in the development of his long stories is obvious. How far does he rely upon the symbol in any one of his more effective shorter stories?

Glance over several short stories to see if any can be found in which action is not subordinated to its effect on the character who commits it.

Read a selected chapter or two, such as the earlier ones in " The House of the Seven Gables," for observation on Hawthorne's style, particularly on the quiet play of humor in it.

CHAPTER XVII

JOHN GREENLEAF WHITTIER

Whittier (1807–1892) stands in decided contrast both in upbringing and in career with the other great New England contemporaries. All the rest were college men, graduates of either Bowdoin or Harvard between 1821 and 1838, and all were familiar from youth with the world of books. Whittier was a farm boy, sprung from untutored farming stock, and in the way of formal schooling had only two terms at Haverhill Academy, paid for with his own hard earnings. He was no less retiring in disposition than the Concord group, yet he was early drawn into the antislavery conflict, and through all his middle years (from 1833 to 1865) he was an untiring man of affairs. Emerson's interest in politics ended with the symbolical value of the Concord town meeting; Thoreau's was registered in his spectacular protest (see p. 224) at a pernicious national policy; Hawthorne's was limited to the performance of duties in posts at the disposal of his political friends; but Whittier undertook the achievement of national ideals through the adoption of wise political measures. The same American to whom Emerson spoke as a thinker Whittier addressed as a voter. In consequence of this his immediate social value became greater, though the verse written in behalf of reform was inferior.[1] In spite of his active rôle in public life, however, Whittier was very much less a man of the world than Lowell, Holmes, or Longfellow. These latter were all men of family, with advantages of college training and foreign travel. They were conscious members of the intellectual aristocracy, bred in polite usages and steeped in polite literature. When Whittier came to Boston for his first

---

[1] See his own acknowledgment in the " Proem " to the poems of 1842.

brief editorial experience it was not to the Boston of the charmed circle to which they and their like belonged. It was not until he had won independent fame that he became their honored friend. By birth he represented an old and stalwart element in New England life — the comparatively unlettered pioneers who made up the silent majority of the population.

He was in every sense an Essex County man. He was born in 1807 in the township of Haverhill, to which his ancestors had come in 1638, on the farm they had owned since 1647, in the house they had built in 1688. He lived in the little three-mile strip between the Merrimac and the New Hampshire line for all his eighty-five years, first at his birthplace, and for the last fifty-six years at Amesbury, a few miles nearer the Atlantic. He thus became in a way an embodiment of local tradition. He felt the strong attachment to his small part of the world that develops in a group whose memories and interests are almost wholly local, and he felt an allegiance to the soil that could respond to Emerson's " Earth Song " :

> They called me theirs,
> Who so controlled me;
> Yet every one
> Wished to stay, and is gone,
> How am I theirs,
> If they cannot hold me,
> But I hold them ?

As a consequence he described the homely beauties that surrounded him, recorded the traditions of the region, and quite unconsciously, as his rimes often prove, wrote in its dialect (see p. 263). His sense of the reality of his state's division into counties is best indicated in the stirring roster which he calls in " Massachusetts to Virginia " (ll. 67–80).

Two other fundamental conditions prevailed in Essex County, though no more strongly than throughout the entire state. It was a time and place of splendid opportunities. In the colonial centuries, hardly more than completed when Whittier was born, pioneer America had barely coped with the elementary problems of settlement. There still remained almost everything that had to do with the alleviations of life — with the nicer refinements, material, intellectual, and æsthetic. For any young man who could combine the will to do with some degree of action, the chance for achievement was exhilarating, — as the Essex boys Garrison and Whittier were to prove. The religious impulse of the day was closely related to these other stimulating conditions. It had the momentum of the generations behind it and the stir of the nineteenth century in it. It was old like the country and new like the period. It was dedicated to a high purpose, but its purpose was more than the personal salvation of the communicant; it was the salvation of Church and State, the bringing of God's kingdom "on earth as it is in heaven."

Whittier grew up, then, in simple and unlettered surroundings, comparable to those of Carlyle, much more propitious than those of Lincoln. Like many another boy of the time when "child hygiene" was undreamed of, he probably suffered from insufficient clothing, unsuitable food, and undue exertion on the farm. At any rate his vigor was impaired and he matured, as often has happened, with just the fragility of health that responded to enforced care and resulted in long life. The reading supplied at home was arid, — a few narratives of frontier adventure, a few religious books, "the Bible towering o'er the rest," and a number of biographies.

> The Lives of Franklin and of Penn,
> Of Fox and Scott, all worthy men.
> The Lives of Pope, of Young, and Prior,
> Of Milton, Addison and Dyer;
> Of Doddridge, Fénelon and Gray,
> Armstrong, Akenside and Gay.
> The Life of Burroughs, too, I 've read,
> As big a rogue as e'er was made;
> And Tufts, who, I will be civil,
> Was worse than an incarnate devil.

Poetry came to Whittier through the chance visit of a Yankee gypsy, "'a pawky auld carle' of a wandering Scotchman. To him I owe my first introduction to the songs of Burns. After eating his bread and cheese and drinking his mug of cider he gave us Bonny Doon, Highland Mary, and Auld Lang Syne." When the boy was fourteen his first schoolmaster, Joshua Coffin, brought a volume of Burns one day to the house and was persuaded to leave it for a while as a loan. With that closer introduction to the world of poetry Whittier's own verse-writing began.

At eighteen he composed the first bit that was destined to appear in print. It was an imitation of Moore, "The Exile's Departure," which was sent without his knowledge to William Lloyd Garrison's *Free Press* at Newburyport and published in June, 1826. The young editor, himself only twenty-one, was greatly impressed by the promise of these lines and hunted up the author, coming to the farm just when the embarrassed youth was hunting out a stolen hen's nest under the barn. Garrison's interest was of the greatest importance. Whittier was encouraged to write the nearly one hundred pieces of verse which appeared in the *Haverhill Gazette* in 1827 and 1828, and to earn by shoemaking the money necessary for his first summer term in the new Haverhill Academy in 1827. The little learning he thus secured he converted by school-teaching into enough to take him for another term the next year, and then in 1828, through the continuing influence of Garrison, he was given his first position as an editor, on the *American Manufacturer* in Boston. He was still a simple country boy, and his published address, "to the young mechanics of New England," suggests that he had not been encouraged to forget this fact during his first four months in town.

He has felt, in common with you all, the injustice of that illiberal feeling, which has been manifested toward mechanics by the wealthy and arrogant of other classes. He has felt his cheeks burn, and his pulse quicken, when witnessing the open, undisguised contempt with which his friends have been received — not from any defect in their moral character, their minds, or their persons, but simply because they depended upon their own exertions for their means of existence, and upon their own industry and talents for a passport to public favor.

He held his post here only from January to August, 1829, when he was summoned home by his father's illness. Editorship of the *Haverhill Gazette* followed for the first half of 1830, when he was called to the *New England Review* in Hartford, Connecticut. This position he occupied with one interruption until the end of 1831, at which time he took his leave of journalism.

He was twenty-four years old — in the restless period between youth and real manhood. He had known little but hardship and had come out of it with impaired health. There was little to cheer him in the tragic career of Burns, in the almost desperate enthusiasm of Garrison, or in the cynicism of Byron, to which he had lately become subject. To cap all, he had been "crossed in love." He could not even have the grim comfort of realizing that he was passing through a youthful phase when he wrote to a friend:

Disappointment in a thousand ways has gone over my heart, and left it dust. Yet I still look forward with high anticipations. I have placed the goal of my ambitions high — but with the blessing of God it shall be reached. The world has at last breathed into my bosom a portion of its own bitterness, and I now feel as if I would wrestle manfully in the strife of men. If my life is spared, the world shall know me in a loftier capacity than *as a writer of rhymes*. There — is not that boasting? — But I have said it with a strong pulse and a swelling heart, and I shall strive to realize it.

This temporary abandonment of poetry was after all only an evidence of his regard for it. With all the other young writers of his day, he was hoping for new achievement in American literature and wondering in the back of his mind if he were not to be a contributor to it. At the moment Bryant had turned to journalism, the New England group were not yet articulate, and the call of politics was loud. "There was nowhere in America a writer of verse with more immediate promise than Whittier, [yet] he was a sick man in the old house at the back of Job's Hill, disgusted with poetry and planning how he could best get to Congress."

Once more Garrison's influence was to determine him. The general inclination toward humanitarian reform had stirred him to the establishment of the *Liberator*, and when he declared, " I am in earnest—I will not equivocate—I will not excuse—I will not retreat a single inch — AND I WILL BE HEARD," he found a natural ally in Whittier. The great step came in 1833 with the poet's publication at his own expense of the pamphlet "Justice and Expediency," with its wider circulation through reprints by sympathizers, with the controversial sequels, and with his share in the founding of the American Anti-Slavery Society. In the years to come he said, " I set a higher value on my name as appended to the Anti-Slavery Declaration of 1833, than on the title-page of any book." It was the deepest test of courage. In the first place it meant that a sensitive young poet who had already felt the injustice of the conservative classes must lay himself open to their contempt and ridicule. It was a bitter time to do this, for never was a day when the miscellaneous inclination to reform offered so great an array of amusing causes and champions. Emerson's derisive list, " Madmen, madwomen, men with beards, Dunkers, Muggletonians, Come-outers, Groaners, Agrarians, Seventh-Day-Baptists, Quakers, Abolitionists, Calvinists, Unitarians and Philosophers," is evidence of the degree to which the general idea of reform had been discredited even in the most liberal minds. For there is no doubt that many of the projects were foolish or that the hopes reposed in them as social cure-alls were ridiculous. But the adoption of the abolition cause involved far more than ridicule — nothing less than the completest disapproval of most good citizens. Considered in the large, lawyers and clergymen are conservatives by profession, deeply committed to the past; and here was slavery sanctioned in the law and the gospel. The prosperous merchant and banker are never markedly eager for a change from the conditions which have fostered their prosperity; and here was a whole economic system, from the plantations of the South to the financial houses of Wall Street and State Street, erected on a foundation of slave labor. According to Emerson cotton thread held the Union together. Men might devote their lives to the substitution of hooks and eyes for buttons or the adoption of a vegetarian diet, and get their pay in laughter, but when they threatened to disturb the industrial system they were pelted and hated and cursed. All this Whittier foresaw when he followed his own counsel of later years, " My lad, if thou wouldst win success, join thyself to some unpopular but noble cause." The history of his participation in the abolition movement does not belong to such a chapter as this except for a record of how he used his literary powers for the good of the cause, and for a comment on the kind of poetry that inevitably resulted from such use.

Between 1831 and 1833 Whittier had become intelligently interested in politics; indeed, had he been a few months older in the autumn of 1832 it is possible that he might have been elected to Congress as a compromise candidate when Caleb Cushing was unable to secure the seat for himself, though strong enough to prevent the choice of an opponent. The young poet had thus learned a good deal about the value of public opinion and about the power of publicity in molding and wielding it. When the American Anti-Slavery Society was formed he had at his hand a great megaphone that could project his voice to the far districts of the country. As a writer of propagandist verse he was endowed with what in an orator would be a "natural speaking voice." His convictions were deep and sincere, he had an easy command of simple rhythms, and he was used to thinking and speaking in the language of the people. He was in no danger of falling into academic subtlety or erudition. So, like his greatest American predecessor in this field—Freneau (see pp. 72–77)—he spoke again and again and always with telling effect.

As a good journalist and rhetorician he made his issues plain and simple — much simpler in fact than they really were, avoiding embarrassing qualifications. He appealed to the Northerners as a people unanimously opposed to human bondage and not as a half-hearted and divided group. In a generation when the sense of statehood was infinitely stronger than it is now he assumed a high level of altruism in Massachusetts, while he stimulated a sense of state resentment against Virginia or South Carolina. With the memories of the Revolution refreshed by a series of recent semicentennials, he employed the conventional language of protest against tyranny; the antislavery verses resound with vituperative allusions to chains, fetters, yokes, rods, manacles, and gyves, with Scriptural idiom and with scorn for the repudiation of Revolutionary principles of freedom. In the opening lines of " The Crisis " he was skillfully suggestive by his paraphrase of the missionary hymn " From Greenland's Icy Mountains," and in the " Letter from a Missionary of the Methodist Episcopal Church, South, in Kansas to a Distinguished Politician " he turned to contempt the perversion of the Scriptures in defense of slavery.

> " Go it, old hoss ! " they cried, and cursed the niggers —
> Fulfilling thus the word of prophecy,
> " Cursed be Canaan."

All this was justifiable, though it frequently was anything but high art. At times, however, the heat of passion led Whittier to write lines for which there was little or no excuse. His disappointment at Webster's famous " Seventh of March " compromise speech in 1850 led him to the extreme of reproach which was felt by most of the North — an extreme from which he shared the common reaction of later years and for which he made the manly atonement of " The Lost Occasion," moved by "the consciousness of a common inheritance of frailty and weakness." The lowest level of his war verse is reached in the most familiar "Barbara Frietchie." This has all the attributes that are usually to be found in popular favorites. It is conventional in form, easily intelligible, a narrative of picturesque tableaux, and capped with an applied moral. The only charge that can be fairly brought against it is, however, a fundamental one — that it is essentially false to the facts. The middle third of the poem that has to do explicitly with Stonewall Jackson is partly libelous and partly ridiculous. Jackson was an honest and devoted man, but he is represented as coming through the town like a stock-melodrama villain, blushing with remorse at the challenge of Barbara and capping the climax with a burst of cheap and unsoldierly rhetoric. No doubt it expressed at the moment what the passions of war could lead even a gentle Quaker to believe; no doubt also it was good war journalism; but granting these concessions, it stands as a deplorable evidence of the depths to which noble talents can be degraded in the times that try men's souls.

"The Waiting," a poem of 1862, is in the loftier vein of one who does not reënforce himself through disparagement of his enemies. It is a lament of unfulfilled endeavor in behalf of an ideal cause. As a really great lyric should be, it is both personal and general in its application. It expresses the despondency of the enfeebled and aging poet that he could not join "the shining ones with plumes of snow" in the good fight; and in its reference to "the harder task of standing still" it alludes not only to his resignation at the moment but also to the patient policy which in former years had estranged the extremest abolitionists from him. It also must have been an immediate source of consolation to thousands who have been confronted by urgent duties they could not perform; while at the same time in a broader way it has expressed the faith of "Ulysses" and "Abt Vogler," of "In

Memoriam" and "Saul" and "Asolando," that "good but wished with God is done."

Like Freneau (see pp. 71–81), but to a more marked degree, Whittier was most popular at first for his journalistic, controversial poems, though his most permanent work has nothing to do with either noble or ignoble strife. He followed the example of Burns, who inspired his first literary passion, in writing simple lyrics and narratives of his own countryside. These included many of the legends of Boston, like "Cassandra Southwick"; of Hartford, like "Abraham Davenport"; or of his beloved district north of Boston, like "The Wreck of Rivermouth," "The Garrison of Cape Ann," and "Skipper Ireson's Ride." As a rule he was not inclined to tell stories without some clear moral implication, and all too often he expounded this implication, sermon-wise, at the end. Thus he tells with dignity and fine effect the story of the Indian specters of Cape Ann, who were finally driven away by the prayers of the devout garrison after repeated volleys from their musketry had failed. In eighty lines the tale is told; an added stanza calls attention to the fact that there is a moral in the ancient fiction; and two more in a sort of sub-postscript indulge in a final burst of poetical exegesis. "Skipper Ireson," the best of Whittier's ballads, is no less moralistic, but is done with more art, for the ethical point is developed within the account instead of being tacked on after it.

In poems such as "Hampton Beach," "The Lakeside," "The Last Walk in Autumn," and "At Eventide" Whittier pictures the nature surroundings of his long lifetime; and in a generous succession, from "Memories" of 1841 to "In School-Days," of nearly thirty years later, he takes his readers along the borderlands of autobiography. Preëminent among his recollections of persons and places is "Snow-Bound." The snowstorm, which Emerson celebrated as a thing in itself, Whittier adopted as the background for a winter idyl. The "Flemish pictures of old days" which he drew of his Haverhill homestead were annotated in great detail by the poet, but their virtue lies not so much in the fact that they are true to a given set of conditions, as that they are essentially true to the rural life of Whittier's New England — just as the pictures in "The Cotter's Saturday Night" are true to the Scotland of Burns, and the pictures of "The Deserted Village" to the landlord-ridden Ireland of Goldsmith. And to the attentive reader the contrasts between the peasant life of Great Britain and the nearest thing to it that can be found in America are abiding witnesses to the practical virtues of a democracy. In this simple idyl, written with "intimate knowledge and delight," Whittier combined truth and beauty as in no other of his poems.

For summarized criticism of Whittier's poetry there are few better passages than his own "Proem" to the collected poems of 1849 and the comment in Lowell's "Fable for Critics," of the preceding year. Whittier acknowledges the lack in his lines of "mystic beauty, dreamy grace" or of psychological analysis converted into poetry; Lowell confirms the judgment with

> Let his mind once get head in its favorite direction
> And the torrent of verse bursts the dams of reflection,
> While, borne with the rush of his metre along,
> The poet may chance to go right or go wrong,
> Content with the whirl and delirium of song.

Whittier lays his best gifts on the shrine of freedom with an avowal of his love for mankind and his hearty and vehement hatred of all forms of oppression, and Lowell properly qualifies the value of these gifts with the statement that the Quaker's fervor has sometimes dulled him to the distinction between "simple excitement and pure inspiration." Whittier deprecates the harshness and rigor of the rhythms which beat "Labor's hurried time, or Duty's rugged march," but Lowell says that at his best the reformer-poet has written unsurpassable lyrics. And both pronounce strictures on his rimes which have been conventionally repeated by most of the later critics who have commented on them at all.

Many of Whittier's apparently false rimes, however, — as the author of the " Biglow Papers " should have recognized — are perfect if uttered according to the prevailing pronunciation of his district. Lowell passes for a scrupulous dialect expert when he writes, " This heth my faithful shepherd ben," but Whittier is derided for allowing the same final verb to rime with " Of all sad words of tongue or pen," whereas the sole difference is that one recognized the pronunciation in his spelling and the other took it for granted. If Whittier had employed Lowell's method, in transcribing " Barbara Frietchie," for example, he would have written,

> Quick, as it fell, from the broken sta 'af
> Dame Barbara snatched the silken sca 'af,

and he would have concluded with

> Peace and odda and beauty drawr
> Reound thy symbol of light and lawr ;

> And evva the stahs above look deown
> On thy stahs below in Frederick teown !

For the *ou* sounds belong to Essex County, and all the others to Boston and even to hallowed Cambridge. False rimes Whittier wrote in abundance, but by no means all of the apparently bad ones should be condemned at first glance.

Until the publication of " Snow-Bound " in 1866 Whittier's verse, though widely circulated, had brought him in but little money return. For twenty years, he later recalled, he had been given the cold shoulder by editors and publishers ; but as the hottest prejudices began to wane they could no longer afford to neglect his manuscripts, for these had in them the leading characteristics of " fireside favorites," the only sort of poetry that is always certain of the sales to which no publisher is indifferent. In the first place, their form is simple ; common words and short sentences are cast in conventional rhythms with frequent rime. They are therefore easy to commit to memory. In content they are easy to understand, not given to subtleties of analysis or to philosphical abstractions. More often than not they are either narratives like the war ballads and the New England chronicles or strung on a narrative thread like " Snow-Bound." Almost always they contain vivid pictures ; mention of " Skipper Ireson " or " Telling the Bees " or " The Huskers " or " Maud Muller " recalls tableaux first and then the ideas connected with them. And finally they contain the applied moral which the immature or the unliterary mind dearly loves, the very feature which proves irksome to the bookish reader serving as an added attraction to the unsophisticated one. It is not difficult to adduce popular favorites which do not include all of these traits, but beyond doubt the great majority of poems that are beloved by the multitude contain most if not all of them. When, in addition to these features, poems are essentially and permanently true to life and to the best there is in life their vogue is likely to be lasting as well as widespread. People cherish them as they do the melodies to which some of them are fortunately set, or as they do certain bits from Beethoven, Mendelssohn, Chopin, and Schubert, which belong to the repertory of every pianola or talking machine. On the other hand, the intricate beauties of Browning and Wagner or the austerities of Milton and Brahms will always be " caviar to the general."

The last third of Whittier's life brought him the rewards he had earned and the serenity he deserved. He lived quietly at Amesbury under his own roof or with his cousins at near-by Danvers. He was on friendly terms with the eminent literary men and women of his day. A long protraction of ill-health from boyhood on had developed him into a fragile, gentle old man, a little shy and reticent and to all appearances quite without the fighting powers which he had displayed when there was need for them. If one chooses to recall Whittier from a single portrait, it should be from one taken in his middle rather than in his later life, for the earlier ones are far more rugged.

As the years passed they were marked by a succession of public tributes. At seventy the most famous of the annual "*Atlantic Monthly* Dinners" was arranged in his honor. At eighty his home state officially celebrated his birthday. The anniversaries that followed were recognized in the public schools of many states; and so with "honor, love, obedience, troops of friends" he came to the end in 1892.

BOOK LIST

Individual Author

JOHN GREENLEAF WHITTIER. Works. Riverside Edition. 7 vols. (I–IV, Poetical works; V–VII, Prose.) Standard Library Edition. 9 vols. (Includes content of the Riverside Edition plus the life by S. T. Pickard.) 1892. The best one-volume edition of the poems is the Cambridge Student's Edition. 1914. His works appeared in book form originally as follows: Legends of New England, 1831; Moll Pitcher, 1832; Justice and Expediency, 1833; Mogg Megone, 1836; Poems written between 1830 and 1838, 1837; Ballads, Anti-Slavery Poems, etc., 1838; Lays of my Home, 1843; The Stranger in Lowell, 1845; Supernaturalism in New England, 1847; Voices of Freedom, 1849; Old Portraits and Modern Sketches, 1850; Songs of Labor, 1850; The Chapel of the Hermits, 1853; Literary Recreations and Miscellanies, 1854; The Panorama, 1856; Home Ballads, 1860; In War Time, 1863; National Lyrics, 1865; Snow-Bound, 1866; The Tent on the Beach, 1867; Among the Hills, 1868; Miriam, 1870; The Pennsylvania Pilgrim, 1872; Hazel Blossoms, 1874; Centennial Hymn, 1876; The Vision of Echard, 1878; The King's Missive, 1881; The Bay of Seven Islands, 1883; Saint Gregory's Guest, 1886; At Sundown, 1892.

Bibliography

Cambridge History of American Literature, Vol. II, pp. 436–451.

Biography and Criticism

The standard life is by Samuel T. Pickard. 1894. 2 vols.

BURTON, RICHARD. John Greenleaf Whittier. 1901.
CARPENTER, G. R. John Greenleaf Whittier. 1903. (*A. M. L. Ser.*)
CLAFLIN, MRS. MARY B. Personal Recollections of John Greenleaf Whittier. 1893.
FIELDS, MRS. ANNIE. Authors and Friends. 1896.
FLOWER, B. O. Whittier, Prophet, Seer and Man. 1896.
HAWKINS, C. J. The Mind of Whittier. 1904.

HIGGINSON, T. W. Cheerful Yesterdays.

HIGGINSON, T. W. Contemporaries.

HIGGINSON, T. W. John Greenleaf Whittier. 1902. (*E. M. L. Ser.*)

KENNEDY, W. S. John Greenleaf Whittier, his Life, Genius and Writings. 1882.

LAWTON, W. C. Studies in the New England Poets. 1898.

LINTON, W. J. Life of John Greenleaf Whittier. 1903.

PAYNE, W. M. Cambridge History of American Literature, Vol. II, Bk. II, chap. xiii.

PICKARD, S. T. Whittier Land. 1904.

RICHARDSON, C. F. American Literature, Vol. II, chap. vi.

STEDMAN, E. C. Poets of America. 1885.

TAYLOR, BAYARD. Critical Essays and Literary Notes. 1880.

UNDERWOOD, F. H. John Greenleaf Whittier: a Biography. 1884.

WENDELL, BARRETT. Stelligeri and Other Essays. 1893.

WHITMAN, WALT. Specimen Days. April 16, 1881.

TOPICS AND PROBLEMS

Read the poems in Whittier the titles of which suggest local treatment of Essex County life and scenes. Compare these with similar poems in Burns.

Read such poems as " First-Day Thoughts," " Skipper Ireson's Ride," " The Garrison of Cape Ann," " The Waiting," " The Eternal Goodness," and " Our Master " for evidences of Whittier's religion.

Read Emerson's essay on " The New England Reformers," remembering that Whittier was one of these.

Compare the war poetry of Whittier and Freneau.

In Whittier's controversial poetry note the different levels of " Barbara Frietchie," " Expostulation," and " The Waiting," and cite other poems which may fairly be located in these three classes.

Read Whittier's ballads with the comments on page 261 concerning his inclination to expound. Compare and contrast Whittier's " Snow-Bound " with Burns's " Cotter's Saturday Night."

Apply the tests for popular fireside poetry to those poems of Whittier's which you regard as general favorites.

CHAPTER XVIII

HENRY WADSWORTH LONGFELLOW

It is a matter of common practice to mention Henry Wadsworth Longfellow (1807–1882) as a member of "the Cambridge group," with the suggestion that there was some such agreement in point of view as existed between the men who lived and wrote in Concord. Yet there was no such oneness of mind among Longfellow, Lowell, and Holmes as among Emerson and his younger associates. Between Longfellow and Lowell the real point of contact was their scholarship, and particularly their enthusiasm for the writings of Dante; between Lowell and Holmes there was neighborly regard but no real intimacy of feeling. The Cambridge men, to be sure, were different from the men of Concord. The fathers of all three were professional gentlemen of some distinction, all were college bred, ripened by residence abroad, and holders of professorships in Harvard College. All enjoyed and deserved social position as members of the " Brahmin caste," [1] all were frequenters of the celebrated Saturday Club, and all contributed to the early and lasting fame of the *Atlantic Monthly*. But as far as their deeper interests in life were concerned they went their several ways. Lowell was a representative first of New England and the North and later of the country as a whole; Holmes belonged far more to Boston than to the college town across the Charles; so that, of the three, Longfellow, the only one not born there, was most closely associated with Cambridge, less clearly allied with any other part of the world. In the literary vista, therefore, the local relationship should not loom too large. Longfellow should be

---

[1] See the first chapter of Holmes's " Elsie Venner " for a discussion of this New England aristocracy of birth and learning rather than of wealth.

considered as belonging to the same decades with Poe and Hawthorne; his greatest productive period was at its height when Poe was living, and was over before the death of Hawthorne, and his attitude toward life was similar to theirs in its sentimental fervor and in its artistic detachment. Lowell, in contrast, was a factor in the issues leading into and out of the Civil War, and Holmes's richest years bridged the '60's.

Longfellow was born in Portland, Maine, in 1807, the second of eight children. The matters of conventional record are that on his mother's side he was descended from John and Priscilla Alden, and that his father was a lawyer with a good practice and a modestly well-équipped library. Able tutoring fitted the boy to matriculate as a sophomore in Bowdoin, in the class with Hawthorne, who was three years older. For a coming man of letters his record as a student was exceptionally good. Instead of being unsettled by vague dreams, he was stirred by a very definite ambition for " future eminence in literature." His whole soul, he wrote to his father at the age of seventeen, burned most ardently for it, and every earthly thought centered in it. Then, just at the time when he was resigning himself to the law, in order not to be, like Goldsmith, " equally irreclaimable from poetry and poverty;" the trustees of Bowdoin, emulating the example of Harvard, established a professorship of modern languages, offered it to Longfellow, and set as a condition that he should prepare himself by study abroad. In the three years from 1826 to 1829 his mastering of the Romance languages was perhaps less important than his breathing the cultural atmosphere of the Old World. Life in America up to the nineteenth century had been a busy and self-centered experience. The chief consciousness of England and Europe had been a consciousness of other governments and of unsympathetic and conflicting loyalties ; and now was beginning to arise an awareness not only of how other peoples were ruled but also of how they lived and what they were thinking about. Longfellow had little to say of foreign unfriendliness which was still disturbing

Irving and Cooper and Bryant (see pp. 111–114). In preparing to teach foreign languages and literatures he yielded to the spell of their richly picturesque traditions; and his first work, "Outre-Mer" (1833), was an effort to expound these to his countrymen. This, too, Irving and Cooper had done, and from now on the refrain was to be taken up by most of the widely read American writers.[1]

As an impressionable young American he fell into the declining sentimentalism of the period and wrote characteristically to his mother: "I look forward to the distant day of our meeting until my heart swells into my throat and tears into my eyes. I cannot help thinking that it is a pardonable weakness." He was so absorbed by all he was seeing and learning that he wrote no verse, letting the days go by until he concluded with the overwhelming seriousness of twenty-two that his poetic career was finished. As a matter of fact he was just complementing his native American feeling with a sense of the glamour of Old World civilization, and was on the way toward combining the two as poet and professor. Returning to his old college he taught there until in 1836 he was invited to succeed Professor George Ticknor at Harvard, again with the condition — implied if not imposed — that he go abroad for study. On his second sojourn he extended his knowledge to the Germanic languages, mastering them as thoroughly as he had French, Spanish, and Italian. In the end he is said to have had a fluent speaking control of eight tongues, with the power to "get along in" six more, and to read yet another six. Until 1854 he was engaged in his duties at Harvard, giving no little instruction, engaging

---

[1] A short list of the chief titles will include Longfellow's "Hyperion" (1839), Willis's "Loiterings of Travel" (1840), Taylor's "Views Afoot" (1846), Curtis's "Nile Notes of a Howadji" (1851), Mrs. Stowe's "Sunny Memories of Foreign Lands" (1854), Emerson's "English Traits" (1856), Bryant's "Letters from Spain and Other Countries" (1859), Norton's "Notes of Travel and Study in Italy" (1859), Hawthorne's "Our Old Home" (1863), Howells's "Venetian Life" (1866), Mark Twain's "Innocents Abroad" (1869), and so on down to and beyond Holmes's "Our Hundred Days in Europe" (1887).

all his assistants, and personally supervising their teaching. It
was an irksome routine against which he began to rebel many
years before he shook himself free. "It is too much to do for
one's daily bread, when one can live on so little," he wrote in
1839. "I must learn to give up superfluous things and devote
myself wholly to literature." And in the same year he referred in another letter to "poetic dreams shaded by French
irregular verbs."

If the distractions of his professorship had actually prevented
all writing, he would doubtless not have held it eighteen years;
but in spite of handicaps his output was fairly steady throughout, and his most richly productive period — 1847–1863 —
half overlapped his Harvard service. Aside from his fruitful
activities in formulating books and methods for language study,
and aside from his unimpressive prose volumes "Outre-Mer,"
"Hyperion," and "Kavanagh," his poetry was abundant and in
a way progressive. Most memorable among the early types was
a sizeable group to which he referred in his diary and letters
as "psalms." Of these, of course, "A Psalm of Life" is best
known. Like all the others of its sort, it has the traits that
are sure to endear it to the multitude. It is in a conventional
ballad meter, alternating lines of four and three stresses with alternating rimes, it is easy to understand, it is constructed around
one vivid picture, and it conveys a wholesome moral lesson.
It is a general counsel to industry and fortitude. Its message
is formulated in a closing stanza of "The Light of Stars,"

> And thou, too, whosoe'er thou art,
>   That readest this brief psalm,
> As one by one thy hopes depart,
>   Be resolute and calm,

and its "act in the living present" is echoed in the daily
achievement of the village blacksmith.

Longfellow's labors as a translator began early and continued
throughout his career, but it is interesting to see that in the

earlier efforts a sober ethical note prevails, whereas many of
the later translations are marked by simple charm and some
by sheer frivolity. "The Coplas de Don Jorge Manrique " is
a transparently veiled homily on the vanity of human wishes ;
others from the Spanish are on " The Good Shepherd " and
" The Image of God " and from Dante on " The Celestial
Pilot " and " The Terrestrial Paradise "; there is an Anglo-
Saxon passage on " The Grave " and a fragment from a
German ballad in which a ribald discussion of " The Happiest
Land " is interrupted by the landlord's daughter who points
to heaven and says :

> ... " Ye may no more contend, —
> There lies the happiest land ! "

In January, 1840, the poet wrote to his friend George Greene :

I have broken ground in a new field ; namely, ballads ; beginning
with the " Wreck of the Schooner Hesperus " on the reef of Norman's
Woe. . . . I think I shall write more. The *national ballad* is a virgin
soil here in New England ; and there are great materials. Besides,
I have a great notion of working on the *people's* feelings.

In 1842, consequently, there appeared his " Ballads and Other
Poems." Longfellow had first intended calling the volume "The
Skeleton in Armor," but the collection grew in number until
this poem was overbalanced by the weight of the whole, and
until — which is more significant — the native ballads were
crowded by the introduction of poems from the German and
Swedish and Danish. The change of plan, though slight, was
indicative of what was taking place in Longfellow's development.
He inclined, in the fashion of his day, to foster American subject matter, but he was full of the spirit and content of European literature which was unknown to his countrymen. Some
years were to pass before he could hold his gaze away from
" outre-mer." Another letter to George Greene shows how he
was vacillating at this time.

A national literature is the expression of national character and thought; and as our character and modes of thought do not differ essentially from those of England, our literature cannot. Vast fields, lakes and prairies cannot make great poets. They are but the scenery of the play, and have much less to do with the poetic character than has been imagined. . . . I do not think a "Poets' Convention" would help the matter. In fact the matter needs no helping.

"Excelsior" is a complete poetic fulfillment of this idea. There is nothing essentially American in the aspiration of youth. Longfellow therefore "staged" the ballad in the Alps, partly because the Alps doubtless first occurred to mind and partly because in America no mountain heights were topped by the symbolic monastery from which the traveler could be found still aspiring in death. Again, lyrics like "The Day is Done," "The Old Clock on the Stairs," and "The Arrow and the Song" belong to no time or place but are meditative moments in the life of any thoughtful man. And finally, "The Bridge" is a representative combination of native and foreign material. The bridge with wooden piers used to stand exactly as described over the Charles River between Boston and Cambridge. It was so near the ocean that the tides swept back and forth under it as they do not under any bridge in London or Paris or on the German Rhine. Yet in the second stanza the likeness of the moonlight to "a golden goblet falling and sinking into the sea" is evidently an allusion to a picture in Schiller's "König in Thule," a literary allusion but not a false one, for the moonlight might well look the same on the tide-tossed Charles as on the streaming Rhine. In his "Seaweed" Longfellow seems to have been half explaining and half defending such poetic processes:

> So when storms of wild emotion
> Strike the ocean
> Of the poet's soul, erelong
> From each cave and rocky fastness,
> In its vastness,
> Floats some fragment of a song.

The one point to accept with caution from all Longfellow's poems of self-analysis is the oft-recurring reference to heroic strife. Whatever heroism he felt or displayed "in the world's broad field of battle" was more quietly enduring than spectacular. The real Longfellow learned "to labor and to wait"; if wild emotion ever struck the ocean of his soul he possessed himself for the tumult to subside. The finest of all his lyrics, "Victor and Vanquished," cannot be confirmed from the visible evidences of his career. The "Poems on Slavery," for example, attest only to the passive courage of his convictions. In 1842 it was no small matter to come out clearly in public opposition to human bondage (see p. 257). Longfellow did not hesitate to risk his growing popularity by issuing this little volume. He was, and he continued to be, the devoted friend of Charles Sumner. Yet his antislavery heroism began and ended with these seven poems, and their value lay more in the bare fact that he had written them than in any ethical or emotional appeal.

The period from 1847 to 1863 was, all things considered, quite the most fruitful for Longfellow; and this contained no five titles to rival "Evangeline" (1847), "The Song of Hiawatha" (1855), "The Courtship of Miles Standish" (1858), "The New England Tragedy" (first form, 1860), and "Tales of a Wayside Inn" (1863). Thus, although he by no means abandoned Europe and the thoughts of Europe, he came at last and altogether naturally to the development of American tradition and the American scene. The immediate success of "Evangeline" (for five thousand copies were sold within two months) is easy to understand. The material was fresh and the story was lovely. Longfellow's reading-public, accustomed to certain charms and qualities in his work, found these no less attractively displayed in the long story than in his brief lyrics. The pastoral scene at the start, the dramatic episode of the separation, the long vista of American scenes presented in Evangeline's vain search, and the final rounding out of the story plot, all belong to a "good seller"; and as it happened there was in America in 1847 no widely popular novelist. The field belonged to the author of " Evangeline " even more completely then a half century earlier it had belonged to the author of " Marmion," on the other side of the sea.

In the journal of 1849 appears the entry, " And now I hope to try a loftier strain, the sublimer Song whose broken melodies have for so many years breathed through my soul in the better hours of life." This was a reference to " The Golden Legend," which appeared in 1851, and which was in the end to become part of " Christus," completed not until 1872. In a sense this was the most ambitious and least effective of all his undertakings. It was too scholastic for the public; it was not a fit avenue to the feelings of " the *people* " whom in 1840 he had resolved to stir. By 1854 Longfellow entered in the journal, " I have at length hit upon a plan for a poem on the American Indians, which seems to me the right one and the only." This was to do with the traditions of the red man what Malory had done with the Arthurian story and what Tennyson was soon to be reweaving into the " Idylls of the King." Schoolcraft's Indian researches put the material into his hands, and the Finnish epic " Kalevala " supplied the suggestion for the appropriate measure. It appeared in 1855 and was demanded by the public in repeated printings.

" Hiawatha " has a double assurance of wide and lasting fame in the fact that it appeals to young and old in different ways. It appeals to children because it is made up of a succession of picturesque stories of action. Their lack of plots is no defect to the youthful reader — nothing could be more plotless than the various parts of " Gulliver's Travels " — and on the other hand few children detect or care for the scheme underlying them as a whole. They are as vivid and circumstantial as " Gulliver " or as " Pilgrim's Progress." Furthermore they deal with human types which belong to all romantic legend : Hiawatha, the hero ; Minnehaha, the heroine ; Chibiabos, the sweet singer, or artist ; Kwasind, the strong man, or primitive force; Pau-Puk-Keewis, the mischief-maker, or the comic spirit, — any child will recognize them for example in Robin Hood, Maid Marian, Allan-a-Dale, Will Scarlet, and Friar Tuck. Again, these human types are extended over into the animal world and even to the forces of nature, the latter, by the way, supplying frequently the place of the indispensable villain or obstacle between the hero and the achievement of his purposes.

Unhappily the average adult who has read it in early life assumes that he has advanced beyond " Hiawatha," that he can put it away with other childish things, not realizing how much more than meets the eye resides within its lines. Moreover, some grown-ups who do attempt a second reading are dissatisfied because their minds have stopped between childhood and maturity, stunted by too heavy a diet on obvious fiction and the daily newspapers. For the later reading of " Hiawatha " demands the kind of intellectual maturity that can cope with " Paradise Lost " or " Sartor Resartus " or " In Memoriam " or the classics which are quite beyond the child. The genuinely mature reader appreciates that the legends and the ballads of a people are never limited to external significance and that, whoever may happen to be the hero, it is the people who are represented through him. So the epic note emerges for him who can hear it. A peace is declared among the warring tribes; Hiawatha is sent by Mudjekeewis back to live and toil among his people; he is commended by Mondamin because he prays " For advantage of the nations "; he fights the pestilence to save the people; he divides his trophies of battle with them; and he departs when the advent of the white man marks the doom of the Indian. And so the ordering of the parts is ethnic, tracing the Indian chronicle through the stages that all peoples have traversed, from the nomad life of hunting and fishing to primitive agriculture and community life; thus come song and festival, a common religion and a common fund of legend, and finally, in the tragic life of this people, come the decline of strength, in the death of Kwasind, the passing of song with Chibiabos, and the departure of national heroism as Hiawatha is lost to view,

> In the glory of the sunset,
> In the purple mists of evening.

It is no mean achievement to write a children's classic, but the enduring fact about " Hiawatha " is that it is a genuine epic as well.

No other poem of Longfellow's is so well adjusted in form and content. The fact of first importance is not that Longfellow derived the measure from a Finnish epic but that the primitive epic form is perfect because it is the natural, unstudied way of telling a primitive story. The forms of literature that go back nearest to the people in their origins are simple in rhythm and built up of parallel repetitions. This marks a distinction between the epics about nations written in a later age, such as the Iliad and the Æneid and the works of Milton, and the epics of early and unknown authorship, such as the " Nibelungenlied " and " Beowulf." It was Longfellow's gift to combine the old material with a fittingly primitive measure, joining as only poet and scholar could

> . . . legends and traditions
> With the odors of the forest,
> With the dew and damp of meadows,
> With the curling smoke of wigwams,
> With the rushing of great rivers,
> With their frequent repetitions,
> And their wild reverberations,
> As of thunder in the mountains.

With " The Courtship of Miles Standish " Longfellow returned to New England and told his first long story of his own district and of his own immediate people. Both " Evangeline " and " Hiawatha " were narratives that ended with themselves. The glory of the Acadians and of the Indians was departed. But "Miles Standish" was like the "New England Tragedies" in dealing with a people who were very much alive. For the early Puritan, Longfellow felt a thorough and abiding respect which was not untinged with humor. For his self-righteousness, his stridency, and his arid lack of feeling for beauty the poet showed an amused contempt, but for the essential qualities of rectitude and abiding persistence he was quite ready to acknowledge his admiration. There is a pleasant personal application in this story which he who runs is likely to overlook. Miles Standish was a worthy man, says Longfellow ; he was stalwart, vigorous, practical, and when put to the test he was magnanimous, too. But he was sadly one-sided. It was not enough to be like his own howitzer,

> Steady, straightforward, and strong, with irresistible logic,
> Orthodox, flashing conviction right into the hearts of the heathen.

He was of the sort who banished the birds of Killingworth with costly consequence. The worthier character was John Alden — "my ancestor" — who was like the Preceptor of Killingworth in his feeling for beauty in nature and in poetry and in song. "Miles Standish" is his most amiable picture of the Puritans. In "The New England Tragedies" Governor Endicott's death is a poetic and divine retribution for his persecution of the Quakers, and Giles Corey's sacrifice to the witchcraft mania is a horrid indictment of bigotry unbridled.

From 1863 on Longfellow continued in the various paths which he had already marked out, but his work in the main was in sustained narrative and in translation. His rendering of Dante is the preëminent piece of American translation, at once more poetic and more scholarly than Bryant's "Iliad" or Bayard Taylor's "Faust." It was a labor of love, extending over many years, the fruit of his teaching as well as of his study, and in its final form the product of nightly counsels with his learned neighbors, Charles Eliot Norton and James Russell Lowell. Age, fame, and the affectionate respect of the choicest friends saw him broaden and deepen in his philosophy of life. Little psalms and ballads no longer expressed him. Life had become a great outreaching drama at which he hinted in his cyclic " Christus : a Mystery." His last lyrics opened vistas instead of supplying formulas, and quite appropriately he left behind as an uncompleted fragment his dramatic poem on the greatest of dreamers and workers, Michael Angelo.

There is no possibility of debate as to Longfellow's immense popularity. The evidence of the number of editions in English and in translation, the number of works in criticism, the number of titles in the British Museum catalogue, the number of poems included in scores of " Household " and " Fireside " collections, and the confidence with which booksellers stock up in anticipation of continued sales,[1] tells the story. But these facts in themselves do not establish Longfellow's claim to immortality, for there is no necessary connection between such popularity and greatness. There was little evidence in him of the genius which takes no thought for the things of the morrow. Until after the height of his career he never wrote in disregard of the public. " The fact is," he sent word to his father, when he was but seventeen, " I most eagerly aspire after future eminence in literature." And even earlier he had laid down his program when he wrote, " I am much better pleased with those pieces which touch the feelings and improve the heart, than with those which excite the imagination only." He had the good sense and the honesty not to pretend to inspiration. On the contrary he was continually projecting poems and continually sitting down, not to write what he had thought but to think what he should write. He was an omnivorous but acquiescent reader, and what his reading yielded him was literary stuff rather than vital ideas. He accepted and reflected the ways of his own time and did not modify them in any slightest degree. He was never iconoclastic, rarely even fresh.

[1] See pages 2-7 in T. W. Higginson's " Longfellow," *American Men of Letters Series.*

He had something of Pope's gift for well-rounded utterances on life, something of Scott's ability to tell a good story well, and withal his own benevolent serenity.

This was not a supreme endowment, but it was a very large one, and he developed it to a lofty degree. There will always be a case for Longfellow in the hands of those who value the inspirer of the many above the inspirer of the wise. There are ten who read Longfellow to every one who reads Whitman or Emerson. His wholesomeness, his lucidity, his comfortable sanity, his very lack of intense emotion, endear him to those who wish to be entertained with a story or soothed and reassured by a gentle lyric. Edmund Clarence Stedman wrote finely of him: "His song was a household service, the ritual of our feastings and mournings; and often it rehearsed for us the tales of many lands, or, best of all, the legends of our own. I see him, a silver-haired minstrel, touching melodious keys, playing and singing in the twilight, within sound of the rote of the sea. There he lingers late; the curfew bell has tolled and the darkness closes round, till at last that tender voice is silent, and he softly moves unto his rest."

BOOK LIST

Individual Author

HENRY WADSWORTH LONGFELLOW. Works. Riverside Edition. 1886. 11 vols. Poetry, Vols. I–VI, IX–XI. Prose, Vols. VII, VIII. Standard Library Edition. 14 vols. (Includes content of Riverside Edition plus the life by Samuel Longfellow.) The best single volume is the Cambridge Edition. His work appeared in book form originally as follows: Miscellaneous Poems from the *United States Literary Gazette* (with others), 1826; Coplas de Manrique, 1833; Outre-Mer, Vol. I, 1833, Vol. II, 1834; Hyperion, 1839; Voices of the Night, 1839; Ballads and Other Poems, 1842; Poems on Slavery, 1842; The Spanish Student, 1843; Poems, 1845; The Belfry of Bruges and Other Poems, 1846; Evangeline, 1847; Kavanagh, 1849; The Seaside and the Fireside, 1850; The Golden Legend, 1851; Hiawatha, 1855; Prose Works, 1857; The Courtship of Miles Standish, 1858; The New England Tragedy, 1860; Tales of a Wayside Inn, 1863; Flower-de-Luce, 1867; Dante's

Divina Commedia (translated), 1867; The New England Tragedies, 1868; The Divine Tragedy, 1871; Three Books of Song, 1872; Aftermath, 1873; The Masque of Pandora, 1875; Kéramos, 1878; Ultima Thule, 1880; In the Harbor, 1882; Michael Angelo, 1883.

Bibliography

A bibliography of first editions compiled by Luther S. Livingston. Privately printed 1908. See also Cambridge History of American Literature, Vol. II, pp. 425–436.

Biography and Criticism

The standard life is by Samuel Longfellow. 3 vols. These first appeared as The Life, 1886 (2 vols), and Final Memorials, 1887 (1 vol).

AUSTIN, G. L. Longfellow: his Life, his Works, his Friendships. 1883.

CARPENTER, G. R. Henry Wadsworth Longfellow. 1901.

DAVIDSON, THOMAS. H. W. Longfellow. 1882.

FIELDS, MRS. ANNIE. Authors and Friends. 1896.

GANNETT, W. C. Studies in Longfellow, etc. 1898. (*Riv. Lit. Ser., No. 12.*)

HENLEY, W. E. Views and Reviews. 1890.

HIGGINSON, T. W. Henry Wadsworth Longfellow. 1902.

HOWELLS, W. D. My Literary Friends and Acquaintances. 1900.

HOWELLS, W. D. The Art of Longfellow. *North American Review*, March, 1907.

KENNEDY, W. S. Henry Wadsworth Longfellow. 1882.

LAWTON, W. C. A Study of the New England Poets. 1898.

LOWELL, J. R. A Fable for Critics, passim. 1848.

NORTON, C. E. H. W. Longfellow: a Sketch. 1907.

PERRY, BLISS. Park Street Papers, The Centenary of Longfellow. 1908.

POE, E. A. In Literati: Mr. Longfellow and Other Plagiarists; Mr. Longfellow, Mr. Willis, and the Drama; Longfellow's Ballads.

RICHARDSON, C. F. American Literature, Vol. II, chap. iii.

ROBERTSON, E. S. Life of Henry Wadsworth Longfellow. 1887.

ROSSETTI, W. M. Lives of Famous Poets. 1878.

STEDMAN, E. C. Poets of America. 1885.

TRENT, W. P. Longfellow and Other Essays. 1910. Cambridge History of American Literature, Vol. II, Bk. II, chap. xii.

UNDERWOOD, F. H. Henry Wadsworth Longfellow: a Biographical Sketch. 1882.

WINTER, WILLIAM. Old Friends. 1909.

TOPICS AND PROBLEMS

Read fifty pages at random from "Outre-Mer." Compare them in tone and style with a passage of equal length from the essays on English life in "The Sketch Book" or from "Innocents Abroad" or from Howells's "London Films."

Apply the tests for popular fireside poetry referred to on pages 263 and 270 to the poems of Longfellow which you regard as general favorites.

Read from three to six of Longfellow's ballads and compare them with a similar number by Tennyson or Dante Gabriel Rossetti or Whittier.

What was there in Longfellow's education and profession to lead him to the contention in 1840 that there was no difference in the characters and modes of thought of Englishmen and Americans?

See Whitcomb's " Chronological Outlines of American Literature " for the years 1845 to 1850 for the absence of any strikingly popular fiction in the period when " Evangeline " was published.

Read " Hiawatha " for the broad view of ethnic life which naturally escapes the attention of the child reader. Compare in general the measures of " Hiawatha " and of " Beowulf " (in the original or in metrical translation).

Note Longfellow's characterizations of the Puritans in the poems mentioned on page 277 and compare these with Hawthorne's.

Read " The Prelude," " The Day is Done," " Seaweed," and " Birds of Passage " for Longfellow's comments on the poet and the poetic art.

CHAPTER XIX

JAMES RUSSELL LOWELL

James Russell Lowell (1819–1891) was born in Cambridge, the youngest of six children. His father, the Reverend Charles Lowell, a Harvard graduate, was pastor of the West Church in Boston, three miles away. Elmwood was an ample New England mansion with the literary atmosphere indoors that is generated by the presence of good books and good talk. The boy was one of a few day scholars at an excellent boarding school in town, from which he entered college in the class of 1838. Like many another man of later distinction in letters, he was more industrious than regular as a student, wasting little time in fact, but often neglecting his assigned work and sometimes lapsing into mild disorder to the extent of falling under college discipline. Toward the end of senior year he was actually " rusticated " for a combination of petty offenses. Under this form of punishment the boy, who was for a time suspended from college, was assigned to a clergyman in some country town and required to keep up in his studies until his reinstatement. It happened that Lowell was sent to Concord, and that here (while in charge of a clergyman with the ominous name of Barzillai Frost) he was fretting over the class poem, in which he commented with youthful cynicism on Carlyle, Emerson, the abolitionists, and the champions of total abstinence and of woman's rights. It was an outburst on which he looked back with quiet amusement in later years :

> Behold the baby arrows of that wit
>> Wherewith I dared assail the woundless Truth!
> Love hath refilled the quiver, and with it
>> The man shall win atonement for the youth.

And the proof that the boyish gibes were hardly more than a result of the impatience at his ungrateful weeks in Concord is contained in his record of the inspiration which he owed in student days to Emerson the lecturer (see p. 211).

In the first years out of college, from which he graduated in 1838, he passed through the oft-trod vale of troubled indecision as to what he should do with his life. He rejected at once his father's profession of preaching and abandoned thoughts of the law after he had earned his LL.B. degree in 1840. And then, following a brief and frustrated romance, he entered upon an acquaintance which culminated in his marriage to Maria White and resulted in his becoming a soberer and a wiser man. She was already deeply interested in the social movements toward which his mind was maturing. His devotion to her took permanent form in his first volumes of poems, " A Year's Life " (1841) and " Poems '" (1843), and her influence on him is shown in his zeal for the very reforms which he had derided in his class poem three years earlier. He founded a new magazine, *The Pioneer*, which lived for three months in 1843 ; he contributed copiously to *The Boston Miscellany*, *Graham's Magazine*, and *Arcturus*; and, what was much more momentous, he threw in his lot with the abolitionists by becoming a regular contributor to *The Pennsylvania Freeman*. In the meanwhile, also, in addition to his purely poetic work and to his reform enthusiasm, he took his first step toward scholastic achievement with his " Conversations on Some of the Old Poets," which appeared in a volume of 1844. From now to the end of his life Lowell continued to distribute his energies among the fields of poetry, civics, and scholarship.

In 1845, 1846, and 1847 he wrote abundantly, widening his relations with the magazines of the day and apparently finding no trouble in marketing his wares. One piece of verse is preëminent in this period for both immediate and lasting appeal — " The Present Crisis." It was Lowell's way of protesting at the national policy in the war with Mexico and, in its contrast with Thoreau's method (see p. 224), throws light on the reformer's later strictures upon the recluse. It was repeated on every hand during the next twenty years and was given special emphasis through its frequent use by such orators as Wendell Phillips and Charles Sumner. It was in 1848, however, that he came to the fullness of his powers, contributing some forty articles to four Boston periodicals and publishing four books "Poems (Second Series)," "A Fable for Critics," "The Biglow Papers," and "The Vision of Sir Launfal." He was only ten years out of college, and at that was only twenty-nine years old, but he showed secure taste, confident judgment, and a seasoned ease of humor which belong to middle life. In the first and last, the more literary volumes, there is perhaps more evidence of youth. It appears in the effusive grief on the loss of his little daughter, and in "Sir Launfal" Lowell seems to be working too clearly after the somewhat confused formula laid down in the introduction to *The Pioneer*. Americans were to attempt a natural rather than a national literature. They were to remember that "new occasions teach new duties." "To be the exponent of a young spirit which shall aim at power through gentleness . . . and in which freedom shall be attempered to love by a reverence for all beauty wherever it may exist, is our humble hope." So in order not to be too aggressively national, he derived a theme from the literature of chivalry and adorned it with a democratic, nineteenth-century moral.

"A Fable for Critics" is less consciously ambitious and more mature. Just how remarkable a piece of discrimination it was can be seen from a comparison of the writers criticized in it with those in Poe's "Literati" of two years earlier. Lowell's subjects are familiar to the modern general reader; he omitted no man of permanent reputation and included almost no one who has been forgotten. Poe's selections, on the other hand, are quaintly unfamiliar as a whole to all but the professed student of literary history. His judgments on them are mostly sound, but his judgment in choosing them for treatment is open to one of two criticisms: either that he could not recognize permanent values or that, for personal and editorial reasons, he preferred to ignore them. In the "Fable" Lowell for the first time put to public use his ready command of impromptu verse. His pen was a little erratic, but when it would work at all, it was likely to work with happy fluency. The jaunty treatment of his contemporaries was quite literally a series of running comments, trotting along in genial anapæstic gait, stumbling sometimes on a pun, scampering with light foot across extended metaphors, and taking the barriers of double and triple rime without a sign of exertion. In point of method the "Fable" was a single exercise in writing the journalistic verse of which Lowell proved himself master in the two series of "Biglow Papers" (1846–1848 and 1862–1866). It was exactly deserving of Holmes's friendly comment, "I think it is capital — crammed full and rammed down hard — powder (lots of it) — shot — slugs — very little wadding, and that is guncotton — all crowded into a rusty-looking sort of a blunderbuss barrel, as it were — capped with a percussion preface — and cocked with a title-page as apropos as a wink to a joke." Different as it is from "The Literati" in scale, tone, individual subjects, and method of circulation, the two deserve mention together as antidotes both to Anglomania and to wholesale praise of everything American.

With "The Biglow Papers" Lowell returned to the attack which he had begun in "The Present Crisis." He wrote in 1860:

I believed our war with Mexico (though we had as just ground for it as a strong nation ever has against a weak one) to be essentially a war of false pretences, and that it would result in widening the boundaries and so prolonging the life of slavery. . . . Against these and many other things I thought all honest men should protest. I was born and bred in the country, and the dialect was homely to me. I tried my first "Biglow Paper" and found that it had a great run. So I wrote the others from time to time in the year which followed, always very rapidly, and sometimes (as with "What Mr. Robinson Thinks") at one sitting.

He wrote the nine numbers of the series not only in the dialect of the countryside but from the viewpoint of a forthright, hard-headed, Puritan-tinged Yankee; and he put them out as the compositions of Hosea Biglow under the encouragement of Parson Wilbur, without the use of his own name. He was surprised by the cordial reception of the volume, fifteen hundred copies of which were sold in the first week. If he had put on the cap and bells to play fool to the public, he said, it was less to make the people laugh than to win a hearing for certain serious things which he had deeply at heart. "The Biglow Papers" were undoubtedly Lowell's great popular success. They carried the fight into the enemies' camp in the abolition struggle, they were resumed with new success with the outbreak of the Civil War, and they widened the reading public for his more sober political prose and for his more elevated verse.

However, Lowell was not satisfied to be only a fighter. In a letter of January, 1850, he wrote to a friend:

My poems hitherto have been a true record of my life, and I mean that they shall continue to be. . . . I begin to feel that I must enter on a new year of my apprenticeship. My poems thus far have had a regular and natural sequence. First, Love and the mere happiness of existence beginning to be conscious of itself, then Freedom — both being the sides which Beauty presented to me — and now I am going to try more *wholly* after Beauty herself. . . . I have preached sermons enow, and now I am going to come down out of the pulpit and *go about among my parish.* . . . I find that Reform cannot take up the whole of me, and I am quite sure that eyes were given us to look about us with sometimes, and not to be always looking forward. . . . I am tired of controversy.

Out of such a mood as this came the natural decision to make his first and long-deferred trip to Europe, a sojourn of fifteen months in 1851–1852 with his wife and children. His wide reading of foreign literatures gave the keys to an understanding of the peoples among whom he traveled, and especially to an understanding of Roman culture. His comments from Rome furnish an interesting contrast with Emerson's ("Written at Rome," 1833). The reaction of the Concord philosopher had been wholly personal. Lowell's was wholly national.

Surely the American (and I feel myself more intensely American every day) is last of all at home among ruins — but he is at home in Rome. . . . Our art, our literature, are, as theirs, in some sort exotics; but our genius for politics, for law, and, above all, for colonization, our instinct for aggrandizement and for trade, are all Roman. I believe we are laying the basis of a more enduring power and prosperity, and that we shall not pass away until we have stamped ourselves upon the whole western hemisphere.

On his return to America he plunged eagerly into writing, but the springs of utterance were soon sealed by the death of his wife. Following on the losses of his mother and two of his children this was the fourth and most crushing bereavement within a very few years. His recovery of working powers was aided by the distraction that came from an invitation to deliver the distinguished Lowell Lecture Series in Boston in the winter of 1854–1855. These were to be twelve in number, on poetry in general and English poetry in particular. The task appealed to him as combining the beauty and truth to which he inclined to turn after his years of conflict. He threw himself wholeheartedly into the preparation and delivery of the lectures and succeeded admirably with his hearers; but the greater result was an indirect one. While they were in progress Longfellow offered his resignation of the Smith Professorship "of the French and Spanish Languages and Literatures . . . and of Belles Lettres in Harvard College," a post he had filled since 1836. Seven candidates of no mean ability presented themselves for the vacant position, but the appointment was offered to Lowell, who had not applied for it, in preference to them all. He spent another year abroad before undertaking the work in the autumn of 1856, and held the position actively until 1877 and as emeritus professor until his death in 1891.

In this work he was a scholar and a critic rather than a teacher. He gave almost no elementary instruction in the languages, and his methods with his classes were casual to the neglect of the usual college traditions. What he did for his students was to share with them his own broad experience of life and letters and to show them how the study of foreign literatures was one with the study of history and philosophy.

Lowell's course of life, however, could never be restricted to any single channel. If he had found in 1850 that reform could not take up the whole of him, he now discovered that scholarship was not all-absorbing. As early as 1853 the question of establishing a new Boston magazine had been in the air. When its chief promoter, Francis H. Underwood,[1] had made certain of its start, Lowell was secured as first editor and carried it through the most critical period, until in 1861 it passed into the publishing hands of Ticknor and Fields and under the editorship of the junior member of that firm, James T. Fields. In the editorial office, as at Cambridge, Lowell was relieved from the heaviest humdrum labor (especially of correspondence) and was enabled to give his best energies to creative planning, yet it is interesting to see how effective were some of the detail criticisms accepted by poets like Emerson and Whittier and how vigilant he was in his reading of manuscripts and proof sheets. Throughout it all he kept up a spring-flow of boyish jollity, no different in spirit from that in his letters of college days.

An unpremeditated bit in one of his letters shows how the mind of professor and literary editor reverted to the excitement of politics on the eve of the war. It is in a fragment of burlesque on the type of love story submitted to the *Atlantic*: "Meanwhile the elder of the two, a stern-featured man of some forty winters, played with the hilt of his dagger, half drawing and then sheathing again the Damascus blade *thin as*

[1] See Bliss Perry's "Park Street Papers," "The Editor who Never was Editor," pp. 205–277.

the eloquence of Everett and elastic as the conscience of Cass." From 1858 to 1866 he printed some sixteen vigorous and substantial political articles, besides many shorter notes and reviews, and during the latter four years resumed the "Biglow Papers," repeating and building upon his original success. The aggressive fighting spirit which he carried into the discussion of definite men and measures did not blind him to the permanent values of the matters in dispute. The consequence was that his political writings were limited to the Civil War only in the facts he cited, and that they apply to any war in the principles to which he appealed. There is no better illustration than " Mason and Slidell : a Yankee Idyll." In this the Concord Bridge and Bunker Hill Monument bring the spirit of the Revolution to the discussion of a Civil War issue, and between them they utter almost all the basic contentions of the World War which broke out fifty years later. They anticipate the vital things that have recently been said for and against military preparedness, international jealousies, the changes made necessary in international law by the progress of invention, the appeals to national hatred and to a tribal or national God, the viciousness of an indeterminate peace, and the essential values of democracy.

From this ordeal by battle Lowell seems to have risen into a broader and nobler serenity. He balanced the prose essay on " The Rebellion : its Cause and Consequences " with the Harvard " Commemoration Ode "; the next prose volumes, " Among my Books " (1870 and 1876) and " My Study Windows " (1871), with the odes on " Agassiz " (1874) and " The Concord Centennial " (1875) and the " Three Memorial Poems " of 1877. In all the poems he looked to the past, the struggle being over, for some evidences of strength and beauty in American life and for some assurances for its future; and in the literary essays he looked beyond nationalism to the permanent and universal values in literature. His political writings had appeared mainly in the *North American Review,* which he had edited (1864–1872) in coöperation with Charles Eliot Norton; and at this point younger admirers called him into public appearances as presiding officer, as committee chairman, as delegate to a Republican national convention, and as presidential elector. It even took some insistence to carry through his refusal to run for Congress. Finally, in 1877 he entered as foreign minister on eight years of the highest service to his country, the first two and a half at Madrid and the remainder at London. Few men in America could have equaled him in his qualifications for the Spanish mission. He had taught the language and the literature and was especially well-versed in the drama, and temperamentally there was much in him which responded to the national character. He wrote to Mr. Putnam, "I like the Spaniards very well as far as I know them, and have an instinctive sympathy with their want of aptitude for business"; and to Professor Child, "There is something oriental in my own nature which sympathizes with this 'let her slide' temper of the hidalgos." Both of which statements should be taken as partly true to the letter and partly indicative of the adjustability which distinguishes the American from the Englishman.

The most compact tribute to his five and a half years at the court of St. James was the remark of a Londoner that he found all the Britons strangers and left them all cousins. Lowell was one of the two extreme types of American whom Victorian England chose to like and admire. One, of the Mark Twain and Joaquin Miller sort, was free and easy, smacking of the wild West, completely in contrast with the English gentleman; the other, in the persons of men like Lowell and Charles Eliot Norton, was the nearest American approach to cultivated John Bull. In diplomatic circles Lowell's tact always mollified his firmness, even leading to criticism from some of his countrymen because he never defied nor blustered. And in his immensely important appearances as the representative of the United States at all manner of social occasions, he charmed his hosts by the grace and pertinence of his public speech.

His speech was the happiest, easiest, most graceful conceivable, with just the right proportion of play to seriousness, the ideal combination of ingredients for a post-prandial confection. . . . He was pithy without baldness and full without prolixity. He never said too much, nor said what he had to say with too much gravity. His manner, in short, was perfection; but the real substance that his felicity of presentation clothed counted for still more. . . . And in England his unexampled popularity was very largely due to this gift.[1]

In the years remaining to him, with eager audiences awaiting him, he literally uttered much of the best that he wrote. He was no longer an eager producer, but he could be stimulated to speak by special invitations. So he delivered addresses out of the fullness of his experience at Birmingham University, at Westminster Abbey, at the celebration of Forefathers' Day in Plymouth, at the 250th Anniversary of the founding of Harvard, before the reform leagues of Boston and New York, and at a convention of the Modern Language Association of America. These, with his last volume of verse, "Heartsease and Rue" (1888), became his valedictory. He died in 1891.

The outstanding feature of Lowell's career is that he was a poet in action. His first and last volumes were lyrics. In the forty-seven years between their issues he was always the artist. He brought his emotional fervor and his sense of phrase to his essays, addresses, and occasional poems and to his pursuit of scholarship. His natural first interests were in the printed page and in the wielding of the pen; measured by weeks and months his life was largely lived in retirement, but the step from reading and writing to active citizenship was an easy one, and in the world of action he seemed to make few waste motions. What he did not only counted in itself but it

[1] W. C. Brownell, "American Prose Masters," pp. 271, 272.

enriched his mind as much as what he read. And back of all his activity were certain qualities that contributed to his effectiveness. He was a representative man, a fact acknowledged by his classmates who elected him their poet. He had the journalistic gift of saying excellently what others were on the verge of thinking. He did little thinking of his own that was original but much that was independent, and as a sane radical he was sure of the hearing he richly deserved. He was clever and charming, with a glint of errant unexpectedness, which was ingratiating even when it was far-fetched or even wantonly malapropos. His quips are like the gifts and favors of old-time children's parties — hidden all over the house and just as likely to defy search as to turn up under a napkin or in the umbrella of a departing guest. And behind all, Lowell was prevailingly American, with the combined trust in democracy and fear for it that belonged to his group in his generation.

From 1820 on, Irving, Cooper, Bryant, and their followers had protested more and more frequently (see pp. 111–114) at the certain condescension in foreigners to which Lowell addressed himself in his essay of 1865. Yet all these men, and cultured America as a whole, played up to this condescension and encouraged it by evidently expecting it — stimulating it by the peevish feebleness of their protests. Lowell, though loyal, was always apologetic, always hoping to gain confidence in his countrymen. His intimate friend, Charles Eliot Norton, was deferent toward all things British or European, and, while working valiantly to establish sound canons of taste, felt a distress for the crudities of American life that was only a refinement upon the snobbishness of the Effinghams in Cooper's " Homeward Bound " and " Home as Found." The fact is that the refined American of the mid-nineteenth century was afraid to contemplate the incarnation of America. He knew that Uncle Sam was too mature for it; he feared that it was like Tom Sawyer; he did what he could to mold it into the image of Little Lord Fauntleroy; and he apologized for

Whitman. When Mark Twain visited William Dean Howells in Cambridge in 1871 they were both young sojourners from what was to Cambridge an undiscriminated West. Young Mr. Clemens did not care at all, and young Mr. Howells did not care as far as he was concerned, though he cared a great deal in behalf of his friend, who was so incorrigibly Western. And in recording his anxiety he recorded a striking fact of that generation : that American culture was afraid even of the rough-and-ready Americans whom Europe was applauding. "I did not care," said Mr. Howells of Mr. Clemens, "to expose him to the critical edge of that Cambridge acquaintance which might not have appreciated him at, say, his transatlantic value. In America his popularity was as instant as it was vast. But it must be acknowledged that for a much longer time here than in England polite learning hesitated his praise. . . . I went with him to see Longfellow, but I do not think Longfellow made much of him, and Lowell made less." [1]

In habits of intellectual nicety, in manners, and in social inclination Lowell was an aristocrat ; yet in spite of these tendencies, and quite evidently in spite of them, he was in principle a stanch democrat, and when put to the test that sort of democrat is the most reliable. The conflict is interestingly apparent throughout his writings. The address on "Democracy" of 1888 need not be gravely cited as proof of Lowell's belief in government by the people ; it is only the final iteration of what he had all his life been saying. Yet after his usual leisurely introduction he approached his subject with the smile of half apology which had become a habit to him : "I shall address myself to a single point only in the long list of offences of which we are more or less gravely accused, because that really includes all the rest." It crops out in the Thoreau essay, apropos of Emerson : "If it was ever questionable whether democracy could develop a gentleman, the problem has been affirmatively solved at last " ; and in the

[1] W. D. Howells, " My Mark Twain," p. 46.

Lincoln essay: "Mr. Lincoln has also been reproached with Americanism by some not unfriendly British critics; but, with all deference, we cannot say that we like him any the worse for it." In the ode on Agassiz he heaved a sigh of relief that the great naturalist was willing to put up with New England conditions; and even in the Harvard "Commemoration Ode" he broke out suddenly with:

> Who now shall sneer?
> Who dare again to say we trace
> Our lines to a plebeian race?

The point is not in the least that Lowell did not believe in democracy; every deprecating remark of this sort was prefatory to a fresh defense of it. The point is that, as with a quarrel, it takes two to make a condescension and that Lowell did his part. It is difficult to imagine the young foreigner of "German-silver aristocracy" condescending with success to Lincoln or Emerson or to Mark Twain or Whitman.

The frequent expression of this self-defensive mood is an illustration of another leading trait in Lowell—his spontaneity. Since he felt as he did there would have been no virtue in concealing the fact, and Lowell seldom concealed anything. He wrote readily and fully, often beyond the verge of prolixity. He gave his ideas free rein as they filed or crowded or raced into his mind, not only welcoming those that came but often seeming to invite those that were tentatively approaching. Only in a few of his lyrics did he compact his utterance. Most of the introductions to essays and longer poems proceed in the manner of the "musing organist" of the first stanza in "Sir Launfal," "beginning doubtfully and far away," and what follows is in most cases somewhat lavishly discursive. The consequences of this manner of expression of a richly furnished mind are not altogether fortunate. Much of his writing could have been more quickly started and more compactly stated, and practically all of it could have been more firmly constructed. Emerson's essays lack firm structure because they were not written to a program, but were aggregations of paragraphs already set down in his journals. Lowell's essays, although deliberately composed, were equally without design. His method was to fill himself with his subject of the moment and then to write eagerly and rapidly, letting "his fingers wander as they list." His productions were consequently poured out rather than built up. They have the character of most excellent conversation which circles about a single theme, allows frequent digression, admits occasional brilliant sallies, includes various "good things," and finally stops without any definitive conclusion. In this respect, while Lowell was by no means artless in the sense of being unsophisticated, he was also by no means artful in the sense of calculating his effects upon the reader. The only reader of whom he seems to have been distinctly conscious was the bookish circle of his own associates. He would fling out recondite allusions as though in challenge, and he wrote in a flowing, polysyllabic diction which was nicely exact but which rarely would concede the simpler word.

This same surging spontaneity was both the strength and weakness of his poetry. He inclined too much to foster the theory of inspiration. "'T is only while we are forming our opinions," he once wrote, "that we are very anxious to propagate them"; and as he indited most of his poems while he was in this state of "anxiety" they became effusions rather than compositions. His first drafts, in fact, were fulfillments of Bryant's injunction in "The Poet":

> While the warm current tingles through thy veins
> Set forth the burning words in fluent strains.

But in his revisions he was unable to follow the instructions to the end:

> Then summon back the original glow, and mend
> The strain with rapture that with fire was penned.

As a consequence his poems when published were as invertebrate as when he first wrote them, and of the revisions in detail many were shifted back to their original form. The degree to which he tempered the wind of self-criticism to his own poetical lambs is the more noteworthy on account of the acumen with which he commented as editor on the work of his fellow-poets.

On the other hand, his easy command of versification, his gift of phrasing, and his rich poetic imagination resulted in very many passages of beauty and feeling, particularly in the later odes like the Commemoration and Agassiz poems, into which he poured the fine fervor of his patriotism. In these his sincerity, his intellectual solidity, his idealism, and his nature-feeling combined with "the incontrollable poetic impulse which is the authentic mark of a new poem" and which Emerson ascribed to him in a journal entry of 1868.

BOOK LIST

Individual Author

JAMES RUSSELL LOWELL. Works. Riverside Edition. 1890. 11 vols. Elmwood Edition. 1904. 16 vols. (Contains one more volume of literary essays, one more of poetry, and the three volumes of letters. C. E. Norton, editor. 1904.) These appeared in book form originally as follows: Class Poem, 1838; A Year's Life, 1841; Poems, 1844; Conversations on Some of the Old Poets, 1845; Poems, Second Series, 1848; A Fable for Critics, 1848; The Biglow Papers, 1848; The Vision of Sir Launfal, 1848; Fireside Travels, 1864; The Biglow Papers, Second Series, 1867; Under the Willows and Other Poems, 1869; The Cathedral, 1870; Among my Books, 1870; My Study Windows, 1871; Among my Books, Second Series, 1876; Three Memorial Poems, 1877; Democracy and Other Addresses, 1887; Political Essays, 1888; Heartease and Rue, 1888; Latest Literary Essays and Addresses, 1891; The Old English Dramatists, 1892; Last Poems, 1895; Impressions of Spain, 1899.

Bibliography

A volume compiled by George Willis Cooke. 1906. Cambridge History of American Literature, Vol. II, pp. 544–550.

Biography and Criticism

The standard life is by H. E. Scudder. 1901. 2 vols.

BENTON, JOEL. Lowell's Americanism. *Century*, November, 1891.

BROWNELL, W. C. American Prose Masters. 1909.
CURTIS, G. W. Orations and Addresses, Vol. III. 1894.
GODKIN, E. L. The Reasons why Mr. Lowell should be Recalled. *Nation*, June 1, 1882.
GREENSLET, FERRIS. Lowell: his Life and Work. 1905.
HALE, E. E. Lowell and his Friends. 1898.
HALE, E. E., JR. Lowell. 1899.
HIGGINSON, T. W. Book and Heart. 1897.
HIGGINSON, T. W. Old Cambridge. 1899.
HOWELLS, W. D. A Personal Retrospect of Lowell. *Scribner's*, September, 1900.
HOWELLS, W. D. Literary Friends and Acquaintances. 1900.
JAMES, HENRY. Essays in London. 1893.
MABIE, H. W. My Study Fire. *Ser. 2.* 1894.
MEYNELL, ALICE. The Rhythm of Life and Other Essays. 1893.
NORTON, C. E. James Russell Lowell. *Harper's*, May, 1893.
NORTON, C. E. Letters of Lowell. *Harper's*, September, 1893.
SCUDDER, H. E. Mr. Lowell as a Teacher. *Scribner's*, November, 1891.
STILLMAN, W. J. The Autobiography of a Journalist, chap. xiv. 1901
STODDARD, R. H. Recollections Personal and Literary. 1903.
TAYLOR, BAYARD. Critical Essays. 1880.
THORNDIKE, A. H. Cambridge History of American Literature, Vol. II, Bk. II, chap. xxiv.
UNDERWOOD, F. H. Lowell; a Biographical Sketch. 1882.
UNDERWOOD, F. H. The Poet and the Man. 1893.
WENDELL, BARRETT. Stelligeri. 1893.
WILKINSON, W. C. A Free Lance in the Field of Life and Letters. 1874.

TOPICS AND PROBLEMS

Read "The Present Crisis" as determining the temper in which Lowell wrote his essay on Thoreau in view of their different reactions to the same national situation.

Read what Poe, Longfellow, and Lowell had to say concerning overemphasis on the American quality of American literature as noted on pages 177, 272, and 284. Is there any clear reason for this common dissent?

Compare the people discussed in Lowell's "Fable for Critics" and in Poe's "Literati," published within two years of each other.

Read the connecting prose passages between the "Biglow Papers" for interesting evidence of Lowell's attention to and knowledge of linguistic detail.

Read " Mason and Slidell: a Yankee Idyll " in " Biglow Papers," Second Series, as a commentary on the Great European War.

Analyze the structure of a selected long poem and of a literary essay with a view to studying its firmness or looseness.

Read any one of Lowell's five great odes and note the rhetorical fitness of meter and subject as contrasted with the artificiality of Lanier's later poems.

Read " The Shepherd of King Admetus," " Invita Minerva," " The Origin of Didactic Poetry," and the passages on Lowell and his fellow-poets for his comments on poetry and poetic art.

CHAPTER XX

The name of Harriet Beecher Stowe (1811–1896) is not so well known as the title of her most famous novel, "Uncle Tom's Cabin," though certain of her stories of New England life are superior as works of art to her great war document. She entered literature by the pathway of reform. "The heroic element was strong in me, having come down . . . from a long line of Puritan ancestry, and . . . it made me long to do something, I knew not what : to fight for my country, or to make some declaration on my own account." Then, when she had developed her story-telling gift she continued to use it for its own sake.

She was born in Litchfield, Connecticut, one of the five children of the Reverend Lyman Beecher, two years before her famous brother, Henry Ward Beecher. The death of her mother when she was but four years old resulted in her having a succession of homes during childhood, in all of which she lived under kindly protection and in somewhat literary surroundings, breathing an atmosphere which was heavy with the exhalations of the old-school Calvinistic theology. In 1832, when Harriet was twenty-one years old, her father, after a six-year pastorate of a Boston church, went to Cincinnati as president of the Lane Theological Seminary, and the two daughters joined him there.

While the father was occupied with his pioneer work in the new institution the daughters started a school for girls ; but Harriet was not to be a schoolmistress for long. In 1833 she was winner of a fifty-dollar prize in a short-story competition conducted by the *Western Monthly*, and in 1836 she married the Reverend Calvin E. Stowe, her father's colleague in Lane

Seminary. How she persisted to combine authorship and maternity in the next sixteen years is a marvel; none the less so because since the days of Anne Bradstreet an occasional woman has succeeded. In 1842 her first volume, a collection of stories, was published by Harpers; but by 1848 she was the mother of six children, the oldest only eleven, and no more books had appeared.

Nevertheless she was not to sink under the tide of home drudgery. She had visited in the South, seeing the more kindly aspects of slavery, and in her own town had witnessed the pursuit of fugitives, the conscientious defiance of law by abolitionists, and the violence of proslavery mobs. In these exciting times it came to her more and more insistently that she must turn her writing to good account. So it was a natural result of her dreamings and longings that in the early winter of 1851 there appeared to her, as in a vision, the scene of the death of Uncle Tom.

The story came out serially in the *National Era*, an anti-slavery journal, from June, 1851, to April of the next year. Although the publishers were skeptical about its success in book form, three hundred thousand copies were sold in America within the first year, and the circulation in England and on the continent was unprecedented for an American book. Mrs. Stowe's "fortune was made" of course; but, more important to her, her influence was made in the great fight in which she enlisted. Whittier wrote to Garrison: "What a glorious work Harriet Beecher Stowe has wrought. Thanks for the Fugitive Slave Law! Better would it be for slavery if that law had never been enacted: for it gave occasion for ' Uncle Tom's Cabin.' " And Garrison wrote in turn to Mrs. Stowe: " I estimate the value of anti-slavery writing by the abuse it brings. Now all the defenders of slavery have let me alone and are abusing you." The volume of objection was so great, and so much of it was directed at the honesty of the work, that the author reluctantly compiled soon after a " Key to Uncle Tom's Cabin," in which she presented documentary evidence for every kind of fact used in the story ; and of this she was able to write : "not one fact or statement in it has been disproved as yet. I have yet to learn of even an *attempt* to disprove."

The only fair basis for criticising "Uncle Tom" is as a piece of propagandist literature. It was not even a "problem novel." It was a story with an avowed "purpose": "to awaken sympathy and feeling for the African race, as they exist among us ; to show their wrongs and sorrows, under a system so necessarily cruel and unjust as to defeat and do away with the good effects of all that can be attempted for them, by their best friends, under it." Mrs. Stowe felt no pride in it as a story, referring with perfect composure to the criticisms on its artistry. But as a popular document she composed it with the greatest of art. With a moderately developed talent for story writing she happened to have just the tone of mind and level of culture which were attuned to the temper of her day, and she employed them to the utmost effect. Moreover she used them just as Whittier used his powers in some of his moralistic poetry, not relying on her narrative to carry its own burdens, but expounding it as she went along, and appending a chapter of "Concluding Remarks" with various odds and ends of afterthought — matters which do not belong in any novel or even in any well-organized section of an essay, but matters which were doubtless valuable in bringing back to the argument the minds of readers which may have been distracted by the sheer human interest of the story. The success of "Uncle Tom" could not be duplicated, of course. The second antislavery novel, "Dred, a Tale of the Great Dismal Swamp," sold enormously on the strength of its predecessor and on its own merits, but it could only fan the embers which had previously been inflamed. The task had been done ; "Dred" could never be anything but an aftermath to "Uncle Tom."

With a removal to Andover, Massachusetts, in 1852, Mrs. Stowe settled down in comfort among cultured and

orthodox neighbors, and began her best work as an inter-
preter of New England life and character. "The Minister's
Wooing," her first novel in this field, was her contribution as a
serial to the newly established *Atlantic Monthly*. With her
recent successes fresh in the public mind, she was an indispensable "selling feature" for the ambitious magazine. With this
novel she made her first attempt since the days of the forgotten
volume of 1842 to write a story in which the moral should take
care of itself. There was a moral, to be sure, and a striking one,
for it pointed to a distrust of the old New England Calvinism,
and made clear the distinction between a religion that uplifts
and a theology that turns to scorn the religion it assumes to
fortify. In the chapter "Which Treats of Romance," Mrs. Stowe
perhaps did not let the moral wholly take care of itself, since
she came into court as a special pleader for beauty as an ally of
religion and brought an indictment against the niggardliness of
a life founded on a dogmatic dread of eternal fire. The moral
of the book, if one must be given in a sentence, is that love
realized is finer than love renounced.

Like "Uncle Tom" and "Dred," "The Minister's Wooing"
has its element of instruction as well as of edification, for it is
a studied and faithful picture of Rhode Island life just after the
Revolution — a period about as remote from Mrs. Stowe as the
slave-story epoch is from the modern reader. And because it is
less of an allegory the characters are more lifelike, not having
to carry each his Christian's pack of argument on his shoulders.
As Lowell stated,[1] they were set in contrast not by the simple and
obvious method in fiction of putting them in different social ranks
— aristocrat and commoner, master and man, Roundhead and
Cavalier, pioneer, Indian and townsman. Between Mrs. Stowe's
village folk, caste distinctions were of little moment; a careful
realism was taxed to show the vital and homely differences between one individual and another. Her success in this respect
is what gives any distinction to "The Pearl of Orr's Island"

[1] *New York Tribune*, June 13, 1859.

(1862). The Pearl herself, who is a bit of labeled symbolism (chap. xxviii), — a little Eva transported to the Maine coast and thence to heaven,— is almost the only significant character. Moses Pennell, an exotic, is comparatively lifelike, and the actual village people are as real as can be.

"Oldtown Folks" (1869) is Mrs Stowe's most effective and least adulterated novel. The people of the story are many and varied, ranging from Sam Lawson, the village Rip Van Winkle, to the choicest of old Boston adornments of society. While the book had no social purpose it had the avowed narrative "object . . . to interpret to the world the New England life and character in that particular time in its history which may be called the seminal period,"— a statement followed by the complacent and thoroughly provincial assertion that "New England was the seed-bed of this great American Republic, and of all that is likely to come of it."

In "breadth of canvas," to resort to the slang of criticism, "Oldtown Folks" is in Mrs. Stowe's whole output what "Middlemarch" is in George Eliot's. It is filled with popular tableaux — in the old Meeting House, in the Grandmother's kitchen, at the Manor House, in the coach on its grave progress to Boston, in the school and its surroundings; and it is red-lettered with festivals in which the richest flavor of social life in the early nineteenth century is developed. As a life story of the four young central characters it does not linger vividly in mind. One does not recall them and their subjective experiences half so clearly as one does their intellectual and social and material surroundings. Yet the shape of their life experience was determined by just these external influences; and how clearly they belonged to a bygone period appears at a glance of comparison with any similar twentieth-century story.

In the quarter-century remaining to her after the writing of "Oldtown Folks," Mrs. Stowe's life was a quiet fulfillment of her earlier career. From a Florida plantation on which she spent her winters she worked for the welfare of the negro and

the upbuilding of the South. She labored as before in coöperation with the church, but her repugnance for the grimness of
Calvinism led her to become an Episcopalian. As a novelist
she kept on in the exposition of New England to the mild
gratification of a public which she had already won; but her
enduring fame will unquestionably rest on the fact that she was
a story writer of moderate talent who in one memorable instance
devoted her gift to the making of American history.

In 1851, the year when " Uncle Tom " was appearing in the
National Era, there was published in book form another American novel on which the verdict of the years is conferring high
though belated honors. This is " Moby Dick," a strange, great,
ungainly composite, that contains a thrilling narrative, a cyclo-
pedic collection of whaling lore, and a tumult of speculation on
the mystery of life, as deep and varied as the seas on which the
story is launched. The author, Herman Melville (1819–1891),
a grandson of the picturesque subject of Holmes's " The Last
Leaf," was in many respects as baffling and elusive as his greatest work. He was born in New York of conservative and moderately prosperous stock. The decline of the family fortunes
cut his formal schooling short, and led him to gain his higher
education on shipboard and in the far islands of the South Seas.
His first experience was as a common seaman on a voyage to
Liverpool and back in 1837, a venture chronicled in "Redburn."
There followed three years of school teaching; and then in 1841
he shipped on a whaling voyage from New Bedford from which
he was not to return for nearly four years. Rebellious at the
harsh treatment of his captain, he escaped with a companion to
an island in the Marquesas, where for four months he was at
once a captive and a guest of the cannibals in the valley of Taipi.
From this came the story " Typee." After escape he was carried
on an Australian whaler to Tahiti, sailed thence to Honolulu,
and eventually returned to Boston on the frigate " United
States," gaining material on the last lap of the long tour for
" White Jacket."

Between the ages of twenty-six and thirty-two his significant writing was done : " Typee " (1845), his first island adventures, and " Omoo " (1846), a sequel, were so fresh and unfamiliar that they were generally credited with being pure romance. " Mardi " (1849) followed as if in answer to a challenge, a romance of the quest for the unattainable, written in a romping and sardonically inflated style, filled with satirical allegories, a book to read casually in an evening, or painstakingly in a week. " Redburn " (1849) and " White Jacket " (1850) returned to the material and the method of the chronicler ; and then in 1851 came " Moby Dick," which combined the skill of a great story-teller and the close observation of the diarist with the farthest outreachings of the philosopher. Four prose volumes followed on the heels of these more important works : " Pierre " (1852), " Israel Potter " (1855), " Piazza Tales " (1856), " The Confidence Man " (1857), and much later some rather bewildering verse. But with " Moby Dick " Melville's real career was over, and there remained to him forty years of secluded obscurity. His death in 1891 caused hardly a ripple of interest, and it is only within the last few years that a fresh and probably lasting recognition has been accorded him.

Melville's approach to the American reader came at a propitious time and in a propitious way. There was no popular writer of sustained fiction on this side of the Atlantic in 1845. Poe was somewhat known for his sketches and tales, but no more so than for his drastic criticisms. Cooper's highest popularity had been lost during his running controversy with the whole American public (see pp. 153–155), and Hawthorne's " Scarlet Letter " was yet to appear. Moreover, as far as English fiction was concerned, the great day of Sir Walter Scott and Jane Porter was past, Dickens and Thackeray had not reached their height in this country, and Bulwer, Trollope, Reade, Meredith, George Eliot, and Wilkie Collins were still to become widely known. It was a promising moment for an American novelist. Furthermore, even in America Melville's South Sea material was happily chosen. In spite of the often repeated call for the treatment of American subjects by American writers, Cooper had been the sole author to respond with any success, and he had succeeded only when he wrote of past years or of frontier life; native drama, with the exception of Mrs. Mowatt's "Fashion," was drawn from everywhere but home; the only native poet who wrote narrative was working on a tale of other days which ranged from Acadia to the unpopulated shores of the Mississippi; and the American public was content. A book was accepted as a guide to remote and enchanted scenes.

In the circumstances it was not surprising that "Typee" and "Omoo" should have had a great vogue. Though based on fact, they were accepted for romance, as literature about any distant and unfamiliar region always will be. The material of the earlier and better one, "Typee," is full of allurements. The daring flight from shipboard into unknown island passes, the hardships on mountainsides and in the chill ravines, the dangers of a too cordial reception from the cannibal inhabitants, the disappearance of the hero's sole white companion, the charms of Fayaway and the other island maidens, the ominous attentiveness of the captor-hosts, and the thrill of the final escape, all help to make the book the best that has ever been written about the South Sea Islands.

The foreword to "Mardi" suggests that Melville roved away into the land of pure fancy because he wanted to show the difference between what he had seen and what he could conjure up. But the real motive doubtless lay deeper than that. Melville was by nature a satirist, a master of irony, and a speculative philosopher. In the earliest two books he had presented a picture of an idyllic life, a sort of sublimated barbarism on an island where there were traces of an extinct and unlamented civilization; and he had refrained from interpreting the picture. But now in "Mardi" he wrote a kind of metaphysical analogue. Two sailors again escape as in "Typee," but this time, instead of coming into plain prose experiences with actual though unreal people, they set out on a quest for unattainable beauty symbolized in a spirit maiden. This quest is annotated with passages in the mood of Swift and Rabelais, pouring contempt on the pride of existing civilizations ; and in the manner now of Sir Thomas Browne and now of Carlyle, Melville careens along like a rudderless ship before a typhoon. Later he was to pass completely over from the concrete material of narrative to the abstractions of metaphysics, depriving American literature when he did so of one of its most brilliant novelists ; but before he made this unhappy transition his greatest work was to intervene.

This was to be the whaling story " Moby Dick." Like most other great narrative literature, it offers an appeal for youthful readers in the external story alone. This concerns Captain Ahab, who had lost a leg in an encounter with the terror of the South Seas, Moby Dick, the great white whale ; and tells of his consuming hatred for the monster, and of his voyage after revenge, which ends with his death in conflict with the foe. Two thirds of the chapters might be culled to present this relentless sequence in the form of a so-called boys' book. Yet even so presented the story would contain more than meets the eye. However great it is as a straight whaling adventure — and there is nothing equal in literature — in a secondary sense it is just as great a story of life which happens to be told in terms of whales and whalers. This is the story of Eve and of Prometheus, the perennial struggle of man for spiritual freedom in the midst of an externally physical world — his attempt to make a conquest of circumstance. " All visible objects, man," says Captain Ahab, " are but as pasteboard masks. But in each event — in the living act, the undoubted deed — there some unknown but still reasoning thing puts forth its features from behind the unreasoning mask. If man will strike, strike through the mask ! How can the prisoner reach outside, except he thrust through the wall ? " The tale is not an allegory, but it is so innately true that it has all the revealing significance of allegory to him who can perceive it.

As a piece of writing "Moby Dick" serves as a reminder that the greatest stories in literature are never the most neatly constructed. The plot of this one has before it an inevitable ending; one is drawn toward it as down a high-walled stream to the edge of a cataract. Yet all the way along it is told with the utmost leisureliness. While there is no escape, there is no haste. With an inexhaustible literary energy, and an abounding flow of varying emotion, Melville combines thrilling episodes, minute discussions of whaling lore, visionary symbolism, ironic allusion and sustained satire, vivid characterization, and picturesque beauty. The present "Melville revival" can be accounted for partly by the present-day vogue of South Sea literature and partly by the post-war temper of skepticism, but more because in Melville has been rediscovered one of the immensely energetic and original personalities of the last hundred years.

BOOK LIST

HARRIET BEECHER STOWE. Works. The writings of Harriet Beecher Stowe, with biographical introductions. 1899. 16 vols. These appeared in book form originally as follows: Mayflower, 1843; Uncle Tom's Cabin, 1852; A Key to Uncle Tom's Cabin, 1853; Sunny Memories of Foreign Lands, 1854; Dred, 1856; The Minister's Wooing, 1859; The Pearl of Orr's Island, 1862; Agnes of Sorrento, 1862; House and Home Papers, 1864; Little Foxes, 1865; Religious Poems, 1867; Queer Little People, 1867; The Chimney Corner, 1868; Oldtown Folks, 1869; Pink and White Tyranny, 1871; Oldtown Fireside Stories, 1871; My Wife and I, 1871; We and Our Neighbors, 1875; Poganuc People, 1878; A Dog's Mission, 1881.

Biography and Criticism

The standard life is by Charles E. Stowe. 1890. The biographical introductions in the standard set are valuable.

CROWE, MARTHA FOOTE. Harriet Beecher Stowe. 1913.

ERSKINE, JOHN. Leading American Novelists. 1910.

FIELDS, MRS. ANNIE. Life and Letters of Harriet Beecher Stowe. 1897.

STOWE, C. E. and L. B. Life of Harriet Beecher Stowe. 1911.

The more important magazine articles are:

BURTON, RICHARD. *Century*, Vol. XXX, p. 690.

COOKE, G. W. *New England Magazine* (N. S.), Vol. XV, p. 3.

FIELDS, MRS. ANNIE. *Atlantic*, Vol. LXXVIII, p. 15.
HIGGINSON, T. W. *Nation*, Vol. LXIII, p. 24.
LEE, G. S. *Critic*, Vol. XXX, p. 281.
PHELPS (WARD), E. S. *McClure's*, Vol. VII, p. 3.
WARD, W. H. *Forum*, Vol. XXI, p. 727.

HERMAN MELVILLE. Sea Tales, 4 vols. 1900. These appeared originally in book form as follows: Typee, 1845; Omoo, 1846; Mardi, 1849; Redburn, 1849; White Jacket, 1850; Moby Dick, 1851; Pierre, 1852; Israel Potter, 1855; Piazza Tales, 1856; The Confidence Man, 1857. Various reprints of Typee, Omoo, and Moby Dick have been issued since 1918.

Biography and Criticism

The standard life and the best piece of extended criticism is by Raymond M. Weaver, Herman Melville: Mariner and Mystic, 1921.

TOPICS AND PROBLEMS

Contrast the conditions of authorship and the circumstances of publication for Jane Austen and Mrs. Stowe. Compare those of George Eliot and Mrs. Stowe.

Read "Uncle Tom's Cabin" for Mrs. Stowe's attitude toward the people of the South in distinction to her attitude toward the institution of slavery.

Read "Oldtown Folks" or "The Minister's Wooing" for Mrs. Stowe's exposition of the orthodox theology in either.

Compare for the broad picture of a community and of an epoch George Eliot's "Middlemarch" with "Oldtown Folks."

Compare Mrs. Stowe's New England village characters with those of Oliver Wendell Holmes in any of his three novels.

Compare and contrast Melville's treatment of South Sea life with that of Edward O'Brien in "White Shadows in the South Seas," that of Somerset Maugham in the latter half of "The Moon and Sixpence," or of other contemporary writers.

Note in the narrative chapters of "Moby Dick" Melville's characterization of Captain Ahab and his unflagging sense of the outcome of the story in all the words and actions of this leading character.

Note the significance of the preliminary quotations on the whale combined with the chapters of "cetology" in the latter half for both their direct and their symbolic values.

CHAPTER XXI

OLIVER WENDELL HOLMES

In the roster of American men of letters it is hard to think of any other who is so completely the product of a district and the spokesman for it as Oliver Wendell Holmes (1809–1894). His whole lifetime was passed in two neighborhoods — that of Harvard College in old Cambridge and that of Beacon Hill in oldest Boston. He was born in the college town in 1809, the same year with Lincoln. His father, the Reverend Abiel Holmes, was a fine exponent of the old orthodoxy and of the old breeding and a historian of the American Revolution. He was an inheritor of the blood of the Bradstreet, Phillips, Hancock, Quincy, and Wendell families, a kind of youth whose "aspect is commonly slender, — his face is smooth, and apt to be pallid, — his features are regular and of a certain delicacy, — his eye is bright and quick, — his lips play over the thought he utters as a pianist's fingers dance o?er their music." [1] It was a type for whose aptitudes Holmes felt the greatest respect. He thanked God for the republicanism of nature which every now and then developed a "large, uncombed youth" who strode awkwardly into intellectual leadership. He acknowledged a Lincoln when he came to maturity, but he expected more of a Chauncey or an Ellery or an Edwards because of his inheritance.

A prevailing alertness of mind in Holmes's generation offset the natural conservatism which belongs to an aristocracy. For a hundred years Harvard had been more liberal than Yale. The cleavage was already taking place between Unitarian and Trinitarian or Congregational believers. To be sure, the eyes

---

[1] "Elsie Venner," chap. i, "The Brahmin Caste of New England."

of Abiel Holmes were focused on the past, and he sent his son to be schooled under the safe influences of Phillips Andover Academy, which were fostered by the orthodox theological seminary just across the road. But even here Wendell — as he was called — decided against entering the ministry because a certain clergyman " looked and talked so like an undertaker." And when he entered college in his home town, while he faced the traditional required course of classical languages, history, mathematics, and moral philosophy, the wind from over the sea was blowing through it, and he breathed the atmosphere which was passing into the blood of Emerson and Thoreau and George Ripley and the other Transcendentalists-to-be.

In his college days he was a little cheerful student of average performance who refused then as always to take himself soberly, although he did not lack inner seriousness. He practised his gift for writing and was rewarded by the acceptance of some of his efforts in the fashionable Annuals of the day — repositories of politely sentimental tales, sketches, and poems in fancy bindings which ornamented the marble-topped tables in the "best rooms." Under his apparently aimless amiability, however, there was an independence of judgment which twice recorded itself, in 1829 and '30. The first time was on the occasion of an issue in his father's church when the son was forced to agree with the liberal majority, who literally took the pastor's pulpit from him, so that he had to reëstablish himself in North Cambridge. Few harder tests could be devised than one between loyalty to conviction and loyalty to family interests. The other sign of independence was his choice of a profession. A boy of his heritage was socially if not divinely predestined for some sort of intellectual life. If he went to college, assurance was made doubly sure that he would not become a business man. From the outset he rejected the ministry as his "calling." He shrank from the formal complexities of the law as he did from the logic of the theologians. The thought of teaching did not seem to enter his mind. Literature could not afford him a livelihood. By elimination, then, only medicine was left to him, but in his day medicine did not occupy a position of dignity equal with the other professions. Medical science was still in earliest youth, and the practice of " physic " was jointly discredited by the barber, the veterinary, the midwife, the " yarb doctor," and the miscellaneous quack. This young " Brahmin," however, saw the chance for contributing to the progress of a budding science, and made his decision with quiet disregard of social prejudice.

Study in Paris, successful research work, practice in Boston, and a year's teaching at Dartmouth College in New Hampshire led to an appointment on the medical faculty at Harvard which he held actively from 1847 to 1882 and as emeritus until his death. As a practitioner he was not remarkably successful. At the first his extremely youthful appearance and his jocosity of manner stood in the way. People could not be expected to flock to the office of a young man who was known to have said that. " all small fevers would be gratefully received." And later his interest in things literary was regarded with distrust by prospective patients. As a teacher, on the other hand, he was unusually effective because of the traits which made him a poor business-getter. He was vivacious and deft in his methods.` He knew how to put his ideas in order, he was a master hand at expounding them, and he was ingenious in providing neat formulas for memorizing the myriad details of physiology and anatomy.

His profession supplied Holmes with a background of thought which was different from any of his contemporaries. It supplied him with titles and whole poems, such as " Nux Postcœnatica," " The Stethoscope Song," and " The Mysterious Illness," with literary essays, such as " The Physiology of Versification," and with a whole volume of medical essays. It furnished the motives for his three " medicated novels," — prenatal influence in " Elsie Venner," physical magnetism (by its opposite) in " A Mortal Antipathy," and telepathy in " The Guardian Angel." İt was the basis for scores of passages and hundreds of allusions in the four volumes of the " Breakfast Table " series. And, furthermore, in the natural sympathy which it generated in him for every branch of progressive science it gave ground for the felicitous toast :[1] " The union of Science and Literature — a happy marriage, the fruits of which are nowhere seen to better advantage than in our American Holmes." This is not to say that Holmes was alone in his consciousness of science. Thoreau was fully as aware of it in the field of plant and animal study ; all things considered, Emerson and Whitman were more responsive to its deeper spiritual implications. It is rather that Holmes had his special avenue of approach through the lore of the physician.

The Boston to which Holmes removed when he began his professional career was all-sufficing to him for the rest of his life. On Beacon Hill, the stronghold of the old social order, there was an eager, outreaching intellectual life. On its slope was the Boston Athenæum ; just below were the Old Corner Book Store and the little shop maintained by Elizabeth Peabody. The theaters were rising at its foot. Music was being fostered under the wise persistence of James S. Dwight, Washington Allston was doing the best of his painting, and the traditions of good statesmanship were being maintained by men like Wendell Phillips and Charles Sumner. To cap all, good-fellowship reigned and many a quiet dinner became a feast of reason and a flow of soul. " Nature and art combined to charm the senses ; the equatorial zone of the system was soothed by well-studied artifices ; the faculties were off duty, and fell into their natural attitudes ; you saw wisdom in slippers and science in a short jacket." Although Holmes discounted it in the moment of utterance, he was not unfriendly to the dictum : " Boston State-house is the Hub of the Solar

[1] Meeting of the American Medical Association, May, 1853. The response was a poem.

System. You could n't pry that out of a Boston man if you had the tire of all creation straightened out for a crowbar."

Moreover, as the half century of his Boston residence progressed there was no waning in the intellectual life. The obvious leaders, whose names are known to everyone, were surrounded by a large circle of thinking men and women. At the corner of the Common, just across from the Statehouse, was the mansion of George Ticknor, then retired from his Harvard professorship but hospitable in the offer of his rich library to the new generation of scholars. William Ticknor founded a publishing business into which he soon took young James T. Fields, a house which under various firm names has had a distinguished and unbroken career. Elizabeth Peabody was a radioactive center of all sorts of enterprises and enthusiasms — the Pestalozzian Temple School, the "conversations" on history, the book shop, and the temporary publishing of the *Dial*. Francis H. Underwood was the untiring champion of the idea which with perfect unselfishness he handed over to the abler founders of the *Atlantic Monthly*. And scores of others with less definite fruits of no less definite interest in life talked well and listened well and wrote well for the passing reader of the day.

In this community Holmes early took his place as the accepted humorist, and for the first twenty-five years he wrote almost entirely in verse. The fact that two of his earliest and most famous poems were anything but funny reënforces the point rather than gainsays it. For the humorist, in contrast to the joker, is a serious man with a special method which he employs usually but not always. If Holmes had not been capable of blazing with the indignation of "Old Ironsides" or glowing with the sympathy of "The Last Leaf," he would have been a clever dispenser of jollities but not a commentator on life. Much of his youthful composition was of the lighter variety — pleasant extravagances on the level of the "Croaker Papers," not quite up to *Salmagundi* (see pp. 116, 134).

"The Music Grinders," "The Comet," "Daily Trials," and "The Stethoscope Song" belong in this class. More humorous and less jocose are the verse with a definite satirical turn. "The Ballad of the Oysterman" was a gibe at the sentimental lays to be found in all the Annuals. "My Aunt" hit off the Apollinean Institute type of Young Lady Finishing School to which he returned in a chapter of "Elsie Venner"; the sort of subject to which he returned too in his shafts at the Latter-Day Adventists, in "Latter-Day Warnings," and at the decline of Calvinism, in "The Deacon's Masterpiece."

At the same time Holmes won a place as the local laureate, — for his class of 1829, for Harvard, and for every kind of occasion, grave and gay, on which some appropriate verse could point a moral and adorn the program. This is an easy accomplishment for those who have the gift, but both difficult and dull in the hands of many a poet who is capable of higher things. It demands fluency of pen, ready inventiveness, informality, and a confident good humor in its oral delivery. These all belonged to Holmes, and not least of them a gracious social manner. It is far easier to depreciate this kind of verse than it is to be consistently effective in it.

Twice in his early maturity he wrote in verse on the theory of poetry. The first, in 1836, when he was entering the medical profession, was his Phi Beta Kappa poem "Poetry"; the second was "Urania," in 1846, shortly before he accepted his Harvard professorship. The object of "Poetry," he wrote in a preface for its publication, was "to express some general truths on the sources and the machinery of poetry; to sketch some changes which may be said to have taken place in its history, constituting four grand eras; and to point out some less obvious manifestations of the poetic principle." In old age he looked back on this ambitious early effort with kindly indulgence, and allowed it to stand as a matter of biographical interest, although it was so evidently the product "of a young person trained after the schools of classical English verse as

represented by Pope, Goldsmith, and Campbell, with whose lines
his memory was early stocked." When, however, he wrote
"Urania, a Rhymed Lesson" he wore a friendly smile and did
his teaching in a less didactic way. He knew his audience, he
said, and he knew that they all expected to be amused.

> I know a tailor, once a friend of mine,
> Expects great doings in the button line, —
> For mirth's concussions rip the outward case,
> And plant the stitches in a tenderer place,
> I know my audience, — these shall have their ᗡue;
> A smile awaits them ere my song is through!

But, he went on to say, he knew himself, too, and he proposed no more to be the buffoon than to be the savage satirist.
Beneath his smiles there was a kindly seriousness. A dozen
years later, in the fifth of the "Autocrat" papers, he put the
case in a little allegory, the end of which is worth quoting
in full:

The stone is ancient error. The grass is human nature borne down
and bleached of all its color by it. The shapes which are found beneath
are the crafty beings which thrive in darkness, and the weaker organ-
isms kept helpless by it. He who turns the stone over is whosoever
puts the staff of truth to the old lying incubus, no matter whether he
do it with a serious face or a laughing one. The next year stands for
the coming time. Then shall the nature which had lain blanched and
broken rise in its full stature and native hues in the sunshine. Then
shall God's minstrels build their nests in the hearts of a new-born
humanity. Then shall beauty — Divinity taking outlines and color —
light upon the souls of men as the butterfly, image of the beatified
spirit rising from the dust, soars from the shell that held a poor grub,
which would never have found wings, had not the stone been lifted.

By these stages, then, Holmes concluded that he was an
essayist and developed into one. The "Poetry" of 1836 was
entitled "A Metrical Essay," and it was, without intending to
be, distinctly prosaic. "Urania," of 1846, was self-described as
"A Rhymed Lesson" and affected to be nothing more. At

last "The Autocrat of the Breakfast Table" — adopting the title and the form of an unsuccessful beginning in the *New England Magazine* of 1831–1832 — resorted frankly to prose and achieved a wider reputation for Holmes than all the foregoing verse had done.[1] The young person trained through the reading of Pope, Goldsmith, and Campbell was in the end fitted to do his best work after the manner of Addison, Goldsmith, and Lamb. From the appearance of "The Autocrat" Holmes's verse was subordinated in bulk and importance to his prose.

With his assumption of the *Atlantic* editorship, Lowell had set the prime condition that Holmes should become a regular contributor, and it is evident from the motto on the title page, "Every man his own Boswell," that Holmes's conversation had furnished the suggestion for the series. The vehicle was perfectly adapted to the load it was devised to carry. The introduction of a chief spokesman in a loosely organized group made way for the casual drift from topic to topic. The accident of a boarding-house selection justified the domination by one speaker which would have been unnatural in any social group. The continuity of the group gave a chance for characterization and for the spinning of a slight narrative thread comparable to those on which the *Citizen of the World* and the "De Coverley Papers" were strung. And the chief speaker, autocrat that he was, could give vent to his thoughts on the universe without let or hindrance, and when the whim seized him could impose his latest poems upon his always tolerant and usually deferential fellow-boarders. From the publication of the first number Lowell's judgment was vindicated, with the result not only that the Autocrat spoke through twelve issues, but that the thread of his discourse was continued with "The Professor at the Breakfast-Table," in 1859, was resumed with

[1] For a direct statement on the resumption of the old attempt, see "The Autocrat's Autobiography" printed as a foreword to the volume. For an indirect account, see the passages on Byles Gridley and his "Thoughts on the Universe" in Holmes's "The Guardian Angel."

"The Poet at the Breakfast-Table," in 1871, and was not concluded until the conversations " Over the Teacups," in 1890.

The range of topics cannot be better shown than by reference to the index — and the original edition was extraordinary in its day for having one. The "A's," for example, include abuse of all good attempts, affinities, and antipathies, age, animal under air-pump, the American a reënforced Englishman, the effect of looking at the Alps, the power of seeing analogies, why anniversaries are dreaded by the professor, the arguments which spoil conversation, the forming American aristocracy, the use of stimulants by artists, the effect of meeting one of heaven's assessors, and so on. The order in which they fall is hardly more casual than in the index. Witness the eleventh paper : puns, " The Deacon's Masterpiece," slang, dandies, aristocracy, intellectual green fruit, Latinized diction (with the verses " Æstivation "), seashore and mountains, summer residences, space, the Alps, moderate wishes (with the verses " Contentment "), faithfulness in love, picturesque spots in Boston, natural beauties in a city, dusting a library, experiencing life, a proposal of marriage. The difference between their structure and that of the formal essay is simply that they meander like a stream instead of following a predetermined course like a canal.

In the later members of the series, and particularly in the third and fourth, there is an evident response to the current of nineteenth-century thinking. By nature Holmes was a liberal but not a reformer. He took no active part in " movements," though he sympathized with many of them and with the intentions of their wiser promoters. At the same time he preferred for his own part to induce and persuade people into new paths rather than to shock and offend them while they were still treading the old ones. There is a note of considerate caution in his espousal of new ideas. He was the type of man who will always be unsatisfactory to extremists, — a dangerous person to the hidebound conservative and a tentative trifler to the

ultraradical. His open-mindedness is charmingly demonstrated
in the book of his old age, "Over the Teacups." Few men
of eighty succeed in keeping their eyes off the past and their
voices from decrying the present, but Holmes in his latest
years was as interested in the developments of the day as he
had been in the prime of life.

The issues of the Civil War — to return from the tea table
to the breakfast room — showed that Holmes had not lost the
spark for righteous indignation in the thirty years since the
writing of " Old Ironsides." " The Statesman's Secret " was
not as effective a protest at Webster's " Seventh of March
Speech " (1850) as Whittier's " Ichabod," but it was quite as
sincerely outspoken. "Non-Resistance" and "The Moral Bully"
prove that Holmes was as little of a peace-at-any-price man as
Lowell. " Brother Jonathan's Lament for Sister Caroline "
was written in deep sorrow that the war had been precipitated,
but " To Canaan " was militant to the highest degree. Two
other poems, written in the years of the Autocrat and the
Poet, both in lofty seriousness, came from "flowering moments
of the mind " which lost fewest petals as they were recorded in
verse. These were " The Chambered Nautilus " and " A Sun-
Day Hymn."

In all Holmes's writing, whatever the mood or the form,
the prevailing method is cumulative. He is likely to start with
an idea, proceed to a simple analysis of it, and expound it by
a single analogy elaborated at length or a whole series of them
more briefly presented. In the sixth "Autocrat" paper he says,
with some show of self-restraint, "There are some curious
observations I should like to make . . . but I think we are
getting rather didactic." Yet as a matter of fact Holmes's
method was seldom anything but didactic, and his content was
frequently such. He evidently saw at a flash how to com-
municate the idea, but, as he must have done hundreds of
times in the classroom, he developed it with what was at once
spontaneous and painstaking detail. His most famous satires,

"My Aunt," "Contentment," and "The Deacon's Master-piece," are all illustrations of this method. Thus in his "Fare-well to Agassiz," before the naturalist left for South America, Holmes mentioned that the mountains were awaiting his approval, as were also five other natural objects. He wished the traveler safety from the tropical sun and twenty-two other dangers and that he might succeed in finding fossils and seven other things of interest. "Bill and Joe" contains sixty lines built up by the enumerative method on the truth that worldly distinctions disappear for a moment in the light of college friendships. "Dorothy Q" devotes thirty-two lines to the quaint fancy "What would I be if one of my eight great, great grandmothers had married another man?" and "The Broomstick Train" a hundred and forty-six lines to the con-ceit "The Salem Witches furnish the power for the trolley cars." In prose, as a final illustration, his well-known discus-sion of the typical lecture audience in the sixth "Autocrat" is about eight hundred words long : Audiences help formulate lectures. The average is not high. They are awful in their uniformity — like communities of ants or bees — whether in New York, Ohio, or New England — unless some special prin-ciple of selection interferes. They include fixed elements — in age (four)— and in intelligence (the dull elaborated) — making up a compound vertebrate (biological analogy). Kindly elements conceded, but on the whole depressing.

Holmes gave the final epithet to his novels when he referred to them as "medicated." For the other and more eminent American physician, Weir Mitchell, fiction was a resort to another world, but the author of "Elsie Venner" (1861), "The Guardian Angel" (1867), and "A Mortal Antipathy" (1885) was the essayist-physician extending the narrative process a little farther than in the conversational series. The plots were supplied by Dr. Holmes and developed by the Autocrat-Professor-Poet. Several chapters of medical lore were inter-polated in each book, and several more of genial exposition.

These latter are like the work of Mrs. Stowe except that their relation to story development is tenuous or imperceptible, and in characterization his successes, like Mrs. Stowe's, are with the homelier New England types.

In the best sense of the word Holmes was a provincial New Englander. He was proud of the traditions of his district, devoted to its welfare, certain of its capacity for improvement, but sure of its contribution to the integrity of American character. Although he did not share the deeper enthusiasms of Emerson or even fully understand them, he had much more of the milk of human kindness in him. His " message " and his manner of delivering it were popular with the reading public. He was not a leader, but he kept up to the times, and he explained the drift of them to many who might not otherwise have perceived what was going on in the world or in themselves. In the tributes which came from every quarter after his death his geniality was the highest common factor — a wholesome and homely trait which will always be sure of affectionate regard in American literature.

BOOK LIST

Individual Author

OLIVER WENDELL HOLMES. Riverside Edition. 13 vols. Prose, Vols. I-X; Poetry, XI-XIII. 1891. Standard Library Edition, 1892; Autocrat Edition, 1904; both 15 vols. (uniform with Riverside Edition, with added life by J. T. Morse as Vols. XIV and XV). The best single volume of poems is the Cambridge Edition, 1895. His work appeared in book form originally as follows: Poems, 1836; Boylston Prize Dissertations, 1838; Homeopathy, and its Kindred Delusions, 1842; Urania, 1846; Poems, 1849; Astræa, 1850; The Autocrat of the Breakfast-Table, 1858; The Professor at the Breakfast-Table, 1860; Currents and Counter-Currents in Medical Science, 1861; Elsie Venner, 1861; Songs in Many Keys, 1862; Soundings from the Atlantic, 1864; Humorous Poems, 1865; The Guardian Angel, 1867; The Poet at the Breakfast-Table, 1872; Songs of Many Seasons, 1875; John Lothrop Motley, 1879; The Iron Gate, 1880; Medical Essays, 1883; Pages from an Old Volume of Life, 1883; Ralph Waldo Emerson, 1885; A Mortal Antipathy,

1885; Our Hundred Days in Europe, 1887; Before the Curfew, and Other Poems. 1888; Over the Teacups, 1891.

Bibliography

A volume compiled by George B. Ives. 1907. Cambridge History of American Literature, Vol. II, pp. 540–543.

Biography and Criticism

The standard life is by John T. Morse. 1896. 2 vols.

COLLINS, CHURTON. The Poetry and Poets of America.

COOKE, G. W. Dr. Holmes at Fourscore. *New England Magazine*, October, 1889.

CURTIS, G. W. Oliver Wendell Holmes, in *Literary and Social Essays*. 1895.

DWIGHT, THOMAS. Reminiscences of Dr. Holmes as Professor of Anatomy. *Scribner's*, January, 1895.

FIELDS, ANNIE. Personal Recollections and Unpublished Letters, in *Authors and Friends*. 1896.

GILDER, JEANNETTE L. A Book and its Story, in *The Genial "Autocrat." Critic*, May 9, 1896.

HALE, E. E. An Afternoon with Dr. Holmes in *Human Documents*. 1895.

HIGGINSON, T. W. Cheerful Yesterdays. 1898.

HIGGINSON, T. W. Contemporaries. 1899.

HIGGINSON, T. W. Old Cambridge. 1900.

HOWELLS, W. D. Oliver Wendell Holmes. *Harper's*, December, 1896.

HOWELLS, W. D. Oliver Wendell Holmes, in *Literary Friends and Acquaintances*. 1900.

KENNEDY, W. S. Oliver Wendell Holmes, Poet, Litterateur, Scientist. 1883.

LANG, ANDREW. Adventures among Books. 1905.

LODGE, H. C. Certain Accepted Heroes and Other Essays. 1897.

LOWELL, J. R. A Fable for Critics. 1848.

MATTHEWS, BRANDER. Cambridge History of American Literature. Vol. II, Bk. II, in chap. xxiii.

MEYNELL, ALICE. The Rhythm of Life and Other Essays. 1897.

RICHARDSON, C. F. American Literature, Bk. II, chap. vi. 1889.

STEDMAN, E. C. Poets of America. 1885.

VINCENT, L. H. American Literary Masters. 1906.

WOODBERRY, G. E. *Nation*, October 11, 1894.

TOPICS AND PROBLEMS

Read any one of Holmes's " Breakfast-Table." Series or any one of his novels for evidences of his prevailing belief in the virtues of an intellectual aristocracy.

Do the same thing with any of these seven books for the recurrence of illustrations, allusions, or whole passages which only a physician would have been likely to write.

Note in any of these books or in any selected group of his poems evidences of his respect for the broad contributions of science and scientific thought.

Read poems and passages of broadest jocosity and see if you find any wisdom intermixed with their ingenuity and their good nature.

Compare the "society verse" of Holmes with that of Austin Dobson or Brander Matthews.

Read at least a half-dozen poems of Holmes written in satire on contemporary men or movements and generalize on them as you can.

Read "Poetry," "Urania," and "To my Readers" for Holmes's theory of the content and the purpose of poetry. Compare with the theory of some other American or English poet.

Read "Elsie Venner," "The Guardian Angel," or "The Mortal Antipathy" and criticize it for its virtues and defects as a novel.

Read "The Guardian Angel" for the autobiographical material discoverable in the character of Byles Gridley.

CHAPTER XXII

SOME METROPOLITAN POETS

In the metropolitan group of the latter half of the nineteenth century Bryant was dominant until his death in 1878. Other conspicuous representatives were Bayard Taylor (1825–1878), Richard Henry Stoddard (1825–1903), Edmund Clarence Stedman (1833–1908), Thomas Bailey Aldrich (1836–1907) in his early career, and — with a difference — Richard Watson Gilder (1844–1909). None of these men was born and brought up in New York, and none but Gilder partook of the nature of the town as Irving and even Bryant and Halleck had been able to do in the preceding generation when it was more compact and unified. Taylor clung to the idea of establishing a manorial estate at Kennett Square, Pennsylvania, but lived more or less in New York and buzzed restlessly about the literary market until he died a victim of overwork in 1878. Stoddard, more stable and unexcited than Taylor or than Stedman, was occupied in a succession of uninspired literary ventures. Aldrich, after a few years, returned to Boston, where he was happier, although always consciously a newcomer. Stedman devoted as much time and energy to poetry as his unsuccessful efforts to become independently rich would allow him. These men were in a way the first American literary victims to "Newyorkitis." Only Richard Watson Gilder succeeded in coping with the great city. The others were not only unable to impress their stamp on the city of their adoption but were engulfed by it. In the midst of the turmoil they could not enjoy the serenity which prevailed in those same days in the Boston or the Charleston where cultural pursuits were held in higher esteem than commercial activity.

They were in the midst of a different cultural atmosphere. Bryant, Irving, Halleck, and Greeley led the way for a succeeding group of self-educated men. The New England writers of the day had been schooled at Harvard and Bowdoin and certain German universities, and the cultured men of Charleston were going abroad for study and travel in increasing numbers. In the midst of all the hurly-burly of New York there was no dominant circle who were disposed to take time for the leisurely contemplation of the finer things in art and life, and the art and life of New York suffered in consequence. In spite of all that had been said for generations about the employment of American subject matter, these men turned away from either the romance or the realities of the town. Except in rare instances they did not even satirize it. Instead they took refuge in sentimentalism and in remote times and places. "The Ballad of Babie Bell," "Ximen, or the Battle of the Sierra Morena, and Other Poems," "Poems of the Orient," "The Blameless Prince," "Poems Lyric and Idyllic," "Königsmark, and Other Poems," "The King's Bell," and "The Book of the East" were the natural output of such a group. Moreover, the plays were of the same sort. "Tortesa the Usurer," "The Merchant of Bogota," "Francesca da Rimini," and "Leonora, or the World's Own" represented the majority. "Fashion" and "Rip Van Winkle" were quite the exceptions.

Of his generation Stoddard was perhaps more devoted than any other in his worship of a fanciful and unvitalized Muse. The criticisms of Lowell and Holmes served as correctives for the artificialities of Stedman and Aldrich, but Stoddard made no poetic response either to the Civil War or to the march of science or to the religious changes that attended it. To the end of his career he was the complete product of the influences surrounding his youth. He had been brought to New York at the age of ten by his widowed mother and kept in school only until he was fifteen. For nine years he worked as an artisan, cultivating literature and literary people in his leisure hours. From 1853 to 1870 he held a post in the New York Customhouse, and from 1860 on, literary editorships with the *New York World*, the *Aldine* and the *New York Mail and Express*.

Stoddard's poetry is altogether detached from this life, ignoring or avoiding the facts of daily existence ; and even in the little lyrics of pleasure there is the lovely detachment of the orchid. Though now and again they show signs of becoming mildly erotic, they have no passion in them. Rather they exhibit the chaste delights of the virtuoso, who takes up one object after another from the glass-covered cabinets in the museum which his fancy has furnished, looks it over fondly, admires its form and color, and sets it back with even pulse until such time as he shall choose to gaze on it again. These lyrics are sometimes nature descriptions and sometimes nature fantasies. Often they are about the idea of love — rather than about love itself — and about wine — but not about conviviality. In the philosophical ones there is a negative tone, as in

> Man loses but the life he lives
> And only lives the life he loses.

or in

> There is no life on land or sea
> Save in the quiet moon and me ;
> Nor ours is true, but only seems
> Within some dead old World of Dreams.

And this dream world was an abandoned unreality and not a hope for something better.

Taken at its best, his verse is chiefly excellent for its form. As it does not spring from any vivid experiencing of life, it is conventional and reminiscent rather than spontaneous and original. It suggests many measures from many periods. In only a few poems, which purport to be themselves imitations from the East, he writes what seems fresh and new. His real gift was in the composition of little poetic cameos, bits of from four to a dozen lines, the dainty ornaments of literature.

The career of Thomas Bailey Aldrich was closely interwoven with the whole fabric of professional authorship in America. Like Bryant and Willis before him, and like Stedman, Stoddard, and Winter of his own generation, he established himself in New York, although he was a New England boy; but unlike all the others he fulfilled his career in Boston. It was an accident of dollars and cents that kept him out of Harvard and put him into a New York office. A love of literature led him then successively into the adventurous byways of Bohemian New York, the secure dignity of magazine editorship in Boston, and the fair prospects of independent literary success as enjoyed on Beacon Hill.

To be explicit, he was born in Portsmouth, New Hampshire, in 1836. His father's pursuit of fortune took Aldrich as a child to many parts of the country, but brought him back to Portsmouth at the age of thirteen. For the next three years he lived there the life which provided the basic facts for "The Story of a Bad Boy." Lack of funds prevented his entering Harvard, and in 1852 he undertook a clerkship in the office of a New York uncle. In 1855, when he was still only nineteen, he published his first volume of poetry and became junior literary critic on the *Evening Mirror*. In the next several years he held a sub-editorship in New York on the *Home Journal* and the *Saturday Press* and literary adviserships to several minor publishing houses, capping off with the editorship of the *Illustrated News*, which had become a thing of the past when, in 1866, he was called to Boston to become editor of *Every Saturday*. This post he held for nine years. For the six years up to 1881 he was an abundant contributor to the *Atlantic Monthly* and for the next nine, 1881–1890, he was the editor. During the remainder of his life he held no literary position.

During his fifteen years in New York, Greeley and Bryant, two newspaper editors, were perhaps the dominant figures in the literary and intellectual stratum, Willis and Halleck the most popular, Henry Clapp, Jr., and Charles T. Congdon the cleverest, and " Bohemia," with its rallying point at Pfaff's restaurant, the visible rallying place for the authors.[1] Aldrich gravitated toward this group, but never really belonged to it. Just why he did not can be inferred from a sentence by Howells, whose nature was very like his own: " I remember that, as I sat at that table, under the pavement, in Pfaff's beer-cellar, and listened to the wit that did not seem very funny, I thought of the dinner with Lowell, the breakfast with Fields, the supper at the Autocrat's, and felt that I had fallen very far." [2]

The men who gathered at Pfaff's were very conscious of Boston, though their consciousness came out in various ways. The most violent said that the thought of it made them as ugly as sin ; others loved it though they left it, as Whitman did " the open road " ; and some, on the outskirts of " Bohemia," were not too aggressively like Stedman, who admitted much later, " I was very anxious to bring out my first book in New York in Boston style, having a reverence for Boston, which I continued to have." Aldrich was of like mind, and readily accepted Osgood's invitation to " the Hub " and to the editorship of *Every Saturday*. Years after he wrote to Bayard Taylor, who could understand : " I miss my few dear friends in New York — but that is all. There is a finer intellectual atmosphere here than in our city. . . . The people of Boston are full-blooded

[1] For varying sentiments about " Bohemia " see the following passages : Ferris Greenslet, " Life of Thomas Bailey Aldrich," pp. 37-47 ; W. D. Howells, " Literary Friends and Acquaintances," pp. 68-76 ; Stedman and Gould, " Life of Edmund Clarence Stedman," pp. 208, 209 ; William Winter, " Old Friends," pp. 291-297.

[2] In reply to this and like passages William Winter wrote : " No literary circle comparable with the Bohemian group of that period, in ardor of genius, variety of character, and singularity of achievement, has since existed in New York, nor has any group of writers anywhere existent in our country been so ignorantly and grossly misrepresented and maligned " (" Old Friends," p. 138).

readers, appreciative, trained." And later, to Stedman : " In
the six years I have been here, I have found seven or eight
hearts so full of noble things that there is no room in them for
such trifles as envy and conceit and insincerity. I did n't find
more than two or three such in New York, and I lived there
fifteen years. It was an excellent school for me — to get out
of ! " Boston was his native heath, in spite of his own saying :
" Though I am not genuine Boston, I am Boston-plated."

Aldrich's literary career began and ended with the writing
of poetry, but what he did in the interims of poetical silence
contributed to the peculiar character of his work even though
it was a source of distraction and sometimes of prolonged
interruption. As a reader and editor he was schooled from
very young manhood in the exercise of a peculiarly fine artistic
taste, a taste so exacting in detail that the *Atlantic* under his
direction was described by a foreign critic as " the best edited
magazine in the English language." He did not reserve the
exercise of this rectitude of judgment for the work of others,
but applied it with perhaps increased austerity to himself. His
verse will consequently endure close examination, and the later
collections will show the virtues and defects of scrupulous
rejection and of the revision in each succeeding publication
of the work which he chose to preserve.

The virtues of work so carefully perfected are evident. His
effects are, in the end, all calculated, for he gave no quarter
to what he had produced with zest if it did not ring true to
his critical ear. His poetic machinery is therefore well oiled
and articulated. His metaphors are sound and his diction
happily adjusted. " The vanilla-flavored adjectives and the
patchouli-scented participles " criticized by his kindly senior,
Dr. Holmes, are pared away. So in the little steel engravings
that are the best expressions of his peculiar talent there is
a fine simplicity, but it is the simplicity of an accomplished
woman of the world rather than of a village maid. And herein
lie the shortcomings of Aldrich's poetry — that it is the poetry

of accomplishment. As a youth in New York, writing while Halleck's popularity was at its height, he was not independent enough to be more original than his most admired townsman. The verses in "The Bells: a Collection of Chimes" are most of them clearly imitative; and from the day of "Babie Bell" on, whatever of originality was Aldrich's belonged to the library and the drawing-room and the literary club rather than to the seas, woods, and mountains.

It is logical, then, that his longer narrative poems have least of his own stamp in them. From a literary point of view they are well enough, but they are literary grass of the field and have no more claim on the primary attention of a modern reader than do the bulk of prose short stories written in the same years by Aldrich and his fellows. The only one that stands out is "Pauline Pavlovna," and that because it has the dramatic vigor and the startling unexpectedness of conclusion which mark the best of his prose tales. It is logical, too, that in his more ambitious odes — such as "Spring in New England" and the "Shaw Memorial Ode," which open and close the second volume of his poems — he did not appear to the best advantage. Memorials of the Civil War are adequate only if written with epic vision, but the best that Aldrich did with such material was to make it the ground for heartfelt tributes to the nobility of his fallen friends. Read Moody's "Ode in Time of Hesitation" beside Aldrich's slender lyric based on the same man and the same memorial, and the difference is self-evident. Aldrich's biographer has commented on the rarity of his æsthetic sense, "among modern poets with their preoccupations, philosophical, religious and political." In this not unjust criticism of Aldrich — which marks a distinction rather than a superiority — lies the reason why he should have left the writing of national odes to poets who were sometimes capable of such preoccupation.

In writing on personal and local and occasional themes Aldrich dealt with more congenial material. When celebrating his fellow-authors and the places he loved he could invoke beauty with an unpreoccupied mind; and he did so with unvarying success, addressing the choicest of the limited public in which he was really interested. The kind of folk he cared for " Drank deep of life, *new books* and hearts of men," like Henry Howard Brownell. As a youth he wrote delightedly of a certain month when he could see " her " every day and browse in a library of ten thousand volumes. He was a literary poet for literary people. As such he was most successful in poems which ranged in length from the sonnet to the quatrain. In the tiny bits like " Destiny," " Heredity," " Identity," " Memory," " I 'll not confer with Sorrow," " Pillared Arch and Sculptured Tower," he achieved works as real as Benvenuto's jewel settings. It was a fulfillment of the wish recorded in his " Lyrics and Epics ":

> I would be the lyric
> Ever on the lip,
> Rather than the epic
> Memory lets slip.
> I would be the diamond
> At my lady's ear
> Rather than a June rose
> Worn but once a year.

No more charming tribute was ever paid Aldrich than this of Whittier's narrated by a friend who had been visiting for a week with the poet in his old age : " Every evening he asked me to repeat to him certain short poems, often " Destiny," and once even ' that audacious " Identity," ' as he called it ; but at the end he invariably said, ' Now thee knows without my saying so that I want " Memory," ' and with his wonderful far-off gaze he always repeated after me : ' Two petals from that wild-rose tree.' "

In his address at a meeting held in memory of Edmund Clarence Stedman in January, 1909, Hamilton Mabie struck the main note in two complementary statements : " Mr. Stedman belongs with those who have not only enriched literature with works of quality and substance, but who have represented it in its public relationships," and, " Stedman was by instinct and temperament a man of the town." He elected to live in Manhattan just as deliberately as Aldrich elected to live in Boston ; and in this distinction lies something much broader than the mere difference between the two men.

Stedman was born in Hartford, Connecticut, in 1833. After the death of his father and the remarriage of his mother, he was brought up from 1839 to 1850 under charge of an uncle. A member of the class of 1853 at Yale, he was "rusticated" (see p. 282) and then expelled for persistent misbehavior. Until 1863 he was in journalism, as petty proprietor in two Connecticut towns, and later as member of the *New York Tribune* staff, ending with two years as war correspondent. In 1863 he went into Wall Street, and in 1869 became a member of the New York Stock Exchange. From this date to the end of his life in 1908 he knew little real repose, oscillating from over-exertion in business to over-exertion in writing, with occasional enforced vacations. His work as poet was inseparable from his labors as editor and critic. In this field he wrote " Victorian Poets," 1875, " Poets of America," 1885, and " The Nature and Elements of Poetry," 1892 ; and edited the " Library of American Literature " (with Ellen Hutchinson) 1888–1889, " A Victorian Anthology," 1895, and " An American Anthology," 1900.

Stedman took the consequences of settling in the commercial capital of the United States. While the members of the Saturday Club were lending distinction to Boston, the members of the Ornithorhyncus Club and the Bohemians were receiving the impress of New York. Men came to the Saturday luncheons from Salem and Haverhill, Concord, and Cambridge as well as near-by Brookline and Boston itself, but the New York groups congregated into literary neighborhoods in the " Unitary Home "

or "on the south side of Tenth Street." Thus it came about
that Aldrich contributed to Boston what he brought there, but
that Stedman was "made in New York." As a result Aldrich
was more frankly absorbed in the concerns of the enlightened
reader, and Stedman relatively more interested in a broader
society. Both were war correspondents, but Aldrich admitted
the war into his poetry only rarely, and then without much
success. On the other hand, the first eighth of Stedman's collected poems are entitled "In War Time," and with the poems
of Manhattan, of New England, and of special occasions amount
to nearly one half the volume. Moreover, of the poems by
Stedman which are generally known and quoted, quite the
larger portion are included in utterances which are representative
of literature "in its public relationships."

A timely admonition from Lowell, as valuable as the one
from Holmes to Aldrich, helped keep him out of the byways
in which he was inclined to stray. In 1866 Stedman was
proud of his "Alectryon," a blank-verse poem on a classic
theme which had appeared in one of his books three years before.

When Mr. Lowell praised the volume in *The North American Review*
I was chagrined that he did not allude to my *pièce de résistance*, and
finally hinted as much to him. He at once said that it was my "best
piece of work," but "no addition to poetic literature," since we already
have enough masterpieces of that kind — from Landor's "Hamadryad"
and Tennyson's "Œnone" down to the latest effort by Swinburne or
Mr. Fields. So I have never written since upon an antique theme.
Upon reflection, I thought Lowell right. A new land calls for new song.

The best of Stedman's nature poems are directly drawn from
boyhood reminiscence or from a voyage and vacation in the
West Indies, and many of his songs and ballads are derived
from contemporary backgrounds and episodes.

Stedman did his work as a poet, however, in full consciousness of all the wealth of continental literature and the splendors
of Old World tradition. Perhaps there was no single work into
which he put more ambition than into his uncompleted metrical

version from the Greek of the Sicilian Idyllists. His "Victorian Poets " and the anthology which followed were undertaken by way of making a workmanlike approach to the poetry of his own countrymen. As a reader he had the scholar's attitude toward literature ; as a poet he felt a respect approaching reverence for the established traditions of his art. And yet — and in this respect Stedman is lamentably rare among critics and artists — his conviction that the centuries had achieved permanent canons for the poetic art did not lead him into slashing abuse of those who dissented from his views. He wrote no single essay which better demonstrated his wisdom, his sanity, and his charming suavity of mind and manner than his discussion of Walt Whitman. Although he felt a native distaste for much of Whitman's writing and for the way most of it was done, he succeeded in applying a fair mode of criticism, and he did it in the manner of an artist and not as a counsel for the plaintiff. Instead of beginning with cleverness and ending with truculence Stedman did himself the honor of coming out magnanimously with ". . . there is something of the Greek in Whitman, and his lovers call him Homeric, but to me he shall be our old American Hesiod, teaching us works and days." The measure of Stedman's poetry should therefore be made in the light of two characteristics : his instinctive and temperamental love of the town, as this determined his choice of subject matter, and his widely read appreciation of the older poets, as this affected his sense of artistic form.

Although some of it was very popular at the moment and not altogether negligible to-day, his less important work was the succession of verses which were written in the spirit and, in some cases, at the speed of the journalist. "The Diamond Wedding," for example, was done in an evening and was the talk of the town thirty-six hours later. But, more than that, it was actually good satire, — as good a piece of its kind as had appeared in New York since Halleck's "Fanny." So, too, "Israel Freyer's Bid for Gold " was published three days after the idea had first occurred to him. These, like the " Ballad of Lager Bier " and " The Prince's Ball " and even " How Old Brown Took Harper's Ferry " represented the high spirit of youth rollicking on paper in the fashion of the young authors of the " Salmagundi " and " Croaker " satires.

" Bohemia " and " Pan in Wall Street," though composed in this same general period, are far more sober, deliberate, and genuinely poetical. In both Stedman dealt with the romantic rather than with the ridiculous or contemptible in city life. From the years of his work on " The Victorian Poets " to the end two developments took place. He inclined more to refine on the form of his poems, giving over at last all fluent satire, and he progressed in subject matter, first to what literature and the past suggested and then, with advancing years, to consider-ations of age and death. The changes are not abrupt, but they are pervasive and evident.

During the last dozen years of his life poetry could not be his natural form of expression, for the world was too much with him. A great deal of the time when he was not getting or losing on Change (he seems to have lost rather more than he spent) he devoted to service on all sorts of boards and councils of good works, speaking and versifying for special occasions, editing miscellaneously, — even a " Pocket Guide to Europe," — and giving advice and encouragement to younger poets. He was admirably representing literature in its public relationships and paying the price which is always exacted of an ambassador of any sort in the complete sacrifice of independent leisure. There is something pathetic in his oft-repeated protests in these latter years at being called a " banker-poet " or " broker-poet," for he had failed to become rich as he had hoped, and he had enjoyed on the whole less security than many of his acquaint-ances who had attached themselves to literature in some pro-fessional way. This, however, had been a mistake not so much of judgment as of temperament. Unless his voluminous biography utterly misrepresents him he had no true capacity for leisure.

He was an intellectual flagellant; and his poetry, although he was in theory devoted to it, was in reality a proof of the love of art which continually tantalized and distracted him but never won his complete allegiance.

Richard Watson Gilder was born in Bordentown, New Jersey, in 1844. He studied there in Bellevue Seminary, founded by his father, intending to practice law. He was in brief active service during the war when Pennsylvania was invaded. On his father's death he entered journalistic work, first with two Newark newspapers and then with *Hours at Home* in New York. From its founding in 1870 he was associate editor of the old *Scribner's Monthly* (since 1881 *The Century*) and from 1881 was its editor in chief. He became increasingly important in New York as contributor to civic welfare, and at the same time held his own as editor and poet. Thus he was first president of the Kindergarten Association of New York and a founder of the Authors' Club. He was identified with the leading agencies for cultural and humanitarian ends, was in demand as laureate on special occasions, and was recipient of many honorary degrees.

Gilder was almost exclusively a lyric poet. His units are very brief, — there are more than five hundred in the one-volume "Complete" edition, — very few extending to the one hundred lines ordained by Poe. Even among lyrics, moreover, he set distinct boundaries to his field. Among his metropolitan fellows — Taylor, Stoddard, Aldrich, Stedman, and the others — he was notable in not writing imitative and reminiscent poetry. These men must have been rather definitely in the back of his mind when he wrote:

> Some from books resound their rhymes —
>   Set them ringing with a faint,
>   Sorrowful, and sweet, and quaint
> Memory of the olden times,
> Like the sound of evening chimes.

And too many of his contemporaries did not follow as well as he the admonition,

> Tell to the wind
> Thy private woes, but not to human ear.

There was still a world of beauty left for him, first of all in songs of love. It is a chaste and disembodied passion that he celebrated in frequent groups of song. The lady is a delight to the eye, modest, timid, and yet all-generous; the lover eager, gentle, adoring, and inspired to nobility. What Gilder recorded in one of the earliest of these lyrics seems in large measure to hold true of them all. After an enumeration of the lady's charms and the charm she bestowed upon earth and sky, he continued:

> I love her doubting and anguish;
> I love the love she withholds;
> I love my love that loveth her
> And anew her being molds.

A poet of so rarefied a sentiment as this hangs on the brink of sentimentalism, but Gilder seldom fell over, for his nicety of feeling could not easily be led into mawkishness.

His regard for nature was refined and sophisticated. One passes from the exquisite " Dawn " with which his first volume opened, past " Thistle-Down " and " The Violet " to the poems of Tyringham, his summer home; and then to " Home Acres " and " The Old Place," which had no rival; and ends " In Helena's Garden " between " The Marble Pool " and " The Sundial," to drink tea with eleven pretty girls at a round table made from a granite millstone. The sun shines brightly, the flowers are in bloom, their odor mingling with that of the souchong, the conversation is facile, and everybody is amiable and complacent. From such a catalogue one might expect sappy and emasculated nature poems, but once again Gilder's sanity rescues him. Even in Helena's garden he is rather a strong man at ease than a sybarite.

In his enjoyment of the allied arts his taste was generous. Music appealed to him most of all. He chanted the praises of Handel and Chopin, Rubinstein and Tschaikowsky, but of Beethoven still more, and of Wagner most of all. He told of the thrill he caught from the various instruments, but of the deeper thrill from the singer and from the chorus. The art of "Madame Butterfly" appealed to him, but not so deeply as the power of the drama, even if played "In a little theater, in the Jewry of the New World." Naturally he wrote much of his own art, revealing his high seriousness in his poems about the poet. Poetry was not solely the record or the evidence of beauty for him. Although his only markedly personal allegiance in poetry was an allegiance to Keats, it was a fealty to Keats taken off before his prime. Gilder lamented the wrong fate had done the youthful genius and did not content himself with reiterating that "a thing of beauty is a joy forever."

For Gilder never, even in his most ecstatic moods, indulged in the fallacy of setting art above life. Though his work does not show the marked changes which have developed in many evolving careers, there is a clear emergence of philosophic and then social and civic interest in his progressive volumes. His sense for the need of a brave integrity comes to the surface in such poems as "Reform," "The Prisoner's Thought," "The Heroic Age," "The Demagogue," "The Tool," "The New Politician," "The Whisperers," and "In Times of Peace." To such themes as these and to his poems of heroism and of the reunited country Gilder brought the same delicacy of touch as to his poems of love and art and nature, and he brought into view in them the latent vigor which saved the others from being merely pink and mellifluous.

In poetry written on the scale of Gilder's there is need of finest workmanship. There is no chance for Turneresque effects :

> The foreground golden dirt,
> The sunshine painted with a squirt.

These paintings are like miniatures which must submit to scrutiny under the reading glass. In this connection his craftsmanship becomes interesting in the history of versification. For Gilder was at once a master of the more complex forms of traditional verse and an early experimenter in the free, rhythmic forms which are the subject of spirited controversy to-day. Some rhythmic prose appears in his earliest volume, but the sonnet prevails at the beginning of his authorship, and at the end it almost utterly disappears in favor of the freest sort of blank verse, irregular and unrimed iambic measures, poems which are suggestive of but distinct from Whitman's, and frank prose-poetry, not even " shredded prose " — in the language of Mr. Howells — but printed in solid paragraphs. Except for the sonnet, Gilder had no favorite measure or stanza in his earlier volumes. Few poems are in exactly similar measures. There are lines of from three to seven feet, quatrains of various sorts, and rhythms from that of the heroic couplet to that of the so-called Pindaric ode. But whatever the measure he adopted, he was scrupulously consistent to it, though he employed it easily, seldom conceding an awkward or prosaic locution to the exigencies of lilt or rime. So he seems to have been equally at home in the use of sundry forms — in the antiphonal ballad like " The Voyager," within the pale of " The Sonnet," in the anapæstic flow of "A Song of Early Autumn," in the swift-moving iambics of "A Woman's Thought," with its intricate double and triple rimes, or in the psalmlike sibilations of " The Whisperers."

The philosophy of Gilder was the philosophy of his most enlightened contemporaries. There is in it much of Emerson, whom he called the " shining soul " of the New World, and there is much of Whitman, though it is not clear whether their likeness does not lie in their common accord with Emerson rather than in a direct influence from " the good gray poet " to Gilder. The immanence of God in nature and in the heart of man (see " The Voice of the Pine ") ; the unity of all natural

law (see " Destiny ") ; the conflict between religion and theology
(see " Credo ") ; and a faith in the essentials of democratic life,
— these are the wholesome fundamentals of modern thinking
shared alike by Emerson and Whitman and Gilder. Gilder is
not their most impressive or prophetic expositor. He is a lesser
voice in the choir. The point of real distinction for him is
that he combined so finely the discriminating work of a literary
editor with the unwearying life of a good and courageous
citizen and still kept the current of his song serene and clear.

BOOK LIST

Individual Authors

RICHARD HENRY STODDARD. Works. Complete Poems. 1 vol. His
verse appeared in book form originally as follows : Footprints, 1849 ;
Poems, 1852 ; Songs of Summer, 1857 ; The King's Bell, 1862 ;
Abraham Lincoln : an Horatian Ode, 1865 ; The Book of the East,
and Other Poems, 1871 ; The Lion's Cub, with Other Verse, 1890.

Collections

BOYNTON, PERCY H. American Poetry, pp. 542–554, 680–684.
STEDMAN and HUTCHINSON. Library of American Literature, Vol.
VIII, pp. 226–238.

Biography

Recollections Personal and Literary, by Richard Henry Stoddard.
Ripley Hitchcock, editor. 1903.

THOMAS BAILEY ALDRICH. Works. The Writings of, in 9 vols. 1907.
(Vols. I–II, Poetry ; Vols. III–IX, Prose.) The best single volume
of the poetry is Poems. 1906. His works appeared in book form
originally as follows : The Bells, 1855 ; The Ballad of Babie Bell,
1856 ; Daisy's Necklace, 1857 ; Pampinea and Other Poems, 1861 ;
Out of his Head, 1862 ; The Story of a Bad Boy, 1869 ; Marjorie
Daw, and Other People, 1873 ; Prudence Palfrey, 1874 ; Cloth of
Gold, 1874 ; Flower and Thorn, 1876 ; The Queen of Sheba, 1877 ;
The Stillwater Tragedy, 1880 ; From Ponkapog to Pesth, 1883 ;
Mercedes, and Later Lyrics, 1883 ; Wyndham Towers, 1889 ; The
Sisters' Tragedy, 1891 ; Two Bites at a Cherry, 1893 ; An Old Town
by the Sea, 1893 ; Unguarded Gates, and Other Poems, 1895 ; Later
Lyrics, 1896 ; Judith and Holofernes, 1896.

Collection

STEDMAN and HUTCHINSON. Library of American Literature, Vol.
IX, pp. 377–399.

Bibliography
A chronological list of Aldrich's works is appended to the Life. See Biography, below.

Biography
The Life of Thomas Bailey Aldrich is by Ferris Greenslet. 1908. See also The Story of a Bad Boy, by Aldrich himself.

EDMUND CLARENCE STEDMAN. Works. The Poems of. 1908. These appeared in book form originally as follows: The Prince's Ball, 1860; Poems Lyrical and Idyllic, 1860; The Battle of Bull Run, 1861; Alice of Monmouth, 1863; The Blameless Prince, and Other Poems, 1869; Victorian Poets, 1875; Hawthorne and Other Poems, 1877; Poets of America, 1885; The Nature and Elements of Poetry, 1892; A Victorian Anthology, 1895; An American Anthology, 1900; Mater Coronata, 1901.

Bibliography
An excellent chronological list is contained in Vol. II of the Life.

Biography
The Life and Letters is by Laura Stedman and George M. Gould. 1910. 2 vols. See also A New England Childhood: the Story of the Boyhood of Edmund Clarence Stedman. Margaret Fuller. 1916.

RICHARD WATSON GILDER. Works. The Poems of. Household Edition. 1908. These appeared in book form originally as follows: The New Day, 1875; The Celestial Passion, 1878; Lyrics, 1878; The Poet and his Master, and Other Poems, 1878; Two Worlds, and Other Poems, 1891; Great Remembrance, and Other Poems, 1893; For the Country, 1897; In Palestine and Other Poems, 1898; Poems and Inscriptions, 1901; A Christmas Wreath, 1903; In the Heights, 1905; A Book of Music, 1906; Fire Divine, 1907; Lincoln the Leader, 1909; Grover Cleveland, 1910.

Collection
STEDMAN and HUTCHINSON. Library of American Literature, Vol. X, pp. 252–259.

Biography
Letters of Richard Watson Gilder. Rosamond Gilder, editor. 1916.

TOPICS AND PROBLEMS

Read the biographical passages cited in the text relative to the difference of literary atmosphere in New York and Boston. Read W. D. Howells's "A Hazard of New Fortunes" for a further contrast between the two cities.

Read Stoddard's poems with a view to marking definite literary influences as shown in poems which seem evidently imitative.

Read a group of the four-line and eight-line poems of Aldrich and compare them in spirit and execution with similar bits by Stoddard and by Emerson.

Read Stedman's critical essays on one or two of the New England poets and on two or three of his fellow New Yorkers. Read his essay on Walt Whitman. Does Stedman's own verse confirm the theory of his criticisms of Whitman?

Read Gilder's poems in the newer verse forms and compare them with one of the contemporary poets mentioned in the last chapter of this book.

Is there a legitimate connection to be mentioned between Gilder's poems on civic themes and the movement for better citizenship in the 1890's? Can you cite political events and characters and novels or plays on political life which belong to this period?

CHAPTER XXIII

THE POETRY OF THE SOUTH

The non-mention of any Southern writers for nearly two centuries in a history of American literature is likely to mislead the unthinking reader. Certain qualifying facts should be reckoned with in drawing any deductions. The first and most specific is that Poe, although born in Boston and largely active in Philadelphia and New York, belongs to the South. His poems and tales are without time and space, but his criticisms are often vigorously sectional; yet he was really an isolated character, speaking for himself without associates or disciples.

For the comparative withdrawal of the South during a long period from the writing and publishing of poems, essays, and stories, there are two main reasons. One is the general nature of the early settlement (see pp. 3, 4, 6). The spread of the population over a wide area and the consequent lack of large towns gave no encouragement to printers and publishers before the Revolution and furnished no such gathering places as Boston, New York, and Philadelphia. Literature, like all the other arts, thrives best in fellowship. With the Revolution and after it the richest culture of the South devoted itself to statesmanship and expressed itself in oratory. John Adams, governmental specialist, regretted that he had no leisure for the arts (see p. 69), but Thomas Jefferson, his successor in the White House, was a creative educator, a linguist, an architect, and not unversed in music. Southern gentlemen from the days of Jefferson and Madison to those of Abraham Lincoln read " Mr. Addison " and " Mr. Steele " and " Mr. Pope," fashioned their speech and writing after those courtly

343

models, and, when they wrote at all, circulated their efforts among friends, not submitting them to the sordid touch of the publisher.

Moreover, the literary consciousness of the South is shown in the history of the American theater. The earliest performances of which there is record were given on Southern estates in the second quarter of the eighteenth century. The Hallam company of players, arriving from England in 1752, secured their first hearing in Maryland and Virginia. Smaller Southern communities held their own with New York and Philadelphia in the patronage of the stage, while surviving Puritan prejudice made New England an arid field for the drama until well into the next century. Again, the founding of the University of Virginia, preëminent though not the oldest among Southern colleges, was a doubly important event in American education, for it was first among state universities, with a curriculum recognizing the demands of citizenship, and it was unique in the beauty of its housing. Finally, journalism was not neglected in the South, keeping pace with the progress in the rest of the country; and the *Southern Literary Messenger* (1834–1865) held an enviable place among American periodicals during its thirty years of life.

From 1850 the natural course of events in the South began to develop literary centers, of which Charleston, South Carolina, was the most notable. At this date William Gilmore Simms (1806–1870) was in the high prime of life and was the unchallenged leader by virtue of age, literary achievement, and force of personality. He had appeared before the public with two volumes of poems in 1827, without foregoing poetry had gone on to prolific writing of adventure stories, and had produced at the rate of more than a book a year. He was an aboundingly vigorous, somewhat turbulent man, with a stimulating gift for talk and a very generous interest in all men of literary feeling and especially in younger aspirants. Around him and John Russell, the bookseller, there gathered by social gravitation a group who became for Charleston what the frequenters of the Old Corner Book Store were to Boston and rather more than what the "Bohemians" of Pfaff's restaurant were to New York. Russell's became a rendezvous for the best people during the daytimes — perhaps to buy, perhaps only to talk — and in the evenings the men gathered in the spirit of a literary club, though without organization or name. *Russell's Magazine* was the natural fruit of the group-spirit thus engendered, just as the *Atlantic Monthly* (see p. 288) was of similar associations in Boston or as the *Dial* had been of the Transcendental Club in 1840 (see p. 195).

It was a further consequence of this plowing of the cultural soil that two Charleston boys born in 1829 and 1830 were encouraged as young men not only to write but to publish their poems and that one became the first editor and the other a frequent contributor to the local periodical. These were Henry Timrod and Paul Hamilton Hayne. Of the two friends, somewhat as in the case of Halleck and Drake, Timrod, the one who showed promise of finer things, was the victim of an early death. As a youth he was given to the introspective seriousness and the grave extravagances of the growing poet — characteristics which are not wholly sacrificed in the grown poet, as they are in the average "sensible" man. His inclination to extol emotion as an end in itself, however, was fostered by a native hospitality toward sentimentalism for which there was little to correspond in the more prosaic North. In fact "the susceptibility of early feeling" which Irving wished to keep alive (see p. 126) and which was the central thread in Jane Austen's "Sense and Sensibility" was, and still is, a cue to certain prevailing Southern traits. Whatever may have been the origin of Southern speech and manners, they have continued in some measure to resemble those which we associate with English literature of the mid-eighteenth century. Both have a touch of courtly formality, a tendency toward the oratorical style, an explicit insistence on honor and chivalry, a display of deference to womanhood and to all beauty, and both are in constant danger from the insincerity which besets a speech or a literature which relies on conventional phrasing until the original locutions lose their original vitality.[1]

Timrod as a youthful versifier passed through his period of unconvincing extravagance, and even in his earlier work showed by occasional flashes that he had his own gift for expression as well as a receptive mind for poetry. In 1859 his first book of poems was published. It had the coveted distinction of the Ticknor and Fields, Boston, imprint, but it was indubitably the utterance of a Charleston poet. The sonnet "I know not why, but all this weary day" is full of genuine feeling, and in its ominous despair foretells the coming war :

> Now it has been a vessel losing way,
> Rounding a stormy headland ; now a gray
> Dull waste of clouds above a wintry main ;
> And then, a banner, drooping in the rain,
> And meadows beaten into bloody clay.

Timrod's two greater poems were dedicated to the Confederacy. They are the outpourings of loyalty to the shortlived nation, full of passion, no freer from hate and recrimination than the average poems from the North, but positive in their ardent faith in the beneficent part the Confederacy was to play in future history. Like all other war poets he suffered from the embittering effects of the conflict. His first inclination was to think more about his hopes for the South than about his hatred of the North ; yet even in "The Cotton Boll" and in "Ethnogenesis" he saw red at times, as any human partisan was bound to do. The newly federated South was to send out from its whitened fields an idealized cotton crop that "only bounds its blessings by mankind." The labors of the

---

[1] A corresponding danger on the other hand is that a people who abjure all such phrases will abjure also the things for which they stand, until they become irredeemably prosaic and matter of fact.

planter were to strengthen the sinews of the world. Yet into
this finely altruistic mood came the acrid thought of the war
which was in progress, and in a moment he was vilifying the
" Goth " in the same breath that he was resolving to be
merciful. Timrod endured without flinching as an individual.
As a confederate patriot he dreamed

> Not only for the glories which the years
> Shall bring us ; not for lands from sea to sea,
> And wealth, and power, and peace, though these shall be ;
> But for the distant peoples we shall bless,
> And the hushed murmurs of a world's distress.

But when the war was over, in his " Address to the Old Year "
(1866) he was all for complete and speedy reconciliation.

> A time of peaceful prayer,
>   Of law, love, labor, honest loss and gain —
>   These are the visions of the coming reign
> Now floating to them on this wintry air.

Fortunately, in the slow approach toward this millennial conclusion Timrod was spared the brutal blunders of the Reconstruction period, for he died within the next twelvemonth,
serene in his hopes.

Paul Hamilton Hayne (1830–1886), a man of moderate
talents and of achievement that was greater in bulk than
quality, was whole-heartedly devoted to literature. With the
founding of *Russell's*, while the bookseller supplied the capital
and Simms the general stimulus, Hayne was the obviously
willing and capable young man to carry the editorial routine.
If the war had not cut short the life of the magazine within
three years, Hayne might have fulfilled a long and useful
career in its guidance. Moreover, the kind of criticism to
which his work would have accustomed him might have
refined his own verse and reduced its quantity as it did for
Aldrich and Gilder. But a career like theirs was denied him

when *Russell's* was discontinued, and he was forced into the precarious existence of living by his pen without the assurance of any regular salary. Though this may be a sordid detail, it is not a negligible one, for the lack of a certain income not only disturbs the artist's mind but goads him to writing for monetary rather than artistic ends. This result is apparent in Hayne's work. He had to force himself, and he wrote in consequence the only kind of poetry that industry and good will can produce.

Much of it was for special occasions. He wrote on demand for everything, from art exhibits to cotton expositions, always conscientiously without any special lightness or felicity. He fell into the conventional nineteenth-century habit of writing on romantic subjects located in parts of the earth which he knew only from other men's poetry. His best work, of course, sprang more directly from his experience. Some of his war lyrics are stirring, though seldom up to Timrod's best. Some of his protests after the war are spirited and wholly justified by the stupid clumsiness of Northern control. " South Carolina to the States of the North " and " The Stricken South to the North " suggest in verse what Page's " Red Rock " and Tourgée's " A Fool's Errand " present through the detail of extended novels. Hayne's tributes to other poets, particularly to Longfellow and Whittier, are full of generous admiration, and his nature poems ring finely true. Most of all the Southern pine fascinated him by its perennial grace and strength and its mysterious voice. A pine-tree anthology could be culled from his verse.

To be the poet of a class or a district and no more than that is ordinarily not a notable achievement, but the fact that they represented an epoch as well as a section emphasizes the significance of Timrod and Hayne. They were products of freshly stimulating conditions in the South ; before the war they began to sing for a neighborhood that had long been comparatively silent. And when the war came on, and after its conclusion, they were not only its best singers but they were remarkable in war literature for the fineness of their positive spirit and their relative freedom from abusive rancor. They reaped in love and praise the reward that their impoverished constituency could not pay them in money.

Sidney Lanier was born in Macon, Georgia, in 1842. He was therefore twelve or thirteen years younger than Hayne or Timrod, and his productive period was correspondingly later, namely, in the 70's. He could trace his Lanier ancestry back to the court musicians of the Stuarts, and beyond them to a conjectured past in France. His mother sang and played in the home, and his father, a courtly and refined lawyer, was a " gentle reader " of the old Southern school. Macon was a town of extreme orthodoxy where "the only burning issues were sprinkling versus immersion, freewill versus predestination," but where the rigors of Calvinism were mollified by innocent merrymaking and the amenities of Southern hospitality. From here Lanier went, in 1857, to Oglethorpe University as a member of the sophomore class, graduating from the modest college with first honors in 1860. Though successful in scholarship, he had found his chief enjoyments in wide reading of romantic literature and in flute-playing. He was convinced that his talents were in music, but his strong ethical bias led him to check them because he could not satisfactorily answer the question, What is the province of music in the economy of the world ? On his appointment as tutor at Oglethorpe he decided to remain in college-teaching, rounding out his preparation by two years at Heidelberg. When the war broke he seemed to be well started on the path trod by Longfellow and Lowell.

In " Tiger Lilies," his early romance, he described how the " afflatus of war " swept the South as it sweeps any land in the first hours of decision. " Its sound mingled with the serenity of the church organs and arose with the earnest words of preachers praying for guidance in the matter. It sighed in the half-breathed words of sweethearts, conditioning impatient lovers with war services. It thundered splendidly in the impassioned words of orators to the people. It whistled through the streets, it stole into the firesides, it clinked glasses in barrooms, it lifted the gray hairs of our wise men in conventions, it thrilled through the lectures in college halls, it rustled the thumbed book leaves of the schoolrooms. . . . It offered tests to all allegiances and loyalties, — of church, of state ; of private loves, of public devotion ; of personal consanguinity, of social ties." In 1861 Lanier enlisted in the first Georgia regiment to leave for the front. Four years later he returned with health permanently impaired by the hardships of service and of a prison camp.

Even though wrecked in health, he came out from the war saddened but not embittered, and convinced as early as 1867 that the saving of the Union had been worth the ordeal. His insistence that hatreds should be buried was maintained in face of every influence to the contrary. The countryside had been devastated and business brought to a stop. Libraries had been destroyed and colleges closed. As recuperation began the magnanimous influence of Lincoln waned, and the reign of the " carpetbaggers " inflamed the worst elements in the South, drove some of the better in despair to other parts of the country, and reduced the rest to bruised and heartsick indignation. Lanier could not be unaffected by such conditions. He took refuge in grinding work : first in teaching and then in several years of law practice in the examination of title deeds. " Tiger Lilies " was published in 1867 by Hurd and Houghton in New York, and a number of poems were printed there in the *Round Table* during 1867 and 1868. But depression and drudgery tended to silence him, and might have done so if the music in him had succumbed with the poetry and if the poetry had not been revived by the stimulating friendships of two older men, Paul Hamilton Hayne and Bayard Taylor.

Music gained a new hold on him during an enforced health trip to Texas in the winter of 1872–1873. He had reveled in the concerts he had heard in different visits to New York after the war, but in San Antonio he fell in with a group of musicians for whom he was a player as well as an auditor. Without any formal instruction in the flute he had achieved such a command of the instrument that it had become a second voice for him. In the autumn of '73 he met and played for Hamerick, Director of the Peabody Conservatory of Music in Baltimore, and in December he went in triumph to his initial rehearsal as first flutist in the newly organized Peabody Symphony Orchestra. For the rest of his life music was his most reliable means of support and a source of pleasure that amounted to little less than dissipation. As a performer he was in great demand for extra local engagements, from which he seemed to gain quite as much enjoyment as he gave — for he played in a kind of ecstasy; he "felt in his performance the superiority of the *momentary inspiration* to all the rules and shifts of mere technical scholarship." As an auditor, whether of his own music or that rendered by others, his appreciation was almost wholly sensuous, an experience of raptures, thrills, and swooning joys. "Divine lamentations, far-off blowings of great winds, flutterings of tree and flower leaves and airs troubled with wing-beats of birds or spirits; floatings hither and thither of strange incenses and odors and essences; warm floods of sunlight, cool gleams of moonlight, faint enchantments of twilight; delirious dances, noble marches, processional chants, hymns of joy and grief: Ah, midst all these I lived last night, in the first chair next to Theodore Thomas' orchestra." From such a comment one is prepared for frequent references to the more modern composers, few to Beethoven, and none at all to Bach and Brahms; and one is helped to understand also the mistakenly limited dictum — too often quoted — that "Music is love in search of a word." Music was immensely important in Lanier's emotional life;

the kind that he most enjoyed, and the kind of enjoyment he derived from it, furnished the cue for an interpretation of much of his poetry — a cue which is the clearer when compared with what music meant to Browning.

The development of a Baltimore orchestra in 1873 was an expression of the reawakening of artistic life from Baltimore to the Gulf. By 1870 the call was repeatedly sounded for a new literature and a new criticism in the South. Short-lived magazines sprang up and were flooded with copy before their early deaths. Much was written that was ostentatiously sectional in tone, but much by men like Hayne and Cable and Page that approached the standard set by Joel Chandler Harris in his appeal for a literature which should be "intensely local in feeling, but utterly unprejudiced and unpartisan as to opinions, traditions, and sentiment. Whenever we have a genuine Southern literature, it will be American and cosmopolitan as well." Equally in the interest of the South was Hayne's demand for criticism which should put a quietus on the fatuous scribblers who had nothing to say and said it badly. "No foreign ridicule," he wrote in the *Southern Magazine* in 1874, "can stop this growing evil, until our own scholars and thinkers have the manliness and honesty to discourage instead of applauding such manifestations of artistic weakness and artistic platitudes as have hitherto been foisted on us by persons uncalled and unchosen of any of the muses."

At the same time a generously enterprising spirit led several of the leading Northern editors to accept and even solicit contributions from the South. In 1873 *Scribner's Monthly* projected and secured a widely advertised series of articles on "the great South." *Harper's* had a series of its own. The *Atlantic*, with Howells as editor, followed conservatively, and the *Independent* opened its columns to the poetry of the men whom it had condemned in most aggressive terms a dozen years earlier. More important to Lanier than any of these was *Lippincott's*, in which "Corn," "The Symphony," and "The

Psalm of the West," with certain shorter poems, were published in 1875, 1876, and 1877 — poems by which his wide reputation was established.

The encouragement given him by Hayne in the dark days of the law, when he had no time to write, was followed by a Northern friendship of even greater value to him when the *Lippincott* poems were brought to the kindly attention of Bayard Taylor. This busy and large-hearted man of letters seems to have been the literary friend of his whole generation. He was on terms of easy acquaintance with the most renowned of his day. He was a companion of publishers, editors, and journalists, and he showed a most generous interest in the fortunes of promising younger men. His literary status is summarized in his relation to the literary ceremonies of the Centennial Exposition at Philadelphia in 1876. He wrote the Ode for the Fourth of July celebration after the honor had been declined by Bryant, Lowell, and Longfellow, and he had sufficient influence to gain for Lanier the distinction of writing the Cantata for the opening ceremonies. The exchange of letters between the two in connection with their efforts is unsurpassed as a record of detailed processes in poetic composition, criticism and rejoinder, and final revision.

Lanier's conscious command of a poetic theory was a product of his habits of study and led to his appointment by President Daniel Coit Gilman as lecturer in English literature at Johns Hopkins University.[1] From youth Lanier had been an extensive reader of the early English classics, and in Baltimore he eagerly used the resources of the Peabody Library, which was maintained especially for research students. He was keenly interested in stimulating general intelligence in literature among the adult public and also in promoting exact and technical study by qualified scholars. In 1878 he plunged once

---

[1] This was the second time that President Gilman had placed a poet in the position of teacher, for he had already done this with Edward Rowland Sill at the University of California (see p. 397).

more into study, planned lecture courses, projected a research program for himself, and early in the next year received the Hopkins appointment. He approached his work with the utmost zest and, as long as his strength lasted, lectured effectively and worked on the critical texts and treatises which the scholarship of his time was just beginning to supply. Now, however, when he had established working relations with the orchestra and the university, he sank under the strain of all the preceding struggle, and in 1881 he died before reaching his fortieth year.

Lanier's abiding conviction put the poet on the same plane with the prophet and the seer. He was far from according with Poe's total subordination of intellect and moral sense to the feeling for beauty. He seldom or never wrote a didactic poem, but he usually composed over a strong moralistic counterpoint. In " Corn " the poet

> leads the vanward of his timid time
> And sings up cowards with commanding rhyme.

In " The Bee " he will wage wars for the world. In " The Marshes of Glynn " he is

> the catholic man who hath mightily won
> God out of knowledge and good out of infinite pain.

The poet's judgments are, therefore, certain to surpass those of his age, certain to reap a harvest of derision and abuse, and certain to approach the right because they are made in the light of eternity rather than in the ephemeral shadow of any passing day.

The tolling of the bell of time which resounds throughout Lanier's poems does not deafen him to the harmonies or the discords of the moment. With all his consciousness of literary tradition he was far more alive to the present than many of his Southern contemporaries, who were not so genuinely literary as imitatively bookish. " Corn " tells the tale of the improvident cotton-grower who becomes "A gamester's catspaw and a banker's slave." "The Symphony" is an arraignment of the industrial system.

> If business is battle, name it so:
> War-crimes less will shame it so,
> And widows less will blame it so.

"Acknowledgment" (first sonnet) and "Remonstrance" were written of the troublous period which was wracked between doubts that merely disturbed and dogmas which were still advocated with all the subtleties of persecution that — in an enlightened age — will substitute ostracism for the stake and social boycott for excommunication.

In the modest volume of his collected work — for his writing was mainly done in his last eight years, and he was not a garrulous poet — there is a marked variety. "The Revenge of Hamish" is a clear reflection of his zest for heroic story. It is one of the notably successful attempts of his day to emulate the old ballad, and it is the better for restoring the spirit of balladry without imitating the manner. "How Love Looked for Hell," without being imitative of anyone, is distinctly pre-Raphaelite in tone. Rossetti might have written it. In "The Stirrup-Cup" there is an Elizabethan note, and "Night and Day" and the "Marsh Song — at Sunset" are literary lyrics for the readers of "Othello" and "The Tempest." These and their like give token of Lanier's versatility, just as the "Song of the Chattahoochee" displays his command of certain obvious devices in diction and rhythm; but the poems most distinctive of Lanier and most generally quoted are the longer meditations already mentioned, and, in particular, "The Symphony" and "The Marshes of Glynn." Of these the earlier is much quoted by social reformers for the vigor of its protests at the exploitation of labor; by musicians, because of the sustained metaphor — though it might better have been named "The Orchestra"; and by those who love a certain fulsomeness of sensuous appeal in verse. This last trait gains friends also for "The Marshes of Glynn," though its supreme passage, the last forty lines, is free from the decorative elaborations which in the earlier portion distract the reader from the content they adorn.

In the development of artistic power the formative period is the most open to influence and the most likely to be formal and self-conscious. Early and full maturity bring the nicest balance between the thing said and the manner of saying it; and a later period often is marked by overcompression or over-elaboration, a neglect of form in favor of content. Lanier, who died on the approach to middle life, had just published "The Science of English Verse" and was studiously aware of poetic processes, from the ingenious conceits of the "Paradise of Dainty Devices" to the metrical experiments of Swinburne and his contemporaries. In the compound of factors which were blending into the matured Lanier there was still a good measure of Elizabethan ingenuity. He felt a pleasant thrill in riding a metaphor down the page. He played repeatedly, for example, with the concept of the passage of time. In the second sonnet of "Acknowledgment" this age is a comma, and all time a complex sentence (four lines); in "Clover" the course-of-things is a browsing ox (twenty-five lines); in "The Symphony" the leaves are dials on which time tells his hours (three lines); in the first of the "Sonnets on Columbus" prickly seconds and dull-blade minutes mark three hours of suspense (three lines); and in "The Stirrup-Cup" death is a cordial compounded by time from the reapings of poets long dead (twelve lines). These all are picturesquely suggestive, but they are rather imposed on the idea than derived from it. Other poets, to be sure, have erred in the same way and then perhaps redeemed themselves. Lanier, however, said nothing so fundamentally true and compact as Pope's "Years following years *steal something* every day," or Shakespeare's "And that *old common arbitrator*, Time," or his "*whirligig* of time." There is a similar reaching for effect in the rhythmical quality of many well-known passages. The twelve-line description of the velvet flute-note in " The Symphony " is more deft and intricate than convincing. The figures stumble on each other's heels, and the alliterations, assonances, and three- and five-fold rimes are intrusively gratuitous. In like manner the opening lines of " The Marshes of Glynn " illustrate the over-luxuriance of Lanier. He delighted in tropical exuberance; he rioted in his letters with less restraint than in his verse, and in one written to his wife in 1874 he confessed parenthetically : " In plain terms — sweet Heaven, how I do abhor these same plain terms — I have been playing ' Stradella.' " When he wrote this Lanier was thirty-two. Before his death he had approached the point of liking the plain term better and employing it oftener.

" The Marshes of Glynn " is a personal utterance of Lanier in its form, in its sensuous opulence, in its social sympathies, and in its religion; but in these latter respects it is emphatically the utterance also of the period that produced Lanier. It was written in 1878, the year of Bryant's death; it was written in the structural sequence of Bryant's " Thanatopsis "; and in its applications it indicates the changes that had taken place in religious thought since Bryant's youth. In the earlier poem the various language that Nature speaks is expounded in general terms, before " Thoughts of the last bitter hour " lead to the monody on death and the resolve so to live that death shall have no fears. The latter poem differentiates the tones of Nature, lingering first in the cloistral depths of the woods during the heat of a June day. In the cool and quiet the poet's

. . . heart is at ease from men, and the wearisome sound of the stroke
Of the scythe of time and the trowel of trade is low,
And belief overmasters doubt.

So, toward sunset, he leaves the protected green colonnades and goes out unafraid to face the expanse of " a world of marsh that borders a world of sea." Here Nature, who has consoled him in the forest, fills him with a great exhilaration.

Oh, what is abroad in the marsh and the terminal sea?
Somehow my soul seems suddenly free
From the weighing of fate and the sad discussion of sin,
By the length and the breadth and the sweep of the marshes of Glynn.

From the marshes he learns a lesson of life rather than of death — the spiritual value of aspiration and the emancipating gift of a broad faith. "Thanatopsis" ends with a nobly stated but restraining admonition; "The Marshes" with a song of liberty:

I will fly in the greatness of God as the marsh-hen flies
In the freedom that fills all the space 'twixt the marsh and the skies:
By so many roots as the marsh-grass sends in the sod
I will heartily lay me a-hold of the greatness of God.

This is written in the positive mood — and in the measure, too — of Browning's "Saul." Both poems record the throwing off of paralyzing restraint and the substitution of hope for dread that resulted from the religious struggles of the nineteenth century.

Lanier went far toward representing the South by the best of all methods, which is to write as a citizen of the world and not as a sectionalist. He was not at the height of his maturity, and he wrote at times with the exuberance and at times with the self-consciousness that he would in all likelihood have outgrown in the fullness of years. He was an aggressive thinker. Only the indifference of his generation to poetry can account for the fact that he was not persecuted for the courage of many utterances. And he was essentially the poet in artistry as well as in vision.

BOOK LIST

General References

Collections

CLARKE, JENNIE T. Songs of the South (Introduction by J. C. Harris). 1913.

FULTON, N. G. Southern Life in Southern Literature. 1917.

KENT, C. W. (literary editor). Library of Southern Literature. 1907. 15 vols.

MANLY, LOUISE. Southern Literature. 1895.

MOORE, FRANK. Songs and Ballads of the Southern People. 1886.
TRENT, W. P. Southern Writers. Selections in Prose and Verse. 1905.
WAUCHOPE, G. A. Writers of South Carolina, 1910.

History and Criticism

BASKERVILL, W. M. Southern Writers: Biographical and Critical
Studies. 1898–1903. 2 vols.
DAVIDSON, J. W. Living Writers of the South. 1869.
DE MENIL, A. N. Literature of the Louisiana Territory. 1904.
HOLLIDAY, CARL. History of Southern Literature. 1906.
LINK, S. A. Pioneers of Southern Literature. 1903. 2 vols.
ORGAIN, KATE A. Southern Authors in Poetry and Prose. 1908.
PAINTER, F. V. N. Poets of the South. 1903.
PAINTER, F. V. N. Poets of Virginia. 1907.

Among periodical articles some of the more important are as
follows:

BASKERVILL, W. M. Southern Literature. *Pub. Mod. Lang. Assoc.*,
Vol. VII, p. 89.
COLEMAN, C. W. Recent Movement in Southern Literature.
Harper's, Vol. LXXIV, p. 837.
HENNEMAN, J. B. National Element in Southern Literature.
Sewanee Review, Vol. XI, p. 345.
MABIE, H. W. The Poetry of the South. *International Monthly*,
Vol. V, p. 200.
SMITH, C. A. Possibilities of Southern Literature. *Sewanee Review*,
Vol. VI, p. 298.
SNYDER, H. N. The Matter of Southern Literature. *Sewanee
Review*, Vol. XV, p. 218.
TRENT, W. P. Dominant Forces in Southern Life. *Atlantic*, Vol.
LXXIX, p. 42.
WOODBERRY, G. E. The South in American Letters. *Harper's*,
Vol. CVII, p. 735.

Individual Authors

HENRY TIMROD. Works. Memorial Edition. 1899, 1901. These appeared in book form originally as follows: Poems, 1860. Complete
edition (edited by Paul Hamilton Hayne), 1873, 1874; Katie, 1884.

Biography and Criticism

Memoir prefixed to editions of 1899 and 1901. Sketch with edition
of 1872, by P. H. Hayne.
AUSTIN, H. Henry Timrod. *International Review*, September, 1880.
HAYNE, P. H. Sketch with edition of 1872.
ROSS, C. H. The New Edition of Timrod. *Sewanee Review*, October,
1899.
ROUTH, J. E. Some Fugitive Poems of Timrod. *South Atlantic
Quarterly*, January, 1903.

WAUCHOPE, G. A. Henry Timrod, Laureate of the Confederacy. *North Carolina Review*, May 5, 1912.
WAUCHOPE, G. A. Henry Timrod: Man and Poet, a Critical Study. 1915.
See also volumes of history and criticism under General References, above.

PAUL HAMILTON HAYNE. Works. Poems of. Complete edition (his own selection), with biographical introduction by Margaret Preston. 1882. The work appeared in book form originally as follows: Poems, 1855; Sonnets, and Other Poems, 1857, 1859; Avolio, 1860; Legends and Lyrics, 1872; The Mountain of the Lovers, 1875; Life of Robert Y. Hayne, 1878; Life of Hugh S. Legare, 1878.

Biography and Criticism

There is no adequate biography of Hayne.

ALLAN, ELIZABETH PRESTON. The Life and Letters of Margaret Junkin Preston. 1903.
BROWN, J. T., JR. Paul Hamilton Hayne. *Sewanee Review*, Apr., 1906.
LANIER, SIDNEY. Essays. 1899.
MIMS, E. Sidney Lanier. 1905.
PRESTON, MARGARET JUNKIN. Introduction to edition of 1882 (see above).
See also the Library of Southern Literature, in which the introduction to the selections from Hayne is well supplemented by his own reminiscences reprinted from the *Southern Bivouac*. See also Paul Hamilton Hayne (edited by S. A. Link) and the passages in the survey histories.

SIDNEY LANIER. Works. Poems of Sidney Lanier, edited by his wife, with a memorial by William Hayes Ward. 1884. Select poems of Sidney Lanier, edited with an introduction, notes, and bibliography, by Morgan Callaway. 1895. (The critical edition.) Lanier's works appeared in book form originally as follows: Tiger Lilies, a Novel, 1867; Florida, its Scenery, Climate, and History, 1876; Poems, 1877; The Boy's Froissart, 1878; The Science of English Verse, 1880; The Boy's King Arthur, 1880; The Boy's Mabinogion, 1881; The Boy's Percy, 1882; The English Novel, 1883; Music and Poetry: Essays, 1898; Retrospects and Prospects, 1899; Shakespeare and his Forerunners, 1902.

Bibliographies

A bibliography prepared for the Southern History Association by G. S. Wills, July, 1899.
A bibliography appended to Select Poems of Lanier (edited by Morgan Callaway). 1895. Also Cambridge History of American Literature, Vol. II, pp. 600–603.

Biography and Criticism

The standard life is by Edwin Mims. 1905. (*A. M. L. Ser.*)

See also Letters of Sidney Lanier. Selections from his Correspondence, 1866–1881. 1911.

CARROLL, C. C. Synthesis and Analysis of the Poetry of Sidney Lanier. 1910.

CLARKE, G. H. Some Reminiscences and Early Letters of Sidney Lanier. 1907.

GILMAN, D. C. Sidney Lanier, Reminiscences and Letters. *South Atlantic Quarterly*, April, 1905.

GOSSE, EDMUND. Questions at Issue. 1893.

HIGGINSON, T. W. Contemporaries. 1899.

KENT, C. W. A Study of Lanier's Poems. *Pub. Mod. Lang. Assoc.*, Vol. VII, pp. 33–63.

MOSES, M. J. The Literature of the South. 1910.

NORTHRUP, M. H. Sidney Lanier, Recollections and Letters. *Lippincott's*, March, 1905.

TOLMAN, A. H. Views about Hamlet and Other Essays.

TRENT, W. P. Southern Writers. 1905.

TOPICS AND PROBLEMS

Read the poems or passages alluded to in the text on sentimentalism by Irving (p. 126), Cooper (p. 148), Bryant (p. 163), Longfellow (p. 269), and compare with the statement on Timrod.

Compare Timrod's " Cotton Boll " with Bryant's " The Sower " or Lanier's " Corn " for the imaginative grasp of what had ordinarily been considered a prosaic subject.

Read the war lyrics of Timrod or Hayne and compare in subject, treatment, and temper with the corresponding work of a Northern poet.

Read several poems of Lanier taken at random for the allusions to music.

Read Lanier for the evident influence of Shakespeare in supplying him with poetic material. Is there evidence that he was affected by Shakespeare's poetic form?

Read the Taylor-Lanier correspondence with reference to the Centennial Cantata. Does the poem fulfill Lanier's intentions?

Read Lanier's poems and passages on poetry and the poet and compare them with similar passages in the work of another poet.

Read Lanier, Timrod, or Hayne for the presence of nature allusions which would be natural only for a poet of the South.

CHAPTER XXIV

WALT WHITMAN

Walt Whitman (1819–1892) and Mark Twain are the two authors whom the rest of the world have chosen to regard as distinctively American. They are in fact more strikingly different from European writers than any other two in their outer and inner reaction against cultural tradition, though it is an error to regard Americanism as an utterly new thing instead of a compound of new and old elements. Whitman was born on Long Island in 1819:

My tongue, every atom of my blood, form'd from this soil, this air,
Born here of parents born here, from parents the same, and their
    parents the same.

They were simple, natural, country people, — the mother, mild-mannered and competent, and the father, " strong, self-sufficient, manly, mean, anger'd, unjust," — people with the kind of stalwart naïveté who would christen three of their sons Andrew Jackson, George Washington, and Thomas Jefferson. Walt was the second of nine children. From boyhood he was quite able to take care of himself — amiable, slow-going, fond of chatting with the common folk of his own kind, and happy out of doors, whether on the beach or among the Long Island hills. At twelve he began to work for his living — in a lawyer's office and a doctor's, in printing shops and small newspaper offices, and in more than one school. Newspaper work included writing as well as typesetting and everything between, and writing resulted in his sending accepted contributions to such respected publications as the *Democratic Review* and George P. Morris's popular *Mirror*.

From 1841 to 1850 he was more steadily using his pen. He wrote some eighteen stories for the periodicals and, though he worked in defiance of the usual schedule, made his way in journalism to the point of becoming editor of the *Brooklyn Daily Eagle*. In 1848 he moved in a wider orbit, going down to New Orleans through the Ohio valley to work on the new *Crescent*, and coming back by way of the Mississippi and the Great Lakes. In 1850 he was living with his family in Brooklyn. By this time he had done a great deal of reading, starting with " The Arabian Nights " and Scott, and moving on by his own choice through the classics. Always, when he could, he read alone and out of doors ; but seldom has man more completely fulfilled Emerson's behest to compensate for solitude with society, for he was one of the great comrades of history. He found his society in places of his own selection — on the Broadway stages, in the Brooklyn ferryboats, and in the gallery at the Italian opera.

Here is his own testimony : " — the drivers — a strange, natural quick-eyed and wondrous race — (not only Rabelais and Cervantes would have gloated upon them, but Homer and Shakspere would) — how well I remember them, and must here give a word about them. . . . They had immense qualities, largely animal — eating, drinking, women — great personal pride, in their way — perhaps a few slouches here and there, but I should have trusted the general run of them, in their simple good-will and honor, under all circumstances." And of the harbor : " Almost daily, later ('50 to '60), I cross'd on the boats, often up in the pilot-houses where I could get a full sweep, absorbing shows, accompaniments, surroundings." There was a time when he affected fine clothes, but as he matured his dress and the dress of his ideas became strikingly informal, more like that of his comrades.

Of the five years before the " Leaves of Grass " appeared too little is known. At thirty-one he was a natural Bohemian, independent enough not even to do the conventional Bohemian things like drinking and smoking, but he had shown no marked promise of achieving anything more than his own personal freedom. His writing and public speaking had been commonplace, and his journalistic work respectably successful. Then in 1855 came the evidence of an immensely expansive development, a development so great and so unusual that it met the fate of its kind, receiving from all but a very few neglect, derision, or contempt. John Burroughs tells of the staff of a leading daily paper in New York, assembled on Saturday afternoon to be paid off, greeting the passages that were read aloud to them with "peals upon peals of ironical laughter." Whitman's family were indifferent. His brother George said he "did n't read it at all — did n't think it worth reading — fingered it a little. Mother thought as I did . . . Mother said that if 'Hiawatha' was poetry, perhaps Walt's was." Obscure young men like Thoreau and Burroughs were moved to early admiration, but their opinion counted for nothing with the multitude. Emerson was the single man of influence to "greet [Whitman] at the beginning of a great career." The larger public paid no attention to him; the smaller, artistic public did what they always do to a defiantly independent artist. Whitman determined his own reception when he wrote,

> Bearded, sunburnt, gray-neck'd, forbidding, I have arrived,
> To be wrestled with as I pass for the solid prizes of the universe,
> For such I afford whoever can persevere to win them.

In 1856, in a new form and with added material but under the same title, there came a second edition that received more attention and correspondingly more abuse. His frank and often wanton treatment of sex gave pause to almost every reader, qualifying the approval of his strongest champions. Emerson wrote to Carlyle: "One book, last summer, came out in New York, a nondescript monster, which yet had terrible eyes and buffalo strength, and was indisputably American

— which I thought to send you; but the book throve so badly with the few to whom I showed it, and wanted good morals so much, that I never did. Yet I believe now again I shall." In the meanwhile the ultra-respectable — of the Jaffrey Pyncheon type — were eager to hound Whitman and his publishers out of society. Undoubtedly the advertising given by his enemies contributed no little to the circulation of the third and again enlarged edition of 1860. Of this between four and five thousand copies were sold in due time.

In 1862, when his brother George was seriously wounded at Fredericksburg, Whitman became a hospital nurse in Washington. With his peculiar gifts of comradeship and his life-long acquaintance with the common man, he was able to give thousands of sufferers the kind of personal, affectionate attention that helped all, who were not doomed, to fight their way to recovery. From every side has come the testimony as to his unique relationship with them. One must be quoted:

Never shall I forget one night when I accompanied him on his rounds through a hospital, filled with those wounded young Americans whose heroism he has sung in deathless numbers. There were three rows of cots, and each cot bore its man. When he appeared, in passing along, there was a smile of affection and welcome on every face, however wan, and his presence seemed to light up the place as it might be lit by the presence of the Son of Love. From cot to cot they called him, often in tremulous tones or in whispers; they embraced him, they touched his hand, they gazed at him. . . . He did the things for them which no nurse or doctor could do, and he seemed to leave a benediction at every cot as he passed along. The lights had gleamed for hours in the hospital that night before he left it, and as he took his way towards the door, you could hear the voice of many a stricken hero calling, "Walt, Walt, Walt, come again! come again!"

The fruits in poetry from these years of duress were in some ways the richest of his lifetime. They were included in the edition of 1865 under the title "Drum-Taps." Here were new poems "of the body and of the soul," telling of his vigils on the field and in the hospital, not shrinking from details of horror and death ; and here also were poems that dealt with the implications of the war and of nationalism militant. " Drum-Taps "—the title poem—and " Beat! Beat! Drums! " sound the call to arms. " The Song of the Banner at Daybreak " contrasts the patriotism of the philistine with the patriotism of the idealist. " Pioneers! O Pioneers! " sings of America for the world, with its thrillingly prophetic fourth stanza,

> Have the elder races halted ?
> Do they droop ánd end their lesson, wearied, over there beyond
>   the seas ?
> We take up the task eternal, and the burden, and the lesson,
>   Pioneers! O pioneers!

And " President Lincoln's Burial Hymn " (" When Lilacs last in the Door-yard Bloom'd ") with " O Captain! My Captain! " are preëminent among the multitude of songs in praise of Lincoln. Whitman wrote fairly in a letter : " The book is therefore unprecedently sad (as these days are, are they not?), but it also has the blast of the trumpet and the drum pounds and whirrs in it, and then an undertone of sweetest comradeship and human love threads its steady thread inside the chaos and is heard at every lull and interstice thereof. Truly also, it has clear notes of faith and triumph."

There were other fateful fruits of his hospital service. It is the salvation of the surgeon and the nurse that they adopt a professional attitude toward their tasks ; they save individual lives in their struggle to save human life. But it was the essence of Whitman's work among the soldiers that he should pour out his compassion without stint. The drain of energy forced him more than once to leave Washington for rest at home, and assisting at operations resulted in poisonous contagions. He seemed to recover from these, only to give way in 1873 to a consequent attack of paralysis, and, though he had nineteen years to live, he was never quite free from the shadow of this menace.

During the latter years, however, public respect increased as his strength waned. Popularity this self-elected poet of the people never gained, but he became a poets' poet. A Whitman vogue developed among the consciously literary, just as a Browning vogue did in the same decades. It is rather a misfortune than otherwise for any art or artist to be made the subject of a fad, but the growth of Whitman's repute was slow and was rooted in the regard of other artists. In the years near 1870 essays and reviews in England and Germany showed how deeply " Leaves of Grass " impressed the small group of men who knew what the essentials of poetry were and were not afraid to acknowledge their great debt to this strange innovator. The timid culture of America at first shrank as usual from any native work which was un-European in aspect, and lagged behind foreign indorsement of something freshly American just as it did in the cases of Mark Twain and " Joaquin " Miller (see pp. 293 and 403). When it did begin to take Whitman seriously, the heartfelt admiration of Freiligrath in Germany and of William Michael Rossetti and John Addington Symonds in England, the published charge that America was neglecting a great poet, and the public offer of assistance from English friends combined to build up for " the good gray poet " a body of support to which the belated interest of the would-be intellectuals was a negligible addition. From 1881 to his death eleven years later the income from his writings was sufficient to maintain him in " decent poverty."

In " Myself and Mine " Whitman delivered an admonition in spite of which he has been discussed in a whole alcoveful of books and in innumerable lectures :

I call to the world to distrust the accounts of my friends, but listen
    to my enemies — as I myself do ;
I charge you, too, forever reject those who would expound me —
    for I cannot expound myself ;
I charge that there be no theory nor school founded out of me ;
I charge you to leave all free, as I have left all free.

The comment and the controversy which have accumulated around his poems and himself center about two nodal points: one is the relatively obvious consideration of the objections to his poetic form, his subject matter, and his conduct, and the other — far more complex and subtle — is the statement and appraisal of his philosophy of life.

Prejudice and ignorance have had altogether too much to say about Whitman's versification, — as they still have in connection with the freer verse forms of the present day. Two or three simple facts should be stated at the outset, by way of clearing the ground. His earliest poetry was written in conventional form; the form of "Leaves of Grass" was the result neither of laziness nor of inability to deal with the established measures. Throughout his work there are recurrent passages in regular rimed meter. "O Captain! My Captain!" (1865), "Ethiopia Saluting the Colors" (1870), and the song of "The Singer in the Prison" (1870) are deliberate resorts to the old ways. More likely to escape the attention are unlabeled bits scattered through poems in Whitman's usual manner. The opening of the "Song of the Broad-Axe" is in eight measures of trochaic tetrameter with a single rime — it sounds like Emerson's; and the first four lines of section 14 in "Walt Whitman," or the "Song of Myself," are iambic heptameters, a perfect stanza. Furthermore, he was not utterly alone in his generation. Similar experiments by some of his contemporaries are almost forgotten, because there was no vital relation between form and content; because there was nothing vital in them; but Whitman's rhythms survive because they are as alive as the wind in the tree tops.

He theorized out his art in detail and referred to his lines as apparently "lawless at first perusal, although on closer examination a certain regularity appears, like the recurrence of lesser and larger waves on the sea-shore, rolling in without intermission, and fitfully rising and falling." His feeling, — and this is the right word for a question of artistic form, which should not be determined primarily by the intellect,

— his feeling was that the idea which is being expressed should govern from moment to moment the form into which it is cast, since any pattern imposed on a long poem must handicap freedom. In many a descriptive passage there is a succession of nice adjustments of word and rhythm to the thing being described. The flight of birds, the play of waves, the swaying of branches, the thousandfold variations of motion, are easy to reproduce and easy to perceive, but Whitman went far beyond these to the innate suggestions of things and of ideas. At the same time — not to be occupied in a search for variety which becomes merely chaos — he adopted a succession of pattern rhythms, taking a simple, free measure and modifying it in the reiterative form frequently used by Emerson and common to " Hiawatha." There was some acumen in Mrs. Whitman's comparison, for Longfellow's assumption of " frequent repetitions" was a reverting to the parallelism that prevails in most folk poetry, the same parallelism which is the warp of Whitman's patterns. Whitman was just as conscious in his choice of diction as in his selection of measures. Poetry, he agreed with Wordsworth, was choked with outworn phrases ; the language of the people should be the source of a poetic tongue. From this he could evolve a " perfectly clear, plate-glassy style."

In execution he was, of course, uneven. He wrote scores upon scores of passages that were full of splendor, of majesty, of rugged strength, of tender loveliness. In general it is true that the lines which deal with definite aspects of natural and physical beauty are most effective — lines of which " Out of the Cradle Endlessly Rocking " are the purest type ; but many of the poems and sections in which concrete imagery is summoned to the explication of a general idea are often finely successful — as in his stanzas on the poet, or on himself, "the divine average," for example :

> My foothold is tenon'd and mortis'd in granite ;
> I laugh at what you call dissolution ;
> And I know the amplitude of time.

To the hostile critic he offered an abundance of lines for unfriendly quotation, as almost every prolific poet has done. Furthermore, he opened to attack all the series of "catalogue," or "inventory," passages, in which he abandoned the artistic habit of selective suggestion and overwhelmed the reader with an avalanche of detail. It is not necessary to defend these vagaries or excesses; they are obvious eccentricities in Whitman's workmanship, as are also the wanton barbarisms of wording into which he occasionally lapsed. There are good English equivalents for *omnes* and *allons* and *dolce* and *résumé*, and better ones than *promulge, philosoph,* and *imperturbe.*

The most violent objections launched at Whitman were based on his unprecedented frankness in matters of sex. It was the habit of the Victorian period, whether in England or in America, to shroud in an unwholesome silence the impulse to beget life and the facts surrounding it as if they were shameful matters. In consequence a central element in social and individual 'experience tended to become a subject of morbid curiosity to young people and one of furtive self-indulgence to adults. This bred vicious ignorance, distorted half-knowledge, and, among other things, hysterical protestations at any open violation of the code in action or in speech. People seemed to feel that they were vindicating their own probity by the voluminousness of their invective. So Whitman was made a scapegoat, just as Byron was at an earlier date; and the merits of the controversies are obscured by the fact that however much in error the poets may have been, their accusers were hardly less in the wrong. Out of the babel of discussion one clearest note emerged in the form of a letter from an Englishwoman to W. M. Rossetti, who had lent her "Leaves of Grass":

I rejoice to have read these poems; and if I or any true woman feel that, certainly *men* may hold their peace about them. You will understand that I still think that instinct of silence I spoke of a right and beautiful thing; and that it is only lovers and poets (perhaps only lovers and *this* poet) who may say what they will — the lover to his own, the poet to all because all are in a sense his own. Shame is like a very flexible veil that takes faithfully the shape of what it covers — lovely when it hides a lovely thing, ugly when it hides an ugly one. There is not any fear that the freedom of such impassioned words will destroy the sweet shame, the happy silence, that enfold and brood over the secrets of love in a woman's heart.

This single judgment naturally cannot serve as a universal ultimatum, but it should serve as a warning for those who jump to the conclusion that only one mood is possible for the writer or reader of such passages. Those who are disturbed by them should be willing not to read the few score lines that are responsible for all the turmoil.

The only other charge against Whitman worth mentioning — the complaint at his " colossal egotism " — is a subject more for interpretation than for defense. Properly understood, it leads far toward an understanding of the whole man. In the first place, if all his "I's" should be taken literally they would amount to no more than an unusual frankness of artistic expression. Every creative artist is of necessity an egotist. He is bound to believe in the special significance of what he is privileged to utter in words or tones or lines and colors. The whole anthology of poems on the poet and his work is a catalogue of supreme egotisms, even though most of them are written in the third person rather than the first. Whitman cast aside the regular locution without apology. But, as a further caution to the supersensitive, his "I's" do not always mean the same thing. Sometimes they are explicitly personal, as in,

> I, now, thirty-six years old, in perfect health, begin,
> Hoping to cease not till death.

Sometimes they stand just as explicitly for " the average man." This he explained in the preface to the 1876 edition : " I meant ' Leaves of Grass,' as published, to be the poem of average Identity (of *yours*, whoever you are, now reading these lines). . . . To sing the Song of that law of average Identity, and of Yourself, consistently with the divine law of the universal, is a main purpose of these ' Leaves.' "

Finally, the egotistic " I " is often a token of the religious mysticism at the back of his faith. Without an understanding of this factor in Whitman he cannot be known. " Place yourself," said William James in his lecture on Bergson, " at the center of a man's philosophic vision and you understand at once all the different things it makes him write or say. But keep outside, use your post-mortem method, try to build the philosophy up out of the single phrases, taking first one and then another, and seeking to make them fit, and of course you fail. You crawl over the thing like a myopic ant over a building, tumbling into every microscopic crack or fissure, finding nothing but inconsistencies, and never suspecting that a centre exists." It is James again who gives the exact cue to Whitman's mysticism, this time in a chapter of " Varieties of Religious Experience." It is the experience of the mystic, he explains, to arrive in inspired moments at a height from which all truth seems to be divinely revealed. This revelation is not a flashlight perception of some single aspect of life, but a sense of the entire scheme of creation and a conviction that the truth has been imparted direct from God. It is clear, like the view from a mountain top, but, like such a view, it is incapable of adequate expression in words, — " an intuition," and now the words are Whitman's, " of the absolute balance, in time and space, of the whole of this multifarious, mad chaos of fraud, frivolity, hoggishness — this revel of fools, and incredible make-believe and general unsettledness, we call *the world*; a soul-sight of that divine clue and unseen thread which holds the whole congeries of things, all history and time, and all events, however trivial, however momentous, like a leashed dog in the hand of the hunter." It was the fashion of speech of the Hebrew prophets, when thus inspired, to preface their declarations with " Thus saith the Lord ";

Whitman, with his simpler, "I say" or "I tell you," regarded himself no less as mouthpiece of the Most High. The vision made him certain of an underlying unity in all life and of the coming supremacy of a law of love; it made him equally certain of the mistakenness of human conditions and unqualifiedly direct in his uttered verdicts.

This sense of the wholeness of life — a transcendental doctrine — made all the parts deeply significant to him who could perceive their meaning. The same mystic consciousness is beneath all these passages, and all the others like them:

I celebrate myself,
And what I assume you shall assume,
For every atom belonging to me as good belongs to you.

. . . .

The wild gander leads his flock through the cool night;
Ya-honk! he says, and sounds it down to me like an invitation;
(The pert may suppose it meaningless, but I listen close;
I find its purpose and place up there toward the wintry sky.)

. . . .

I believe a leaf of grass no less than the journey-work of the stars,
And the pismire is equally perfect, and a grain of sand, and the egg
    of the wren,
And the tree-toad is a chef-d'œuvre for the highest,
And the running blackberry would adorn the parlors of heaven,
And the narrowest hinge in my hand puts to scorn all machinery,
And the cow crunching with depress'd head surpasses any statue,
And a mouse is miracle enough to stagger sextillions of infidels,
And I could come every afternoon of my life to look at the farmer's
    girl boiling her iron tea-kettle and baking short-cake.

It explains, too, the otherwise bewildering excesses of the "inventory" passages, which, for all their apparent unrelatedness, are always brought up with a unifying, inclusive turn. In the universe, then, — and Whitman thought of the word in its literal sense of a great and single design, — man was the supreme fact to whom all its objects "continually converge"; as man was God-created, Whitman was no respecter of persons, but a lover of the common folk, in whom the destiny of human-kind resided more than in presidents or kings. And since he considered the race in the light of ages upon ages, the generating of life seemed to him a matter of holiest import.

For the carrying out of such a design the only fit vehicle is the purest sort of democracy; all other working bases of human association are only temporary obstacles to the course of things; and as Whitman saw the nearest approach to the right social order in his own country, he was an American by conviction as well as by the accident of place. Governments, he felt, were necessary conveniences, and so-called rulers were servants of the public from whom their powers were derived. The greatest driving power in life was public opinion, and the greatest potential molder of public opinion was the bard, seer, or poet. This poet was to be not a reformer but a preacher of a new gospel; he was, in fact, to be infinitely patient in face of " meanness and agony without end " while he invoked the principles which would one day put them to rout.

I hear it was charged against me that I sought to destroy institutions;
But really I am neither for nor against institutions;
(What indeed have I in common with them? — Or what with the
    destruction of them?)
Only I will establish in the Mannahatta, and in every city of These
    States, inland and seaboard,
And in the fields and woods, and above every keel, little or large,
    that dents the water,
Without edifices, or rules, or trustees, or any argument,
The institution of the dear love of comrades.

To the bard he attributed knowledge of science and history, — the learning of the broadly educated man, — but, beyond that, wisdom :

He bestows on every object or quality its fit proportion, neither more
    nor less. . . .
He is no arguer, he is judgment — (Nature accepts him absolutely;)

He judges not as the judge judges, but as the sun falling round a
    helpless thing;
As he sees farthest, he has the most faith.

He is no writer of "poems distilled from foreign poems";
he is the propounder of

the idea of free and perfect individuals,
For that idea the bard walks in advance, leader of leaders,
The attitude of him cheers up slaves and horrifies foreign despots.

In America, whose "veins are filled with poetical stuff,"
Whitman was certain not only of the need for poets but of
their ultimate power; for *in* America, the cradle of the race,
and *through* the bards God's will was to be done.

Whitman arrived at the acme of self-reliance. With the
mystic's sense of revealed truth at hand, and a devout conviction that it was the poet's duty — his duty — to show men
a new heaven and a new earth, he went on his way with perfect faith. Emerson wrote of self-reliance in general, "Adhere
to your act, and congratulate yourself if you have done something strange and extravagant, and broken the monotony of a
decorous age." Yet he remonstrated with Whitman, and in
the attempt to modify his extravagance used arguments which
were unanswerable. Nevertheless, said the younger poet, "I
felt down in my soul the clear and unmistakable conviction to
disobey all, and pursue my own way"; in doing which he
bettered Emerson's instructions by disregarding his advice.
Hostile or brutal criticism left him quite unruffled. It reënforced him in his conclusions and cheered him with the
thought that they were receiving serious attention. After
Swinburne's fiercest attack says Burroughs: "I could not
discover either in word or look that he was disturbed a par-
ticle by it. He spoke as kindly of Swinburne as ever. If he
was pained at all, it was on Swinburne's account and not on
his own. It was a sad spectacle to see a man retreat upon
himself as Swinburne had done."

His daily preoccupation with "superior beings and eternal interests" gave him some of the elevations and some of the contempts of the Puritan fathers. It leads far to think of Whitman as a Puritan stripped of his dogma. It accounts for his daily absorption in things of religion, for his democratic zeal, his disregard for the adornments of life, even for his subordination of the sentiment of love to the perpetuation of the race. In these respects he dwelt on the broad and permanent factors in human life, regarding the finite and personal only as he saw them in the midst of all time and space. And this leads to the man in his relation to science, with which Puritan dogma was at odds. Whitman was not in the usual sense a "nature poet." The beauties of nature exerted little appeal on him. He had nothing to say in detached observations on the primrose, or the mountain tops, or the sunset. But nature was, next to his own soul, the source of deepest truth to him, a truth which science in his own day was making splendidly clear. The dependence of biological science on the material universe did not shake his faith in immortality. He simply took what knowledge science could contribute and understood it in the light of his faith, which transcended any science. Among modern poets he was one of the earliest to chant the pæan of creative evolution.

Rise after rise bow the phantoms behind me,
Afar down I see the huge first Nothing — I know I was even there,
I waited unseen and always, and slept through the lethargic mist,
And took my time, and took no hurt from the fetid carbon.

Before I was born out of my mother, generations guided me,
My embryo has never been torpid — nothing could overlay it.
For it the nebula cohered to an orb,
The long, slow strata piled to rest it in,
Vast vegetables gave it sustenance,
Monstrous sauroids transported it in their mouths, and deposited it
    with care.
All forces have been steadily employed to complete and delight me,
Now I stand on this spot with my Soul.

It is impossible, as all critics agree, to compass Whitman in a book or essay or compress him into a summary. He was an immensely expansive personality whose writings are as broad as life itself. It is almost equally impossible for one who has really read over and through and under his poems to speak of him in measured terms. The world is coming round to Whitman much faster than he expected. Every great step in human progress is a step in the direction he was pointing. His larger faith, whether so recognized or not, is yearly the faith of more and more thinking people. And in an immediate way his influence on the generation of living poets is incomparably great.

BOOK LIST

Individual Author

WALT WHITMAN. Works. Selections from the prose and poetry of Whitman. O. L. Triggs, editor. 1902. 10 vols. The best single volumes are Leaves of Grass, Complete Poetical Works, and Complete Prose Works. (Small, Maynard.) 1897 and 1898. During Whitman's lifetime ten successive enlarged editions of Leaves of Grass were published: in 1855, 1856, 1860, 1867, 1871, 1876, 1881 (Boston), 1881 (Philadelphia), 1888, 1889, 1891. Other titles are as follows: *Drum-Taps, 1865; *Passage to India, 1871; *Democratic Vistas, 1871; Memoranda during the War, 1875; Specimen Days and Collect, 1882, 1883; Two Rivulets, 1876; *November Boughs, 1888; *Good-bye, My Fancy, 1891. (Titles with the mark * were included as new sections in the next forthcoming edition of Leaves of Grass.)

Bibliographies

Selections from Whitman. O. L. Triggs, editor. 1898.
Library of Literary Criticism of English and American Authors, Vol. VIII, pp. 129–153. C. W. Moulton, editor. 1905. Cambridge History of American Literature, Vol. II, pp. 551–581.

Biography and Criticism

There is no complete standard biography. The best single volume surveys are Walt Whitman, by G. R. Carpenter, 1909 (*E.M.L. Ser.*); and Walt Whitman: his Life and Works, by Bliss Perry, 1906 (*A.M.L. Ser.*).
BINNS, H. B. A Life of Walt Whitman. 1905.

BOYNTON, P. H. **Whitman's Idea of the State.** *New Republic*, Vol. VII, p. 139.

BROOKS, VAN WYCK. America's Coming of Age. 1915.

BURROUGHS, JOHN. Notes on Walt Whitman as Poet and Person. 1867.

BURROUGHS, JOHN. Whitman: a Study. 1896.

CARPENTER, EDWARD. Days with Walt Whitman. 1906.

CHAPMAN, J. J. Emerson and Other Essays. 1892.

DART, W. K. Walt Whitman in New Orleans. *Pub. Louisiana Hist. Soc.*, Vol. VII, pp. 97–112.

ELLIOT, C. N. Walt Whitman as Man, Poet, and Friend. 1915.

FERGUSON, J. D. American Literature in Spain. 1916.

FOERSTER, NORMAN. Whitman as Poet of Nature. *Pub. Mod. Lang. Assoc. of Amer.*, Vol. XXI (N. S.), pp. 736–758.

GOULD, E. P. Anne Gilchrist and Walt Whitman. 1900.

GUMMERE, F. B. Democracy and Poetry. 1911.

HOLLOWAY, EMORY. Cambridge History of American Literature, Vol. II, Bk. II, chap. i.

JONES, P. M. Influence of Whitman on the Origin of "Vers Libre." *Modern Language Review*, Vol. XI, p. 186.

JONES, P. M. Whitman in France. *Modern Language Review*, Vol. X, p. 1.

LANIER, SIDNEY. The English Novel. 1883.

LEE, G. S. Order for the Next Poet. *Putnam's Magazine*, Vol. I, p. 697; Vol. II, p. 99.

MACPHAIL, ANDREW. Walt Whitman, in *Essays in Puritanism*. 1905.

MORE, P. E. Walt Whitman, in *Shelburne Essays*. Fourth Series. 1906.

PATTEE, F. L. American Literature since 1870, chap. ix. 1915.

PERRY, BLISS. Walt Whitman: his Life and Work. 1906 and 1908.

SANTAYANA, GEORGE. Walt Whitman, in *Interpretations of Poetry and Religion*. 1900.

STEDMAN, E. C. Poets of America. 1885.

STEVENSON, R. L. Familiar Studies of Men and Books. 1882.

SWINBURNE, A. C. Studies in Prose and Poetry. 1894.

TRAUBEL, H. L. *In re* Walt Whitman. 1893.

TRAUBEL, H. L. With Walt Whitman in Camden, p. 473. 1906. (This is Vol. I of Traubel's diary notes made during Whitman's life. Vol. II, 1908; Vol. III, 1914. Vol. IV is announced for early publication, and the whole work, when completed, will fill eight or ten volumes.)

WALLING, W. E. Whitman and Traubel. 1916.

TOPICS AND PROBLEMS

Select and discuss poems and stanzas in Whitman which are written in conventional rhythms.

Select and discuss passages in which he employs changing rhythms adjusted to the persons or objects in hand.

Study Whitman's diction with reference to his use of the average man's speech and to his occasional use of foreign words, corrupted words (whether foreign or English), and coined words.

List and discuss poems which are clearly autobiographical. Does this list include any personal lyrics?

List and discuss poems written in the first person but intended as poems of "the divine average."

Select and discuss poems and passages on the theme of companionship.

Select and discuss poems and passages which express his sense of universal law.

Read his longer poems for passages on the subject of the state, the rulers, and public opinion.

Read and discuss his utterances on poetry and the poet, noting especially "The Song of the Banner at Daybreak" and "As I sat by Blue Ontario's Shore."

Read and discuss Whitman's utterances on war and nationalism.

Read for an estimate of his feeling for the beauties of nature.

CHAPTER XXV

THE WEST AND MARK TWAIN

There is a valid parallel between the beginnings of American literature and the early stages of its development in the West, for in both instances it followed on the wave of pioneer settlement. The earliest writers came from the East and were only temporary sojourners in the new country, Bret Harte and Mark Twain corresponding in different degrees to colonists like John Smith and Nathaniel Ward. A more permanent allegiance developed in a second group who lived out their lives in the land of their adoption, such, for example, as Joaquin Miller and Increase Mather. And the final stage is fulfilled by those whose whole lives belonged to the maturing frontier, like most of the second generation. The parallel exists too in the fact that the early authors wrote usually with one eye on the older community, eager for approval and half resentful of criticism — an attitude of West toward East which still survives in the timider element along the chain from London to New York to Chicago to San Francisco to Honolulu. The obvious contrasts between the motives for settlement, the character of the settlers, and the nature of their writings only serve to emphasize the underlying similarities. Manners change, but human nature changes so much more slowly that it seems almost a constant.

Bret Harte (1839–1902) is the outstanding writer who lived for a while in the far West, turned it to literary account, failed in any deep sense either to sympathize with its spirit or to represent it, and left it permanently and with apparent relief. He was an Eastern town-bred boy of cultured parentage who aspired to become a poet. At eighteen he went to California where, before he was twenty-one, he saw life as tutor, express

380

messenger, typesetter, teacher, and drug clerk. During half of the next fourteen years in San Francisco he was secretary of the California mint, and during all of them he was primarily interested in authorship. He wrote for periodicals East and West and had a manuscript accepted by the *Atlantic* as early as 1863. With the founding of the *Overland Monthly* in 1868 he became editor, and with the publication of " The Luck of Roaring Camp " in the second number he jumped into fabulous popularity. In 1871 he went to New York, and in 1878 he went abroad, where he lived till his death in complete estrangement from all his old associates. These latter facts deserve mention only as they stress the lightness of his contact with the West. He found fresh material there which he used with great narrative adroitness, contributing definitely to the progress of short-story technique. But his tales are deftly melodramatic, built on a sort of paradox formula, and greatly indebted in detail and mannerisms to the example of Charles Dickens. Harte was beyond any question a good craftsman ; his wares would still find a ready magazine market, for they would be modern in execution, but there is no soul in what he wrote. He was a reporter with a gift for rapid-moving, close-knit narrative. He was greatly interested in facts, but very little concerned with the truth. He wrote some clever stories, but he seems like a trinket shop at the foot of Pike's Peak as Mark Twain looms above him.

The life of Mark Twain (Samuel Langhorne Clemens, 1835–1910) probably touches American life at more points than that of any other author. The first half has been very definitely written into his books, and the whole has been told with his help in one of the best of American biographies.[1] It involves indirectly his Virginia parentage and the pioneer experiences of his father and mother in the Tennessee mountains ; his own residence in the Mississippi valley and on both seacoasts ; his activities as printer, river-pilot, journalist, lecturer,

[1] " Mark Twain, a Biography," by Albert Bigelow Paine. 3 vols. 1912.

and publisher; his friendships with all sorts and conditions of men from California miners to the crowned heads of Europe; the joys and sorrows of a beautiful family life ; the making and losing of several fortunes ; and an old age crowded with honors and popularity, yet overshadowed by a tragic cloud of doubts and griefs.

His parents, who had been dissatisfied with their attempted settlement in a Tennessee mountain town, left it in 1835 with four children for Florida, Missouri, allured to the move by the optimism of a relative, as it worked on their own pioneer restlessness. The conditions they left are vividly described in the first eleven chapters of "The Gilded Age." In a little town of twenty-one dwellings the boy was born in the autumn of 1835. When he was four years old the family moved to Hannibal, a river town. Sam Clemens was an irresponsible, dreamy, rather fragile child, a problem to parents and teachers and given to associating with the boys presented in "Tom Sawyer," the most notable of whom was Tom Blankenship, the original of "Huckleberry Finn." His father, consistently unsuccessful, was made justice of the peace and finally was elected clerk of the circuit court, only to die in 1847 from exposure in the campaign. For the next ten years young Clemens was engaged in the printing business, first under his brother Orion on a Hannibal journal (see "My First Literary Venture," in "Sketches, New and Old," pp. 110–114); then during fifteen months in New York, Philadelphia, and Washington, and next in Keokuk, Illinois, and Cincinnati, Ohio.

Finally, in April, 1857, he began to "learn the river" from Horace Bixby, pilot of the *Paul Jones*. His experience on the river, the basis for "Life on the Mississippi," was early marked by the tragic destruction of the *Pennsylvania*, on which his younger brother, Henry, suffered a fearful death, the first of the personal sorrows which were deeply scored into his life. His career as pilot was ended by the closing of river traffic in the spring of 1861, but it gave him, with many other bequests, his pen name, derived from one of the calls used in sounding the depth of the ever-shifting channel. Piloting during war times did not appeal to him. " I am not very anxious to get up into a glass perch and be shot at by either side. I 'll go home and reflect on the matter." And after reflection he chose the better part of valor and stayed on land. In the next three months there followed his amusing adventures recorded in " The Private History of a Campaign that Failed " (see " The American Claimant," pp. 243–265) ; and in July, 1861, he went with his brother Orion to serve with J. W. Nye, territorial governor of Nevada. The life of the next months went into "Roughing It," first at Carson City, then at Humboldt, until, in August, 1862, he began his journalistic work in California on *The Virginia City Enterprise*. At twenty-five he had secured his first view of the country from coast to coast and all down the central artery, he had been schooled in the exacting discipline of the printer's trade (see pp. 47, 48) and in the still more rigorous responsibilities of river piloting, and he had begun to write for a living. Two more steps remained in the growth of his acquaintance with the external world, and these followed after five years of shifting fortunes on California newspapers. The first was his trip to Honolulu as correspondent for the *Sacramento Union*, on the new steamer *Ajax*, and the second, in 1867, was his trip to the Holy Land on the steamship *Quaker City* for the tour which was to be immortalized in "Innocents Abroad," first as a series of newspaper letters and then in book form.

With the publication of " The Innocents " in the summer of 1869 Mark Twain came to the halfway point. Out of his wide experience he had developed the habits of an observer and he had learned how to write. He had earned a reputation as a newspaper man, and he had published his most famous short story, " The Jumping Frog," using his talent in spinning a yarn [1] after his own fashion. His lecturing had met

[1] See his essay " How to Tell a Story " in " The Man that Corrupted Hadleyburg," pp. 225–230.

with unqualified success; the new book was selling beyond all expectation — 67,000 copies in the first year; and he was happily married to Olivia Langdon, his balance wheel, his severest critic, and the friend of all his closest friends.

The story of the rest of his life is a record of varied and spectacular fortunes. His home from 1871 to 1891 was in Hartford, Connecticut, where he was a neighbor of Charles Dudley Warner and an intimate of the Reverend Joseph Twitchell (the original of Harris in "A Tramp Abroad"), and where William Dean Howells, his friend of over forty years, often visited him. There was a kind of lavishness in everything he did. He built a mansion, made money with ease, spent it profusely, and invested it with the care-free optimism of Colonel Sellers himself. New inventions fascinated him and made him an easy victim for the fluent promoter, so that what was left from his ventures with the *Buffalo Express* and the Webster Publishing Company went into other enterprises, of which the Paige typesetting machine was the most disastrous for this ex-printer. After his failure for a large amount, a later friend, Henry H. Rogers, took his affairs in hand and by good management enabled Mark Twain to meet all debts and enjoy a very handsome income during his later years.

The ups and downs of business distracted him but did not baffle him. He traveled extensively, living abroad during most of the decade between 1891 and 1901. He made cordial friends wherever he went, but he was not weaned by them away from the old cronies of the Mississippi Valley and the Pacific coast. He accepted honors from Yale twice and from the University of Missouri, and in 1907 was the subject of a four-weeks' ovation from all England when he went over to receive the degree of Doctor of Letters from Oxford. His opinion was sought on public questions and he was importuned for speeches on every sort of occasion; but his last years were shadowed by a succession of bereavements. In 1904 Mrs. Clemens died. Two children died in childhood, a third under tragic circumstances in 1909, and the surviving daughter was married and far away most of the time. His chief personal solace was found in his friendships with several schoolgirls.

> During those years after my wife's death I was washing about on a forlorn sea of banquets and speech-making in high and holy causes, and these things furnished me intellectual cheer and entertainment; but they got at my heart for an evening only, then left it dry and dusty. I had reached the grandfather stage of life without grand-children, so I began to adopt some.

He died of angina pectoris in 1910.

Mark Twain's reputation was built on his humor. He came to his maturity in a fruitful decade just after the Civil War, when a crop of newspaper men were coming out with a reck-lessly fresh, informal jocularity which was related to the old American humor, but a great departure from it. They were all unconscious of making any contribution to American litera-ture. They never could have written books which would have won the attention of Irving's readers and the perusers of the old Annuals and the admirers of the Knickerbocker courtliness. They wrote for the world of Horace Greeley and the elder James Gordon Bennett, caring nothing for beauty of style or for any kind of literary tradition. They wrote under odd pen names like " John Phœnix," who preceded them by ten years—" Petroleum V. Nasby," " Artemus Ward," " Orpheus C. Kerr," " Max Adler," and " M. Quad " serving as fancy dress for Locke, Browne, Newell, Clark, and Lewis. They drew their material from the common people, as Lincoln had done with all his anecdotes, putting it in the idiom of the common people and frequently distorting it into illiterate spelling, as Lowell had done in "The Biglow Papers." This disturbed and shocked the lovers of a refined literature — men like Stedman, for example, who wrote to Bayard Taylor, " The whole country, owing to *contagion* of our American newspaper ' exchange ' system, is flooded, deluged, swamped, beneath a muddy tide of slang, vulgarity, inartistic [bathos], impertinence, and buffoonery that is not wit." But it was an irresistible tide that threw up on its waves something more than froth or flotsam, in the shape of a few real treasures from the deep — and the rarest was Mark Twain.

Had there been no such journalistic tide this original genius would still have gone on his original way. What these other men did was much more to put the public into a humor for Mark Twain than to lead Mark Twain in his approach to the public. He started as the others did, allowing an undercurrent of seriousness to appear now and then in the flow of his extravagance. His platform experience taught him by the immediate response of the audience what were the most effective methods.

> All Tully's rules and all Quintilian's too,
> He by the light of listening faces knèw.
> And his rapt audience, all unconscious, lent
> Their own roused force to make him eloquent.[1]

He was quite deliberate in the employment of them. His essay on "How to Tell a Story" is an evidence of what he knew about structure, and his letter to the young London editorial assistant (see Paine's "Mark Twain" pp. 1091–1093) is only the best of many passages which show his scrupulous regard for diction. He did not indulge in the usual vagaries of spelling; he had, to paraphrase his own words, "a singularly fine and aristocratic respect for homely and unpretending English"; and he treated punctuation as a "delicate art" for which he had the highest respect. People who carelessly think of Mark Twain as a kind of literary swashbuckler can disabuse themselves by an attentive reading of any few pages.

While they are doing it, they can discover in addition to the points just mentioned that he was essentially clean-minded. Vulgar he was, to be sure, at times, in the sense of not

---

[1] James Russell Lowell, "Ode on Agassiz."

indulging always in drawing-room talk or displaying drawing-room manners, as, for instance, in his repeated references to spitting, — to use the homely and unpretending word, — but he never partook of the nature of his rough and ready human subjects to quite the extent that Franklin or Lincoln did. His pages are utterly free from filth. He drew a line, no doubt assisted by Mrs. Clemens, between what he wrote for the public and his private speech and correspondence. "He had," Mr. Howells wrote, " the Southwestern, the Lincolnian, the Elizabethan breadth of parlance, which I suppose one ought not to call coarse, without calling one's self prudish ; and I was always hiding away in discreet holes and corners the letters in which he had loosed his bold fancy to stoop on rank suggestion ; I could not quite bear to burn them, and I could not, after the first reading, quite bear to look at them. I shall best give my feeling on this point by saying that in it he was Shakespearian, or if his ghost will not suffer me the word, then he was Baconian."

His humor relied on his never-failing and often extravagant use of the incongruous and the irrelevant. Often this came out in his similes and metaphors. "A jay has n't got any more principles than a Congressman." " His lectures on Mont Blanc . . . made people as anxious to see it as if it owed them money." It emerged in his impertinent personalities, as in the instance of his first meeting with Grant, when he said after a moment of awkwardness : " General, I seem to be a little embarrassed. Are you ? " or as in the case of his reply to a query as to why he always carried a cotton umbrella in London, that it was the only kind he could be sure would not be stolen there. It appeared too in his sober misuse of historical facts with which he and his readers or auditors were well acquainted. And it was developed most elaborately in " hoax " passages where, in his violation of both fact and reason, the canny author looked like the innocent flower but was the serpent under it.

A particular charm attached to his work because it was so apparently uncalculated and spontaneous. What he wrote seemed to be for his own delectation, and what he spoke to be the casual improvisation of the moment. At times, of course, he did improvise — with all the art of a musician whose mastery of technique is no less the result of great labor because he has it completely in hand; but often the utterance which his hearers took for an extempore speech had been composed to the last syllable and then delivered with an art that concealed its own artistry. No doubt for the multitudes who bought up the editions of "Innocents Abroad" the salient feature of Mark Twain's writing was its jovial extravagance. The first feeling of the public was that he had out-Phœnixed "Phœnix" and beaten "Petroleum Nasby" at his own game. Beyond question he literally "enjoyed himself" when he was giving hilarious enjoyment to others; the free play of his antic fancy was a kind of self-indulgence. The best evidence is offered in "Joan of Arc." The story is approached, pursued, and concluded in a spirit of admiration often amounting to reverence. Yet in the character of "The Paladin," Edmond Aubrey, the old *miles gloriosus* of Roman comedy, and in Joan's uncle, the historian reverted to his broadest jocosities. There are interpolated pages of pure farce. There are scenes in "Joan" that are companion pieces with portions of the sardonic "Man that Corrupted Hadleyburg." On his seventy-third birthday he wrote, "I like the 'Joan of Arc' best of all my books; and it *is* the best; I know it perfectly well." Yet this serious chronicle, with its occasional outbursts of fun, was of a piece with his best-known book of nearly thirty years earlier, the laugh-invoking "Innocents Abroad." The books are not alien to each other; the difference is simply in the prevailing moods.

For under all the frolicsome gayety and beneath the surface ironies of this log of "The Quaker City" there is a solid sense of the realities of human life. Over against the pure fun of such episodes as the Fourth of July celebration on the high seas is a steady run of satire at the traditionalized affectations of the American who pretended to enjoy the things that he ought and attempted to shake off the manners of Bird City when he registered in his Paris hotel. His gibes at cultural insincerity, however, did not degenerate into a fusillade of cheap cynicisms at everything old. Whatever contempt he felt for the antiques of the tradesmen was overshadowed by the solemnity with which the evidence of the passing centuries impressed him. He may not have rendered the " old masters " their full deserts, but he entered a cathedral with respect, walked in reverent silence among the ruins of the Holy Land, and felt in the Alps the presence of the Most High. " Notwithstanding it is only the record of a picnic," he wrote in the preface, " it has a purpose, which is, to suggest to the reader how *he* would be likely to see Europe and the East, if he looked at them· with his own eyes instead of the eyes of those who traveled in those countries before him." So he wrote this book out of the fullness of his heart as well as out of the abundance of his humor. There was in him a natural acumen which for want of a better name we may call wisdom. His instinctive perceptions were usually right.

The fundamental Mark Twain was an increasingly serious man. Before he was fifty years old his precocious daughter had written in her journal, " He is known to the public as a humorist, but he has much more in him that is earnest than that is humorous." And again : " Whenever we are all alone at home nine times out of ten he talks about some very earnest subject (with an occasional joke thrown in), and he a good deal more often talks upon such subjects than upon the other kind. He is as much a philosopher as anything, I think." There were many external reasons for his turn of mind. His romantic passage through life from obscure poverty to wealth and fame, with the depressing chapters of his temporary business reverses, heightened his native respect for the few blessings that are really worth while. His repeated travels, culminating with his trip around the world, the honors that came to him, the social distinctions that were showered on him, his friendships with thinking men, his bereavements, all contributed to the same end of making him consider the ways of the world and of the maker thereof. In a further comment his astute little daughter went near to the heart of the matter when she wrote quaintly, " I think he could have done a great deal in this direction if he had studied while young, for he seems to enjoy reasoning out things, no matter what ; in a great many such directions he has greater ability than in the gifts which have made him famous." " If he had studied while young" Mark Twain might have gained a knowledge of the progressions in philosophic thought that would have steadied him in his own thinking. Yet possibly it would have made little difference, for his thinking was at the same time all his own and altogether in the drift of nineteenth-century thought.

With an initial distrust of conventionalized thinking he came to his own analysis of the prevailing religious views. His reason was alert to challenge theology wherever it was at odds with science. He found nothing in the Bible to question the assumption that Man was the crowning triumph of his Creator, but everything in evolutionary doctrine to suggest that Man was only a link in a far-evolving succession of higher forms. He found a God in the Old Testament who was " an irascible, vindictive, fierce and ever fickle and changeful master," though in the ordering of the material universe he appeared to be steadfast, beneficent, and fair. His reason thus unseated his faith in the Scriptures and thereby his confidence in the creeds founded upon them. He lost the God of the Hebrews only to find his own " in the presence of the benignant serenity of the Alps," . . . " a spirit which had looked down, through the slow drift of ages, upon a million vanished races of men, and judged them ; and would judge a million more — and still be there, watching unchanged and unchangeable, after all life should be gone and the earth have become a vacant desolation."

For the after-life he could find no such assurance as he could for a Creator. For many men of his generation, and the one just before, the solution when they found themselves in such a quandary was to take refuge in the authority of the dogmas they had set out to question ; many of the most radical came back with relief to the protection of the Roman Catholic faith ; but Mark Twain could not find his way into the harbor, glad as he might have been for the anchorage. There is a deep pathos in the many passages of which the following is a type :

To read that in a book written by a monk far back in the Middle Ages would surprise no one ; it would sound natural and proper ; but when it is seriously stated in the middle of the nineteenth century, by a man of finished education, an LL. D., M. A., and an archæological magnate, it sounds strangely enough. Still I would gladly change my unbelief for Neligan's faith, and let him make the conditions as hard as he pleased.

In spite of all his yearnings he never could achieve for himself the assurance "of things hoped for, the evidence of things not seen "; so that his most clearly formulated profession of faith was in reality a pathetic profession of doubts :

I believe in God the Almighty . . . . I think the goodness, the justice and the mercy of God are manifested in his works ; I perceive they are manifested toward me in this life ; the logical conclusion is that they will be manifested toward me in the life to come, if there should be one.

Here again, as in his discrimination between " antiques " and antiquity, Mark Twain kept clear of a despairing cynicism and held to the distinction between what Emerson called "historical Christianity" and the ideals from which its adherents have fallen away. He judged the religion of his countrymen by its social and national fruits, and he was filled with wrath at the indignity of an Episcopal rector's refusal to perform the burial service of the actor George Holland and at the extortionate demands of the missionaries for indemnities after the Boxer

Rebellion in China. On the national ideals of Christendom he spoke in bitter prophecy in 1908:

The gospel of peace is always making a deal of noise, always rejoicing in its progress but always neglecting to furnish statistics. There are no peaceful nations now. All Christendom is a soldier camp. The poor have been taxed in some nations to the starvation point to support the giant armaments which Christian governments have built up, each to protect itself from the rest of the Christian brotherhood, and incidentally to snatch any scrap of real estate left exposed by a weaker owner. King Leopold II of Belgium, the most intensely Christian monarch, except Alexander VI, that has escaped hell thus far, has stolen an entire kingdom in Africa, and in fourteen years of Christian endeavor there has reduced the population from thirty millions to fifteen by murder and mutilation and overwork, confiscating the labor of the helpless natives, and giving them nothing in return but salvation and a home in heaven, furnished at the last moment by the Christian priest. Within the last generation each Christian power has turned the bulk of its attention to finding out newer and still newer and more and more effective ways of killing Christians, and, incidentally, a pagan now and then; and the surest way to get rich quickly in Christ's earthly kingdom is to invent a kind of gun that can kill more Christians at one shot than any other existing kind. All the Christian nations are at it. The more advanced they are, the bigger and more destructive engines of war they create.

Such doubts as to the future and depression at surrounding events have led many an inquirer to a relaxation in his moral standards and in his personal conduct; but in Mark Twain his rectitude was as deeply grounded as his humor — both, indeed, flowing from the same source. Throughout his books he upheld the simple virtues — common honesty; fidelity to the family; kindness to brutes, to the weak or suffering, and to the primitive peoples. His ironies and his satires were always directed at unworthy objects, the varied forms of selfishness and insincerity; and his answer to "What is Happiness?" is contained in the admonition, "Diligently train your ideals upward and still upward, toward a summit where you will find your chiefest pleasure in conduct which, while contenting you, will be sure to confer benefits upon your neighbor and the community."

Not until the last years of his life did readers begin to take Mark Twain seriously; now they are coming to appreciate him. He has been fortunate in his literary champions — biographers, critics, and expositors — and incomparably so in the loving interpretation, "My Mark Twain," by his intimate friend, William Dean Howells. This concludes: "Out of a nature rich and fertile beyond any that I have ever known, the material given him by the Mystery that makes a man and then leaves him to make himself over, he wrought a character of high nobility upon a foundation of clear and solid truth. . . . It is in vain that I try to give a notion of the intensity with which he pierced to the heart of life, and the breadth of vision with which he compassed the whole world, and tried for the reason of things, and then left trying. . . . Next I saw him dead. . . . I looked a moment at the face I knew so well; and it was patient with the patience I had so often seen in it; something of puzzle, a great silent dignity, an assent to what must be from the depths of a nature whose tragical seriousness broke in the laughter which the unwise took for the whole of him. Emerson, Longfellow, Lowell, Holmes — I knew them all — and all the rest of our sages, poets, seers, critics, humorists; they were like one another and like other literary men; but Clemens was sole, incomparable, the Lincoln of our literature."

BOOK LIST

Individual Authors

BRET HARTE. Works. Standard Library Edition. 20 vols. During his lifetime his works were issued in forty-nine successive volumes between 1867 and 1902. Of these seven were poetry, and of the prose works two were novels. The remainder were made up of short units, mostly narrative.

Biographies

BOYNTON, H. W. Bret Harte. 1905.

MERWIN, H. C. The Life of Bret Harte, with some Account of the California Pioneers. 1911.

PATTEE, F. L. American Literature since 1870, chap. iv. 1915.
PEMBERTON, T. E. Life of Bret Harte. 1903.

MARK TWAIN. Works. Writings of Mark Twain. 1910. 25 vols. (These have been supplemented by various posthumous articles in *Harper's Magazine* which have been published, and will doubtless be further added to, in supplementary volumes.) His works appeared in book form originally as follows: The Jumping Frog, 1867; The Innocents Abroad, 1869; Autobiography and First Romance, 1871; Roughing It, 1872; The Gilded Age (with C. D. Warner), 1873; Sketches New and Old, 1875; Tom Sawyer, 1876; The Stolen White Elephant, 1878; A Tramp Abroad, 1880; The Prince and the Pauper, 1881; Life on the Mississippi, 1883; Huckleberry Finn, 1884; A Connecticut Yankee in the Court of King Arthur, 1889; The American Claimant, 1892; Tom Sawyer Abroad, 1894; Pudd'n-head Wilson, 1894; Joan of Arc, 1896; Tom Sawyer Detective, and Other Stories, 1896; Following the Equator, 1897; Christian Science, 1907; Captain Stormfield's Visit to Heaven, 1907; Is Shakespeare Dead, 1909.

Bibliography

A volume by M. Johnson. 1910.
Chronological list of Mark Twain's work published and otherwise, Appendix X, Vol. III, of Mark Twain, by A. B. Paine (see below).

Biography and Criticism

The standard life is by Albert Bigelow Paine. 1912. 3 vols.

The following list does not attempt to represent the periodical material except for one symposium in *The Bookman*. See the Reader's Guide to Periodical Literature. The volume for 1910–1914 alone contains seventy-six items.

CLEMENS, W. M. Mark Twain: his Life and Work. 1892.
HENDERSON, ARCHIBALD. Mark Twain. 1912.
HOWELLS, W. D. My Mark Twain. 1910.
Mark Twain's Letters (edited by A. B. Paine). 1917.
MATTHEWS, BRANDER. Inquiries and Opinions. 1907.
PAINE, A. B. A Boy's Life of Mark Twain. 1916.
PATTEE, F. L. American Literature since 1870, chap. iii. 1915.
PHELPS, W. L. Essays on Modern Novelists. 1910.
SHERMAN, STUART. Fifty Years of American Idealism (edited by Gustav Pollak). 1915. Also in On Contemporary Literature. 1918.
WALLACE, ELIZABETH. Mark Twain and the Happy Island. 1913.
The Bookman, Vol. XXXI, pp. 363–396: Mark Twain in San Francisco, by Bailey Millard; Mark Twain, an Appreciation, by

Henry M. Alden. Best Sellers of Yesterday: The Innocents Abroad, by A. B. Maurice; Mark Twain in Clubland, by W. H. Rideing; Mark Twain a Century Hence, by Harry Thurston Peck; The Story of Mark Twain's Debts, by F. A. King.

TOPICS AND PROBLEMS

Note, as you read any one of Mark Twain's longer stories, passages which are evidently autobiographical. Do these throw any light on the history of his neighborhoods and his period or are they purely personal in their interest?

Read the essay "How to tell a Story" and test it by Mark Twain's method in one of his shorter stories and in one of his after-dinner speeches as printed in the appendix to Vol. III of A. B. Paine's "Life."

Read a few pages at random for observations on Mark Twain's diction. Is it more like Emerson's or Lowell's, more like Whitman's or Longfellow's?

Does Mark Twain's consistent interest in history appear in his writing through the use of allusion and comparison?

Read for the employment of unexpected humor. Are passages in which it suddenly appears the result of forethought or merely the result of whim?

Read for Mark Twain's resort to serious satire. To what objects of satire does he most frequently revert?

Do you find a distinction between Mark Twain's attitude toward religion and his attitude toward religious people?

Mark Twain is held up as an example of Americanism. Do his writings give evidence of patriotism in the usual sense of the word?

CHAPTER XXVI

THE WEST IN SILL AND MILLER

In the development of a Western literature Sill and Miller, like Bret Harte and Mark Twain and like all the other adult Californians in the pioneer period, were imported from the East, but they were not such temporary sojourners as the two prose writers. Sill, after an Eastern education, enjoyed two prolonged residences in California, and in his journeyings back and forth became a kind of cultural medium, bringing something of Eastern tradition to the Pacific coast and interpreting the West to the East. Of the four men Joaquin Miller was the most completely and continuously Western. He went out almost as early as Mark Twain did, lived during boyhood in far more primitive circumstances, and, after varied travels in the East and in Europe and intimate association with the world of letters, returned to the West for his old age, dying on "The Hights" in sight of the Golden Gate.

EDWARD ROWLAND SILL (1841–1887)

Sill was born in Windsor, Connecticut, in 1841. In 1861 he was graduated from Yale, where he had developed more clearly than anything else a dislike for narrowly complacent orthodoxy of thought and conduct and had acquired a strain of mild misanthropy which characterized him for the next several years. His health sent him West, by sailing-vessel around Cape Horn, and he stayed in California occupied in a variety of jobs until 1866. A winter's study satisfied him that he should not enter the ministry, and a shorter experiment that he could not succeed in New York journalism. In 1868 he published the only volume of poems during his lifetime, the little duodecimo entitled " The Hermitage." From this year to 1882 he was occupied in teaching — first in the high schools at Cuyahoga Falls, Ohio, and Oakland, California, and from 1874 on in the department of English in the University of California. Here he had the double distinction of serving under President Daniel C. Gilman and over Josiah Royce, whom he secured as assistant. A letter of 1882 gives as the reason for his resignation that his " position had become intolerable for certain reasons that are not for pen and ink," in spite of which ill health is usually assigned as the cause. In 1883 a second volume, "The Venus of Milo, and Other Poems" was privately printed. For the rest of his life he lived at Cuyahoga Falls again, writing frequently under the name of Andrew Hedbrook for the *Atlantic*, whose pages were opened to his prose and verse through the appreciative interest of the editor, his fellow-poet, Thomas Bailey Aldrich. He died in 1887.

During his last thirty years, from his entrance to Yale in 1857 to his death in 1887, Edward Rowland Sill experienced American life in a variety of ways which were not exactly paralleled in the career of any of his contemporaries. He did not belong to any literary group. Because of a certain timidity, which was probably more artistic than social, he did not even become acquainted with the well-known authors who were his neighbors while he was in Cambridge and New York City; but his natural inclination to find his proper place and do his proper work led him to partake of the life on both coasts and in the Mississippi Valley and to contribute richly to the leading periodicals of the East and the West — the *Atlantic* and the *Overland Monthly*.

By inclination he was from the outset a cultured radical. He loved the best that the past had to offer, he wanted to make the will of God prevail, and he was certain that between lethargy and crassness the millennium was being long delayed. It was lethargy which characterized Yale and New Haven for him.[1] The curriculum was dull in itself and little redeemed by any vital teaching or by reference to current thought. The faculty, wrote one of his classmates, "gave us a rare example of single-hearted, self-sacrificing, and unswerving devotion to duty, as they saw it. But they had not the gift to see much of it, and so their example lacked inspiration. It is astounding that so much knowledge (one-sided though it was) and so much moral worth could have existed side by side with so much obtuseness." The natural consequence was that Sill picked up what crumbs of comfort he could from miscellaneous reading, was "rusticated" for neglect of his routine duties, wrote Carlylesque essays of discontent, and went out from graduation with a deep feeling of protest against what he supposed was the world. "Morning" and "The Clocks of Gnoster Town, or Truth by Majority" are the chief poetical results of this experience.

California offered him a relief, but too much of a relief. He was always loyal to his closest college friends and to his ideals for Yale. The license of a frontier mining country did not in any sense supply the freedom which New Haven had denied him. His greatest pleasure out there was in the companionship of an intellectual and music-loving "Yale" family. And so his revolt from the world and his return to it, which are motivated in "The Hermitage" by the charms of a lovely blonde, had a deeper cause in the facts of his spiritual adolescence. All this pioneering was in the nature of self-discovery. For a while he inclined to the study of law because he thought the discipline of legal training would lead him toward the truth. Then after returning to the East he came by way of theological study and journalism to his final work: ". . . only the great schoolmaster Death will ever take me through these higher mathematics of the religious principia — this side of his schooling, in these primary grades, I never can preach. — I shall teach school, I suppose."

[1] See chap. ii, " His Life at College," in W. B. Parker's Life.

Now that he had left it, however, the charm of California was upon him. Although he was later to write in sardonic comment on the dry season,

> Come where my stubbly hillside slowly dries,
> And fond adhesive tarweeds gently shade,

he was really in love with the great open vistas, the gentleness of the climate, and with the Californians' "independence of judgment; their carelessness of what a barbarian might think, so long as he came from beyond the border; their apparent freedom in choosing what manner of men they should be; their ready and confident speech." "Christmas in California," "Among the Redwoods," and "The Departure of the Pilot" are examples of much more California verse and of the spirit of many and many of his letters. Yet for this radical thinker institutional life was somewhat cramping even here. It is an unhappy fact that colleges and universities, devised as systems for educating the average by the slightly more than average, have rarely been flexible enough in their management to give fair harborage for creative genius either in front of or behind the desk. Sill's experience was not unusual; it only went to prove that in academic America East was West and West was East and that the two had never been parted. So finally the young poet, still young after two periods of residence on each coast, settled down again to quiet literary work in the little Ohio town. There were only five years left him.

Throughout his work, but increasingly in these later years, there is a fine and simple clarity of execution. The something in him which withheld him from calling on Longfellow and the others when in Cambridge, or even on his fellow-collegian Stedman in New York, made him slow to publish, rigorous in self-criticism, and eager to print anonymously or under a pseudonym. He wrote painstakingly, followed his contributions to the editors with substituted versions, and revised even in the proof. Although he was a wide reader, he was usually independent of immediate models, and always so in his later work. He avoided the stock phrases of poetry, but often equaled the best of them himself : "the whispering pine, Surf sound of an aërial sea," "Struck through with slanted shafts of afternoon," "When the low music makes a dusk of sound," are representatives of his own fresh coinage.

A reading of Sill's poetry would reveal much of his life story without other explanation. An acquaintance with his biography makes most of the rest clear. The poems relate in succession to his college experience, his lifelong search for truth, his Western voyage, his revolt against the world and his return to it, his residence in California. They show in parts of "The Hermitage" and in "Five Lives" his rebellion at the incursions of science. They show, however, that in his own mind a greater conflict than that between science and religion was the conflict, as he saw it, between religion and the church.

For my part I long to "fall in" with somebody. This picket duty is monotonous. I hanker after a shoulder on this side and the other. I can't agree in belief (or expressed belief — Lord knows what the villains really think, at home) with the "Christian" people, nor in spirit with the Radicals, etc. . . . Many, here and there, must be living the right way, doing their best, hearty souls, and I'd like to go 'round the world for the next year and take tea with them in succession.

The tone of this letter, written in 1870, was to prevail more and more in his later years. He had passed out from the rather desperate seriousness of young manhood. He had found that on the whole life was good. He was no less serious at bottom than before, but in the years approaching the fullness of his maturity he let his natural antic humor play without restraint. As a consequence the poems after 1875 tend as a group to deal more often with slighter themes and in lighter vein. The human soul did not cease to interest him, but the human mind interested Sill the husband and the teacher more than they had interested Sill the youthful misanthrope. Thus the confidence in "Force," the subtlety in "Her Explanation," the mockery in "The Agile Sonneteer," and the whimsical truth of "Momentous Words" were all recorded after he was forty years of age.

It is impossible not to feel the incompleteness of his career. It was cut off without warning while Sill was in a state of happy relief from the perplexities of earlier years. He was gaining in ease and power of workmanship. There was a modest demand, in the economic sense, for his work. There was everything to stimulate him to authorship and much to suggest that in time he would pass beyond this genial good humor into a period of serene and broadening maturity. Possibly in another decade he would have come into some sense of nationalism which would have illuminated for him the wide reaches of America which he had passed and repassed. The Civil War had meant nothing to him : "What is the grandeur of serving a state, whose tail is stinging its head to death like a scorpion ! " Since war times he had passed out of hermitage into society, and with the Spanish War he might have seen America and the larger human family with opened eyes. But at forty-six the arc of his life was snapped off short.

JOAQUIN MILLER (1841–1913)

Cincinnatus Hiner Miller was born in 1841. "My cradle was a covered wagon, pointed west. I was born in a covered wagon, I am told, at or about the time it crossed the line dividing Indiana from Ohio." His father was born of Scotch immigrant stock — a natural frontiersman, but a man with a love of books and a teacher among his fellow-wanderers. In 1852, moved by the same restlessness that had taken the Clemens family to Missouri seventeen years earlier, the Millers started on the three-thousand-mile roundabout journey to Oregon, finding their way without roads over the plains and mountains in a trip lasting more than seven months. It was from this that the boy gained his lasting respect for the first pioneers.

O bearded, stalwart, westmost men,
So tower-like, so Gothic built!
A kingdom won without the guilt
Of studied battle, that hath been
Your blood's inheritance. . . . Your heirs
Know not your tombs: The great plough-shares
Cleave softly through the mellow loam
Where you have made eternal home,
And set no sign. Your epitaphs
Are writ in furrows.

After two years in the new Oregon home the coming poet ran away with a brother to seek gold. They seem to have separated, and in the following years the one who came to celebrity survived a most amazing series of primitive experiences and primitive hardships among the Indians. Part of his time, however, with "Mountain Joe" preserved his contact with books, for this man, a graduate of Heidelberg, helped him with his Latin. The boy returned to Oregon early enough to earn a diploma at Columbia University in 1859, — an institution in which the collegiate quality was doubtless entirely restricted to its name. According to Miller the eagerness of study there was no less intense than the zest for every other kind of experience among the early settlers. In the next decade he had many occupations. For a while he was express messenger, carrying gold dust, but safe from the Indians, who had become his trusted friends. "Those matchless night-rides under the stars, dashing into the Orient doors of dawn before me as the sun burst through the shining mountain pass, — this brought my love of song to the surface." Later he was editor of a pacifist newspaper which was suppressed for alleged treason. But the largest proportion of his time was spent at the law. From 1866 to 1870 he held a minor judgeship.

Throughout all this time — he was now nearly thirty — Miller's primary passion had been for poetry and for casting in poetic form something of the rich, vivid romance of the great

West and Southwest. In 1868 a thin booklet, "Specimens,"
was issued and in San Francisco, in 1869, "Joaquin et al."
For naming his book in this fashion instead of "Joaquin and
Other Poems," his legal friends repaid him with a derisive nickname that finally became the one by which the world knows
him. Bret Harte, then in an influential editorship, gave the
book a fair review, but in general it was slightingly treated.

Impulsive in mood and accustomed to little respect for the
hardships of travel, Miller started East, and three months
later, as he records, was kneeling at the grave of Burns with
a definite resolve to complete his life in the country of his forefathers. In the volume of poems of his own selection he wrote
of "Vale! America," "I do not like this bit of impatience
nor do I expect anyone else to like it, and only preserve it
here as a sort of landmark or journal in my journey through
life." But for the moment in his sensitiveness he doubtless
wrote quite truly:

> I starve, I die,
> Each day of my life. Ye pass me by
> Each day, and laugh as ye pass; and when
> Ye come, I start in my place as ye come,
> And lean, and would speak, — but my lips are dumb.

He had, of course, no reputation in London, where he soon
settled near the British Museum, and the period was an unpro-
pitious one for poetry. A descendant and namesake of the
John Murray who had refused to deal with "The Sketch
Book" (see p. 118) gave a like response to Miller's offer of
his "Pacific Poems." But Miller carried the risk-taking spirit
of the pioneer to the point of privately printing one hundred
copies and sending them broadcast for review, with the result
of an immediate and enthusiastic recognition. The "Songs of
the Sierras" were soon regularly published in London, and the
poet was received in friendliest fashion as a peer of Dean
Stanley, Lord Houghton, Robert Browning, and all the pre-
Raphaelite brotherhood.

The period from 1873 to 1887 is distinctly a middle zone in Miller's career. The restless eagerness of his formative years still dominated him, but it led him for the most part to rapid changes, most of which were in the world of men and many of which were in the largest cities. His moves on both continents are difficult to follow and have not been clearly unraveled by any biographer. One can get a fairly clear idea of their nature if not of their order by an attentive reading of his poems and particularly of the chatty footnotes with which he accompanied the collections he edited. He continued to use the frontier experience of the early days. His most character-istic poems were stories of thrilling experience in the open. In " My Own Story," " Life Amongst the Modocs," " Unwritten History, Paquita," and " My Life Among the Indians " he recorded the same material in prose. In certain other poems, particularly the " Isles of the Amazons " and " The Baroness of New York," he set in contrast the romance of the forest with the petty conventions of the metropolis, and in " The Song of the South " he attempted — not to his own satisfaction — to do for the Mississippi what he had done for the moun-tains. Shorter lyrics show his response to world events such as the death of Garfield and the American war with Spain. In two poems of 1901 he wrote in withering condemnation of England's policy toward the Boers.

In all the material of this middle period the dominant feature is his praise of the elemental forces of nature. Nature itself for him was always dynamic. The sea and the forest at rest suggested to him their latent powers. His best scenes deal with storm, flood, and fire, and when occasionally he painted a calm background, as in the departure of " The Last Taschastas," the burnished beauty of the setting is in strong contrast with the violence of the episode. In human experience he most admired the exertion of primitive strength. It is this which endeared the early pioneers to him. Man coping with nature thrilled him, but for human conflict he had little sympathy.

His women were Amazonian in physique and character — a singularly consistent type, almost a recurrence of one woman of various complexions. In the judgment of Whitman — his Washington intimate of two years — he must have fallen from grace in his treatment of love. If he did not vie (to paraphrase Burroughs) "with the lascivious poets in painting it as the forbidden" passion, he did compete with the fleshly school in depicting all its charms. Yet even here in that strange concluding romance "Light" he struggled to overcome the sensuous with the spiritual element.

The form of all this mid-period work was quite conventional and, in view of the content, smacked strangely of the library and the drawing room. He ran as a rule to four-stressed lines, indulged in insistent riming, rarely missing a chance, and cast his stanzas into a jogging and seldom-varied rhythm. In their assault on the ear his verses have little delicacy of appeal. They blare at the reader like the brasses in an orchestral fortissimo. They clamor at him with the strident regularity of a Sousa march. This dominant measure accords well with the rude subject matter of his poems, — the march of the pioneer, the plod of oxen yoked to the prairie schooner, the roar of prairie fire or of the wind through the forest; and, with a difference, the hoof-beat of galloping horses or of stampeding buffalo. And it expresses the rhetorical magniloquence which is the natural fruit of life in a country of magnificent distances. At the same time Miller found a poetical justification for his style in the narrative rhythms of Scott and Byron and Coleridge, by whom he was often and evidently influenced. Until he was well past mid-career he was boyishly open to direct literary influences. He had no theory of prosody; his originality was inherent in the harmony between himself and his wild material; so he tried his hand at writing in the manner of this, that, and the other man.

In his final revisions, however, he was ruthless in rejecting his imitative passages and in his reduction of earlier work to

what was unqualifiedly his own. This is best illustrated by
what he did to " The Baroness of New York " before he had
done with it. In its original form of 1877 it filled a whole
volume, a poem — not a novel, as often erroneously stated —
in two parts. The former is a sea-island romance of love and
desertion after the manner of Scott; the sequel presents Adora
in New York as the Baroness du Bois, where she lives in scorn-
ful indifference until the original lover turns up with a title
of his own and carries her off in triumph ; this second part
is in the manner of Byron. When Miller included this poem
in his collected edition of 1897, he dropped all the Byronic,
metropolitan portion and reduced the rest to less than half —
the fraction that was quite his own.

Such a revision was in the fullest sense the work of matured
judgment. Miller was now in his last long period of picturesque
retirement on " The Hights," looking back over his prolific
output of former years, recognizing the good in it, and depend-
ing upon the public to reject what had no right to a long life.
At times he still wrote poem-stories located in settings of
tumultuous abundance, but he supplemented these with more
and more frequent short lyrics, and he studied continually to
achieve that simplicity which is seldom the result of anything
but perfected artistry. In 1902 he wrote :

Shall we ever have an American literature ? Yes, when we leave
sound and words to the winds. American science has swept time and
space aside. American science dashes along at fifty, sixty miles an
hour ; but American literature still lumbers along in the old-fashioned
English stage-coach at ten miles an hour ; and sometimes with a red-
coated outrider blowing a horn. We must leave all this behind us.
We have not time for words. A man who uses a great, big, sounding
word, when a short one will do, is to that extent a robber of time.
A jewel that depends greatly on its setting is not a great jewel.
When the Messiah of American literature comes, he will come singing,
so far as may be, in words of one syllable.

In the main his hope now was to pass from objective poetry
to " the vision of worlds beyond," — a vision which he more

nearly approached in "Sappho and Phaon" than in any other
poem, and a vision for which the motive is stated in the second
stanza of "Adios":

> Could I but teach man to believe —
> Could I but make small men to grow,
> To break frail spider-webs that weave
> About their thews and bind them low;
> Could I but sing one song and slay
> Grim Doubt; I then could go my way
> In tranquil silence, glad, serene,
> And satisfied, from off the scene.
> But ah, this disbelief, this doubt,
> This doubt of God, this doubt of good, —
> The damned spot will not out.

In the meanwhile, by way of a practical application of his
ideals, Miller was attempting to lead his life sanely and, by an
association that suggests the old Greek academy, to point the
way for the younger generation of poets. In his final note to
the 1902 edition he described himself as living on "a sort of
hillside Bohemia." No lessons were taught there except, by
example, the lesson of living. Three or four "tenets or principles of life" were insisted upon: that man is good; that
there is nothing ugly in nature; that man is immortal; that
nature wastes no thing and no time; and that man should
learn the lesson of economy. So in a way he returned to
the simple conditions in which his earliest life had grounded
his affections.

Miller naturally invites comparison with Mark Twain and
Walt Whitman. The likeness starts with the simple origins
of all three and with the rough-and-ready circumstances of
their upbringing. It continues with their resultant sympathetic
feeling for the common men and women who make up the
mass of humankind. It is maintained in their conscious personal picturesqueness: Whitman gray-bearded, open-collared,
wearing his hat indoors or out; Mark Twain in his white
serge, regardless of season; and Miller with long hair, velvet

jacket, and high boots, — evidence of the humanizing personal vanity in each which was quite apart from the genuine bigness of their characters. It follows in the high seriousness of all three. And it is confirmed in the fact of their early recognition in England and their less respectful reception at home (see pp. 293 and 367). Miller, like these others, was in the 70's what the Old World chose to think the typical American ought to be. He was fresher to them than those other Americans whom their countrymen were eagerly describing as "the American Burns," "the American Wordsworth," "the American Scott," and "the American Tennyson"; and to this degree — though he was not a representative of the prevailing American literature — he was actually a representative of the country itself and especially of the vast stretch from the Mississippi to the Pacific. For Miller and the America he knew best were both full of natural vigor, full of hope and faith, conscious of untold possibilities in the nearer and the remoter future, and, withal, relatively naïve and unformed.

BOOK LIST

Individual Authors

EDWARD ROWLAND SILL. Works. The Political Works of. 1906. 1 vol. His works appeared in book form originally as follows: The Hermitage and Other Poems, 1867; Venus of Milo, and Other Poems, 1883; Poems, 1887; The Hermitage, and Later Poems, 1889; Christmas in California: a Poem, 1898; Hermione, and Other Poems, 1899; Prose, 1900; Poems (Special Edition), 1902; Poems (Household Edition), 1906.

Biography and Criticism

The best biographical study is Edward Rowland Sill: his Life and Work, by W. B. Parker. 1915. See also Modern Poets and Christian Teaching (Gilder, Markham, Sill), by D. G. Downey. 1906.

JOAQUIN MILLER. Works. Bear Edition. 1909–1910. 6 vols. A single-volume "complete" edition was published in 1892, 1897, and 1904. These appeared in book form originally as follows: Specimens, 1868; Joaquin et al., 1869; Pacific Poems, 1870; Songs of the Sierras, 1871; Songs of the Sunlands, 1873; Unwritten History: Life Amongst the Modocs (with Percival Mulford), 1874; The Ship in the Desert, 1875; First Families of the Sierras, 1875; Songs of the Desert, 1875; The One Fair Woman, 1876; The Baroness of New York, 1877; Songs of Italy, 1878; The Danites in the Sierras, 1881; Shadows of Shasta, 1881; Poems (Complete Edition), 1882; Forty-nine: a California Drama, 1882; '49: or, the Gold-seekers of the Sierras, 1884; Memorie and Rime, 1884; The Destruction of Gotham, 1886; Songs of the Mexican Seas, 1887; In Classic Shades and Other Poems, 1890; The Building of the City Beautiful: a Poetic Romance, 1893; Songs of the Soul, 1896; Chants for the Boer, 1900; True Bear Stories, 1900; As It Was in the Beginning, 1903; Light: a Narrative Poem, 1907.

Biography and Criticism

There is no adequate biography or even biographical study. Of the historians of American literature only Churton Collins, C. F. Richardson, G. E. Woodberry, and F. L. Pattee ("American Literature since 1870") accord Miller serious attention. The autobiographical preface to the Bear Edition and the same material scattered through the one-volume editions are the raw stuff for interpretation of Miller's character and aim. These can be supplemented by his own article in the *Independent* on "What is Poetry?" See also *Current Literature*, Vol. XLVIII, p. 574.

See the historians above mentioned and the following review articles: *Academy*, Vol. II, p. 301; Vol. LIII, p. 181; *Arena*, Vol. XII, p. 86; Vol. IX, p. 553; Vol. XXXVII, p. 271; *Current Opinion*, Vol. LIV, p. 318; *Dial*, Vol. LIV, p. 165; *Fraser's*, Vol. LXXXIV, p. 346; *Godey's*, Vol. XCIV, p. 52; *Lippincott's*, Vol. XXXVIII, p. 106; *Munsey's*, Vol. IX, p. 308; *Nation*, Vol. XXVII, p. 336; Vol. XIII, p. 196; Vol. XVIII, p. 77; Vol. XCVI, pp. 169, 187, 230, 544.

TOPICS AND PROBLEMS

Compare the use of California and California life by Sill with use of the same material by Joaquin Miller or Bret Harte or Mark Twain.

Compare Sill's "Hermitage" with Robert Frost's "A Boy's Will." What is the likeness in the general drift of the two and what are the essential differences in the treatments of the theme?

Read W. B. Parker's "Life of Sill" with especial reference to Sill's letters and the degree to which they reveal his humor and his seriousness. Note poems which correspond in spirit or in content with given letters.

Compare the treatment of primitive Western life and adventure by Miller with use of the same material by Mark Twain or Bret Harte.

Read Miller for evidences of literary influence upon him of Scott or Byron or Coleridge or Browning.

Read Miller's " Song of the South " and his explanatory remarks on it and compare Longfellow's treatment of the Mississippi; or compare Masters's preface to his volume " Toward the Gulf " and his poems on the same subject.

Note the insistence of Miller on the idea that life is power and in his later poems the increasing respect for reflection.

Compare Miller's " Columbus " with Lowell's " Columbus " and Lanier's " Sonnets on Columbus."

CHAPTER XXVII

THE RISE OF FICTION; WILLIAM DEAN HOWELLS

It is very seldom in the history of literature that important developments take place without long preliminaries. From period to period new emphasis is placed on old ideas, and old forms are given the right of way in literary fashion. In the course of American literature, roughly speaking, the dominating forms of literature have been in succession : exposition and travel during the colonial period ; poetry, satirical and epic, in the Revolutionary period ; poetry in all its broader aspects during the first two thirds of the nineteenth century. After the Civil War for fifty years fiction came to the front ; from about 1900 on a new emphasis was given to the stage and the playwright ; at present the most striking fact in world literature is the broadening and deepening of the poetic currents again. Yet all of these forms are always existent. To speak of the rise of fiction, then, is simply to acknowledge the increased attention which for a period it demanded.

It is frequently said that America's chief contribution to world literature has been the short story as developed since the Civil War. Yet in America the ground had been prepared for this development by many writers, — among them, as already mentioned in this history, Washington Irving with "The Sketch Book" in 1819 (see pp. 118–131), Hawthorne with "Twice-Told Tales" in 1837 (see pp. 240 and 243), Poe with his various contributions to periodical literature in the 1840's (see pp. 185–187), Mark Twain with "The Jumping Frog" of 1867, Bret Harte with "The Luck of Roaring Camp" of 1870 and the great bulk of his subsequent contributions (see p. 381), and Thomas Bailey Aldrich with "Marjorie

Daw " of 1873 and his other volumes of short stories. In the meanwhile the novel had had its consecutive history — from Brockden Brown beginning with 1798 (see pp. 100–109) to Cooper in 1820 (see pp. 141–157), William Gilmore Simms from 1833 (see p. 344), Hawthorne from 1850 on (see pp. 236–251), Mrs. Stowe from 1852 (see pp. 299–309), and Holmes from 1861 (see pp. 320, 321). And these writers of short and long fiction are only the outstanding story-tellers in America between the beginning of the century and the years just after the Civil War.

In a chapter such as this no exhaustive survey is possible, for it involves scores of writers and hundreds of books. The vital movement started with a fresh and vivid treatment of native American material, and it moved in a great sweeping curve from the West down past the Gulf up through the southeastern states into New England, across to the Middle West, and back into the Ohio valley until every part of the country was represented by its expositors. The course of this newer provincial fiction is suggested by the mention of Mark Twain's "Jumping Frog " (1867, California), "The Luck of Roaring Camp " of Bret Harte (1870, California), G. W. Cable's " Old Creole Days " (1879, Louisiana), Harris's " Uncle Remus : his Songs and his Sayings " (1880, Georgia), " In the Tennessee Mountains," by Charles Egbert Craddock (1884), " In Ole Virginia," by Thomas Nelson Page (1887), " A New England Nun," by Mary E. Wilkins Freeman (1891), "Main-Traveled Roads," by Hamlin Garland (1891, the Middle West), "Flute and Violin," by James Lane Allen (1891, the Ohio valley).

WILLIAM DEAN HOWELLS (1837–1920)

The preëminent figure in the field of American fiction during the last half century has been William Dean Howells, a man who is widely representative of the broad literary development in the country and worthy of careful study as an artist and as a critic of life. Although he has been an

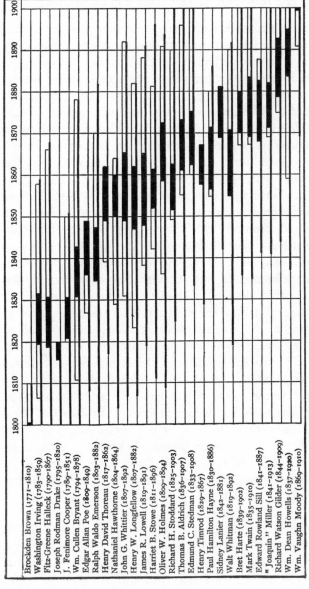

CHRONOLOGICAL CHART II. AMERICAN LITERATURE IN THE NINETEENTH CENTURY

= Length of life, as far as included in this century

= Period of authorship

= Most important period of authorship

Easterner by residence for nearly half a century, he is the greatest contribution of the West — or what was West in his youth — to Eastern life and thought.

He was born in 1837 at Martins Ferry, Ohio, — the second of eight children. Perhaps the richness of his character is accounted for by the varied strains in his ancestry. On his father's side his people were wholly Welsh except his English great-grandmother, and on his mother's wholly German except his Irish grandfather. His mother he has described as the heart of the family, and his father as the soul. The family fortunes were in money ways unsuccessful. His father's experience as a country editor took him from place to place in a succession of ventures which were harrassed by uncertain income and heavy debts. These were always paid, but only by dint of unceasing effort. The Howells family were, however, happy in their concord and in their daily enjoyment of the best that books could bring them. Unlike many another youth who has struggled into literary fame, William Dean found a ready sympathy with his ambitions at home. His experience was less like Whitman's than Bryant's. From childhood the printing office was his school and almost his only school, for the district teachers had little to offer a child of literary parentage "whose sense was open to every intimation of beauty." Very early his desire for learning led him into what he called "self-conducted inquiries" in foreign languages; and with the help of a "sixteen-bladed grammar," a nondescript polyglot affair, he acquired in turn a reading knowledge of Latin, Greek, Spanish, German, French, and Italian. In the meanwhile he was reading and assimilating the popular English favorites. It was typical of his experience that Longfellow led him to his first studies of the Spanish language, bringing him back to Spain, where he had traveled in fancy with Irving. Always he was writing, for his life was "filled with literature to bursting," and always imitating — now Pope, now Heine, now Cervantes, now Shakespeare.

As a printer on country journals he had the opportunity to place his own wares before the public, often composing in type without ever putting pen to paper. His father encouraged him to contribute to journals of larger circulation, and the experience naturally led him into professional journalism before he was of age. It led him also to Columbus, the state capital, where he reported the proceedings of the legislature and in time rose to the dignity of editorial writer. During these years of late youth and early manhood his aspirations were like Bret Harte's, all in the direction of poetry, and his earliest book was a joint effort with James J. Piatt, "Poems of Two Friends," 1859. This was a typical experience in literary history. Again and again at the period of a change to a new form or, better, a revived artistic form, the literary youth has started to write in the declining fashion of his day and has been carried over into the rising vogue. "Paradise Lost" was first conceived of as a five-act tragedy. "Amelia" and "Tom Jones" were preceded by twenty-odd unsuccessful comedies. "The Lay of the Last Minstrel" and "Marmion" and "The Lady of the Lake" were all preliminary to "Waverley" and the tide of novels that followed. In 1860 Howells had five poems in the *Atlantic* and had no expectation of writing fiction; and it was another full decade, after the publication of several volumes of sketches and travel observations, before he was fairly launched on his real career.

In Columbus he had come by 1860 to a full enjoyment of an eager, book-loving group. He was working enthusiastically as a journalist, but his knowledge of politics and statecraft did not bring him to any vivid sense of the social order. "What I wished to do always and evermore was to think and dream and talk literature, and literature only, whether in its form of prose or of verse, in fiction, or poetry, or criticism. I held it a higher happiness to stop at a street corner with a congenial young lawyer and enter upon a fond discussion of, say, De Quincey's essays than to prove myself worthy the respect of any most eminent citizen who knew not or loved not De Quincey." There was a succession of fellow-journalists with whom he could have this sort of pleasure, and there were houses in town where he could enjoy the finer pleasure of talking over with the girls the stories of Thackeray and George Eliot and Dickens and Charles Reade as they appeared in rapid sequence in book or serial form. "It is as if we did nothing then but read late novels and current serials which it was essential for us to know one another's minds upon down to the instant; other things might wait, but these things were pressing." During these years he developed a liking for the social amenities, of which an enjoyment of polite literature was a natural expression. Literature was an adornment of life and, as he saw it, was confined to an interpretation of individual experience.

With the presidential candidacy of Lincoln, Howells became one of his campaign biographers, and after the election and a period of anxious waiting he received the appointment as United States consul to Venice. Upon his return to this country he became an Easterner, settling happily in Boston as assistant editor and then as editor in chief of the *Atlantic Monthly* from 1866 to 1881. This was a fulfillment beyond his highest hopes. The great New England group were at the height of their fame, and his connection with the unrivaled literary periodical of America brought him into contact with them all. He was ready to begin his own work as a writer of novels.

For the next twenty years he was a thoroughly conventional artist, gaining satisfaction and giving pleasure through the exercise of his admirable technique. In this period he wrote always, to borrow an expression originally applied to Tennyson, as though a staid American matron had just left the room: a matron who had been nurtured on the reading which gave rise to his own literary passions — Goldsmith, Cervantes, Irving, Longfellow, Scott, Pope, Mrs. Stowe, Dickens, and

Macaulay; a matron, in short, who was the Lady of the Aroostook at forty-five, the mother of a numerous family, and aggressively concerned that no book which fell into the hands of her daughters should cause the blush of shame to rise upon the maiden cheek. He wrote not only on an early experience in the life of this lady but on "A Modern Instance," "A Woman's Reason," "Indian Summer," and, best of them all, "The Rise of Silas Lapham." He was giving ground to Mr. Crothers's pale-gray pleasures as a reader in the time when, as he said: "I turned eagerly to some neutral tinted person who never had any adventure greater than missing the train to Dedham, and I . . . analyzed his character, and agitated myself in the attempt to get at his feelings, and I . . . verified his story by a careful reference to the railroad guide. I . . . treated that neutral tinted person as a problem, and I . . . noted all the delicate shades in the futility of his conduct. When, on any occasion that called for action, he did not know his own mind, I . . . admired him for his resemblance to so many people who do not know their own minds. After studying the problem until I came to the last chapter . . . I . . . suddenly gave it up, and agreed with the writer that it had no solution." Had nothing occurred to break the sequence, he was on the way to wasting his energy, as Henry James did, "in describing human rarities, or cases that are common enough only in the abnormal groups of men and women living on the fringe of the great society of active, healthy human beings."

The books of this period, in other words, were all the work of a well-schooled, unprejudiced observer whose ambition was to make transcripts of life. "Venetian Life" and "Italian Journeys" were the first logical expression of his desire and his capacities — books of the same sort as "Bracebridge Hall" and "Outre-Mer" and "Views Afoot" and "Our Old Home" (see p. 269, note). "A Foregone Conclusion" and "A Fearful Responsibility" simply cross the narrow bridge between exposition and fiction but employ the same point of view and the same technique. Howells was interested in American character and in the nice distinctions between the different levels of culture. In " Silas Lapham," his greatest novel written before 1890, the blunt Vermonter is set in contrast with certain Boston aristocrats. He amasses a fortune, becomes involved in speculation, in business injustice, and in ruin. But whatever Howells had to say then of social and economic forces, he said of powers as impersonal as gravitation. Business was business, and the man subjected to it was subjected to influences as capricious but as inevitable as the climate of New England.

More and more as a realist he devoted himself to the presentation of character at the expense of plot. " The art of fiction," he wrote in his essay on Henry James in 1882, " has become a finer art in our day than it was with Dickens or Thackeray. We could not suffer the confidential attitude of the latter now nor the mannerism of the former any more than we could endure the prolixity of Richardson or the coarseness of Fielding. These great men are of the past — they and their methods and interests ; even Trollope and Reade are not of the present." He dismissed moving accidents and dire catastrophes from the field of the new novel, substituting for fire and flood the slow smolder of individual resentment and a burst of feminine tears. With " April Hopes " of 1887 he deliberately wrote an unfinished story, following two young and evidently incompatible people to the marriage altar, but leaving their subsequent sacrifice to the imagination of the reader, who must imagine his own sequel or go without.

However, when he was past fifty he underwent a social conversion. And when he wrote his next book about his favorite characters, the Marches, he and they together risked " A Hazard of New Fortunes." He and they were no longer content to play at life under comfortable and protected circumstances. They went down into the metropolis, competed with strange and uncouth people, and learned something about poverty and something about justice. In fact they learned what went into "Annie Kilburn" and "The Quality of Mercy" and "The World of Chance" and "A Traveler from Altruria" and "The Eye of a Needle," learning it all through the new vision given by the belated reading of a great European. Writing from his heart of this conversion Mr. Howells says, in "My Literary Passions":

It is as if the best wine at this high feast, where I have sat so long, had been kept for the last and I need not deny a miracle in it in order to attest my skill in judging vintages. In fact I prefer to believe that my life has been full of miracles, and that the good has always come to me at the right time, so that I could profit most by it. I believe that if I had not turned the corner of my fiftieth year, when I first knew Tolstoy, I should not have been able to know him as fully as I did. He has been to me that final consciousness, which he speaks of so wisely in his essay on Life. I came in it to the knowledge of myself in ways I had not dreamt of before, and began at last to discern my relations to the race, without which we are nothing. The supreme art in literature had its highest effect in making me set art forever below humanity, and it is with the wish to offer the greatest homage to his heart and mind which any man can pay another, that I close this record with the name of Lyof Tolstoy.

This passage we can hardly overvaluate. Taken by itself, it is merely a punctuation point in one author's autobiography, but seen against its background it records the epoch-marking fact that in the very years when America as one expression of itself was producing such native-born spokesmen as Whitman and Mark Twain and Joaquin Miller, it was also, in the spiritual successor to Longfellow and Lowell, making reverent acknowledgment, not to the splendors of an ancient civilization but to the newest iconoclasm in the Old World. It is not unworthy of comment that the influence of Tolstoy was exerted upon Howells after his removal to New York City, where he has been associated with the editorial staff of *Harper's Magazine* ever since 1881, and that the experiences of the Marches in their hazard of new fortunes is apparently autobiographical.

There was no violent change in the material or method of his fiction-writing. It was simply enriched with a new purpose. To his old power to portray the individual in his mental and emotional processes he added a criticism of the rôle the individual played in society. He added a new consciousness of the institution of which the individual was always the creator, sometimes the beneficiary, and all too often the victim. His maturity as a man and as a writer secured him in his human and artistic equilibrium, and in this degree has distinguished him from younger authors who have written with the same convictions and purposes. He has written no novels as extreme as Sinclair's " The Jungle," which ends with a diatribe on socialism, although he has been a socialist; he has written nothing quite so insistent as Whitlock's " The Turn of the Balance," although he has been keenly aware of the difference between justice and the operation of the legal system. Every story has contained a recognition that life is infinitely complex, with a great deal of redeeming and a great deal of unintelligent and baffling good in it. Furthermore, he has written always out of his own experience and with all his old skill as a novelist, so that he has never done anything so clumsily commendable as Page's " John Marvel, Assistant " or anything so clearly prepared for by painstaking study as Churchill's " The Inside of the Cup."

By 1894 Howells had come to the point where he wished to present his social thesis as a thesis, and he did so in "A Traveler from Altruria," which is not a novel at all but a series of conversations on the nature of American life as contrasted with life in an ideal state. Mr. Homos from Altruria (Mr. Man from Other Land) is the traveler who gets his first impressions of America by visiting a conservative novelist, Mr. Twelvemough, at a summer resort in which the hotel furnishes "a sort of microcosm of the American republic." Here, in addition to the host, are an enlightened banker, a complacent manufacturer, an intolerant professor of economics, a lawyer, a minister, and a society woman " who as a cultivated American woman . . . was necessarily quite ignorant of her own country, geographically, politically and historically "; and here also are the hotel keeper, the baggage porter, a set of college-girl waitresses, and a surrounding population of " natives," as the summer resorter invidiously describes the inhabitants whom he does n't quite dare to call peasants. In the earlier part of the essay the social cleavages are embarrassingly revealed, — the ignominy of being a manual laborer or, worse still, a domestic servant, and the consequent struggle to escape from toil and all the conditions that surround it. This leads quickly to a study of the economic situation in a republic where every man is for himself.

When pinned by embarrassing questions the defenders of the American faith take refuge in what they regard as the static quality of human nature, but are further embarrassed by the Altrurian's innocent surprise at their tactics. He does not understand that it is in human nature for the first-come to be first served, or for every man to be for himself, or for a man " to squeeze his brother man when he gets him in his grip," or for employers to take it out of objecting employees in any way they can. To Mr. Twelvemough it is a matter of doubt as to whether the traveler is ironically astute or innocently simple in his implication that even human nature is subject to development.

The latter two thirds of the book are a composite indictment of an economic system which permits slavery in everything but name and which extols the rights of the individual only as they apply to the property holder. This culminates with the concluding lecture by the Altrurian — an " account of his own country, which grew more and more incredible as he went on, and implied every insulting criticism of ours." The book concludes :

We parted friends; I even offered him some introductions; but his acquaintance had become more and more difficult, and I was not sorry to part with him. That taste of his for low company was incurable, and I was glad that I was not to be responsible any longer for whatever strange thing he might do next. I think he remained very popular with the classes he most affected; a throng of natives, construction hands, and table-girls saw him off on his train; and he left large numbers of such admirers in our house and neighborhood, devout in the faith that there was such a commonwealth as Altruria, and that he was really an Altrurian. As for the more cultivated people who had met him, they continued of two minds upon both points.

These are the convictions which dominate in all the later works. On the whole it is a significant fact that novels of so radical a thesis have attracted so little opposition. Never was an iconoclast received with such unintelligent tolerance. The suavity of his manner, the continued appearance of his books of travel and observation, the recurrence (as in "The Kentons") to his old type of work or the resort (as in the long unpublished "Leatherwood God") to fresh woods and pastures new, and all the while the humorous presentation of his favorite characters, particularly the bumptious young business man and the whimsically incoherent American woman, beguile his readers into a blind and bland assumption of Mr. Howells's harmlessness. Possibly because they have been less skillful and more explicit, novel after novel from younger hands has excited criticism and the healthy opposition which prove that the truth has struck home. Perhaps his largest influence being indirectly exerted, his lack of sensationalism or sentimentalism debar him from the " best-seller " class ; but for fifty years he has been consistently followed by the best-reading class, and no novelist of the newer generation has been unconscious of his work.

Henry James (1843–1916), whose work in some respects has been comparable to that of Howells, was a writer of so distinct an individuality that he has been the subject of much criticism and no little amiable controversy. Born in New York of literary parentage, educated in the university towns of Europe, and resident most of his life abroad, he developed into an international novelist, chiefly interested in the various shades of the contrasting cultures in the Old World and the New. Of his subject matter one story is about as good an example as another, for James was remarkably consistent. The backgrounds are almost always intercontinental or transatlantic. The characters belong to the leisure class. The episodes, where they exist, are adventures of the mind. In the earlier stories, such as "The American" (1877), plot is more eventful and definitive and style is more lucid than in the later ones. In these James seemed to be so fascinated with his intricate discriminations of feeling that he confined himself largely to psychological analysis in a style which became increasingly obscured by subtle indirections. Thus "The Awkward Age" (1899) is a narrative in ten short "books" centering about the marriage and non-marriage of two London girls. Aggie, who has been brought up in the fashion of Richard Feverel translated into feminine terms, is married off to a wealthy and decent man twice her age, and after a short experience turns out to be altogether unfitted for his degree of sophistication. Nanda, wise from the beginning, fails to win the most attractive man of the lot, and in the end is adopted and carried off to the country by a charming old Victorian gentleman. Nothing objective happens. The tale is told in ten long conversations, each entitled for one of the chief characters and occupying most of one of the books. All the characters talk with circuitous elusiveness, and all employ the same idiom, with the single exception of Aggie in her first two appearances, when she is supposed to be hopelessly ingenuous. In his attitude toward these people James put himself in a somewhat equivocal position. With their general social and spiritual insufficiency he had no patience. They represent the world of "Vanity Fair" and "The Newcomes" done down to date. But at the time he betrayed a lurking admiration for them, their ways, and their attitude toward life. Like the rest of his stories, "The Awkward Age" has little to do with the world of affairs in any group aspect. It is like a piece of Swiss carving on ivory. It has the same marvelous minuteness of detail, the same inutility, the same remote and attenuated relationship to any deep emotional experience or vigorous human endeavor. Unless one is devoted to the gospel of art for art's sake, one cannot appreciate the good of this sort of endeavor. In his narrowly limited field Mr. James is a master. For more than forty years and in more than thirty volumes he did the thing that he elected to without compromise in behalf of popularity. Yet admire him as much as they may, most readers turn from him with relief to the literature of activity and of the normal, healthy human beings who are seldom to be encountered in the pages of Henry James.

Before mentioning in detail the types of American realistic novel which have followed on the work of Mr. Howells, something should be said about the very considerable output of romantic fiction of which he has been strangely intolerant; for it is strange that a man of his gentle generosity should be so insistent on the wrongness of an artistic point of view which is complementary to his own, though different from it. Distinctions between romance and realism often lead into a dangerous " no man's land," and discussions of the term are harder to close than to begin. However, Sir Walter Raleigh's contention that the essence of romance lies in remoteness and the glamour of unfamiliarity — though not inclusive of all romance — will serve as an index for grouping here.

In 1879, 1880, and 1882 three men, the first of whom is still producing, set out on long careers of popularity. They were George W. Cable (1844–   ), Joel Chandler Harris (1848–1908), and F. Marion Crawford (1854–1909). Mr. Cable's contribution has been the interpretation of the elusive and fascinating character of the New Orleans creole. Cable was bred in the river port when the old part of the city was less like the decaying heart of a mushroom than it is to-day. He grew up in an understanding of the courtly, high-spirited gentry of this exotic people, not studying either the people or their traditions for the sake of writing them up. He felt the beauty, but no less the futility, of their life. He was in no hurry to write for publication, but when he did so his fame was soon made. His subsequent departure from the South and his settling in New

England seemed to many critics to be an abandonment of the richest field that life had to offer him. It was said for years, until it became one of the literary commonplaces, that Mr. Cable would never again rise to the level of " Old Creole Days " (1879), " The Grandissimes " (1880), or " Madame Delphine " (1881). The fourteen volumes of the next third of a century seemed to fulfill this dreary prophecy. Yet all the time the South was the home of his imagination, and with 1918 he gave the lie to all his Jeremiahs. The " Lovers of Louisiana " has quite as fine a touch as the works of nearly forty years ago. Mr. Cable sees the old charm in this life of an echoing past and the same fatuousness. At this distance into the twentieth century he leads his old characters and their children by new paths into the future, but he presents the graces of their obsolescent life in the familiar narrative style of his early successes — a style as fleeting yet as distinctive as the aroma of old lace.

Joel Chandler Harris, like George W. Cable, did his work in presenting the life of a vanishing race — the antebellum negro. He finished off his formal education, which ended when he was twelve, with the schooling of the printing shop, and passed from this into journalistic work with a succession of papers, of which the *Atlanta Constitution* is best known. Boy life on the plantation gave him his material in the folklore of the negro, and a chance bit of substituting gave him his very casual start as the creator of " Uncle Remus." Northern readers were quick to recognize that Harris had given a habitation and a name to the narrative stuff that folklorists had already begun to collect and collate. The material goes back to the farthest sources of human tradition, but " Uncle Remus " was a new story-teller with a gift amounting to little short of genius. So his stories have the double charm of recording the lore of the negro and of revealing his humor, his transparent deceitfulness, his love of parade, his superstition, his basic religious feeling, and his pathos. Harris seemed to draw his material from a bottomless spring. Starting with " Uncle Remus : his Songs and Sayings " in 1880, Harris produced six other volumes in the next ten years and brought the total to fourteen in folk stories alone before his death in 1908. As the aptest of criticisms on his own work, one of his admirers has well quoted Harris's comment on a book of Mark Twain: "It is history, it is romance, it is life. Here we behold a human character stripped of all tiresome details; we see people growing and living; we laugh at their humor, share their griefs, and, in the midst of it all, behold, we are taught the lesson of honesty, justice and mercy."

The fluent romance of Marion Crawford is of a different and a lower order. He was a sort of professional cosmopolitan, — American by birth, educated largely abroad, widely traveled, and resident for most of his maturity on the Bay of Naples. He could turn off romances of Persia, of Constantinople, of Arabia, of medieval Venice, of Rome, and of England with about equal success. He had no great artistic purpose, admitting complacently that he was not great enough to be a poet or clever enough to be a successful playwright. He had no ethical purpose. He had not even a high ideal of craftsmanship, putting out eight volumes in 1903 and 1904 alone. He deserves mention as a prolific and self-respecting entertainer who converted his knowledge of the world into a salable commodity and established a large market for his superficial romances.

With the turn of the century — almost two decades after the débuts of Cable, Harris, and Crawford — a new interest began to spread from the collegians to the reading public as a whole the same influences which were producing as leaders in the scholastic field Von Holst, Channing, McMaster, Hart, Jameson, and McLaughlin — masters of American history — extending to the people at large. In 1897 appeared Weir Mitchell's "Hugh Wynne." In the spring of 1898 came the war with Spain. In 1899 Ford's "Janice Meredith" and Churchill's "Richard Carvel" were published; in 1900, Mary Johnston's "To Have and to Hold"; and in 1901 Churchill's

" The Crisis "— four novels which by the end of the latter year had reached a combined sale of 1,200,000 copies. For a little while the vogue of the historical romance passed all recent precedent. The natural zest for stories of olden days was reënforced by the revival of national feeling, and the popular authors of the moment reaped a golden harvest from the public, whom they at once charmed and instructed.

In the meanwhile, however, the describers and critics of contemporary American life were by no means on the wane. In the shifting currents of fiction various types of realism have come to the surface and are conspicuous in the tide. They all fall under the definition formulated by Mr. Perry: the sort of fiction that " does not shrink from the commonplace or from the unpleasant in its effort to depict things as they are and life as it is "; but within this definition they may be separated into two main classes. The first is the type that begins and ends with portrayal of human life, deals with the individual, and aims only to please. The second is written with the intent of pronouncing a criticism on the ways of men as they live together, presents its characters against a social and institutional background, and aims to influence the opinions of its readers. The difference between the two is, of course, the difference between the earlier and the later novels of Mr. Howells. In his later studies Mr. Howells is always dealing unaggressively but searchingly with the problem of economic justice, but this is only one of three broad fields. All modern problem and purpose novels are devoted, simply or complexly, to the market — property; the altar — religion; and the hearthstone — domestic life. This classification, which is useful only as long as it is employed cautiously for a general guide, leads to a cross-survey of recent fiction by kinds rather than by individual authors.

The number of more or less successful portrayers of provincial types in American fiction defies even enumeration. The most effective have, however, been unsatisfied with depicting the mere idiosyncrasies of a region heavily propped by dialect and have gone on to the interpretation of life as it might express itself anywhere under similar conditions. Thus the "Old Chester" of Mrs. Margaret Deland (1857–   ) is a study of isolated conservatisms thrown into relief by the wise sanity of Dr. Lavendar. Old Chester, we are told, is in Pennsylvania. It might be in any state or country where narrow respectability could intrench itself. It is an American Cranford. In the "Old Chester Tales" (1898) "The Promises of Dorothea" involve her utterly respectable elopement with Mr. King, whose worst offense in the eyes of her guardian maiden aunts is that he has lived abroad for many years. The implied departure from Old Chester customs is sufficient condemnation. "Good for the Soul" culminates with the doctor's sensible advice to Elizabeth Day, who, at the end of twelve years of happy marriage, is oppressed by the memory of a Bohemian girlhood of which her husband is ignorant. "Suppose," said the doctor, "I had n't found her a good woman, should I have told her to hold her tongue?" "The Child's Mother" is the story of an unregenerate whose baby Dr. Lavendar keeps away from her by a process we should call blackmail if it were not practiced by a saint. Wide and varied as her output is, Mrs. Deland has nowhere shown her artistry more finely than in the two Dr. Lavendar volumes.

The comments of Edith Wharton (1862–   ) on American life are from the cosmopolitan point of view and present a series of pictures of the American woman which for harshness of uncharity are difficult to parallel. As a matter of fact America is so vast and varied that there is no national type of woman. Mrs. Wharton's women are representative of one stratum just as Christy's pictorial girls are. They are the product of indulgence which makes them hard, capricious, and completely selfish. Lily Bart of "The House of Mirth" (1905) begins high in the social scale, compromises reluctantly with moneyed ambition, and in one instance after another defeats herself by delay and equivocation in a declining series of "affairs." More approachable than irreproachable, she suffers from the social beclouding of her reputation and, in the end, as a consequence of her low standards but her lack of shamelessness she succumbs to the circumstances that created her and arrives at a miserable death. Undine Spragg, in "The Custom of the Country" (1913), first married and divorced in a Western town is then brought to New York, introduced into society and "made" by her good looks and her brazen ambition. She wrecks the life of her second husband, a refined gentleman, and then as a result of much foreign residence marries a Frenchman of family. From him she runs away, finally to remarry Moffatt, who, throughout the story, has been her familiar spirit, subtly revealing his intimacy of feeling, and increasing his hold upon her as he rises in the money world. The title gives the cue to the story as a whole and to its several parts. By nature Undine is coarse-grained, showy, and selfish; by upbringing she becomes incorrigible. Her first and last husband is one of her own kind — sufficiently so that he is capable of resuming with her after her streaky, intermediate career. The second is broken on her overweening selfishness; the third, by virtue of his ancient family tradition, is able to save himself though not to mold or modify her. At the end, with Moffatt and all his immense wealth, she is still confronted by "the custom of the country." Because of her divorces "she could never be an ambassador's wife; and as she advanced to welcome her first guest she said to herself that it was the one part she was really made for." This is the Wharton formula: none of her women really triumphs. Lily Bart's downfall is one with her death. She had breathed the stifling atmosphere from her city childhood; what seemed to save Undine was the initial vigor of her Western youth, but even she could not successfully defy the ways of the world.

Hamlin Garland (1860–   ) in 1891 achieved with his "Main-Traveled Roads" as quickly earned a reputation as Cable and Harris had done with their first volumes. The son

of a sturdy Western pioneer, he had passed a boyhood of incessant toil before breaking away to earn his own schooling,
which culminated with several years of self-directed study in
Boston. A vacation return in 1887 to Wisconsin, Dakota, and
Iowa revealed to him the story-stuff of his early life, and during
the next two years he wrote the realistic studies which won
him his first recognition. In them, he explained later, he tried
to embody the stern truth. "Though conditions have changed
somewhat since that time, yet for the hired man and the renter
farm life in the West is still a stern round of drudgery. My
pages present it — not as the summer boarder or the young
lady novelist sees it — but as the working farmer endures it."
To the reader of Mr. Garland's work as a whole it is evident
that the richest part of his life was over with the writing of
this book and "A Spoil of Office" (1892) and "Rose of
Dutcher's Coolly" (1895). With the adoption of city life his
interests became diffuse and miscellaneous, as his writing did
also. The almost startling strength of "A Son of the Middle
Border" (1917) reënforces this conviction, for this late piece
of autobiography is the story of the author's first thirty-three
years and owes its fine power to the fact that in composing
it Mr. Garland renewed his youth like the eagle's. What
he propounded in his booklet of essays, "Crumbling Idols"
(1894), he illustrated in his stories up to that time. In them
he made his best contribution to American literature, except
for this recent reminiscent volume. In almost every quarter
of the country similar expositions of American life were multiplied and to such an extent that Mrs. Deland, Mrs. Wharton,
and Mr. Garland are chosen simply as illustrations of an
output which would require volumes for full treatment.

In the field of realism which is concerned with a criticism of
institutional life, Mrs. Deland wrote a memorable book in "John
Ward, Preacher" (1888). This was the same year in which
Mrs. Humphry Ward's "Robert Elsmere" appeared. Both
were indexes to the religious unrest of the whole Victorian

period, — an unrest apparent in America since the rise of the
Unitarians and the activities of the Transcendentalists, and
recorded in such novels as Mrs. Stowe's "Oldtown Folks"
and Bayard Taylor's "Hannah Thurston," as well as in the
underlying currents of Holmes's Breakfast-Table series. The
explicit story of John Ward is the tragic history of his love
and marriage with Helen Jaffrey. The implicit story is based
on the insufficiency of religious dogma detached from life.
Mrs. Deland's convictions resulted later in the genuine strength
of her best single character, the lovable Dr. Lavendar, and
in the subordinate religious motif of "The Iron Woman"
(1910). In recent years the narrative treatment of the problem
to attract widest attention has been Churchill's "The Inside
of the Cup" (1913), a story which one is tempted to believe
gained its reading more from its author's reputation and the
prevailing interest in the problem than from its artistic excellence. Mrs. Stowe and Mrs. Ward wrote out of long experience in life; Mr. Churchill seems rather to have felt the need
of introducing this theme into his many-volumed exposition of
America and to have read up on the literature of the subject
with the same thoroughness that characterized his preparation
for more strictly historical stories.

The novels of economic life are far more numerous and
more urgent in tone. One of the earliest was John Hay's
"The Breadwinners" (1883). It is significant that this appeared anonymously, the talented poet and politician preferring
not to be known as a story-teller. The labor unrest of the
early 80's disturbed him. Desire for education seemed to result unfortunately, and with a very clear impatience Mr. Hay
expounded the hardships of wealth in the midst of a labor uprising. To go to the root of the difficulty did not seem to occur
to him. Shortly after this early industrial novel Mr. Howells
was to attack the problem in a broader and deeper way (see
pp. 418–421). And while Howells was still making his successive approaches a whole succession of younger men joined

the assault. With many of them there was no such vital experience as their senior had passed through ; they were rather writing as journalists and utilizing the novel, sometimes clumsily and often feverishly. Few have done work which could at all compare with that of Frank Norris (1870–1902). His interrupted trilogy — an epic of the wheat — fulfilled the promise of his early efforts, "Vendover and the Brute" and "McTeague," and made his early death the occasion of a deep loss. Of these three novels "The Octopus" (1901) forms the story of a crop of wheat and deals with the war between the wheat-grower and the railroad trust ; the second, "The Pit" (1903), is a story of the middleman ; the third, "The Wolf" (never written), was to have dealt with the consumption in Europe. Norris's aspiration was no less than that of his own character Presley, the poet. "He strove for the diapason, the great song which should embrace in itself a whole epoch, a complete era, the voice of an entire people. . . ." With a great imaginative grasp he conceived of the wheat as an enormous, primitive force.

The Wheat that had killed Cressler, that had ingulfed Jadwin's fortune and all but unseated reason itself; the Wheat that had intervened like a great torrent to drag her husband from her side and drown him in the roaring vortices of the Pit, had passed on, resistless, along its ordered and predetermined courses from West to East, like a vast Titanic flood, had passed, leaving Death and Ruin in its wake, but bearing Life and Prosperity to the crowded cities and centres of Europe.

The number and the temper of stories written without Norris's breadth of vision or skill brought down on many of their authors the epithet of "muck-raker" in common with the sensational writers of magazine exposures. Among the saner and, consequently, more effective purpose novels the writings of Winston Churchill and Brand Whitlock have helped to offset the shrill cries of Upton Sinclair and Jack London.

The American novels which center about sex and the family have passed through rapid changes during the twentieth century.

In 1902 Mr. Bliss Perry, discussing tendencies of American novelists in his "A Study of Prose Fiction," declared that the American novel was free from equivocal morality, that " people who want the sex-novel, and want it prepared with any literary skill, have to import it from across the water," and concluded with the confident assertion that while American fiction " may not be national, and may not be great, it will have at least the negative virtue of being clean." A few pages later in the same chapter he made an observing comment of which he failed to see the implication when he noted that conversation between writers of fiction was likely to center about men like Turgenieff, and Tolstoi, Flaubert and Daudet, Björnson and D'Annunzio. The influence of these men was soon to be felt, both directly and through the medium of Englishmen from the generation of Hardy to that of Wells and Galsworthy. And within a dozen years it had extended so far that the National Institute of Arts and Letters went on record in warning and protest against the morbid insistency of an increasing number of younger writers. This wave was a symptom not only of a literary influence but, more deeply, of the world-wide attempt to re-estimate the rights and duties and privileges of womankind. There are few subjects on which people of recent years have done more thinking, and few on which they have arrived at less certain conclusions. With the collapse of the great " conspiracy of silence " that has surrounded certain aspects of personal and family life, it has been natural for the present generation to fall into the same errors into which Whitman had fallen. Naturally, too, the evil thinker seized on the occasion for evil speech. There has been every shade of expression from blatant wantonness to high-minded and self-respecting honesty. Thus we can account for Mr. Theodore Dreiser, who seems to feel that freedom of speech should be gratefully acknowledged by indulgence to the farthest extreme. And thus we can account for Mr. Ernest Poole, who, in " His Family," has presented an extraordinarily fine summary of the broad and perplexing theme.

The English novel is nearing the end of its second century of influence. It is a constant in literature which will probably attract more readers than any other single form. Yet it will have its times of greater and lesser popularity, and it seems to have passed the height of a wave shortly after 1900. First the drama came forward with a new challenge to serious attention, and of late poetry has reëstablished itself as a living language.

BOOK LIST

General References

BESANT, SIR WALTER. The Art of Fiction. 1884.
BURTON, RICHARD. Forces in Fiction. 1902.
CRAWFORD, F. MARION. The Novel: what it is. 1903.
CROSS, W. L. The Development of the English Novel. 1899.
FISKE, H. S. Provincial Types in American Fiction. 1903.
GARLAND, HAMLIN. Crumbling Idols. 1894.
HOWELLS, W. D. Criticism and Fiction. 1895.
HOWELLS, W. D. Heroines of Fiction. 1901.
JAMES, HENRY. The Art of Fiction, in *Partial Portraits*.
JAMES, HENRY. The New Novel, in *Notes on Novelists*. 1914.
LANIER, SIDNEY. The English Novel. 1883.
MATTHEWS, BRANDER. Aspects of Fiction. 1896.
MATTHEWS, BRANDER. The Historical Novel and Other Essays. 1901.
NORRIS, FRANK. The Responsibilities of the Novelist. 1901.
PATTEE, F. L. American Literature since 1870, chaps. xi, xii, xvii. 1916.
PERRY, BLISS. A Study of Prose Fiction, chap. xiii. 1902.
PHELPS, W. L. Essays on Modern Novelists. (Howells, Mark Twain.) 1910.

Individual Works

The field is so extensive that no lists of works by the authors mentioned are included here. The novels selected for reading can be taken from the specific references in the text. All the works are in print and easily available.

Magazine Articles

The magazine articles on fiction are extremely numerous. From among those since 1900 the following are of special interest:

1900–1904. New Element in Modern Fiction. N. Boyce. *Bookman*, Vol. XIII, p. 149. April, 1901.
Novel and the Short Story. G. Atherton. *Bookman*, Vol. XVII, pp. 36–37. March, 1903.

Novel and the Theater. *Nation*, Vol. LXXII, pp. 210–211. March 14, 1901.

1905–1909. Confessions of a Best-Seller. *Atlantic*, Vol. CIV, pp. 577–585. November, 1909.

Convention of Romance. *Bookman*, Vol. XXVI, pp. 266–267. November, 1907.

Humor and the Heroine. *Atlantic*, Vol. XCV, pp. 852–854. June, 1905.

Mob Spirit in Literature. H. D. Sedgwick. *Atlantic*, Vol. XCVI, pp. 9–15. July, 1905.

Purpose Novel. F. T. Cooper. *Bookman*, Vol. XXII, pp. 131–132. October, 1905.

1910–1914. American and English Novelists. *Nation*, Vol. XCVIII, pp. 422–423. April 16, 1914.

American backgrounds for fiction :

Georgia. W. N. Harben. *Bookman*, Vol. XXXVIII, pp. 186–192. October, 1913.

North Carolina. T. Dixon. *Bookman*, Vol. XXXVIII, pp. 511–514. January, 1914.

Tennessee. M. T. Daviess. *Bookman*, Vol. XXXVIII, pp. 394–399. December, 1913.

North Country of New York. I. Bacheller. *Bookman*, Vol. XXXVIII, pp. 624–628. February, 1914.

Pennsylvania Dutch. H. R. Martin. *Bookman*, Vol. XXXVIII, pp. 244–247. November, 1913.

American Novel in England. G. Atherton. *Bookman*, Vol. XXX, pp. 633–640. February, 1910.

Recent Reflections of a Novel-Reader. *Atlantic*. Vol. CXII, pp. 689–701. November, 1913. Vol. CXIII, pp. 490–500. April, 1914.

Big Movements in Fiction. F. T. Cooper. *Bookman*, Vol. XXXIII, pp. 80–82. March, 1911.

Characters in Recent Fiction. M. Sherwood. *Atlantic*, Vol. CIX, pp. 672–684. May, 1912.

Fault-Findings of a Novel-Reader. *Atlantic*, Vol. CV, pp. 14–23. January, 1910.

Morality in Fiction and Some Recent Novels. F. T. Cooper. *Bookman*, Vol. XXXVIII, pp. 666–672. February, 1914.

Newest Woman. K. F. Gerould. *Atlantic*, Vol. CIX, pp. 606–611. May, 1912.

Relation of the Novel to the Present Social Unrest. *Bookman*, Vol. XL, pp. 276–303. November, 1914.

Art in Fiction. E. Phillpotts. *Bookman*, Vol. XXXI, pp. 17–18. March, 1910.

1915. American Style in American Fiction. F. F. Kelly. *Bookman*, Vol. XLI, pp. 299–302. May, 1915.

Free Fiction. H. S. Canby. *Atlantic*, Vol. CXVI, pp. 60–68. June, 1915.

Advance of the English Novel. W. L. Phelps. *Bookman*, Vol. XLII, pp. 128–134, 381–388, 389–396. October–December, 1915.

Literary Merchandise. G. Atherton. *New Republic*, Vol. III, pp. 223–224. July 3, 1915.

1916. New York of the Novelists: a New Pilgrimage. A. B. Maurice, *Bookman*, Vol. XLII, pp. 20–41, 165–192, 301–315, 436–452, 569–589, 696–713. September, 1915–February, 1916.

Realism and Recent American Fiction. H. W. Boynton. *Nation*, Vol. CII, pp. 380–382. April 6, 1916.

Russian View of American Literature. A. Yarmolinsky. *Bookman*, Vol. XLIV, pp. 44–48. September, 1916.

Recent Reflections of a Novel-Reader. *Atlantic*, Vol. CXVII, pp. 632–642. May, 1916.

Sex in Fiction. *Nation*, Vol. CI, p. 716. Dec. 16, 1915.

Woman's Mastery of the Story. G. M. Stratton. *Atlantic*, Vol. CXVII, pp. 668–676. May, 1916.

1917. Analysis of Fiction in the United States, 1911–1916. F. E. Woodward. *Bookman*, Vol. XLV, pp. 187–191. April, 1917.

Apotheosis of the Worker in Modern Fiction. L. M. Field. *Bookman*, Vol. XLV, pp. 89–92. March, 1917.

New Orthodoxy in Fiction. L. M. Field. *Bookman*, Vol. XLV, pp. 175–178. April, 1917.

Outstanding Novels of the Year. H. W. Boynton. *Nation*, Vol. CV, pp. 599–601. Nov. 29, 1917.

Sixteen Years of Fiction. A. B. Maurice. *Bookman*, Vol. XLIV, pp. 484–492. January, 1917.

CHAPTER XXVIII

CONTEMPORARY DRAMA

From 1865 to 1900 the American drama occupied a place of so little artistic importance in American life that the literary historians have ignored it. There is no word about it in the substantial volumes by Richardson and Wendell, none in the ordinary run of textbooks, not a mention of playwright, producer, actor, or stage even in the four-hundred-odd pages of Pattee's "American Literature since 1870." This silence cannot, of course, be accounted for by any conspiracy among the historians; it must be acknowledged that in itself the period had almost no dramatic significance. Quinn's collection of twenty-five "Representative American Plays" includes only three produced between these dates. The basic reason for this is that literary conditions did not induce or encourage play-writing in the English-speaking world on either side of the Atlantic. The greatest artistry was expressing itself in poetry, and in America no major poet but Longfellow attempted even "closet drama." The greatest genius in storytelling was let loose in the channel of fiction, and many of the successful novels were given a second incarnation in play form. The names that stand out in stage history in these years are the names of controlling managers, like Lester Wallack and Augustin Daly, or of players, like Charlotte Cushman, Booth, Barrett, Jefferson, and Mansfield; and the writers of plays — encouraged by stage demands rather than by literary conditions — were the theatrical successors of Dunlap and Payne (see pp. 94–96) — men like Dion Boucicault (1822?–1890) with his hundred and twenty-four plays, and Bronson Howard (1842–1908) with his less numerous but no more distinguished array of stage successes. Side by side with these, and quite on a level with them, rose one eminent critic of stagecraft and the drama, William Winter (1836–1917).

With the last decade of the nineteenth century, however, a new generation of playwrights began to win recognition — men who knew literature in its relation to the other arts and who wrote plays out of the fullness of their experience and the depth of their convictions, hoping to reach the public with their plays but not concerned chiefly with immediate "box-office" returns. The movement started in England and on the Continent and — as we can now see — in America as well, but the traditional American neglect of American litera- ture[1] led the first alert critics on this side the Atlantic to lay all their emphasis on writers of other nationalities. Thus in 1905 James Huneker's "Iconoclasts" discussed Norwegian, French, German, Russian, Italian, Belgian, and English dram- atists. E. E. Hale's "Dramatists of To-day" of the same year dealt with four from Huneker's list, substituted one French- man, and added two Englishmen. This selection was quite defensible, for the significant contemporary plays which reached the stage came from these sources. But by 1910 the drift of things was suggested by the contents of Walter Prit- chard Eaton's "At the New Theatre and Others." In this book, of twenty-three plays reviewed, ten were by American authors, and in the third section, composed of essays related to the theater, two of the chief units were discussions of Clyde Fitch and William Winter. And the dedication of Eaton's book is perhaps the single item of greatest historical significance, for it gives due credit to Professor George P. Baker of Harvard as "Founder in that institution of a pioneer course for the study of dramatic composition" and as "inspir- ing leader in the movement for a better appreciation among educated men of the art of the practical theater."

[1] See "American Neglect of American Literature" by Percy H. Boynton. *Nation* (1916), Vol. CII, pp. 478–480.

The field into which we are led is so broad and so near that in a brief excursion we can undertake only a rough classification of the main products and the soil in which they are growing. Such a classification may be found if we consider in turn first the better play written for a better theater, which began to appear about 1890, then the various new types of theater which grew from the people's interest instead of from managerial enterprise, and, finally, the literary drama in poetry or prose which profits from the coöperation of actor and stage-manager, but can survive in print unaided.

"The movement for a better appreciation among educated men of the art of the practical theatre," although led by one college professor, was itself a symptom of fresh developments in the art to which he addressed himself. Omitting — but not ignoring — the rise of the modern school of European dramatists in the 1890's, we must be content for the moment to note that this decade brought into view in America several men who were more than show-makers, even though they were honestly occupied in making plays that the public would care to spend their money for. The significant facts about these playwrights are that they gave over the imitation and adaptation of French plays, returned to American dramatic material, and achieved results that are readable as well as actable. Their immediate forerunners were Steele MacKaye (1842–1894) and James A. Herne (1840–1901) — the former devotedly active as a teacher of budding players and as a student of stage technique, the latter the quiet realist of "Shore Acres" and other less-known plays of simple American life. Coming into their first prominence at this time were Augustus Thomas (1859– and Clyde Fitch (1865–1909).

They both appeared as theatrical craftsmen of the new generation, and like their prototypes in America, Dunlap and Payne (see pp. 96–98), they wrote abundantly, for audiences rather than for readers, and with definite actors and actresses in mind as they devised situations and composed lines. Clyde

Fitch in twenty years wrote and produced on the stage thirty-three plays and adapted and staged twenty-three more — an immense output. In the first ten years the most important were all built on historical themes : " Beau Brummel," " Nathan Hale," and " Barbara Frietchie." It is easy to see and to say that in writing these he was carrying on the tradition of Bronson Howard with his Civil War melodramas, — a half truth, however, since " Beau Brummel " in no way fits the generalization, and other plays of the decade were on contemporary social life. In the second ten years the keynote was struck with " The Climbers," a social satire on a shallow city woman and her two daughters whose social ambition deadens them to any fine impulses or natural emotions. In the long roster of Fitch's successes a few constant traits are obvious. He built his stories well, set them carefully, combined the resources of the playwright who knows how to devise a " situation " with those of the stage-manager who knows how to present it, and cast his stories into simple, rapid-fire, clever dialogue. He took advantage of up-to-date material for the superficial dress of his plays, introducing the background of latest allusion, recently coined turns of phrase, the newest songs, the quips and turns of fashion. And he went beneath the surface to the undercurrents of human motive as in the wifely constancy in " The Stubbornness of Geraldine," the jealousy of " The Girl with the Green Eyes," and the weak mendacity of Becky in " The Truth." Fitch was never profound, never sought to be ; but he was deservedly popular, for he combined no little skill with an alert sense of human values in everyday life, and he brought an artistic conscience to his work. Because he was so successful his influence on other dramatists has been far-reaching ; and those who have been neither too small nor too great to learn from him have learned no little on how to write a play.

Mr. Augustus Thomas has lived in the atmosphere of the theater from boyhood. He began writing plays at fourteen, was directing an amateur company at seventeen, and had his first New York success in his twenty-eighth year. Since 1887 he has been a professional playwright; he has nearly fifty productions to his credit, and he is now art director of the Charles Frohman interests. His first widely known works were the plays of states: "Alabama" (1891), "In Mizzoura" (1893), and "Arizona" (1899) — plays which exerted the same general appeal as "Shenandoah" and "Barbara Frietchie." As a practical man of the theater he adapted and worked over material, dramatizing novels of Mrs. Burnett, Hopkinson Smith, and Townsend. His attractive "Oliver Goldsmith" was built not only around the character of that whimsical man of letters but included as its own best portion an act out of the hero's play "The Good-Natured Man." With the kind of adaptability which belongs equally to the practical man of the theater and to the enterprising journalist, he undertook in time the type of play that deals with questions or problems of modern interest. The same current of speculation that led Mark Twain to write his essay on "Mental Telepathy" and Hamlin Garland his book on "The Shadow World" accounts for Thomas's "The Witching Hour" (1907), which interweaves the strands of hereditary influence and mental suggestion; and he contributed his word on the complex problems of the modern family in "As a Man Thinks" (1911). Up to 1917 he had written and adapted forty-six plays, of which eleven had been published after their production, but his work of real distinction belongs to the period opening with "The Witching Hour." In his later plays he has coupled his highly developed ability to tell a story with a vital feeling for the positive values in life. In "The Harvest Moon" he makes a playwright-character say, "I would willingly give the rest of my life to go back and take from my plays every word that has made men less happy, less hopeful, less kind." And in "The Witching Hour" he declares through Jack Brookfield the text of that and succeeding plays, "You're a child of *the everlasting God* and nothing on the earth or under it can harm you in the slightest degree "— a text which, said of the soul, is immortally true.

In a short chapter it is impossible to discuss in detail any other of the play-writers who have done with less applause but with no less devotion the kind of writing represented by the best of Fitch and Thomas ; and it would be invidious to attempt a mere list of the others, as if a mention of their names would be a sop to their pride. The case must rest here with the statement that these two men were the leaders of an increasing group and that the desire to compose more skillful and more worthy plays was paralleled by a revival of respect for the modern drama and the modern stage. This leads to the middle section of our survey, and turns from the drama itself to the fifteen-year struggle for possession of the American stage — the actual "boards" on which the plays could be presented. It is as dramatic as any play, this story of the conflict between intelligent idealism, — whether in play-wright, actor or theatergoer, and commercial greed, — and it is far from concluded, though a happy dénouement seems to be in sight.

The first step has already been mentioned : the development of a student attitude toward the contemporary play and its production. Professor Baker at Harvard and Professor Matthews at Columbia were looked at by some with wonder and by others with amused doubt when they began as teachers to divide their attention between the ancient and the modern stage. Yet as the study progressed their students became not only intelligent theatergoers but constructive contributors, as critics and creators, to the literature of the stage ; and then in the natural order of events the whole student body came to realize that the older drama 'should be reduced to its proper place and restored to it ; that it was an interesting chapter in literary and social history because it was not a closed chapter, but a preliminary to the events of the present. At the same time modest but important beginnings were being made in the education of the actor, and men like Franklin Sargent, President of the American Academy of Dramatic Arts, opened the way to a professional training for actors that would compare with the training demanded of and by the singer, painter, or sculptor. These beginnings were full of promise, but the promise was to be long held in abeyance by the machinations of the theatrical syndicate.

This commercial trust is the heavy villain of the play, the charge against it being that whereas the business management of the theater was called into being in order to serve the drama, it managed so effectively that by the winter of 1895–1896 it was strong enough to demand that henceforth the drama support the business management. The six men who were able to assume control handled their business according to the approved methods of the trust, trying to get salable goods and to multiply the output of what the public wanted, trying to control all the salesmen (players) and all the distributing points (playhouses) and to put out of business any player or local manager who would not market their choice of goods at their schedule of dates and prices. For nearly fifteen years the syndicate were as effective in their field as the Standard Oil or United Shoe Machinery Companies were in theirs. One actress, Mrs. Fiske, endured every sort of discomfort and, no doubt, heavy losses for the privilege of playing what, when, and where she pleased; but for a while she had her own way only to the extent of appearing in theaters so cheap that they were beneath the contempt of the monopoly. In the meanwhile, however, discontent spread, a rival firm of managers erected rival theaters, and, conducting their business on principles of more enlightened selfishness, in 1910 enlisted twelve hundred of the smaller revolting theaters with them and forced the syndicate to share the field. Since that time the theaters of America have been administered as well, perhaps, as the system will allow; but it is a mistaken system that puts a fine art in the market place and demands that it maintain itself because "business is business."

The first really great attempt to ask anything less of the modern drama in America, to demand no more of the play than is demanded of the opera or the symphony, was the founding of the celebrated and short-lived New Theater in New York (1909–1911). That it failed within two years is not half so important as that it was founded, that others on smaller scales have since been founded and have failed, that municipal theaters have sprung up here and there and are being supported according to various plans, that scores upon scores of little theaters, neighborhood playhouses, and people's country theaters have been founded, that producers like Winthrop Ames and Stuart Walker are established in public favor, that the Drama League of America is a genuine national organization, and that the printing of plays for a reading public is many fold its proportions of twenty years ago. The Napoleonic theatrical managers are still in the saddle in America, and the commercial stage of the country is still managed from Broadway, but the uncommercial stage is coming to be more considerable every season. The leaven of popular intelligence is at work.

With developments of this sort taking place and gaining in momentum, there is a growing attention to the printed literary drama and an encouraging prospect for it in the theater. As far back as 1891, when Clyde Fitch and Augustus Thomas were coming into their reputations, Richard Hovey (1864–1900) published "The Quest of Merlin," the first unit in his "Launcelot and Guenevere," which he described as a poem in dramas. It was a splendidly conceived treatment of the conflict between the claims of individual love and the intruding demands of the outer world. In resorting to the Arthurian legends Hovey "was not primarily interested in them," according to his friend and expounder, Bliss Carman, "for their historic and picturesque value as poetic material, great as that value undoubtedly is . . . the problem he felt called upon to deal with is a perennial one, old as the world, yet intensely modern, and it appealed to him as a modern man. . . . The Arthurian cycle provided Tennyson with the groundwork of a national epic; . . . to Richard Hovey it afforded a modern instance stripped of modern dress." It was to have been completed in three parts, each containing a masque, a tragedy, and a romantic drama; but only the first was completed — "The Quest of Merlin" (1891), "The Marriage of Guenevere" (1891), and "The Birth of Galahad" (1898). Shortly after finishing "Taliesin," the masque for the second part, Hovey died.

Another and greater cycle of poetic dramas which was interrupted by a premature death was a trilogy on the Promethean theme by William Vaughn Moody (1869–1910). The theme is the unity of God and man and their consequent mutual dependency. "The Fire-Bringer" (1904) presents man's victory at the supreme cost of disunion from God through the defiant theft of fire from heaven. "The Masque of Judgment" (1900) is a no less fearful triumph of the Creator in dooming part of himself as he overwhelms mankind. The final part, "The Death of Eve," was to have achieved the final reconciliation, but it was left a fragment at the poet's death in 1910 and so stands in the posthumous edition of his works. It is significant in the literary history of the day that the culminating product of both these young poets was an uncompleted poetic play-cycle. Moody's connection with the stage, however, was closer than Hovey's, for he wrote two prose plays which were successfully produced — "The Great Divide" (1907) and "The Faith Healer" (1909). In "The Great Divide," produced first under the title of "The Sabine Woman," Moody wrote a dramatic story on a fundamental, and hence a modern, aspect of life. The problem of the play is stated flippantly yet truly by the heroine's sister-in-law :

Here on the one hand is the primitive, the barbaric woman, falling in love with a romantic stranger, who, like some old Viking on a harry, cuts her with his two-handed sword from the circle of her kinsmen, and bears her away on his dragon ship toward the midnight sun. Here on the other hand is the derived, the civilized woman, with a civilized nervous system, observing that the creature eats bacon with his bowie knife, knows not the manicure, has the conversation of a preoccupied walrus, the instincts of a jealous caribou, and the endearments of a dancing crab in the mating season. . . . Ruth is one of those people who can't live in a state of divided feeling. She sits staring at this cleavage in her life. . . . All I mean is that when she married her man she married him for keeps. And he did the same by her.

The play was produced in Chicago, put on for a long run in New York and on tour, and presented in London, and in 1917 was revived for a successful run in New York again. "The Faith Healer," the idea for which occurred to Moody in 1898, was completed ten years later, after the success of the first play. The theme is not so close to common experience as that of "The Great Divide," and perhaps because of this as well as the subtler treatment it did not draw such audiences. Both plays end on a high spiritual level, but the second failed to register in the "box office" because the relief scenes are grim rather than amusing and because there is no fleshly element in the love of the hero and the heroine.

Percy MacKaye (1875–   ) embodies the meeting of the older traditions — his father was Steele MacKaye (see p. 439) — and the most recent development in American drama, the rise of pageantry and the civic festival. As a professional dramatist he has been prolific to the extent of some twenty-five plays, pageants, and operas. His acted plays have varied in range and subject from contemporary social satire to an interesting succession of echoes from the literary past — plays like "The Canterbury Pilgrims" (1903), "Jeanne D'Arc" (1906), and "Sappho and Phaon" (1907), which he seems to have undertaken, in contrast to Hovey, for their picturesque and poetic value alone. His special contribution, however, has been to the movement for an uncommercialized civic and national theater through the preparation of a number of community celebrations.

These include the Saint Gaudens Pageant at Cornish, New Hampshire (1905), the Gloucester Pageant (1903), " Sanctuary, a Bird Masque" (1913), "St. Louis, a Civic Masque" (1914), and "Caliban, a Community Masque" (New York, 1916, and Boston, 1917). The fusing interest in a common artistic undertaking has brought together whole cities in the finest kind of democratic enthusiasm, and the effects have not been merely temporary, for in a community such as St. Louis the permanent benefits are still evident in the community chorus and in the beautiful civic theater which is the annual scene of memorable productions witnessed by scores of thousands of spectators.

Charles Rann Kennedy (1871–), the last of the dramatists to be considered here, is a man in whom a technical mastery of the play is combined with a high degree of poetic fervor. He was born in Derby, England, coming from a family which has been famed for classical scholarship.[1] His own education was largely pursued outside of the schools, and he is not a university man, but no element is more important in his preparation for play-writing than his intimate knowledge of the classical and, especially, the Greek drama. Between the ages of thirteen and sixteen he was office boy, clerk, and telegraph operator, but always imaginatively interested in the technical aspects of his jobs. During his early twenties he was a lecturer and writer, and it is a matter of literary as well as personal moment that in 1898 he married Edith Wynne Matthison, widely known for her work with Irving, with Tree, and at the New Theater and as the creator of leading parts in her husband's plays. Since the beginning of his authorship Mr. Kennedy has lived in the United States, of which he is now a citizen.

His dramatic work has fallen into two groups: "The Terrible Meek" and "The Necessary Evil"— Short Plays for

[1] In the "Sketch Book" Washington Irving concludes "Rural Life in England" with a poem by the Reverend Rann Kennedy, A.M., a great-uncle of the dramatist.

Small Casts — and his Seven Plays for Seven Players. As in the cases of Moody and Hovey already cited, his plays are part of an inclusive program — a program which is the more remarkable on account of the fact that it took definite shape in the course of a single discussion with a group of literary friends — G. B. Shaw, Gilbert Chesterton, and Hilaire Belloc among them — before he came to this country. As a result of this discussion he undertook to write seven plays : each for five men and two women, each holding the mean between a heightened and decorative romance and an objective and unimaginative realism, each dealing with a separate great central theme in life, each attempting a new or revived technical difficulty in play construction, and each subjected to the most rigid conformity to the dramatic unities, being written with no break in time sequence or shift of scene.

The series includes (1) " The Winterfeast " (1906), of which the central theme is "The Lie and Hate in Life which destroy"; (2) "The Servant in the House " (1907), on " The Truth and Love in Life which preserve "; (3) " The Idol-Breaker " (1913), on " Freedom "; (4) " The Rib of the Man " (1916), on "The New Woman already in the World, and the New Warrior coming as fast as the European War will let him "; (5) " The Army with Banners " (1917), on " The Coming of the Lord in Power and Glory and the New World now culminating." Of these five, all but the fourth have been produced, " The Rib of the Man " having been withheld temporarily because of its nonmilitant theme and the resultant managerial timidity ; and all but the fifth have been published. The series will be completed with " The Fool from the Hills," the central theme being " The Bread of Life, or The Food Problem "; and the last will be " The Isle of the Blest," on " The Consummation of Life in what Men call Death."

Plays written in such a progression are clearly approached in a spirit of high seriousness and with little regard or any expectation of immediate applause. But they are also written in a spirit of high defiance, with deliberate consciousness of the methods employed, and an inspired certainty that they will be heard at last. Adam — the Idol-Breaker — has thrown down the definite challenge:

"I've told these people things before. Many times. Why, it was me, six years ago, as called them here, and told them of the brotherhood of man." [Cf. "The Servant in the House."]

"Well, didn't they listen to you, that time?" says Naomi.

"Ay, at first," replies Adam, "while I was new to them. Then they turned again to idols; and twisted my plain meaning into tracts for Sunday School. I up and spoke again, and told them of the lies and hate they lived by. [Cf. "The Winterfeast."] Shewed them the death and bitterness of it!— Well, they soon let me know about that. I preached their own God's gospel to them, and brought Christ's Murder to their blood-stained doors. [Cf. "The Terrible Meek."] They spat upon me. I told them of the lusts as fed their brothels; [cf. "The Necessary Evil"] and every red-eyed wolf among them said I lied. Even when they didn't speak, I knew the meaning of their leering silence. This time, it's freedom — the thing they're always bragging of; and as long as I am in the world, they'll have it dinned into their heads, as freedom isn't all a matter of flags and soldiers' pop-guns. It's something they've got to sweat for. Don't you think they're going to get off easy, once I see them stuck in front of me!

"Oh, I make them laugh, all right. They want to be amused. Lot of jaded johnnies! Every one of them thinking I mean his next-door neighbor; and I mean just him!"

In "The Winterfeast" there is no laughter; at most only a smile in the first meeting of the two young lovers. It is a relentless tale of Nemesis following on the path of hatred, set in Iceland of the eleventh century, told in the tone and at times plainly in the manner of Sophocles. All the others of the Seven Plays, however, are put in the present day, with characters who are modern examples of perennial types, with abundant "relief scenes" in confirmation of Adam's "I make them laugh," and with an undertone of irony, — whimsical, derisive, grave, or bitter, as the occasions demand. Of these "The Servant in the House" has been the preëminent popular success because of its appeal to the conventionally religious, who accepted its pervasive beneficence and ignored its strictures on the church.

None of Mr. Kennedy's plays is more completely representative of his spirit, his purpose, and his method than "The Rib of the Man." It is located on an island in the Ægean, amid "the never-ending loveliness of all good Greek things." It is dedicated to the New Woman, to whom a recently unearthed altar inscribed "To the Mother of the Gods" has given the authority of the ages. The persons of the play are morality types, although intensely human. They are "David Fleming, an image of God, the Man; Rosie Fleming, an helpmeet for him, the Rib; Archie Legge, a gentleman, a Beast of the Earth; Basil Martin, an aviator, a Fowl of the Air; Peter Prout, a scientist, the Subtle One; Ion, the gardener, the Voice Warning; and Diana Brand, a spare rib, the Flaming Sword." And finally, the play is written "with an inner and an outer meaning, symbolical, instinct with paradox and irony, leading deeply unto truth."

Only one of Mr. Kennedy's plays has achieved a popular triumph, and the success of that one was due to its limited and somewhat perverted interpretation. They all, however, repay study and disclose new depths with each re-reading. Serious art rarely makes quick conquests. Audiences of spirit and intellect will develop for them as they have for the plays of Ibsen and Maeterlinck. The new audience, the new theater, and the new drama — old as the oldest literature — in due time will come to their own again.

Plays by Individual Men

CLYDE FITCH. The Plays of Clyde Fitch, Memorial Edition, edited by M. J. Moses and Virginia Gerson, 1915.

RICHARD HOVEY. Plays, uniform edition, 1907–1908.

CHARLES RANN KENNEDY. The plays have been published in succession by Harper's.

PERCY MACKAYE. Poems and Plays. 1916. 2 vols.

WILLIAM VAUGHN MOODY. Poems and Plays. 1912. 2 vols.

AUGUSTUS THOMAS. Arizona, Alabama. Dramatic Publishing Co. As a Man Thinks. Duffield. The Witching Hour, Oliver Goldsmith, The Harvest Moon, In Mizzoura, Mrs. Leffingwell's Boots, The Other Girl, The Capitol, and The Earl of Pawtucket. Samuel French.

Collections

DICKINSON, THOMAS H. Chief Contemporary Dramatists. Boston, 1915. (Contains four American plays.)

MOSES, MONTROSE J. Representative Plays by American Dramatists. 3 vols. Vol. I, 1918 (contains ten plays, 1759–1824); Vols. II and III announced.

PIERCE, JOHN ALEXANDER. The Masterpieces of Modern Drama. Abridged in Narrative with Dialogue of the Great Scenes. Preface with a critical essay by Brander Matthews. (Vol. II contains selections from twelve American plays.)

QUINN, A. H. Representative American Plays. 1917. Twenty-five plays, 1769–1911.

Criticism

ANDREWS, CHARLTON. The Drama To-day. 1913.

BURTON, RICHARD. The New American Drama. 1913.

CHENEY, SHELDON. The New Movement in the Theatre. 1914.

CLARK, BARRETT H. The British and American Drama of To-day. 1915.

DICKINSON, THOMAS H. The Case of American Drama. 1915.

EATON, W. P. The American Stage of To-day. 1908.

EATON, W. P. At the New Theatre and Others. 1910.

HAPGOOD, NORMAN. The Stage in America, 1897–1900. 1901.

HENDERSON, ARCHIBALD. The Changing Drama. 1914.

MACKAYE, PERCY. The Playhouse and the Play. 1909.

MACKAYE, PERCY. The Civic Theatre. 1912.

MATTHEWS, BRANDER. Inquiries and Opinions. 1907.

MATTHEWS, BRANDER. The Historical Novel and Other Essays. 1901.

MOSES, M. J. The American Dramatist. 1911.

RUHL, ARTHUR. Second Nights. 1914.

Magazine Articles

The magazine articles on the drama cited in the " Reader's Guide "
are extremely numerous. From among those since 1900 the following are
of special interest:

1900–1904. Development of the drama. B. Matthews. *Nation,* Vol.
LXXVII, pp. 346–347. Oct. 29, 1903.

Poetry and the stage. H. W. Boynton. *Atlantic,* Vol. XCII,
pp. 120–126. July, 1903.

Theater and the critics. *Nation,* Vol. LXXIII, p. 106. August 8.
Outlook, Vol. LXIX, pp. 528–529. Nov. 2, 1901.

Future of drama. B. Matthews. *Bookman,* Vol. XVII, pp. 31–
36. March, 1903.

Makers of the drama of to-day. B. Matthews. *Atlantic,* Vol.
XCI, pp. 504–512. April, 1903.

1905–1909. Literature and the modern drama. H. A. Jones. *Atlantic,* Vol.
XCVIII, pp. 796–807. December, 1906.

Playwright and the playgoers. B. Matthews. *Atlantic,* Vol. CII,
pp. 421–426. September, 1908.

Elevation of the stage. *Atlantic,* Vol. XCIX, pp. 721–723.
May, 1907.

New theatre. M. Merington. *Bookman,* Vol. XXVII, pp. 561–
566. August, 1908.

Theatrical conditions. *Nation,* Vol. LXXXIV, pp. 182–183.
Feb. 21, 1907.

1910–1914. What is wrong with the American drama? C. Hamilton. *Bookman,* Vol. XXXIX, pp. 314–319. May, 1914.

Exotic plays. *Nation,* Vol. XCIV, pp. 142–143. Feb. 8, 1912.

1915. Decay of respectability. F. Hackett. *New Republic,* Vol. II,
p. 51. Feb. 13, 1915.

Work of the Drama League of America. R. Burton. *Nation,*
Vol. XCIX, pp. 668–669. Dec. 3, 1914.

1916. Realism of the American stage. H. de W. Fuller. *Nation,* Vol.
CII, pp. 307–310. March 16, 1916.

The Public and the theater. C. Hamilton. *Bookman,* Vol. XLIV,
pp. 252–257. November, 1916.

The Public and the theater. Reply to Mr. Hamilton. G. R.
Robinson. *Bookman,* Vol. XLIV, p. 401. December, 1916.

1917. Belasco and the independent theater. C. Hamilton. *Bookman,*
Vol. XLV, pp. 8–12. March, 1917.

East and West on the stage. *Nation,* Vol. CIV, p. 321. March 15,
1917.

CHAPTER XXIX

THE LATER POETRY

All of the calculated activities for the promotion of the stage during the last few years in America have as yet been limited and indirect in their results. Among them it is very possible that there was a blazing of the way for another development of great importance which has taken place without any leagues or schools or organized propaganda. This has been the restoration of poetry as a living language. Not only have authors' readings taken the place of dramatic interpretations in the lecture market but the audiences who flock to hear Tagore and Noyes and Masefield and Gibson and Bynner and Lindsay and Frost go to listen to poems with which they are already familiar and to get that sense of personal aquaintance with poets which ten years ago they coveted with playwrights and, further back, with novelists. The dominant fact about the contemporary reading public is its reawakened zest for poetry.

In 1890 the English poetry-reading world was chiefly conscious of the passing of its leading singers for the last half century. It was a period when they were recalling Emerson's "Terminus" and Longfellow's "Ultima Thule," Whitman's "November Boughs" and Whittier's "A Lifetime," Tennyson's "Crossing the Bar" and Browning's "Asolando." There was no group in the prime of life who were adequate successors to this greater choir. Stedman, Aldrich, and Stoddard had courted the muse as a kind of alien divinity and enjoyed excursions into the distant land of her dwelling-place. But their poetry was a poetry of accomplishment; an embellishment of life, and not an integral part of it (see pp. 324–326). It was a period when people were tempted with some reason to dwell on the "good old days," and for a while it seemed as though it would be long before the world would see their like again.

The spirit of the times seemed to be expressed by a group of younger artists who were in conscious revolt against Victorian literature and rather noisily assertive on their favorite theme of art for art's sake. They were occupied in composing intricate and ingenious poems. They were engrossed like Masters's " Petit, the Poet " in inditing

> Triolets, villanelles, rondels, rondeaus,
> Seeds in a dry pod, tick, tick, tick,
> Tick, tick, tick, what little iambics,
> While Homer and Whitman roared in the pines !

Some of them did pastels in prose, and many edited transitory little periodicals like *The Yellow Book*, *The Chap Book*, *The Lark*, and *Truth in Boston*. Fourteen of these came into existence in the United States in the first two months of 1897, and almost none of them survived till the Fourth of July of that year. Probably the only lines in any of them recalled by the readers of to-day are Gelett Burgess's quatrain on the purple cow. The burden of these young poets was many words fairly spoken of " organic growth," " development," " progress," " liberalism," " freedom of speech," and " independent thought " ; and the chief product of their thinking was a frank and free Bohemianism, an honest unconventionality much more real than the diluted thing about which Stedman and Aldrich had rimed thirty years before.

The most vigorous and enduring of the new group was Richard Hovey (1864–1900). He was Western-born, schooled at Washington, and a graduate of Dartmouth in 1885. His next years included study in the General Theological Seminary in New York, an assistantship in a New York ritualistic church, excursions into journalism and acting, and then, after some years as poet and dramatist, a professorship of English literature in Barnard College, Columbia University. Hovey grew perceptibly during his eager enjoyment of these various pursuits. For a while he seemed content to sing the praises of convivial comradeship :

> For we know the world is glorious
> And the goal a golden thing,
> And that God is not censorious
> When his children have their fling;

but he passed before long to the stage in which the good fellowship of youth was a symbol of something far larger than itself — nothing less than the promise of humankind. The ode delivered before his fraternity convention in 1896 quite transcends the sort of effusion usually evoked by such occasions. The spring in the air, in the world, and in the heart of youth culminate in the oft-sung "Stein Song"; and after it the poem goes on to "The first low stirring of that greater spring,"

> Of something potent burning through the earth,
> Of something vital in the procreant air.

This potent something is the "unceasing purpose" of Tennyson, but with a difference, for in Hovey's mind it is not the purpose of a detached God who imposes his will benevolently on mankind from without, but the creative impulse which is inherent in life itself, the evidence of the divine spirit in the heart of man. Comradeship, then, became to Hovey a symbol of altruism, and he looked beyond this springtide of the year and of the youthful collegians to the time when science, art, and religion should emancipate men in the truth that should set them free and bring them, in spite of delays, in the fullness of time to "the greater to-morrow."

Yet while Hovey was uplifted by the fine fervor of such a faith, he experienced a reaction with the outbreak of the Spanish-American War. In the sudden self-righteousness of an inflamed patriotism he nationalized God and deified war. Excited beyond measure by the immediate issue, he not only justified America against Spain but, forgetting all the lessons of evolution, he declared that the race could develop only through the repetition of old experiences.

> By strife as well as loving — strife,
> The Law of Life, —
> In brute and man the climbing has been done
> And shall be done hereafter. Since man was
> No upward-climbing cause
> Without the sword has ever yet been won.

His mistake lay in justifying all wars in order to justify the national altruism of the war with Spain, and his fallacy came in his assumption that biological and physical life were governed by the same laws. For the moment Hovey turned " jingo," as most of his countrymen did, yet even then he invoked the sword for the suppression of tyranny and not in the name of nationalistic ambition.

The home of Hovey's imagination was where the true poet's always is — " far in the vast of sky, . . . too high for sound of strife, or any violation of the town." From this high vantage point he sang the glories of the things he loved the best, but with maturity he moved from the world of material pleasure to the realms of spiritual adventure. In 1893 he wrote

> Down the world with Marna !
> That's the life for me !
> Wandering with the wandering wind,
> Vagabond and unconfined !

Five years later he could no longer catalogue his places on the map, for his goal was "the unknown " and "the wilderness " in pursuit of the high human adventure which Moody was to celebrate in his " Road Hymn for the Start." In a parallel way Hovey's first conception of fellowship rose from the early relish for beer and song to the fellowship of kindred souls of which the fine flowering is the love of man and woman.

> Spirit to spirit finds its voiceless way,
> As tone melts meeting in accordant tone, —

Oh, then our souls, far in the vast of sky,
  Look from a tower, too high for sound of strife
  Or any violation of the town,
Where the great vacant winds of God go by,
  And over the huge misshapen city of life
  Love pours his silence and his moonlight down.

At the age of thirty-six, just on the threshold of maturity, Hovey died.

William Vaughn Moody (1869–1910) was another son of the Middle West. Born in southern Indiana, he lost his mother in his fifteenth year and his father, a river-steamboat captain, in his seventeenth. By alternate study and teaching he prepared himself for Harvard, and entering at somewhat more than the average age he completed his college work in three years and followed these with a year in Europe as private tutor. In addition to a receptiveness for learning he had the capacity for a rich and varied culture which is sometimes mistakenly thought to belong only to blue-blooded inheritors of family tradition. From the close of his residence in Cambridge till his death, seventeen years later, Moody's life included long and extended travels, varied and profound study, eight years' teaching at the University of Chicago, from which President Harper was reluctant to accept his resignation, and distinguished work as painter, poet, and dramatist. Suddenly stricken with a fatal illness, he died in 1910.

Mention has already been made of his work as playwright (see pp. 445, 446). His lyric and narrative poems all have the same breadth of view which is inherent in his poetic dramas. He was familiar with a wide range of the world's art and literature, but in the work which he chose to collect for republication he was imitative of none. His imagination roved freely through all time and space. " Gloucester Moors " were the vantage point from which he conceived the earth as a " vast, outbound ship of souls " ; " Old Pourquoi " challenged the scheme of creation from beneath the Norman sky ; " The Death of Eve "

is derived from the Hebrew past, " The Masque of Judgment "
from the Greek, " A Dialogue in Purgatory " from the Italian,
" The Fountain " from early American legend, " On a Soldier
Fallen in the Philippines " from a current event. Thus he did
not maintain his citizenship of the world by any denial of allegiance to America. In the third section of " An Ode in Time
of Hesitation " he sketched as splendid a pageant of America
as has ever been devised. The Cape Ann children seeking the
arbutus, the hill lads of Tennessee harking to the wild geese
on their northern flight, are one with the youth of Chicago, the
renewing green of the wheat fields, the unrolling of the rivers
from the white Sierras, the downward creep of Alaskan glaciers,
and the perennial palm-crown of Hawaii. It is in very truth

> the eagle nation Milton saw,
> Mewing its mighty youth.

Moody's love of America did not lead him to embrace the
" manifest destiny " illusion. He was quite as conscious of
the misdirection of human leadership as he was of the riches
with which God had endowed the natural land. " Gloucester
Moors " is deeply solicitous for a future which seems to be in-
sured for the grasping capitalist ; " The Brute " is both more
vigorous and more hopeful in its certitude that the factory system in its worst forms is a short-lived social abortion. The
demon of the machine is sure to be caught and subdued :

He must give each man his portion, each his pride and worthy place ;
He must batter down the arrogant and lift the weary face.
On each vile mouth set purity, on each low forehead grace.

These poems were of life within America or without it, but in
" An Ode in Time of Hesitation " and " On a Soldier Fallen in
the Philippines " Moody warned the rulers in Washington that
the country, now awake to its duties in the world, would forgive blindness, but baseness it would smite. Finally, in " The
Quarry " he cried out in pride at America's fine part in preventing

the partitioning of helpless China by the grasping European empires, — the achievement of the poet-diplomat, John Hay.

Throughout all Moody's work is a constant undercurrent of evolutionary thought — not the brutal mechanism associated with the term " Darwinism," but the aspiring impulse within all life which makes it rise not through struggle against outer forces so much as through the innate impulse to develop. In the sardonic " Menagerie " the idea is ironically stated :

> Survival of the fittest, adaptation,
> And all their other evolution terms,
> Seem to omit one small consideration,

which is no less than the existence of souls :

> Restless, plagued, impatient things,
> All dream and unaccountable desire ;

and these souls are expressions of the universal soul which finds its own salvation in unceasing " groping, testing, passing on," — the creative struggle described by Raphael in " The Masque of Judgment " as

> The strife of ripening suns and withering moons,
> Marching of ice-floes, and the nameless wars
> Of monster races laboring to be man.

In his attitude toward and his literary treatment of woman Moody was emphatically modern. He was far beyond the supercilious and hollow amenities with which eighteenth-century poetry was filled, and he was not satisfied with the sincerer expression of deep personal tributes to individual women. In his philosophy woman was the dominant influence in the development of humankind. Eve and Prometheus were one in seeking the knowledge and power to lift man above brute creation and in producing the clash between God and man which was the price of knowledge and the cost of progress. But Prometheus was a poor and defeated character in comparison ; for Moody, in Eve and Pandora, presented woman not only as

the donor and the fulfillment of love but as the final agent of
reconciliation between the human and the divine. In the various poems there are acknowledgments of awe, of reverence,
of spiritual love, and of passion ; taken together they show the
same breadth of view that belongs to the human equation in
which Moody regards woman as the greatest factor. It is most
significant that the dramatic trilogy was planned to conclude with
a song of Eve, and that twice — in " I am the Woman " and
part five of " The Death of Eve " — Moody composed studies
toward that final song that was never perfected. Both progress
through the ages when woman was subtly molded by man's
conception of her, so that her happiness and her very being
consisted in conforming herself to him.

> Still, still with prayer and ecstasy she strove
> To be the woman they did well approve,
> That, narrowed to their love,
> She might have done with bitterness and blame.

And in both she appears as the indomitable Promethean spirit
who in the end was to fulfill that plan which in the beginning
she had endangered. There is no reference to any woman in
in any of Moody's poems which is out of harmony with this
dominating and progressive idea.

For several reasons Moody's poetry is not easy to read and
is therefore undestined to wide popularity (see pp. 263, 264).
He was not interested to compose simple lyrics or narratives.
Seldom does he aid the reader by means of even an implied
narrative thread. The poems inspired by history are not self-
explanatory nor accompanied by footnotes. Moody consistently
employed events, whether actual or imagined, as mere avenues
of approach to emotional and spiritual experiences, and he
expected the reader to contribute to the poems from his own
resourceful imagination. It is because the whole meaning is
not laid out on the surface of his verses — like Christmas-card
sentiments — that Moody has become very largely a poet's poet.

Their instinctive grasp of the figurative deeper meanings, their immediate response to elusive metaphor, and their understanding of his vigorous, exact, but sometimes recondite diction make them his best audience. For they too can most nearly appreciate the distinguished beauties of his work — his wide and intimate knowledge of world literature, the opulence of his style, the firmness of his structure, the scrupulousness of his detail. Through the rising and the risen poets of the present generation Moody's influence is exerted on thousands who are all unconscious of it.

An approach to contemporary American poetry in a fraction of a chapter at the end of a general history can be justified on only one ground : it serves the purpose of a guideboard on a transcontinental highway. American literature was not concluded with the deaths of the great New England group nor has it come to an end since then. The student should recognize this in his respect for the fine promise of what is now being written, and he should recognize that the study of our past literature can bear no richer fruit than a sane understanding of the literature of the day. Furthermore he should be intelligent enough to see that literature need not be old to be fit for study — that it is not only absurd but vicious to assume (as used to be said, with a difference, of the Indian) that there is no good poet but a dead poet. These few pages are therefore devoted to a half-dozen writers who represent tendencies. They are arbitrarily selected as the contemporary dramatists in the preceding chapter were. Yet their weight is greatly reënforced by the many others to whom no allusion can be made. A comparison of the three books on recent American poetry suggests the speed of the literary current. Miss Rittenhouse's "The Younger American Poets" (1904) includes eighteen poets of whom thirteen were born before 1865. Miss Lowell's "Tendencies in Modern American Poetry" (1917) includes six poets, none of whom were mentioned in the earlier book, and the oldest of whom was born in the closing days of 1869. Of the sixteen poets indicated by name in the chapter headings of Mr. Louis Untermeyer's "New Era in American Poetry" (1919), only three were born before 1875.

The reading of contemporary poetry should be done with zest and without calculation, but the study of the same material must be approached with self-conscious deliberateness and with a definite resolve not to be carried away by the cheap and easy generalizations current on the lips of the careless talker. Contemporary poetry is not all of one kind nor is it chiefly characterized by defiant revolt against old forms and old ideas. It is true that in all branches of artistic endeavor new methods and new points of view are being advanced. In music Debussy and Schoenberg, in painting Cézanne and Matisse, in sculpture Rodin and his disciples, in stage setting and costuming Gordon Craig and Leon Bakst, have shocked and surprised quite as many as they have edified, and have given rise to the same sort of querulous protest indulged in by those who talk as if all modern poetry were typified by the most extravagant verses of Alfred Kreymborg, or "Anne Knish." But in poetry most of the recent work has not been wantonly bizarre, most of the more distinguished verse has not been "free," and most of the men and women who have written free verse have shown and have practiced a firm mastery of the established forms. The point, then, is to maintain an open mind and to make sure of conclusions before adopting them, and the surest method of doing these two student-like things is to read and study authors by the bookful and not by the pseudo-royal road of anthologies and eclectic magazines. If you want to become acquainted with a man you will sit down at leisure with him in his study, instead of forming snapshot judgments from contact at afternoon teas, and you will form your own opinion in preference to gleaning it from the conversation of others.

Edwin Arlington Robinson (1869–   ), the oldest of this latter group, was born in the same year with Moody and is now in the prime of life. The Tilbury of many of his poems is really the town of his upbringing — Gardiner, Maine. It is an unusual but not a unique village in America — a colonial old-world village. The atmosphere of Puritanism had not been blown away from it, and it still felt the subtle influence of a preëminent family. When "the squire " passed,

> We people on the pavement looked at him ;
> He was a gentleman from sole to crown,
> Clean-favored, and imperially slim.

It is easy to think of Tilbury as an English town ; it is utterly different from Lindsay's Springfield or Masters's Spoon River. It is not without significance that the clearest single picture presents a little boy of twelve as the companion of " Isaac and Archibald," two old men on the ominous verge of superannuation. It was life in Gardiner that gives so real a sense of the town on the Avon in " Ben Jonson Entertains a Man from Stratford." In 1891 Mr. Robinson entered Harvard, withdrawing at the end of two years and entering business in New York City. Here he remained till 1910, the last five years as an appointee of President Roosevelt in the New York Customhouse, and since the latter date he has lived again in Gardiner, bearing some resemblance in his mellowed maturity, perhaps, to Larry Scammon in his play " The Porcupine."

As a matter of literary history the most striking fact about Mr. Robinson is that the poetry-reading public has been re-developed since he began to write. Although his first volume, " The Children of the Night," appeared in 1897, and his second, " Captain Craig," in 1902, it was possible for him to be omitted from " The Younger American Poets " of 1904. With " The Town down the River " in 1910 his recognition began to come, and with the republication of " Captain Craig " the public became aware of a volume which they could have been reading for full thirteen years.

Miss Lowell displays a mild contempt for the title poem of this book, and Mr. Phelps — in his " Advance of English

Poetry in the Twentieth Century " — echoes her verdict. Yet
for many readers there is a splendor in it and a richness that
brings them back to it again and again. It is doubtless long,
discursive, and condensible. In fact it is already condensed in
such a bit as " Flammonde." It is an elaboration of the title
lyric for " The Children of the Night "; but only a wanton perversion of criticism will discount a philosophical poem for not
submitting to lyric standards. It is a poem of childhood, sunlight, laughter, and hope declaimed by an indomitable old vaga-
bond of eternity who is invincible in death and is fittingly
borne to the grave while the trombones of the Tilbury band
blare the Dead March in " Saul." Captain Craig is a character
who would not be his complete self without his verbosity. His
type, in fact, is never succinct. They are extravagant of time,
of gesture, of vocal and rhetorical emphasis, of words themselves. Out of the abundance of their hearts their mouths
speak all sorts of irresponsible, whimsical, exalted, and splendid
extravagance. They give voice to the dumb, and they amuse
and stimulate the good listeners, but they bore the cleverly
communicative, who dislike any consecutive talk but their own.
Thus, for example, the captain writes on one May day :

>   I have yearned
> In many another season for these days,
> And having them with God's own pageantry
> To make me glad for them, — yes, I have cursed
> The sunlight and the breezes and the leaves
> To think of men on stretchers and on beds,
>
> .   .   .   .
>
> Or of women working where a man would fall —
> Flat-breasted miracles of cheerfulness
> Made neuter by the work that no man counts
> Until it waits undone ; children thrown
> To feed their veins and souls with offal. . . .
>   Yes,
> I have had half a mind to blow my brains out
> Sometimes ; and I have gone from door to door

Ragged myself, trying to do something —
Crazy, I hope. — But what has this to do
With Spring? Because one half of humankind
Lives here in hell, shall not the other half
Do any more than just for conscience' sake
Be miserable? Is this the way for us
To lead these creatures up to find the light,
Or the way to be drawn down to find the dark
Again?

Captain Craig, in a word, is self-expression in very being and condemns in joyous scorn the man who believes that life is best fulfilled through discipline and renunciation. Instead he offers something positive:

Take on yourself
But your sincerity, and you take on
Good promise for all climbing; fly for truth,
And hell shall have no storm to crush your flight,
No laughter to vex down your loyalty.

This is the note throughout all Robinson's poems and plays. His disbelief in negativism leads him often to be impatient and caustic and leads the cloudy minded to timid deprecation of his cynicism, not knowing the difference between this and irony; but Mr. Robinson is never cynical toward the things that are more excellent. He is only convinced that people's Puritan convictions as to what is more excellent result in a perverted estimate; he is only attempting to substitute light for shadow, laughter for gloom; he is only saying with Larry Scammon:

" Stop me if I am too cheerful; but at the same time, if I can instil the fertile essence of Hope into this happy household, for God's sake, let me do it. . . . You had far better — all of you — begin to get yourselves out of your own light, and cease to torment your long-bedevilled heads with the dark doings of bogies that have no real existence."

As a craftsman Mr. Robinson has won distinction by his simple, direct realism. He employs for the most part the old iambic measures, a sentence structure which is often conversational, and a diction which is severe in its restraint. There are few "purple patches" in his poetry, but there are many clear flashes of incisive phrasing. His work is like a May day in his own seacoast town — not balmy, but bracing, with lots of sparkle on the blue, and the taste of the east wind through it all.

Robert Frost (1875–   ) is known as the author of three books of verse: "A Boy's Will," 1913, "North of Boston," 1914, and "Mountain Interval," 1916. He is known also — and rightly — as the voice and embodiment of rural New England. Yet he was born in San Francisco, his mother was born in Edinburgh, he first came to New England at the age of ten, and he lived for the next eight schoolboy years in a mill town, Lawrence, Massachusetts. Nevertheless, in his capacity for receiving impressions, he seemed to have a selective memory which made him sensitive to the aspects of country life in the regions north of Boston — the regions trod by nine generations of forbears on his father's side of the family. And so it was that though his first two volumes were published in London, there is no local trace of the old country in them, nothing in them that he had not known in farm or village between 1885 and 1912, when he set sail with his wife and children toward a residence of two and a half years in England. On his return to America he bought a farm in New Hampshire. From 1916 to 1920 he taught in Amherst College.

The common statement that Mr. Frost is content solely to present the appearances of New England life should be given distinct qualifications in two respects: the first is that his earliest book, "A Boy's Will," is wholly subjective and analytical, completely falling outside the generalization. And the second is that while "North of Boston" and "Mountain Interval" are objective pictures of New England life, the truth in them is by no means limited to New England, but is pertinent to human kind, although deeply tinged with the nue of that particular district.

THE LATER POETRY 467

"A Boy's Will," a little volume, is made up of thirty-two lyrics, each of them complete and most of them lovely. They are not, however, detached, although it is an open question how many readers would see their relationship if this were not indicated in the table of contents. It is the record of a young artist's experience who marries, withdraws to the country, revels in the isolation of winter, in the coming of spring, and in the farm beauties of summer. This isolation, however, cannot satisfy him long. Let the contents for Part Two show what happens: "'Revelation'—He resolves to become intelligible, at least to himself, since there is no help else—'The Trial by Existence'—and to know definitely what he thinks about the soul; 'In Equal Sacrifice'—about love; 'The Tuft of Flowers'—about fellowship; 'Spoils of the Dead'—about death; 'Pan with Us'—about art (his own); 'The Demiurge's Laugh'—about science." With the five lyrics of Part Three, the youth and his bride return to the world with misgivings:

Out through the fields and the woods
    And over the walls I have wended;
I have climbed the hills of view
    And looked at the world, and descended;
I have come by the highway home,
    And lo, it is ended.
.   .   .   .   .   .

Ah, when to the heart of man
    Was it ever less than a treason
To go with the drift of things,
    To yield with a grace to reason,
And bow and accept the end
    Of a love or a season?

This book does not represent the work of Frost as it appears in his later volumes, but it does represent the poet himself:

A lover of the meadows and the woods,
And mountains; and of all that we behold
From this green earth.

The second volume, "North of Boston," is twice as long as "A Boy's Will" and contains half as many titles. There would be nothing in this mathematical formula if it did not carry with it a real difference in content. But this second book is made up not of lyrics, but of unimpassioned vignettes of New England life. This is the grim New England which the poet attempted to shut out in "Love and a Question":

> But whether or not a man was asked,
>   To mar the love of two
> By harboring woe in the bridal house,
>   The bridegroom wished he knew.

The book presents the death of a farm laborer, the maddened bereavement of a mother whose child is buried within sight of the house, the black prospect faced by a household drudge who faces the insanity which is an inherited blight in her blood. They are not amiable pictures, and they offer neither problem nor solution, only the life itself. They are not, however, all equally grim. "The Mountain" tells of a township of sixty voters with only a fringe of level land around the looming pile. It dominates life, limits it, and rises above it, for few have either time or curiosity to reach the top. "The Black Cottage" presents a widowed relict of the Civil War who knew only her sacrifice and whose unthinking orthodoxy was as hazy as her political creed. With liberalism in the parish, the preacher was inclined to omit "descended into Hades" from the ritual:

> .... We could drop them
> Only — there was the bonnet in the pew.
> Such a phrase could n't have meant much to her.
> But suppose she had missed it from the Creed
> As a child misses the unsaid Good-night,
> And falls asleep with heartache — how should I feel?

Of another sort are the poems which have most of outdoor in them: "Mending Wall," the symbol of barriers between properties which the winters throw down; "Blueberries," which

indicates the complex of ownership in a countryside filled with
nature's gifts of uncultivated fruit; "After Apple Picking,"
the weariness forced upon the farmer in his effort to husband
an embarrassment of orchard riches; and "The Woodpile" with
its suggestion of the slow processes of nature contrasted with
the temporal efforts of man. The woodpile is discovered far
out in a swamp, long abandoned and vine-covered:

> . . . . I thought that only
> Someone who lived in turning to fresh tasks
> Could so forget his handiwork on which
> He spent himself, the labour of his axe,
> And leave it there far from a useful fireplace
> To warm the frozen swamp as best it could
> With the slow smokeless burning of decay.

The last volume, "Mountain Interval," is something of a
composite, with elements in both the former two. One reads
Mr. Frost's pages thoughtfully and leaves them in a thoughtful
mood. Not all are grim, but very few are gay. They have the
rock-ribbed austerity of the country from which they spring and
some of its beauty, too. They are suffused with the smoky haze
of an Indian-summer day.

Edgar Lee Masters (1869–   ) was born in Kansas in the
same year with Moody and Robinson. In the next year his
family moved to Illinois, which is his real " native " state. As
a boy he had wide opportunities for reading. At the age of
twenty-one he entered Knox College and plunged with zest
into the study of the classics, but was forced to withdraw at
the end of the year because Mr. Masters, Sr., would acknowledge no value in these studies for the practice of law, toward
which he was directing his son. After a brief experiment
in independence the young man surrendered and eventually
entered on a successful career as a Chicago attorney. Yet the
law did not take complete possession of him; he has always
been a devoted reader of Greek literature. "Songs and Satires,"
published in 1916, contains a few lyrics from a volume of 1898

which was printed, but through an accident of the trade never published. One of these ends with the significant stanza :

> Helen of Troy, Greek art
> Hath made our heart thy heart,
>   Thy love our love.
> For poesy, like thee,
> Must fly and wander free
>   As the wild dove.

Mr. Masters's next venture was a poetic drama in 1900, "Maximilian," a tragedy in verse which was accorded a few sympathetic reviews but no wide reading. Other works followed in the next fifteen years, some in law and some in literature. And finally, in 1915, appeared the "Spoon River Anthology." This is in all probability the most widely circulated book of new poems in the history of American literature ; others may have achieved a greater total of copies during a long career, but it is doubtful whether any others have equaled fifty thousand within three years of publication.

The most valuable single utterance on this much-discussed work is the richly compacted preface of Mr. Masters in "Toward the Gulf," with its inscription to William Marion Reedy. Mr. Masters had submitted various contributions to Reedy's *Mirror*, but had received most of them back with friendly appeals for something fresh. The first five Spoon River epitaphs were written almost casually in answer to this repeated challenge. At the same time they were a more than casual application of a hint from the Greek : a "resuscitation of the Greek epigrams, ironical and tender, satirical and sympathetic," assembled into an ultimate collection of nearly two hundred and fifty brief units, each a self-inscribed epitaph by one of the Spoon River townsfolk. These represent the chief types in an American country town and recognize in particular the usual line of cleavage between those who choose to be considered virtuous and those who do not care what they are considered. Unfortunately the first of these classes includes both the idealist and the hypocrite; and the second, both the conscious radical and the confirmed reprobate. A typical issue which might arise in such a town, as well as a typical alignment of forces, is described in "The Spooniad," the closing mock-heroic fragment and the longest unit in the book.

The "Anthology" has been violently assailed as a wantonly cynical production, each assault on this ground carrying within itself a proof that the censor either had not read the book through or did not understand it. As a matter of fact the most impressive element in the book and the one which bulks largest in the last quarter of it are the victorious idealists. There is Davis Matlock, who decided to live life out like a god, sure of immortality. There is Tennessee Claflin Shope, who asserted the sovereignty of his own soul, and Samuel Gardiner, who determined to live largely in token of his ample spirit, and the Village Atheist, who knew that only those who strive mightily could possess eternal life, and Lydia Humphrey, who in her church found the vision of the poets. In spite of the protests of readers who were so disgusted with the Inferno of the earlier portion that they never progressed to the concluding Paradiso, the book achieved its great circulation among a tolerant public and enviable applause from the most discriminating critics.

"Spoon River" established Mr. Masters's reputation and prepared the public for further thrills and shocks in the volumes to follow. This expectation has been only half fulfilled. The certainty of a public hearing has naturally encouraged the poet to more rapid production, but the subsequent books — "Songs and Satires" and "The Great Valley" of 1916 and "Toward the Gulf" of 1918 — have been divided both in tone and content between the caustic informality for which Mr. Masters was known in his earlier work and the classic finish which is a return to his unknown, earliest style.

In his treatment of sex, however, Mr. Masters has supplied the shocks and thrills expected, dealing with various aspects of passion with a frank minuteness which is sometimes distasteful and sometimes morbid. Usually his discussions of passion are more analytical than picturesque. He assumes its existence as a dominant factor in life and discusses not the experience itself so much as its influence. Frequently whole poems are concerned with it. He takes for granted passionate love without benefit of clergy, recording it without either idealizing it or defending it. Doubtless life has included the material for the " Dialogue at Perko's," for " Victor Rafolski on Art," and for " Widow La Rue," and certainly modern poetry supplies parallels in the works of other men. In a more significant way the sex psychology of Freud crops out in many poems not ostensibly devoted to it, as, for example, in " To-morrow is my Birthday." This soliloquy attributed to Shakespeare in his tercentenary year stands in striking contrast to Mr. Robinson's " Ben Jonson Entertains a Man from Stratford." In these two poems (of about four hundred lines each) Mr. Robinson writes in the manner of Ben Jonson, paying his tribute to Shakespeare at the height of his powers in London, touching on his susceptibility to women but passing this to dilate on his almost superhuman wisdom ; Mr. Masters devotes the last two thirds of Shakespeare's monologue on the night of his last carousal to sex confessions which become increasingly gross as the bard becomes increasingly drunk. Mr. Robinson's passage is only a few lines in length and concludes :

> There's no long cry for going into it,
> However, and we don't know much about it.

Mr. Masters's approaches two hundred and fifty lines, begins with " The thing is sex," continues with

> Give me a woman, Ben, and I will pick
> Out of this April, by this larger art
> Of fifty-two, such songs as we have heard,
> Both you and I, when weltering in the clouds
> Of that eternity which comes in sleep,
> Or in the viewless spinning of the soul
> When most intense,

and ends with common brothel profanity. The popular method
of justifying the Masters treatment is to gibe at the Robinson
reticence as Puritan prudishness, but it is a gibe which for
many enforces the value of reticence even in modern art.

So much for the negative side of Mr. Masters's work — the
so-called cynicism declaimed at by the inattentive reader and
the preoccupation with sex which is fairly open to criticism.
On the positive side the greater weight of his work lies in
poems of searching analysis. " So We Grew Together " is
the changing relations of an adopted son for his Bohemian
father ; " Excluded Middle," an inquiry into the mystery of
inheritance ; " Dr. Scudder's Clinical Lecture," the study of
a paranoiac — dramatic monologues suggestive of Browning in
execution as well as content. The reader of Mr. Masters as
a whole is bound to discover in the end that all these analyses
are searchings into the mystery of life. It appears in " The
Loom " as it does in " The Cry":

> There 's a voice in my heart that cries and cries for tears.
> It is not a voice, but a pain of many years.
> It is not a pain, but the rune of far-off spheres.
>
> .   .   .   .
>
> Deep in darkness the bulb under mould and clod
> Feels the sun in the sky and pushes above the sod ;
> Perhaps this cry in my heart is nothing but God !

And he is bound to confess that Mr. Masters, instead of
being a cynic, is a sober optimist. Take the last lines of the
opening and closing poems in " Toward the Gulf " :

> And forever as long as the river flows toward the Gulf
> Ulysses reincarnate shall come
> To guard our places of sleep,
> Till East and West shall be one in the west of heaven and earth !
>
> .   .   .   .
>
> " And after that ? "
> " Another spring — that 's all I know myself,
> There shall be springs and springs ! "

Nicholas Vachel Lindsay (1879–   ), born in Springfield, Illinois, of which he is the most devoted and distinguished citizen since Lincoln, studied for three years at Hiram College and then for five years as an art student in Chicago and New York. Unfortunately his drawings are accessible only in a quarto pamphlet—"A Letter to Program Managers"—which is not for sale. They show the same vigor and the same antic play of fancy inherent in his verse. In 1906 he took his first long tramp through Florida, Georgia, and the Carolinas, and in 1908 a second through the northeastern states. During these two, as in his latest like excursion through the Western wheat belt, he traveled as a minstrel, observing the following rules :

(1) Keep away from the cities.
(2) Keep away from the railroads.
(3) Have nothing to do with money. Carry no baggage.
(4) Ask for dinner about quarter after eleven.
(5) Ask for supper, lodging and breakfast about quarter of five.
(6) Travel alone.
(7) Be neat, truthful, civil and on the square.
(8) Preach the Gospel of Beauty.

These appeared at the head of a little pamphlet entitled "Rhymes to be Traded for Bread," the only baggage he carried besides a further printed statement called "The Gospel of Beauty." In smiling defense of his course Mr. Lindsay has said that up to date there has been no established method for implanting beauty in the heart of the average American. "*Until such a way has been determined upon by a competent committee,* I must be pardoned for taking my own course and trying any experiment I please." Mr. Lindsay has not limited himself to this way of circulating his ideas. He has posted his poems on billboards, recited them from soap boxes and on the vaudeville stage, and has even descended to select club audiences. He has, however, not allowed the calls of the lyceum managers to convert him from a poet to an entertainer.

His books have been six in number and, according to his own advice, are to be read in the following order : " A Handy Guide for Beggars," " Adventures while Preaching the Gospel of Beauty," " The Art of the Moving Picture," " General William Booth Enters into Heaven," " The Congo," and " The Chinese Nightingale." The first three are prose statements of his social and religious philosophy ; the second three are poems. His seventh volume is announced as "The Golden Book of Springfield." In its title it is a reaffirmation of what appears in many of his poems and of what he stated in " The Gospel of Beauty " (1914) : " The things most worth while are one's own hearth and neighborhood. We should make our own home and neighborhood the most democratic, the most beautiful, and the holiest in the world."

The obvious first point about the poetry of Mr. Lindsay is that in it he lives up to his own instructions. He keeps quite as close to his own district as Mr. Masters and Mr. Frost do and he indulges in as wide a play of imagination as does Mr. Robinson. In the rôle of an apostle he tries to implant beauty in the heart of the average American. Yet " implant " is not the proper word ; his own word is " establish," for he re-enforces a latent sense of beauty in hearts that are unconscious of it and he reveals it in the lives of those whom the average American overlooks or despises. On the one hand, he carries whole audiences into an actual participation in his recitals and, on the other, he discloses the " scum of the earth " as poets and mystics.

Thus " General William Booth Enters into Heaven " tells of Booth's apotheosis as it is seen and felt by a Salvation Army sympathizer. Booth with his big bass drum, followed by a motley slum crowd, leads to the most impressively magnificent place within the ken of a small-town Middle Westerner. This is an Illinois courthouse square. As a matter of fact, it is bleak, treeless, dust-blown, mud-moated — the dome of the courthouse in the middle, flanked on all sides with ugly brick blocks and alternating wooden shacks with corrugated iron false fronts ; but this is splendor to the mind of the narrator. And so in all reverence he says :

(*Sweet flute music*)

Jesus came from out the court-house door,
Stretched his hands above the passing poor.
Booth saw not, but led his queer ones there
Round and round the mighty court-house square.

From this scene General Booth ascends into heaven. "The Congo" is a similar piece of interpretation. Few types could seem more hopeless than the levee negroes, yet through them Mr. Lindsay makes a study of their race. In a drunken saloon crowd he sees the basic savagery which back in the Congo forests displays itself in picturesque poetry stuff. In a group of crapshooters who laugh down a police raid he finds the irrepressible high spirits which carry the negroes in imagination back to a regal Congo cakewalk, and in the exhortations of an African evangelist he sees the same hope of religion which the slave brought with him from his native soil. Once again, "The Chinese Nightingale" is written in the same spirit, this time accounting for the Chinese laundryman's tireless industry through the fact that while his iron pounds in the dead of night he is living in a world of oriental romance.

Mr. Lindsay's poetry has two chief aspects, sometimes separated, sometimes compounded. One of these is an ethical seriousness. He might be called an ideally provincial character. He chooses to express himself in terms of his home and neighborhood, but his interests move out through a series of concentric circles which include his city, his state, America, and the world federation. The poems on Springfield, therefore, are of a piece with the poems on "America Watching the War" and those on "America at War." "The Soul of the City," with Mr. Lindsay's own drawings, is quite as interesting

as any of the poems above mentioned. " Springfield Magical "
suggests the source of his inspiration :

> In this, the City of my Discontent,
> Sometimes there comes a whisper from the grass,
> " Romance, Romance — is here. No Hindu town
> Is quite so strange. No Citadel of Brass
> By Sinbad found, held half such love and hate ;
> No picture-palace in a picture-book
> Such webs of Friendship, Beauty, Greed and Fate ! "

" The Proud Farmer," " The Illinois Village," and " On the
Building of Springfield "— three poems which conclude the
General William Booth volume — are all on his favorite thesis
and were favorites with his farmhouse auditors.

His poems related to the war reveal him as an ardent democrat, a hater of tyranny, a peace-loving socialist, and, in the
end, like millions of his countrymen, a combatant pacifist, but
none the less a pacifist in the larger sense. A pair of stanzas,
" Concerning Emperors," are a very pretty cue both to himself
and his convictions. The first in fervent seriousness prays for
new regicides ; the second states the case unsmilingly, but as
it might be put to any newsboy, concluding :

> And yet I cannot hate the Kaiser (I hope you understand).
> Yet I chase the thing he stands for with a brickbat in my hand.

This leads naturally to his verses of fancy and whimsy, like
the group called the " Christmas Tree," " loaded with pretty
toys," or the twenty poems in which the moon is the chief
figure of speech. And these lead naturally to his distinctive
work in connection with poetic form, his fanciful and often
whimsical experiments in restoring the half-chanted Greek
choral odes to modern usage — what W. B. Yeats calls " the
primitive singing of music " (expounding it charmingly in
the volume " Ideas of Good and Evil "). Mr. Lindsay, in the
" Congo " volume has indicated on some of the margins ways
in which the verses might be chanted. Before many audiences

he has illustrated his intent with awkwardly convincing effectiveness. And with the Poem Games, printed with "The Chinese Nightingale," he has actually enlisted unsuspecting audiences as choruses and sent them home thrilled and amused at their awakened poetic susceptibility. Mr. Lindsay's theories are briefly indicated in the two books just mentioned, in Miss Harriet Monroe's introduction to the former and in the poet's explanation of Poem Games in the latter. They are briefly stated and should be read by every student of his work. Like most of the developments in modern poetry they are very new only in being a revival of something very old, but in their application they are local, and they partake of their author's genial, informal, democratic nature in being very American. Among the contemporary poets who are likely to leave an individual impress on American literature, Mr. Lindsay, to use a good Americanism, is one of the few who "will certainly bear watching."

Miss Amy Lowell (1874–   ) was born in Brookline, Massachusetts. James Russell Lowell was a cousin of her grandfather, and she numbers among her relatives her mother's father, Abbott Lawrence, minister to England, and a brother, Abbott Lawrence Lowell, president of Harvard. In her education general reading and wide travel were the most important factors. In 1902, at the age of twenty-eight, she decided to devote herself to poetry, and for the next eight years she studied and wrote without attempting publication. Her first verse was printed in the *Atlantic Monthly* in 1910, and her first volume, "A Dome of Many-Coloured Glass," was published in 1912. Her further volumes have been "Sword Blades and Poppy Seed" (1914), "Six French Poets" (1915), "Men, Women and Ghosts" (1916), "Tendencies in Modern American Poetry" (1917), and "Can Grande's Castle" (1918), — in all, four volumes of verse and two of prose criticism. She has been a conspicuous personality among contemporary poets in France, England, and America, and though she has not been lacking in self-assertiveness she has been without question chiefly interested in the progress of contemporary poetry and finely generous in both theory and practice in the support of her fellow-poets.

As one of her most recent critics has pointed out, she has been notable and notably American in her zest for argument and in her love of experiment — "a female Roosevelt among the Parnassians." She has championed the cause of modern poetry and has fought the conventions of Victorian verse wherever she has encountered them, and in her liking for experiment and her absorption in technique she has taken up the cudgels successively for free verse, for the tenets of Imagism, and for polyphonic prose. She has been most closely identified with the activities of the Imagist poets, — three Englishmen, two Anglicized Americans, and herself, — and it is therefore well to summarize the six objects to which they committed themselves : (1) to use the language of common speech, but to employ always the exact word, (2) to create new rhythms as the expression of new moods, (3) to allow absolute freedom in the choice of subject (within the limits of good taste), (4) to present an image (hence the name "Imagist"), (5) to produce poetry that is hard and clear, (6) to insist on concentration as the essence of poetry. A stanza from "Before the Altar," the opening poem in her first book, serves to illustrate her technique as an Imagist :

> His sole condition
> Love and poverty.
> And while the moon
> Swings slow across the sky,
> Athwart a waving pine tree,
> And soon
> Tips all the needles there
> With silver sparkles, bitterly
> He gazes, while his soul
> Grows hard with thinking of the poorness of his dole.

The fourth section of "Spring Day," the poem in "Men, Women and Ghosts" which begins with the much-discussed "Bath," is an example of her "polyphonic prose":

MIDDAY AND AFTERNOON

SWIRL of crowded streets. Shock and recoil of traffic. The stock-still brick façade of an old church, against which the waves of people lurch and withdraw. Flare of sunshine down side-streets. Eddies of light in the windows of chemists' shops, with their blue, gold, purple jars, darting colors far into the crowd. Loud bangs and tremors, murmurings out of high windows, whirring of machine belts, blurring of horses and motors. A quick spin and shudder of brakes on an electric car, and the jar of a church-bell knocking against the metal blue of the sky. I am a piece of the town, a bit of blown dust, thrust along with the crowd. Proud to feel the pavement under me, reeling with feet. Feet tripping, skipping, lagging, dragging, plodding doggedly or springing up and advancing on firm, elastic insteps. A boy is selling papers, I smell them clean and new from the press. They are fresh like the air, and pungent as tulips and narcissus.

The blue sky pales to lemon, and great tongues of gold blind the shop-windows, putting out their contents in a flood of flame.

In her essay on John Gould Fletcher, in "Tendencies in Modern American Poetry," Miss Lowell has defined the æsthetic intent of this poetic form: "'Polyphonic' means — many-voiced — and the form is so-called because it makes use of all the 'voices' of poetry, namely: metre, *vers libre*, assonance, alliteration, rhyme and return. It employs every form of rhythm, even prose rhythm at times, but usually holds no particular one for long. . . . The rhymes may come at the ends of the cadences, or may appear in close juxtaposition to each other, or may be only distantly related." These two forms, with the aid of the two formulas, may be tested at leisure from an abundance of passages ; they correspond with their recipes, are distinct from each other, and have certain distinctive beauties. But a further experiment — the attempt to make the cadences of free verse harmonize with the movements of natural objects — is by no means so successful. "If

the reader will turn," says Miss Lowell, in the preface to
"Men, Women and Ghosts," "to the poem 'A Roxbury
Garden,' he will find in the first two sections an attempt to
give the circular movement of a hoop bowling along the
ground, and the up-and-down, elliptical curve of a flying
shuttlecock." The following, presumably, is a segment of the
circular movement:

> "I will beat you Minna," cries Stella,
> Hitting her hoop smartly with her stick.
> "Stella, Stella, we are winning," calls Minna,
> As her hoop curves round a bed of clove-pinks.

It is an example, in fact, of the fruitlessness of dwelling on a
matter of artistic form till it becomes more important than the
artistic content. Miss Lowell admits in this connection that
there flashed into her mind "the idea of using the movement
of poetry." The student, therefore, should not regard the
resultant verses as anything more than experiments in technique, and at the same time he should speculate as to whether
a vital artistic form can ever be imposed upon a subject
instead of springing spontaneously from it.

Yet, although Miss Lowell's reputation rests mainly on her
experiments in novel and striking poetic forms, most of
her work has been written in conformity with classic traditions.
The opening volume is all in common rhythms, and so is most
of the second, and quite half of the third. The last alone is
devoted to a new form; "Can Grande's Castle" contains four
long poems in polyphonic prose. The tendency is clearly in
the direction of the innovations, but thus far the balance
is about even between the new and the old.

As to subject matter, Miss Lowell's thesis is Poe's: that
poetry should not teach either facts or morals, but should be
dedicated to beauty; it is a stained-glass window, a colored
transparency. And the poet is a nonsocial being who

> spurns life's human friendships to profess
> Life's loneliness of dreaming ecstacy.

Like Poe she limits herself to the production of lyrics and tales and resorts not infrequently to grotesques and arabesques. Unlike Poe her resort to horror leads her to the composition of sex infidelities which are sometimes boring, sometimes foul, and rarely interesting. On this point (rule three for the Imagists) Miss Lowell falters awkwardly. "'How can the choice of subject be absolutely unrestricted?' — horrified critics have asked. The only reply to such a question is that one had supposed one were speaking to people of common sense and intelligence." The bounds of taste are assumed; yet these, she hastens to state, differ for different judges, and she illustrates her contention by the extreme extensiveness of her own. Finally, and again like Poe, Miss Lowell is to a high degree bookishly literary in her choice and treatment of subjects.

After all, for the attentive reader of contemporary poetry Miss Lowell's most distinguished service has been in her two books of criticism. In the concourse of present-day poets she is a kind of drum major. One cannot see the procession without seeing her or admiring the skill with which she swings and tosses the baton. But when the parade is past, one can easily forget her until the trumpets blare again. She leads the way effectively, and one is glad to have her do it, — glad that there are those who enjoy being excellent drum majors. Then one pays farewell to her in the words with which she salutes Ezra Pound in her verses headed " Astigmatism " : " Peace be with you, [Sister]. You have chosen your part."

Witter Bynner (1881–   ) was born in Brooklyn and is a graduate of Harvard in the class of 1902. He took the impress of his university and recorded it not only in an " Ode to Harvard " (1907) — reprinted in " Young Harvard and Other Poems " — but also in the two plays that followed, " Tiger " (1913) and " The Little King " (1914), neither of which have anything to do with Harvard, but both of which reflect the intelligent interest in drama encouraged at that seat of learning. Aside from " Iphigenia in Tauris " (1915), his remaining work, in which his real distinction lies, is the single poem "The New World" (1915) and the collection "Grenstone Poems" (1917). Into both of these are woven threads of the same story, — the poet's love and marriage to Celia, the inspiration which comes to him from her finer nature, the birth and loss of their child, the death of Celia, his dull bereavement, the dedication of his life to the democracy which Celia had taught him to understand.

"Grenstone Poems" is a series of little idyls comparable in some respects to Frost's "A Boy's Will." They are wholly individual in tone, presenting in brief lyrics, nearly two hundred in number, the quaint and lovely elements in the humor and the tragedy of life. "The New World," in contrast, contains by implication much of this, but is constructed in nine sections which trace the progressive steps in the poet's idealization of America. Always Celia's imagination leads far in advance of his own. Again and again as he strives to follow, his triumphant ascent reaches as its climax what to her is a lower round in the ladder. Two passages suggest the theme in the abstract, though the beauty of the poem lies chiefly in the far implications of definite scenes and episodes. The first is a speech of Celia's:

> It is my faith that God is our own dream
> Of perfect understanding of the soul.
> It is my passion that, alike through me
> And every member of eternity,
> The source of God is sending the same stream.
> It is my peace that when my life is whole,
> God's life shall be completed and supreme.

The second, with which this volume may well conclude, is in the poet's own words:

> In temporary pain
> The age is bearing a new breed
> Of men and women, patriots of the world
> And one another. Boundaries in vain,
> Birthrights and countries, would constrain

The old diversity of seed
To be diversity of soul.
O mighty patriots, maintain
Your loyalty! — till flags unfurled
For battle shall arraign
The traitors who unfurled them, shall remain
And shine over an army with no slain,
And men from every nation shall enroll
And women — in the hardihood of peace!
What can my anger do but cease?
Whom shall I fight and who shall be my enemy
When he is I and I am he?

Let me have done with that old God outside
Who watched with preference and answered prayer,
The Godhead that replied
Now here, now there,
Where heavy cannon were
Or coins of gold!
Let me receive communion with all men,
Acknowledging our one and only soul!
For not till then
Can God be God, till we ourselves are whole.

BOOK LIST

General References

The Younger American Poets. Jessie B. Rittenhouse, 1904.
Tendencies in Modern American Poetry. Amy Lowell, 1917.
The Advance of English Poetry in the Twentieth Century. W. L. Phelps,
    1918. (Latter half, American Poetry.)
Convention and Revolt in Poetry. G. L. Lowes, 1919.
The New Era in American Poetry. L. Untermeyer, 1919.

Collections

A Little Book of Modern Verse. Edited by Jessie B. Rittenhouse.
Some Imagist Poets (three annual volumes in a completed series),
    1915, 1916, 1917.
An Anthology of Magazine Verse (annual volumes in a continuing
    series). Edited by W. S. Braithwaite, since 1915.
The Poetry of the Future. Edited by W. T. Schnittkin.
A Book of Princeton Verse. Edited by Alfred Noyes and Others.

Works of Individual Men

WITTER BYNNER. Ode to Harvard, 1907; Tiger, 1913; The Little King, 1914; Iphigenia in Tauris, 1915; The New World, 1915; Grenstone Poems, 1917; Any Girl, 1917.

ROBERT FROST. A Boy's Will, 1913; North of Boston, 1914; Mountain Interval, 1916.

RICHARD HOVEY. Plays (uniform edition), 1907-1908.

NICHOLAS VACHEL LINDSAY. General William Booth Enters into Heaven, 1913; Adventures while Preaching the Gospel of Beauty, 1914; The Congo, 1914; The Art of the Moving Picture, 1915; A Handy Guide for Beggars, 1916; The Chinese Nightingale, 1917.

AMY LOWELL. A Dome of Many-Colored Glass, 1912; Sword Blades and Poppy Seed, 1914; Six French Poets, 1915; Men, Women and Ghosts, 1916; Tendencies in Modern American Poetry, 1917; Can Grande's Castle, 1919.

EDGAR LEE MASTERS. Poems, 1898; Maximilian, 1900; The Spoon River Anthology, 1915; Songs and Satires, 1916; The Great Valley, 1916; Toward the Gulf, 1918.

WILLIAM VAUGHN MOODY. Poems and Plays. 1912. 2 vols.

EDWIN ARLINGTON ROBINSON. The Children of the Night, 1897; Captain Craig, 1902 and 1915; The Town down the River, 1910; The Man against the Sky, 1916; Prose plays: Van Zorn, 1914; The Porcupine, 1915; Merlin, 1917.

Magazine Articles

The magazine articles on poetry are extremely numerous. From among those since 1900 the following are of special interest:

1900-1904. Poetry and the Stage. H. W. Boynton. *Atlantic*, Vol. XCII pp. 120-126. July, 1903.
  Poetry of a Machine Age. G. S. Lee. *Atlantic*, Vol. LXXXV, pp. 756-763. June, 1900.

1905-1909. Certain Vagaries of the Poets. *Atlantic*, Vol. C, pp. 431-432. September, 1907.
  On the Slopes of Parnassus. A. Repplier. *Atlantic*, Vol. CII, pp. 397-403. September, 1908.
  Our Strepitous Poets. *Nation*, Vol. LXXXV, pp. 277-278. Sept. 26, 1907.
  Poetry and Elocution. F. B. Gummere. *Nation*, Vol. LXXXIX, pp. 453-454. Nov. 11, 1909.
  State of Pseudo-Poetry at the Present Time. J. A. Macy. *Bookman*, Vol. XXVII, pp. 513-517. July, 1908.

1910-1914. Democracy and Poetry. *Nation*, XCIII, pp. 413-414. Nov. 2, 1911.
  New Poetry. R. M. Alden. *Nation*, Vol. XCVI, pp. 386-387. April 17, 1913.

1910–1914. New Poets and Old Poetry. B. Hooker. *Bookman*, Vol. XXXI, pp. 480–486. July, 1910.

Taking Poetry too Seriously. *Nation*, Vol. XCVI, pp. 173–174. Feb. 20, 1913.

1915. Imagism, Another View. W. S. Braithwaite. *New Republic*, Vol. III, pp. 154–155. June 12, 1915.

Limits to Imagism. C. Aiken. *New Republic*, Vol. III, pp. 204–205. June 26, 1915.

New Movement in Poetry. O. W. Firkins. *Nation*, Vol. CI, pp. 458–461. Oct. 14, 1915.

Place of Imagism. C. Aiken. *New Republic*, Vol. III, pp. 75–76. May 22, 1915.

1916. New Manner in Modern Poetry. A. Lowell. *New Republic*, Vol. VI, pp. 124–125. March 4, 1916.

New Naïveté. L. W. Smith. *Atlantic*, Vol. CXVII, pp. 487–492. April, 1916.

Poetry To-day. C. A. P. Comer. *Atlantic*, Vol. CXVII, pp. 493–498. April, 1916.

Poetry under the Fire Test. J. N. Hall. *New Republic*, Vol. IX, pp. 93–96. Nov. 25, 1916.

1917. From Florence Coates to Amy Lowell : a Glance at Modernity. O. W. Firkins. *Nation*, Vol. CIV, pp. 522–524. May 3, 1917.

Poetry, Education, and Slang. M. Eastman. *New Republic*, Vol. IX, pp. 151–152, 182–184. Dec. 9, 16, 1916.

Singers and Satirists. O. W. Firkins. *Nation*, Vol. CIV, pp. 157–158. Feb. 8, 1917.

Critical Notes on American Poets. E. Garnett. *Atlantic*, Vol. CXX, pp. 366–373. Sept., 1917.

See also the periodicals *Poetry, a Magazine of Verse* (see p. 497), as well as *The Poetry Journal, The Poetry Review of America*, and *Poet Lore*, entire.

1800	1810	1820	1830	1840	1850	1860	1870	1880	1890	1900	1910	1920

New York Evening Post, 1801–
The Portfolio, 1806–1827
North American Review, 1815–
Saturday Evening Post, 1821–
New York Mirror, 1823–1846
New York Review and Athenæum Magazine, 1826–1827
Casket, 1826–1840
Godey's Lady's Book, 1830–1898
New England Magazine, 1831–1835
Liberator, 1831–1865
Baltimore Saturday Visiter, 1833–?
Western Monthly Magazine, 1833–1836
Knickerbocker Magazine, 1833–1865
Southern Literary Messenger, 1834–1865
Western Messenger, 1835–1841
Gentleman's Magazine, 1837–1841
Democratic Review, 1837–1859
Dial (Boston), 1840–1844
Graham's Magazine, 1841–1859
Brooklyn Daily Eagle, 1841–
New York Tribune, 1841–
New Englander, 1843–1892
Littell's Living Age, 1844–
Broadway Journal, 1845
Home Journal, 1847–
Independent, 1848–
Congregationalist, 1849–
Harper's Magazine, 1850–
Putnam's Magazine, 1853–1858, 1868–1870, 1906–1910
Russell's Magazine, 1857–1860
Atlantic Monthly, 1857–
Saturday Press, 1858–1860
Round Table, 1864–1869
Every Saturday, 1865–1874
Nation, 1865–
Galaxy, 1866–1878
Overland Monthly, 1868–1875, 1883–
Lippincott's Magazine, 1868–1916
Scribner's Monthly, 1870–1881
Outlook, 1870–
Southern Magazine, 1871–1875
American Magazine, 1875–
Dial (Chicago-New York), 1880–
Critic, 1881–1906
Century Magazine, 1881–
Scribner's Magazine, 1886–
Poet-Lore, 1889–
Conservator, 1890–
Yale Review, 1892–
McClure's Magazine, 1893–
Everybody's Magazine, 1899–
Poetry Magazine, 1912–
New Republic, 1914–

CHRONOLOGICAL CHART III. LEADING PERIODICALS ESTABLISHED SINCE
1800 WHICH HAVE SERVED AS VEHICLES FOR AMERICAN WRITINGS

INDEX TO LEADING NINETEENTH-CENTURY
PERIODICALS

The following list of periodicals represents a small fraction of those which were established and throve for longer or shorter periods in the United States between 1800 and the present time. The basis of selection has been to include only those which published a generous amount of literature which is still remembered or those of which leading men of letters were editors.

It was intended at first to make the list identical with the periodicals mentioned in the text, but this proved not to be practical. On some of the earlier ones it was not possible to secure exact data concerning length of life, editors, and contributors. Some others mentioned in the text were not of importance enough to justify inclusion. Still others, though not mentioned in the text, were too important to be omitted. The list as it stands, therefore, represents the judgment of the author and would not coincide with that of any other compiler of a list of equal length. It will serve, however, as a fairly representative list and will, perhaps, move some other student of American literature to what is greatly needed — a relatively complete and compact " Who's Who " of American periodicals.

As yet such material is very meager and unsatisfactory. The great number of magazines and the bewildering consolidations, changes of editorship, title, form, period of publication, and place of publication have apparently discouraged anyone's attempting a definitive piece of work. On this account and with this explanation the following brief appendix has been prepared.

AMERICAN MAGAZINE, THE, 1875———. A New York monthly.

Founded in 1875. From 1884 to 1888 the *Brooklyn Magazine*, then resumed its own name, continuing without important developments till it entered on its present régime in 1905. This came with the absorption of *Leslie's* and the assumption of control by Ray Stannard Baker, Lincoln Steffens, and Ida Tarbell, all former staff writers for *McClure's*. In this latter period it has been specially successful in recognizing younger authors. It has printed much by Bynner, O. Henry, Lindsay, Whitlock, and Poole; by Eaton and Hamilton on the drama; by F. P. Dunne ("Mr. Dooley"), George Ade, and Irvin Cobb; and, among foreign authors, by Wells, Bennett, Kipling, and Locke. It is popular in policy and content.

ATLANTIC MONTHLY, THE, 1857——. A Boston monthly.

Founded in 1857, Francis H. Underwood the prime mover, with the intention of setting new standards for a literary magazine of American authorship. Lowell was first editor; the first notable essay series Holmes's "Autocrat of the Breakfast Table"; the first popular serial story, Mrs. Stowe's "Dred." The field has been consistently divided among fiction, essay, and poetry, and the book reviewing has always been scrupulous. The editors have been Lowell, James T. Fields, W. D. Howells, T. B. Aldrich, Horace Scudder, W. H. Page, Bliss Perry, and the present editor and chief owner, Ellery Sedgwick. Early important contributors were Emerson, Holmes, Longfellow, Lowell, Thoreau, Whittier, Hawthorne, Wendell Phillips. Later issues have included Lafcadio Hearn, Edith Wharton, Frank Norris, Agnes Repplier, Gerald Stanley Lee, S. M. Crothers, William Vaughn Moody, Richard Hovey, and most of the contributors to the best traditions in American literature. (See "The Atlantic Monthly and its Makers," by M. A. DeWolfe Howe.)

BALTIMORE SATURDAY VISITER, 1833——(?). A Baltimore weekly.

Started by Lambert A. Wilmer, who continued with it for only six months. In October of this year Poe's "MS. Found in a Bottle" was published as the winner of a prize competition. This was Poe's one contribution and the *Visiter's* sole apparent title to fame.

BROADWAY JOURNAL, 1845. A New York weekly.

Founded by C. F. Briggs ("Harry Franco") in January, 1845. So named according to the first editorial from "the first street in the first city of the New World. . . . We shall attempt to make it entirely original, and instead of the effete vapors of English magazines . . . give such thoughts as may be generated among us." Poe and Briggs were associate editors in the spring, until in July, 1845, it went under the sole charge of Poe, who bought it from Briggs for $50. During this year it was Poe's chief vehicle, printing or reprinting some fifteen of his prose tales and two poems. Its business failure took place at the end of the first year. (See "Life of Poe," by George E. Woodberry.)

BROOKLYN DAILY EAGLE, 1841. A Brooklyn daily.

Isaac Van Anden, first editor and publisher. A democratic newspaper with independent judgment. From 1844 (?) to 1848 Walt Whitman was its editor. From 1885, until his recent death, it was under charge of St. Clair McKelway, a brilliant writer and speaker and a constructive educator.

BURTON'S GENTLEMAN'S MAGAZINE (see *Gentleman's Magazine*).

CASKET, THE (*Graham's Magazine*), 1826–1840. A Philadelphia monthly. Called *Atkinson's Casket*, 1831–1840. Was combined with *Gentleman's Magazine* and became *Graham's Magazine*.

CENTURY MAGAZINE, THE, 1881——. A New York monthly.

A continuation of the older *Scribner's Monthly* (1870–1881) on the assumption of control by Roswell Smith. R. W. Gilder was editor from the second number, till his death in 1907. Its policy was to publish articles, singly and in series, related to broad aspects of American life, exposition and poetry playing a larger part in the earlier years than of late. In travel it published Lowell's "Impressions of Spain" and van Dyke's "Sicily"; in biography large portions of Hay and Nicolay's "Lincoln," Jefferson's autobiography, and a Napoleon series. Riis, Bryce, Darwin, Tolstoy, and Burroughs have contributed from their own fields. Notable fiction series have been contributed by Howells, Mark Twain, Crawford, Weir Mitchell, Garland, London, and Mrs. Wharton; and verse by Emerson, Whitman, Gilder, Moody, Markham, and Cawein. (See also *Scribner's Monthly*, p. 499.)

CONGREGATIONALIST AND CHRISTIAN WORLD, THE, 1849——. A Boston weekly.

Founded in 1816 as the *Boston Recorder* by Nathaniel Willis, father of the more famous Nathaniel Parker Willis, and conducted by him until 1844. From then till about 1890 it was the sectarian organ of the Congregationalists, playing a rôle similar to that of the *Independent* and the *Christian Union*. In the latter part of the nineteenth century it was under the editorship of W. A. Dunning, who was succeeded by the present editor, Horace Bridgman. It has had a consistent career as a religious weekly, changing with the times, but not modifying itself for the sake of a secular circulation so frankly as the other two have done.

CONSERVATOR, THE, 1890. A Philadelphia monthly.

Founded in 1890 by Horace Traubel, an independent exponent of the world movement in ethics. In 1892 W. H. Ketler, Joseph Gilbert, W. Thornton Innes, and James A. Brown added to the editorial staff and enlarged to contain articles of timely interest, a book-review section, and a "Budget" for the reports of the ethical societies. The chief contributors: Stanton Coit, William Salter, Robert Ingersoll, and M. M. Mangasarian. The magazine gradually dropped its study of ethical questions and became an exponent of "the Whitman argument," treated by Bucke, Harned, Kennedy, Platt, and Helena Born. In 1890 Traubel added extensive dramatic criticism and enlarged the book-review department. Since 1898 the magazine has been an expression of Traubel's radical theories. It contains a long editorial "Collect," which is an uncompromising criticism of the times, a long poem by Traubel, and reviews of current books of socialistic tendencies. During the Great War it was frankly pacific, before the entrance of the United States.

CRITIC, THE, 1881–1906. A New York bi-weekly (1881–1882), weekly (1883–1898), and monthly.

Founded as a "fortnightly review of literature, the fine arts, music, and the drama." The best known of its editors were the latest — J. L. and J. B. Gilder. After the first four years art and music notes were dropped and book reviews were made the leading feature, original essays giving place to extracts from other magazines. In 1900 the design was stated to be "an illustrated monthly review of literature, art, and life." From 1905 politics and technical science were dropped. In 1906 it was absorbed by *Putnam's*. Best-known contributors: E. C. Stedman, Edith M. Thomas, R. W. Gilder, John Burroughs, E. E. Hale, F. B. Sanborn, J. C. Harris, Brander Matthews.

DEMOCRATIC REVIEW, THE UNITED STATES, 1837–1859 (?). A Washington and New York quarterly.

A note in Vol. XXXVIII stated that with Vol. XXXIX it would be issued as a newspaper. At the outset it was the most successful political magazine in the country. It was characterized by Carlyle as "*The Dial* with a beard." It was at first partisan, until, with payment for its articles, it became broader. Early contributors and best known were Orestes Augustus Brownson, Bancroft, Whittier, Bryant, and Hawthorne.

DIAL, THE, 1840–1844. A Boston quarterly.

Founded as a quarterly organ for the group of Transcendentalists centering about Emerson. Editors: 1840–1842, Margaret Fuller; 1842–1844, Emerson. The issues of 128 pages contained philosophical essays, discussions of German and oriental thought, comments on contemporary art and literature, book reviews, and poetry. The circulation never reached 300 copies, and at the end of the fourth year it was discontinued, the final debts being paid by Emerson. Leading contributors were the editors: Thoreau, Bronson Alcott, Theodore Parker, George Ripley, C. P. Cranch, J. F. Clarke, and Ellery Channing. There was a reprint by the Rowfant Club, Cleveland, in 1901–1902, with the addition of a historical and biographical introduction. (See introduction to the reprint of *The Dial*, Vol. II, George Willis Cooke, 1902.)

DIAL, THE, 1880——. A Chicago fortnightly and New York monthly.

Founded and edited for a third of a century by Francis F. Browne as a literary review, and able to refer to itself on its thirtieth birthday as "the only journal in America given up to the criticism of current literature" and "the only literary periodical in the country not owned or controlled by a book publishing house or a newspaper." After one or two changes of control, following the death of its founder, *The Dial* was transferred to New York in July, 1918, extending its editorial policy to include, besides the literary features, discussions of internationalism and of industrial and educational reconstruction.

EVERYBODY'S MAGAZINE, 1899———. A New York monthly.

Founded by John Wanamaker and for the first four years a miscellany best characterized by the purchasers in 1903. The Ridgway-Thayer Company on taking control announced their purpose to do away with the "mawkish, morbid, and unreal," to repress questionable advertising, and in general to transform the magazine. Since then *Everybody's* has attempted in content to satisfy all sorts of intellectual tastes and at the same time to have a hand in the social and economic investigation of the period. The most celebrated series, which multiplied the circulation, was Thomas W. Lawson's "Frenzied Finance." Literary contributors in recent years have included Mary E. Wilkins Freeman, O. Henry, Frank Norris, Booth Tarkington, Ernest Poole, Dorothy Canfield, and in poetry Margaret Widdemer, Witter Bynner, and others.

EVERY SATURDAY, 1865–1874. A Boston weekly.

A Ticknor and Field publication; one of the numerous "eclectic" mid-century periodicals made up of selected materials chiefly from English magazines. It is of interest partly as a type and partly because Thomas Bailey Aldrich was editor for the nine years of its life. In 1874 it was merged with *Littell's Living Age* (see p. 493).

GALAXY, THE, 1866–1878. A New York monthly.

"An illustrated magazine of entertaining reading." The first volume illustrated the practice of the day in featuring English authors with a leading serial by Anthony Trollope. The American contributors include Bayard Taylor, Howells, Stedman, and William Winter. Later Charles Reade was accompanied by Henry James, John Burroughs, E. R. Sill, and Paul Hamilton Hayne. With contributors of this substantial secondary rank, later still supplemented by Sidney Lanier and Joaquin Miller, the *Galaxy* completed and died with its twelfth year.

GENTLEMAN'S MAGAZINE, Burton's (1837–1841). A Philadelphia monthly.

Founded by William E. Burton, the actor. Poe was an early, important contributor and in the second year the editor. Although he and Burton separated in 1839, the proprietor saw to it that Poe was reëmployed when in 1841 George R. Graham bought out its circulation of 3500 and merged it with *Atkinson's Casket* as *Graham's Magazine*.

GODEY'S LADY'S BOOK, 1830–1898. A Philadelphia monthly.

Founded by Louis A. Godey, July, 1830, and managed by him as a monthly until 1877. In 1837 it absorbed the Boston *Lady's Magazine* and took over its editor, Sarah J. Hale. Its chief distinction and highest circulation (150,000) came under its first manager. It printed much early work of Longfellow, Holmes, Poe, Bayard Taylor, Mrs. Sigourney, and Harriet Beecher Stowe. In its last years it was renamed *Godey's Magazine*. In 1898 it was absorbed by the *Puritan*.

GRAHAM'S MAGAZINE, 1841–1859. A Philadelphia monthly.

Founded by George R. Graham by combining his *Atkinson's Casket* with his purchase of Burton's *Gentleman's Magazine*. Within a year, largely through Poe's editorial work, the circulation rose from 5000 to 30,000. By 1850 it had reached a circulation of 135,000. Among the later editors were R. W. Griswold, Bayard Taylor, and Charles Godfrey Leland, and among the contributors, Cooper, Longfellow, Poe, Hawthorne, Lowell, N. P. Willis, E. P. Whipple, the Cary sisters, William Gilmore Simms, Richard Penn Smith, and Thomas Dunn English. In January, 1859, *Graham's* became the *American Monthly* (see "Philadelphia Magazines and their Contributors," A. H. Smyth, 1892, and the *Critic*, Vol. XXV, p. 44).

HARPER'S NEW MONTHLY MAGAZINE, 1850——. A New York monthly.

Founded by Harper Brothers in order "to place within the reach of the great mass of the American people the unbounded treasures of the periodical literature of the present day"; thus it was an " eclectic " magazine, and in the early years it supplemented this borrowed magazine material with serials by the most popular English novelists. Within four years it had a circulation of 125,000. During the 1860's it became more American in content, and in the 1870's it included a notable series on the transformed South. In the last thirty years it has drawn on the best-known American authors for single articles and serials : Aldrich, Howells, Lowell, Wister, Mrs. Deland, Mark Twain, James, Harte, Mrs. Wharton, Tarkington, Allen ; and it has shared in the publication of recent significant poetry by Cawein, Le Gallienne, Untermeyer, Bynner, and the Misses Thomas, Teasdale, Widdemer, and Lowell. (See " The House of Harper," J. H. Harper, 1912, and " The Making of a Great Magazine," Harper & Brothers, 1889.)

HOME JOURNAL, THE, 1847——. A New York monthly.

Jointly founded and conducted by George P. Morris and N. P. Willis as a continuation of their *National Press* (founded 1845). Both remained with it till death — Willis, the survivor, till 1865. " It was and is," wrote H. A. Beers in his Life of N. P. Willis (1885), "the organ of japonicadom," the journal of society, and gazette of fashionable literature, addressing itself with assiduous gallantry to 'the ladies.' "

INDEPENDENT, THE, 1848——. A New York weekly.

A periodical "Conducted by Pastors of Congregational Churches"; Leonard Bacon, the first editor; Reverend George B. Cheever and Reverend Henry Ward Beecher, contributing editors. Its purpose was to be a progressive religious journal, particularly for Congregationalists, who protested against conservatism in theology and proslavery politics. Eventually it became an open forum for the liberally minded of all sects, being carefully nonpartisan in politics. From 1870 to 1890 it printed good verse, notably poems by Joaquin Miller and Sidney Lanier. The religious and political viewpoints broadened out from 1873. By 1898 an evident attempt was made to popularize the magazine. Since 1914 it has absorbed the *Chautauquan*, the *Countryside*, and *Harper's Weekly*.

KNICKERBOCKER MAGAZINE, THE, 1833–1865. A New York monthly.

The first editor was Charles Fenno Hoffman. From 1839 to 1841 Irving wrote monthly articles for a salary of $2000. Bryant, Whittier, Longfellow Holmes, Halleck, and most of the secondary writers contributed. The second editor, from 1841 to 1861, was Lewis Gaylord Clark. In its later years the magazine declined, chiefly because it was carrying the tradition of polite and aimless literature into Civil-War times. During its period it stood in the North for the same interests that its contemporary, the *Southern Literary Messenger*, did in the South (see "The Knickerbocker Gallery," 1855, and *Harper's Magazine*, Vol. XLVIII, p. 587).

LIBERATOR, THE, 1831–1865. A Boston weekly.

The most famous and effective abolition journal, founded and edited throughout by William Lloyd Garrison. It was proscribed in the South and denounced in the North. Wendell Phillips and Henry Ward Beecher praised it, but Mrs. Stowe criticized and Horace Greeley misrepresented it. The financial straits it passed through were augmented by the rivalry of other abolition papers. After the Emancipation Proclamation and Lincoln's second Inaugural, announcement of discontinuance was made. The last issue appeared December 29, 1865.

LIPPINCOTT'S MAGAZINE, 1868–1916. A Philadelphia monthly.

One of three magazines founded near 1870 — the others *Scribner's Monthly* and the *Galaxy* — that made an active market for American writers. *Lippincott's*, " a magazine of literature, science, and education," made an unpretentious start and throughout its career published little prose of distinction. Its poetry, however, was excellent. Bayard Taylor and Paul Hamilton Hayne appeared in the first and following numbers. Margaret Preston, Emma Lazarus, Thomas B. Read, George H. Boker, Thomas Dunn English, and Christopher P. Cranch contributed frequently. Whitman, rare in the magazines, wrote in prose, and, most important of all, Lanier found here a channel for much of his verse from 1875 on. In later years a feature of many issues was a complete short novel. In 1916 *Lippincott's* was absorbed by *Scribner's Magazine*.

LITTELL'S LIVING AGE, 1844——. A Boston monthly.

This is the longest-lived of the eclectic, or " scissors and paste-pot," magazines. It has been made up of reprints from foreign periodicals, sometimes quoting from English apparent sources articles which had been borrowed there from original American publications. In 1874 it absorbed *Every Saturday* (see p. 491) and in 1898 the *Eclectic Magazine*. It survives as the *Living Age*.

McCLURE'S MAGAZINE, 1893————. A New York monthly.

S. S. McClure founder and editor. Fiction and poetry have been the dominant features. Contributors (fiction): Kipling, Stevenson, Arnold Bennett, Bret Harte, Mark Twain, Booth Tarkington, Robert Chambers, O. Henry, Jack London; (verse): Wordsworth, Browning, Walt Whitman (reprints), Kipling, Witter Bynner, Edgar Lee Masters, Hermann Hagedorn, Louis Untermeyer. It was the first magazine to sell at the popular price of fifteen cents. The nonliterary articles on affairs of the day were prepared on assignment by expert writers such as Ida Tarbell, Ray Stannard Baker, and Lincoln Steffens, years sometimes being spent on a single series. In 1905 these three assumed control of the *American*, but the policy has been continued to the present.

MIRROR, THE NEW YORK, 1823–1846. A New York weekly.

Founded by George P. Morris and Samuel Woodworth (remembered respectively for "Woodman, Spare that Tree" and "The Old Oaken Bucket"). In 1831 the *Mirror* absorbed the *Boston American Monthly* together with its editor, Nathaniel Parker Willis. In the next year Willis wrote for it the first of his travel series, "Pencillings by the Way," continuing with weekly letters for four years. In 1839 Hawthorne became a contributor. In 1844–1845 Poe was subeditor and critic, his most famous contribution being "The Raven," January, 1845. In 1845 the weekly became a daily — the *Evening Mirror* — and in 1846 it was discontinued.

NATION, THE, 1865————. A New York weekly.

Publishers: Joseph H. Richards, 1865; Evening Post Publishing Co., 1871; E. L. Godkin Co., 1874; *Evening Post*, 1881; *New York Evening Post*, 1902; Nation Press, Inc., New York, 1915. Editors have changed frequently, the most famous being the first, E. L. Godkin, who was in the chair from 1865 to 1881. Oswald Garrison Villard, present editor. It has been devoted to discussions of politics, art, and literature and to reviews of the leading books in these fields. Representative contributors have been Francis Parkman, T. R. Lounsbury, B. L. Gildersleeve, J. R. Lowell, Carl Schurz, James Bryce, William James, Paul Shorey, and Stuart Sherman. (See "Fifty Years of American Idealism," edited by Gustav Pollak. 1915. Also the "Semicentenary Number," 1915.)

NEW ENGLAND COURANT, THE, 1721–1727. A Boston weekly.

Founded by James Franklin and carried on by him and a group of friends known as the Hell-Fire Club. The *Courant* represents a violent and somewhat coarse reaction against the domination of the New England clergy. It was written after the manner of the *Spectator* with frequent paraphrased and a few quoted passages. After the imprisonment of James the paper was carried on by the youthful Benjamin Franklin, who had already contributed the fourteen "Do-Good Papers." The *Courant* gave evidence of much wit and enterprise, but quite lacked the urbanity of its English model.

NEW ENGLAND MAGAZINE, THE, 1831–1835. A Boston monthly.

Founded by Joseph T. Buckingham, former editor of the *Polyanthus*, 1805–1807 and 1812–1814, the *Ordeal*, 1809, the *New England Galaxy*, 1817–1828, and the *Boston Courier*, a daily, 1814–1848. The *New England Magazine*, superior to any of these, was the project of Edwin, a son, who gave it distinction in a single year of editorship before his death, at the age of twenty-two. The father continued in charge for eighteen months, relinquishing it for the final year to Charles Fenno Hoffman and Park Benjamin. These latter took the magazine to New York in January, 1836, renaming it the *American Monthly Magazine*. The younger Buckingham showed enterprise in enlisting well-known contributors and acuteness in securing copy from Longfellow, Whittier, Holmes, and Hawthorne before they were widely known. It was in the *New England* that Holmes originated "The Autocrat of the Breakfast Table" in two numbers of 1832, reviving the theme in his first *Atlantic* series twenty-five years later; and here also Hawthorne printed many stories now in "Twice-Told Tales" and "Mosses from an Old Manse." (See "The First *New England Magazine* and its Editor," by George Willis Cooke, *New England Magazine* (N. S.), March, 1897.)

NEW YORK EVENING POST, THE, 1801——. A New York daily.

A Federal paper at first. Alexander Hamilton and John Jay aided in its establishment. William Coleman, first editor. Bryant began to write for the *Post* in 1826. He was editor from 1829 to 1878.

NEW YORK REVIEW AND ATHENÆUM MAGAZINE, THE, (?)–1827. A New York monthly.

A type of the short-lived magazine which rose and then combined with or absorbed others in a succession of changes. This was first the *Review*, then in March, 1826, it was merged with another periodical into the *New York Literary Gazette or American Athenæum*, and a little later it combined with Parson's old paper, the *United States Literary Gazette*, to form the *United States Review and Literary Gazette*. It is mentioned because of Bryant's contributions and his editorship from 1826 until its discontinuation.

NEW YORK TRIBUNE, THE, 1841——. A New York daily.

Started by Horace Greeley as a reform newspaper in support of President Harrison. In 1847 Greeley enlisted the support of several of the Brook Farm group — George Ripley, Margaret Fuller, Charles A. Dana, and George William Curtis—and secured as later contributors Carl Schurz, John Hay, Henry James, William Dean Howells, Bayard Taylor, Whitelaw Reid, E. C. Stedman, and others. The *Tribune* made much of its literary side, not only in book reviews and discussions of contemporary art and letters but in the inclusion of much significant verse. The *Tribune* was an important ally in securing the election of Lincoln and supporting his policies. It has continued to be one of the leading New York dailies, but its great days were concluded with the resignation of Greeley in 1872.

496 A HISTORY OF AMERICAN LITERATURE

NEW REPUBLIC, THE, 1914——. A New York weekly.

A "journal of opinion" founded with the assistance of Mr. Willard Straight by Herbert Croly and associates. As its subtitle indicates, it is chiefly concerned with problems of national and international import, but, in addition to the articles by editors and contributors on affairs of the day, it includes papers on the art, music, and literature of the present and the recent past, occasional light essays, discriminating book reviews, and verse. Representative contributors have been John Graham Brooks, John Dewey, William Hard, Elizabeth Shipley Sargent, Louis Untermeyer, Robert Frost, Edwin Arlington Robinson, and, from England, Norman Angell, H. M. Brailsford, and H. G. Wells.

NORTH AMERICAN REVIEW, THE, 1815——. A Boston and New York quarterly.

Successor to the *Boston Monthly Anthology*, 1803–1811, being founded by an editor, William Tudor, and several contributors who had been members of the Anthology Club. After three years as a general literary bimonthly it became a quarterly review. Among early contributors, besides well-known leaders in political thinking, were George Ticknor, George Bancroft, Bryant, and Longfellow. Until the founding of the *Atlantic* it was the leading organ of conservative thought in New England. For the decade from 1864 it was under the joint editorship of James Russell Lowell and Charles Eliot Norton. Since 1878 it has been in New York, changing in editorship and periods of publication. It became settled as a monthly under George Harvey. The more purely literary American contributors of the last few years have been Howells, Mabie, Matthews, Woodberry, Miss Repplier, Miss Teasdale, Miss Lowell, Hagedorn, Robinson, Mackaye, and Ficke. (See *North American*, Vol. C, p. 315, and Vol. CCI.)

OUTLOOK, THE, 1870——. A New York weekly.

Founded in 1870 as the *Christian Union*, an undenominational paper, by Henry Ward Beecher. In 1876 he shared his duties as editor with Lyman Abbott, present editor. In 1884 Hamilton Wright Mabie was added as associate editor. Title was changed to *The Outlook* in 1893. Mabie secured contributions from men like James Bryce and Edward Dowden, translations from the works of Daudet and François Coppée. Recent American literary contributors: Ernest Poole, Vachel Lindsay, Cawein, Oppenheim. New political impetus came with contributions from Theodore Roosevelt, beginning 1909. The paper has had more or less of ecclesiastical character all along, but at present may be characterized as seeking to mold public opinion and interpret current events. One number of each month formerly contained special departments; called Illustrated Magazine Number from 1896 to 1905.

PENNSYLVANIA GAZETTE, THE, 1729–1821. A Philadelphia weekly.

The new name and new periodical founded by Benjamin Franklin when he purchased Samuel Keimer's *Universal Instructor* in October, 1729. The news element was slight and unreliable, but the literary, Addisonian essays gave the paper character at once. These gave way later to essays more distinctly peculiar to Franklin's own point of view and kind of humor. The book advertisements supplemented this essay material in contributing to the broader culture of the readers. After Franklin's personal withdrawal the traditions of the *Gazette* were continued. In 1765 Franklin sold out to his partner David Hall. With the death of his grandson, also David Hall, the paper passed into the hands of Atkinson and Alexander and was renamed the *Saturday Evening Post* (p. 498).

POETRY, 1912———. A Chicago monthly.

A magazine of verse. Harriet Monroe, editor. Ralph Fletcher Seymour Co., Chicago, publishers. Advisory committee: H. B. Fuller, Edith Wyatt, and H. C. Chatfield Taylor. It was guaranteed for five years by endowment fund and contained no advertisements at the beginning. It has been a vehicle for poetry from all parts of the world by poets with or without fame. Now it contains book-list awards, reviews, and poetry announcements and advertisements. The original staff is almost unchanged. It seems to be on a sound financial footing.

POOR RICHARD'S ALMANAC, 1733–1748.

Founded by Benjamin Franklin. Its chief feature was its inclusion in the reading matter of the proverbial sayings, the best of which were combined in " The Way to Wealth." It was characterized by a French critic of the day as " the first popular almanac which spoke the language of reason." It was conducted by Franklin until 1748.

PORT FOLIO, THE, 1801–1827. A Philadelphia weekly and monthly.

Founded by Joseph Dennie as a weekly magazine. From 1806 to 1809, though continuing as a weekly, it assumed the character of a literary magazine, and in the latter year became a monthly. Its most distinctive period was in the first eleven years before the death of Dennie. While he was editor the *Port Folio* was a vehicle of " polite letters." It was imitative in style and reminiscent in point of view, but it was wholesome in its honesty about American matters and manners and exerted a strong and healthy influence. The best-known contributors were the editor, " Oliver Oldschool," John Quincy Adams, and Charles Brockden Brown.

PUTNAM'S, 1853–1858, 1868–1870, 1906–1910. A New York monthly.

Publishers, G. P. Putnam and Co., New York. *Putnam's Monthly Magazine* of American literature, science, and art. Established by George P. Putnam with the assistance of George William Curtis and others. In 1857 merged into *Emerson's United States Magazine*, which was continued as *Emerson's Magazine and Putnam's Monthly*. Discontinued November, 1858. January, 1868–November, 1870, *Putnam's Monthly Magazine*. Original papers on literature, science, art, and national interests. Merged into *Scribner's Monthly*, December, 1870. October, 1906–March, 1910, reëstablished and merged with the *Critic*, founded in 1881 ; issued by Messrs. Putnam since 1898. An illustrated monthly of literature, art, and life. Absorbed the *Reader*, March, 1908. Titles vary during this period. A large number of full-page and smaller illustrations. One serial running, small proportion of verse, special articles, comments, and criticisms on literature and the fine arts, science, travel, statesmanship. Alternating emphasis with successive issues on the different arts. Typical contributors and contributions, with illustrations concerning : Lafcadio Hearn, Mark Twain, William Dean Howells, Stedman, Stoddard, Henry James, Longfellow, Franklin, Margaret Deland, Maeterlinck, Thomas Edison, Binet, Corot, Helen Keller, Nazimova, Gladstone, the Bonapartes. Absorbed by the *Atlantic Monthly*, April, 1910.

ROUND TABLE, THE, 1864–1869. A New York monthly.

A literary journal founded in New York in emulation of Boston's *Atlantic* and supported with great interest by Aldrich, Stedman, Bayard Taylor, and their circle. It was suspended during parts of 1864–1865 and discontinued in July, 1869, in spite of the efforts to secure a subsidy for it from the wealthy men of New York.

RUSSELL'S MAGAZINE, 1857–1860. A Charleston monthly.

Founded by John Russell, Charleston bookseller, with Paul Hamilton Hayne as editor. A monthly periodical for the literary group centering around William Gilmore Simms. Contained fiction, sketches, addresses, reviews, and essays on various topics — political, historical, literary, artistic, scientific. These were mainly unsigned, but the leading contributors were Simms, Hayne, Timrod, James L. Petigru, John D. Bruns, and Basil Gildersleeve. With the approach of the Civil War it was discontinued March, 1860. (Lives of P. H. Hayne and W. G. Simms. Three Notable Ante-Bellum Magazines of South Carolina, Sidney J. Cohen, University of South Carolina, *Bulletin 42*.)

SATURDAY EVENING POST, THE, 1821——. A Philadelphia weekly.

A lineal descendant of Franklin's *Pennsylvania Gazette* (see p. 496). It was given its present name in 1821 when Samuel C. Atkinson and Charles Alexander took control, Atkinson being the surviving partner of David Hall, grandson and namesake of Franklin's partner to whom the *Gazette* was sold in 1765. In one hundred and eighty years the only interruption to consecutive issues was during the British occupation of Philadelphia. The *Post* of recent years has been one of the American weeklies of largest circulation. It contains fiction, up-to-date personalia, and brisk articles on the affairs of the moment. Its attitude toward thrift, industry, and the way to wealth is completely consistent with the ethics of Franklin. It is conducted by the Curtis Publishing Company and edited by George H. Lorimer.

SATURDAY PRESS, THE, 1858–1860. A New York weekly.

The special organ of the " Bohemians " — a group of New Yorkers who acknowledged Henry M. Clapp as their leader. Other contributors were Fitz-
James O'Brien, Thomas Bailey Aldrich, R. H. Stoddard, William Winter, and
E. C. Stedman, The *Press* was brilliant but short-lived, announcing in its last
number in early 1860 that it was "discontinued for lack of funds which [was], by
a coincidence, precisely the reason for which it was started." (See H. M. Clapp
in Winter's "Other Days," and "The Life of Stedman," by Stedman and Gould.)

SCRIBNER'S MAGAZINE, 1886——. A New York monthly.

Founded December, 1886, by Messrs. Scribner (entirely distinct from old
Scribner's Monthly), with E. L. Burlingame as editor. Illustrated. Typical
contributors, in the early years: H. C. Bunner, Joel Chandler Harris, Sarah
Orne Jewett, Barrett Wendell, E. H. Blashfield, Richard Henry Stoddard,
Thomas Bailey Aldrich, T. W. Higginson, W. C. Brownell, Charles Edwin
Markham, Robert Louis Stevenson; in recent years: Winston Churchill,
J. L. Laughlin, W. C. Brownell, Meredith Nicholson, John Galsworthy, etc.
Articles of popular interest on art, music, nature, travel, and since 1914 a
section given to the World War. Aim and policy unchanged.

SCRIBNER'S MONTHLY, 1870–1881. A New York monthly.

Founded by Roswell Smith, manager, and J. G. Holland, editor, and published
as *Scribner's*, but not like *Harper's* as a publishing-house magazine. The design
from the first was to deal with matters of social and religious opinion from
the liberal viewpoint. At the outset it absorbed *Hours at Home* and *Putnam's*
and in 1873 Edward Everett Hale's *Old and New*. It was the first to undertake a series on the new South and to encourage Southern contributors, including Lanier, Thomas Nelson Page, George W. Cable, and Joel Chandler
Harris. It published serially, among others, Stockton's " Rudder Grange,"
Jules Verne's " The Mysterious Island," and Charles Dudley Warner's " Back-
Log Studies " before they appeared in book form. *Scribner's Monthly* was a
pioneer in the use of illustrations made by the new mechanical methods of re-
production. The magazine never printed or sold less than 40,000 copies, and
when in 1881 it changed ownership and became the *Century* it had a circulation of 125,000. (See Tassin's " The Magazine in America," pp. 287–301.)

SOUTHERN LITERARY MESSENGER, 1834–1865. A Richmond monthly.

Founded at Richmond, Virginia, in August, 1834, by Thomas W. White, as
a semimonthly, but changed to a monthly almost at once. Poe contributed to the
seventh number and from then on in each number till he became assistant
editor from July, 1835, to January, 1837. During this period the circulation
increased from 700 to 5000. Well established by this time, it continued as the
most substantial and longest lived of the Southern magazines. A vehicle for
literature between the too heavy and the frivolous, and an honest review.

Poe's contributions outrank those of any other writer, but the list of contributors includes N. P. Willis, C. F. Hoffman, R. W. Griswold, J. G. Holland, R. H. Stoddard, W. M. Thackeray, Charles Dickens, G. P. R. James, John Randolph, R. H. Bird, Philip P. Cooke, J. W. Legare, P. H. Hayne, Henry Timrod, John P. Kennedy, and Sidney Lanier. (See "The Southern Literary Messenger," by B. B. Minor.)

SOUTHERN MAGAZINE, THE, 1871–1875. A Baltimore monthly.

The most distinguished of the several short-lived Southern magazines established in the Civil War reconstruction period. It was a continuation of the *New Eclectic*, but included, in addition to the English reprints, original work by many Southern authors. These were, among others, Margaret Preston, Malcolm Johnson, Sidney Lanier, Paul Hamilton Hayne, and Professors Gildersleeve and Price. It could pay nothing for manuscript, however, and the new interest in Southern writing awakened by *Scribner's* in 1873, and responded to by *Harper's*, the *Atlantic*, *Lippincott's*, the *Independent*, and others, furnished support as well as stimulation to its best contributors and hastened its death at the end of five years.

WESTERN MESSENGER, THE (Cincinnati), 1835–1841.

Begun by Reverend Ephraim Peabody. Published by Western Unitarian Society aided by American Unitarian Association. Purposed to make it a vehicle for clear, rational discussion of important and interesting topics. Discussed reform movements, religious questions and creeds, and encouraged expression of all cultural ideas, — literary articles, poetry, book reviews, etc. Contributors: Mann Butler, W. D. Gallagher, James H. Perkins, R. W. Emerson, J. S. Dwight, Elizabeth P. Peabody, Jones Very, James Freeman Clarke, Dr. Lyman Beecher, Professor Calvin E. Stowe, Margaret Fuller, C. P. Cranch. Sought to make it Western in spirit with many Western contributors and articles on history of the West. 1836–1839 in Louisville, under J. F. Clarke, then back to Cincinnati, under William H. Channing, till April, 1841.

WESTERN MONTHLY MAGAZINE, THE (Cincinnati), 1833–1836.

Edited for two and one-half years by James Hall and for six months by Joseph R. Foy. Thirty-seven contributors, of whom six were women and only three from east of the Alleghenies. Harriet Beecher won "the prize tale" in April, 1834, and contributed another story in July. The contents made up largely of expository articles on art, history, biology, travel, education, economics, and modern sociology. The book notices were independent and discriminating.

YALE REVIEW, THE, 1892–1911, 1911——. Issued quarterly.

Continued *New Englander and Yale Review*. G. P. Fisher and others, editors. In 1900 changed from a "journal of history and political science" to a "Journal for the Scientific Discussion of Economic, Political, and Social

Questions "; 1911—— " a quarterly magazine devoted to Literature, Science, History, and Public Opinion." Yale Publishing Association, Inc., Wilbur L. Cross, chief editor. Not an official publication of Yale University. Made up of serious articles and essays, some light essays and verse, and literary criticism. Leading contributors, prose: W. H. Taft, Norman Angell, Walter Lippman, Simeon Strunsky, Vida D. Scudder; verse: Witter Bynner, Louis Untermeyer, Sara Teasdale, Edgar Lee Masters, Robert Frost, John Masefield. Thus its place as a literary periodical has been assumed only within the last decade. The old *New Englander* (1843-1892) was a substantial and dignified journal but included the work of no writer of even minor literary achievement.

INDEX